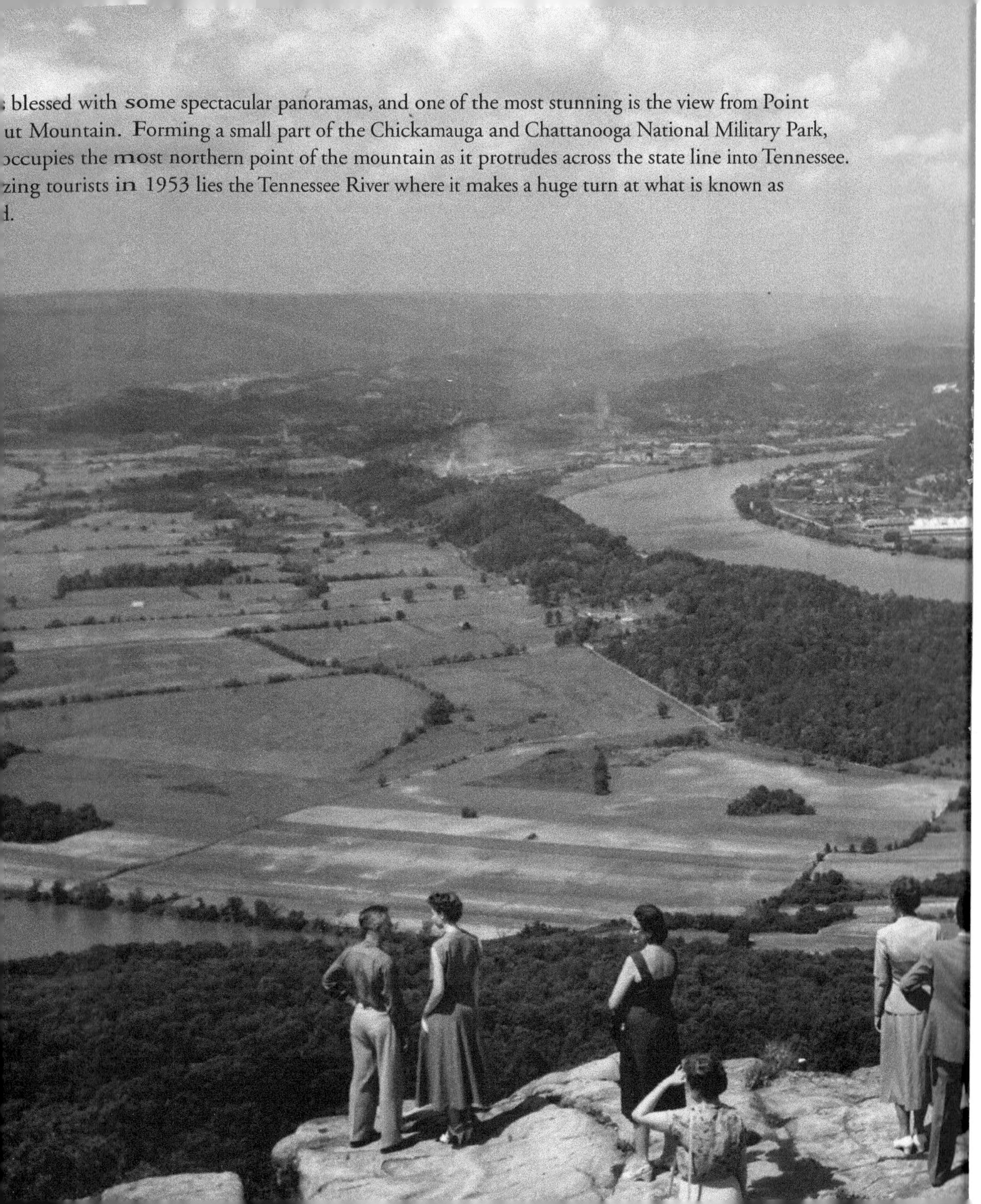

blessed with some spectacular panoramas, and one of the most stunning is the view from Point
ut Mountain. Forming a small part of the Chickamauga and Chattanooga National Military Park,
occupies the most northern point of the mountain as it protrudes across the state line into Tennessee.
zing tourists in 1953 lies the Tennessee River where it makes a huge turn at what is known as
d.

Chattan
Park on
this par
Below t
Moccasi

HISTORIC PHOTOS
CHATTANOO
IN THE 50s, 60s, AN

Text and Captions by
William F. Hull

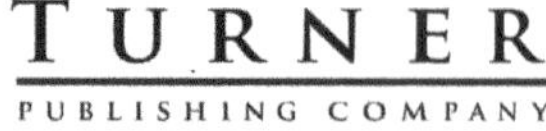

HISTORIC PHOTOS OF CHATTANOOGA IN THE 50s, 60s, AND 70s

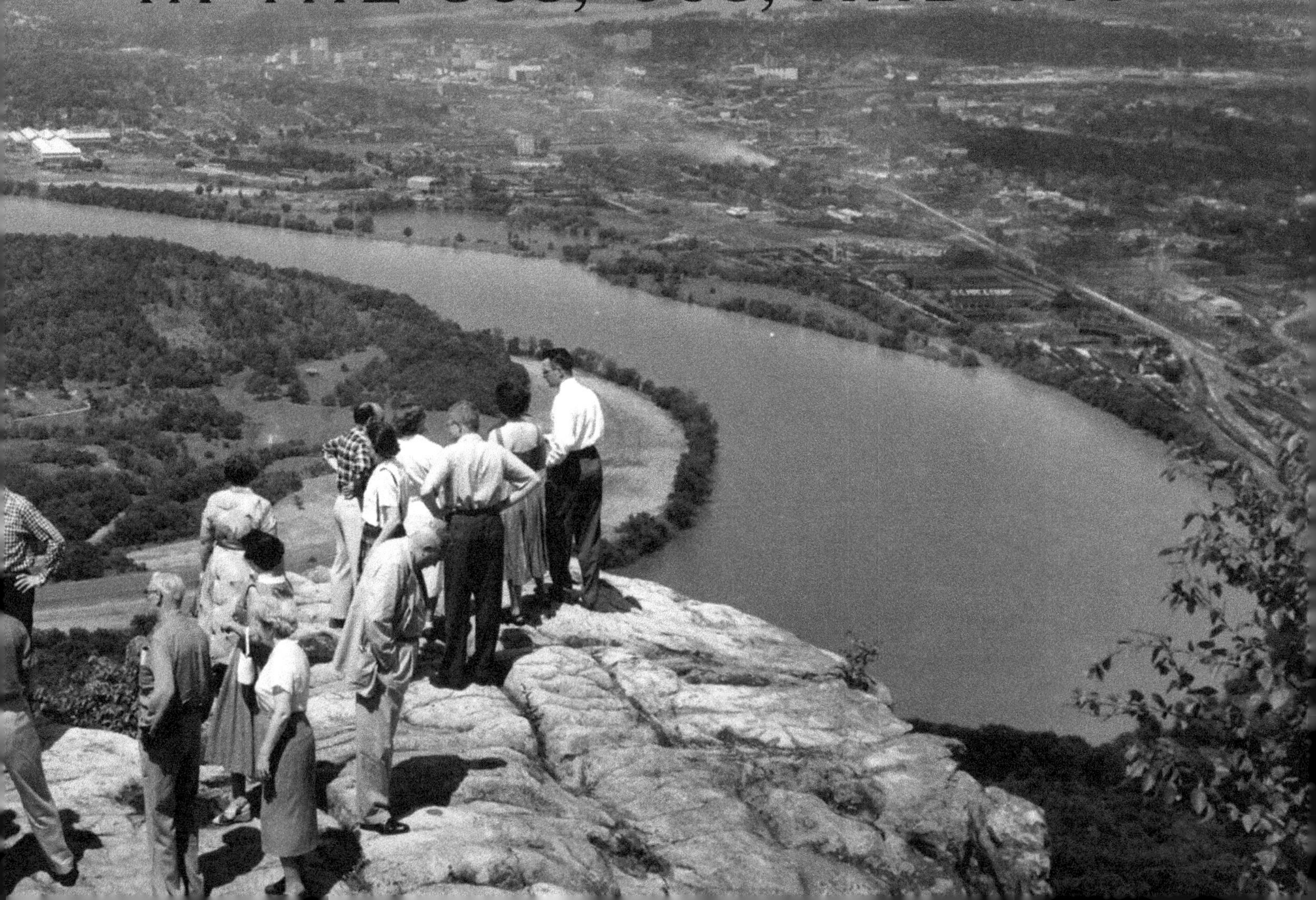

Turner Publishing Company
www.turnerpublishing.com

Historic Photos of Chattanooga in the 50s, 60s, and 70s

Library of Congress Control Number: 2010926752

ISBN: 978-1-59652-743-0

Printed in the United States of America

ISBN 978-1-68442-127-5 (hc)

Contents

Acknowledgments vii

Preface viii

Recasting the City
(1950–1959) 1

Challenges and a Choo Choo
(1960–1969) 105

New Visions of Old
(1970–1979) 151

Notes on the Photographs 201

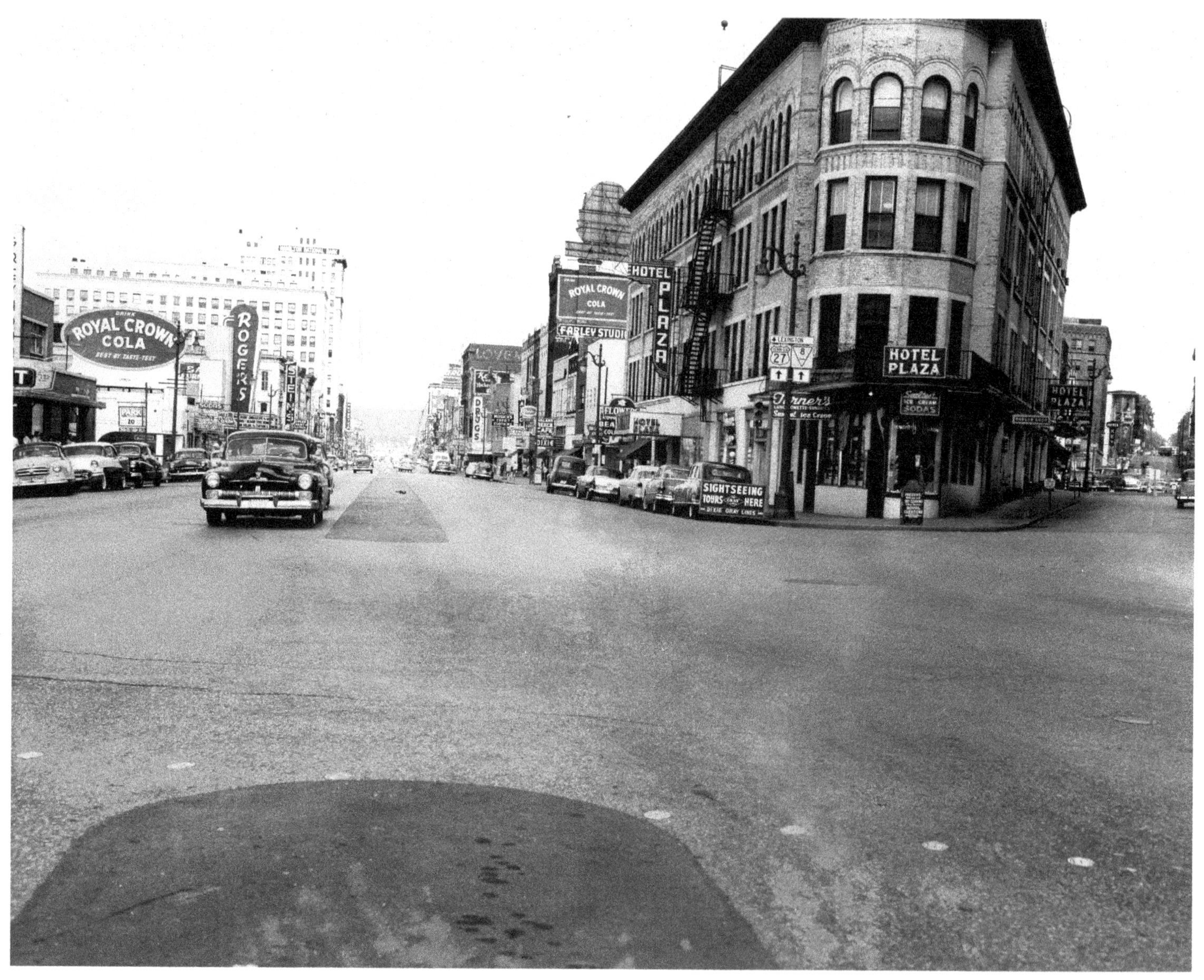

This view faces north on Market Street from Eleventh Street in 1955. Directly in front to the right is the bow-front Plaza Hotel, today the site of the long-running eatery, the Pickle Barrel; Georgia Avenue is to its right. To the far left is an advertisement for a drink called Royal Crown Cola—commonly known as RC Cola. The soft drink is frequently paired with Moon Pies, a Chattanooga institution.

Acknowledgments

This volume, *Historic Photos of Chattanooga in the 50s, 60s, and 70s,* is the result of the cooperation and efforts of many individuals and organizations. It is with great thanks that we acknowledge the valuable contribution of the following for their generous support:

Chattanooga–Hamilton County Bicentennial Library
Cox Family Collection
Tennessee State Library and Archives

We would also like to thank the capable and professional staff in the Local History Department at the Chattanooga–Hamilton County Public Library.

With the exception of touching up imperfections that have accrued with the passage of time and cropping where necessary, no changes to the images have been made.

Preface

In the years after the Second World War, Chattanoogans resumed a life not unlike the one that had predominated in the 1930s. Many men returned to jobs in industry, women became homemakers, and children were expected to finish basic schooling and attend church. In the city, heavy industry abounded, foundries were busy, and small shops were filling orders in the great economic surge that America was undergoing. Outside town and around the valley, small farming was still a way of life. It would be fair to say that most Chattanoogans had "country roots." But new opportunities were on the horizon. The Tennessee Valley Authority was well funded through tax dollars and expanding its work on the river system. A huge new Dupont plant opened near the Chickamauga Dam in 1948, employing 900 local folks around the clock to produce nylon, which would cover everything from upholstery to human beings. The dream of a house and a new car was now within reach of many Chattanoogans. The new prosperity touched a generation that had not known middle-class comforts, while the poverty that pervaded this southern Appalachian region still left a large number of families "barely scraping by."

In Chattanooga, P. R. Olgiati was elected mayor, taking advantage of a new state law which made annexation of the suburbs almost a fait accompli. Some enclaves such as East Ridge and Red Bank incorporated as towns to keep the city at bay, but around them the city limits expanded. Sections of town were removed by way of eminent domain to make way for the modern interstate system being laid across the nation like the railroads of a century before. A downtown landmark, Cameron Hill, would literally lose its top so that its soil could be used as fill dirt for the new highway.

A small art museum fashioned out of the old George Hunter home on the river bluff downtown opened in the 1950s. Concentrating on American art, its collection would grow in depth and its name in respect. A collector with a keen eye for glassware, Anna Safley Houston, left a treasure trove of antiques to the city of Chattanooga itself, which found a home within walking distance of the Hunter Museum for this unique assemblage of Americana. On radio, the voice of Luther Masingill came over the air, a voice of trust for the river city since 1941, bringing news and conversation and reuniting lost dogs with thankful owners. In 2010, Masingill was still broadcasting after 70 years in the business.

As the decade wore on, racial troubles were brewing across the South and in southeast Tennessee. The Atlanta civil rights worker Ralph Abernathy visited the city in the spring of 1956, proclaiming that "it's great to be arrested" to loud applause from his black audience. By 1960, sit-ins in downtown restaurants had become a means to an end. The confrontations were tense, but relatively brief. Ultimately, the conflict in Chattanooga was peacefully resolved, resulting in a push to desegregate local schools and public places citywide.

If Chattanoogans were able to negotiate a racial solution of sorts, the town appeared unable to undo the work of a century of smokestack emissions. An infamous award given in 1969 by the U.S. Health, Education, and Welfare Department branded the Scenic City as America's most polluted town. Profligate polluting by local industry had left a mark on the land and the water and had fouled the air to the point where it plainly stank. Stories of businessmen coming home at noon to change into a clean shirt for an afternoon's work were common. Nevertheless, the city would redeem itself in only three years by enforcing new industrial measures of air quality for the region and sowing the seeds of stewardship that would transform Chattanooga as the century closed.

The nation's economy was changing as well. Symbolic of changes in transportation, after passenger train service ended in 1971, the historic railroad Union Depot near the Read House was razed. Chattanoogans were traveling by automobile and leaving the city for the suburbs. Cheap foreign labor began producing everything from socks to steel. Production orders slowed down and jobs began to disappear. Downtown suffered accordingly as store vacancies became all too common. But by the late 1970s, efforts were under way to turn things around. Terminal Station had been revitalized to become the Chattanooga Choo Choo. Citizens rallied to preserve an old downtown bridge and convert it to a public commons, bringing people together over the river. The natural beauty of the land was seen as something worth preserving, promoting, and guarding; plans for walkways and green areas became an emphatic part of city planning. Conversations about a walkable, livable city were small, but earnest. In the next decade, these dreams would begin to bloom and bear fruit, demonstrating the power of a place to discover renewal and change its destiny.

—William F. Hull

Here around 1955, it's hard to know whether these young women are fascinated with a rock formation or gazing in apprehension at a creature from a science fiction movie. At any rate, the group is descending into the depths of Tennessee's most famous cave, Ruby Falls. An enduring attraction on Lookout Mountain and a landmark for traveling Americans, the cave was discovered in 1928 by Leo Lambert, who named it for his wife, Ruby. "See Ruby Falls" would eventually beckon to motorists across the state from barn roofs everywhere.

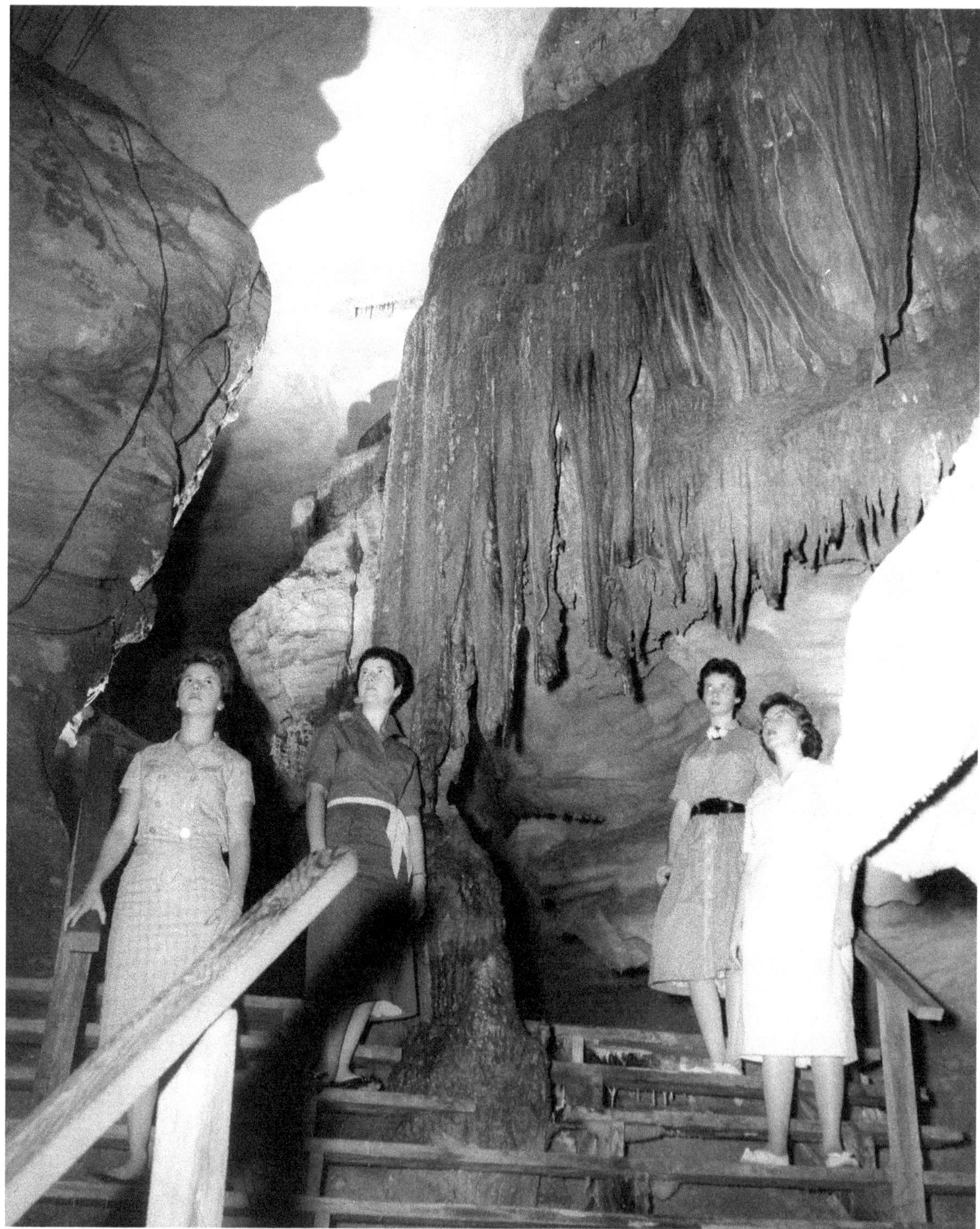

Recasting the City

(1950–1959)

For citizens making a new life after the rigors of the Great Depression and World War II, the 1950s brought expanded opportunities. Dupont located a large facility near the Chickamauga Dam off Hixson Pike to produce that truly modern synthetic wonder, nylon. The Tennessee Valley Authority, which had placed permanent offices in the city in the thirties, continued to grow steadily from the increasing power generation required by a rising middle class. Factories like the Wheland Foundry were busy across the city, as were the mills around town that supported the textile industry that was taking larger shape to the south in Dalton, Georgia.

George Thomas Hunter, an heir to the Chattanooga Coca-Cola Bottling fortune, passed away in 1952. In his will he bequeathed the Faxon Mansion on the city's river bluff to house an art collection that would enrich the cultural life of the city for years to come. Another humanitarian effort, the Siskin Memorial Foundation, began at this time boasting a mission of innovative treatment for those who had suffered debilitating injuries regardless of their ability to pay.

Chattanooga elected a new mayor, P. R. Olgiati, a man who had a vision for the city. He would work to have a new federal interstate completed, I-24, connecting Chattanooga to Atlanta and Nashville. His administration would also oversee massive redevelopment of the west side of town under the guise of "urban renewal," forcing 1,400 families to move and creating a "Golden Gateway" of retail development. Suburbs like Brainerd were whisked into the city through rapid annexation.

Other highlights helped define the decade. Many citizens were galvanized by the youthful fire of the evangelist Billy Graham in a series of local, memorable crusades in 1953. Television came to town when WDEF signed on the air in 1954. Chattanooga congressman Estes Kefauver became a nationally known Tennessee senator and a vice-presidential candidate in 1956. A less public man, Professor Irvine W. Grote, working at the University of Chattanooga, became known as the inventor of Rolaids and Bufferin. And in a public moment of great pride, the University of Chattanooga Mocs football team upset the mighty Vols of Tennessee in their home stadium in Knoxville by a score of 14 to 6, spreading jubilation across the city in the valley.

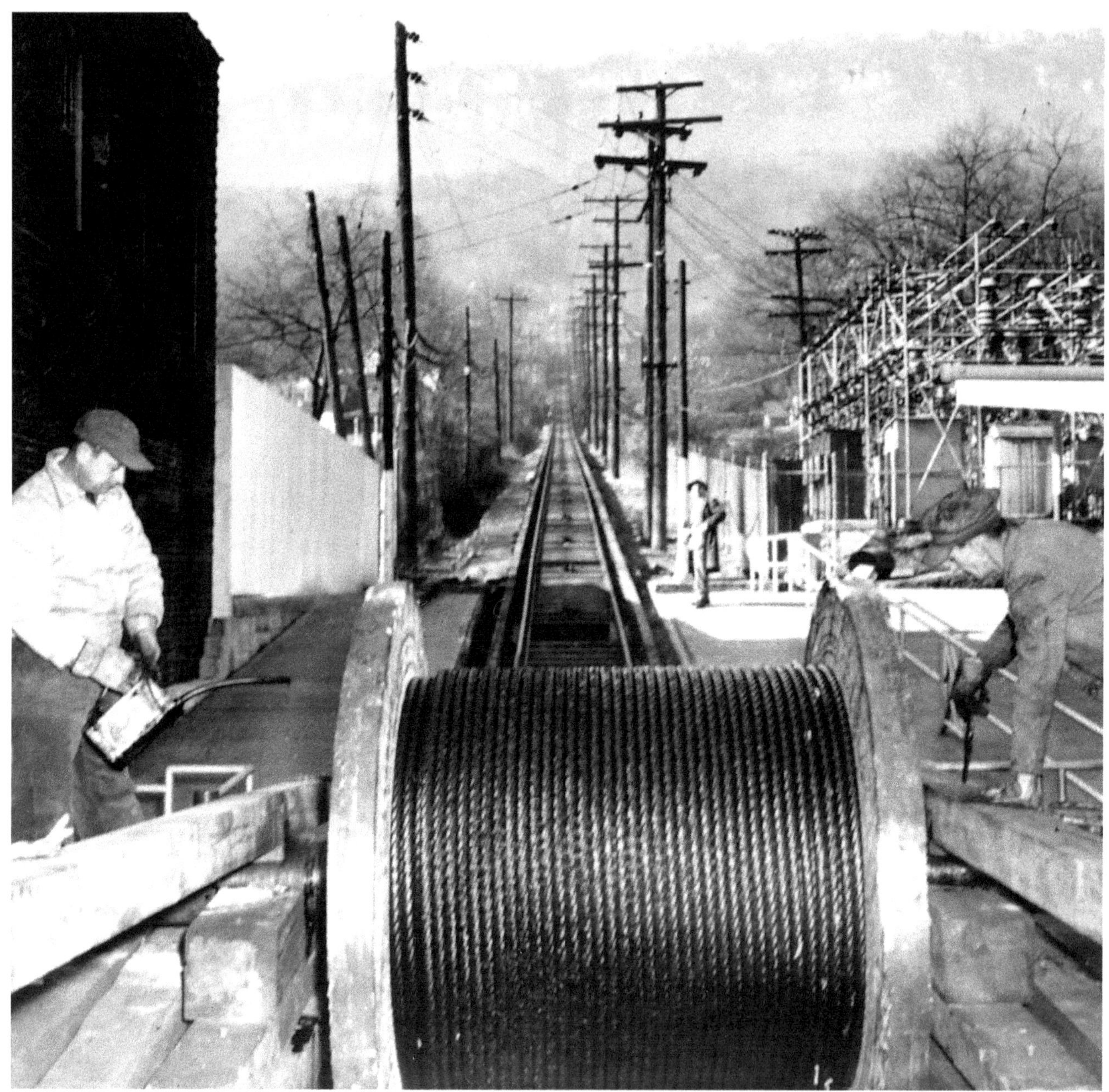

It takes a ton of steel cable to operate the Lookout Mountain Railway Incline—seven tons to be exact. Pivotal to the operation of the cable cars that ascend and descend the mountain with the regularity of a pendulum, this cable was installed in a few short, cold days in January 1950. Here workers oil and tighten the gleaming rope of steel prior to a real-life test of the system.

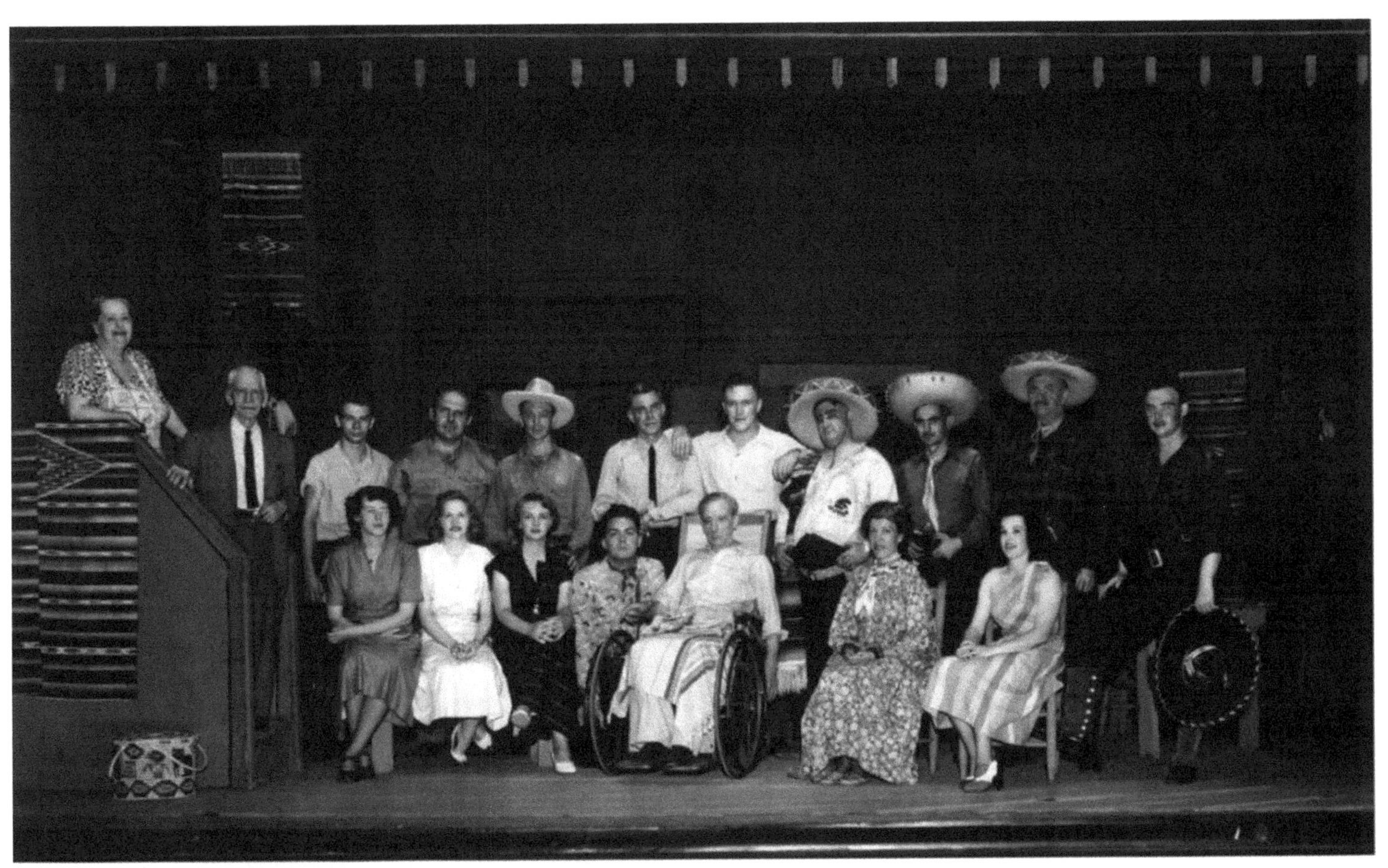

At the turn of the decade, the Chattanooga Little Theatre offered amateur thespians an opportunity to perform for Chattanoogans fond of the stage. This 1949 production of "The Bad Man" was sombrero-studded with talent. Seated, left to right, are Betty Lutz, Bobby Holderman, Betty Zimmerman, Jimmy Garner, Andy Andrews, Frankie Beck, and Marianne Sizer. Standing, left to right, are Ma Peruchi, Pa Peruchi, Bill Jones, Jim Steakley, Don Andrews, Gene Carr, Val Moore, Ed Green, Tom Cox, Raleigh Crumbliss, and Elmer Smith. The Chattanooga Little Theater is one of the longest continuously running community theaters in the nation.

It's not unusual to see Civil War cannons around Chattanooga even in the yards of private residences. Around 1950, this house most likely stands on Missionary Ridge, where Confederate troops once lined the crest. They fought a decisive battle against Federal troops, who assaulted the high ridge and drove Bragg's boys back into Georgia.

The handsome house with its arched windows exemplifies the masterly masonry work of native stone that still graces the city's older neighborhoods.

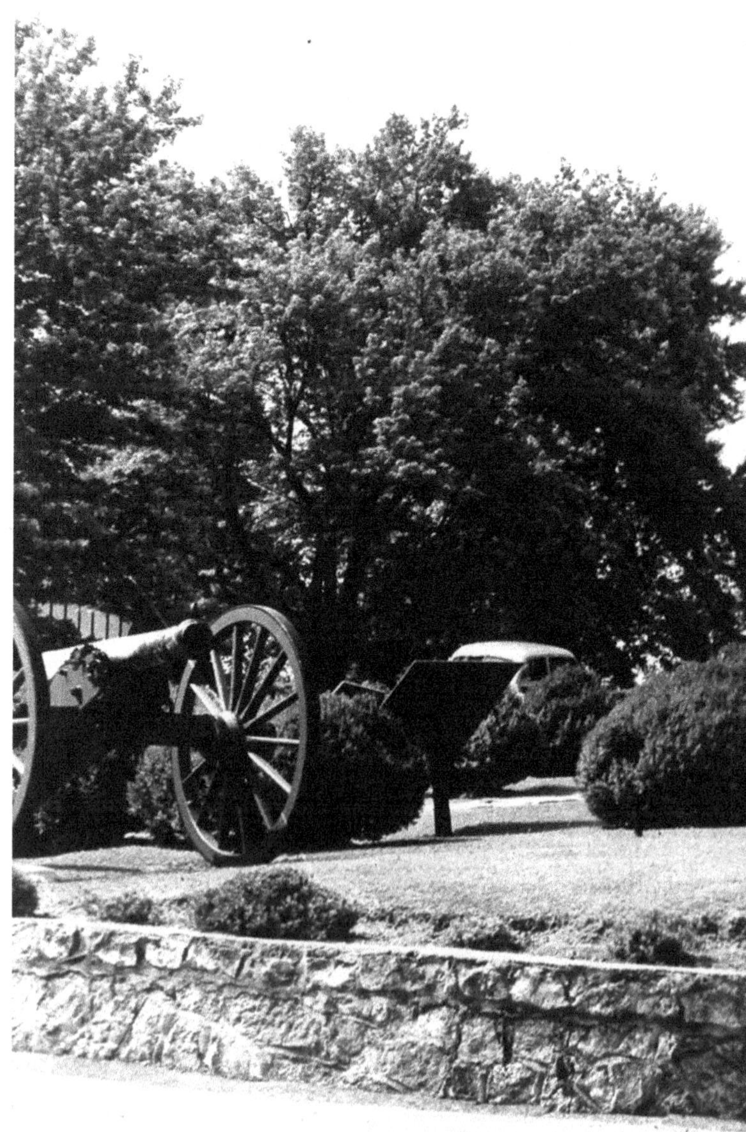

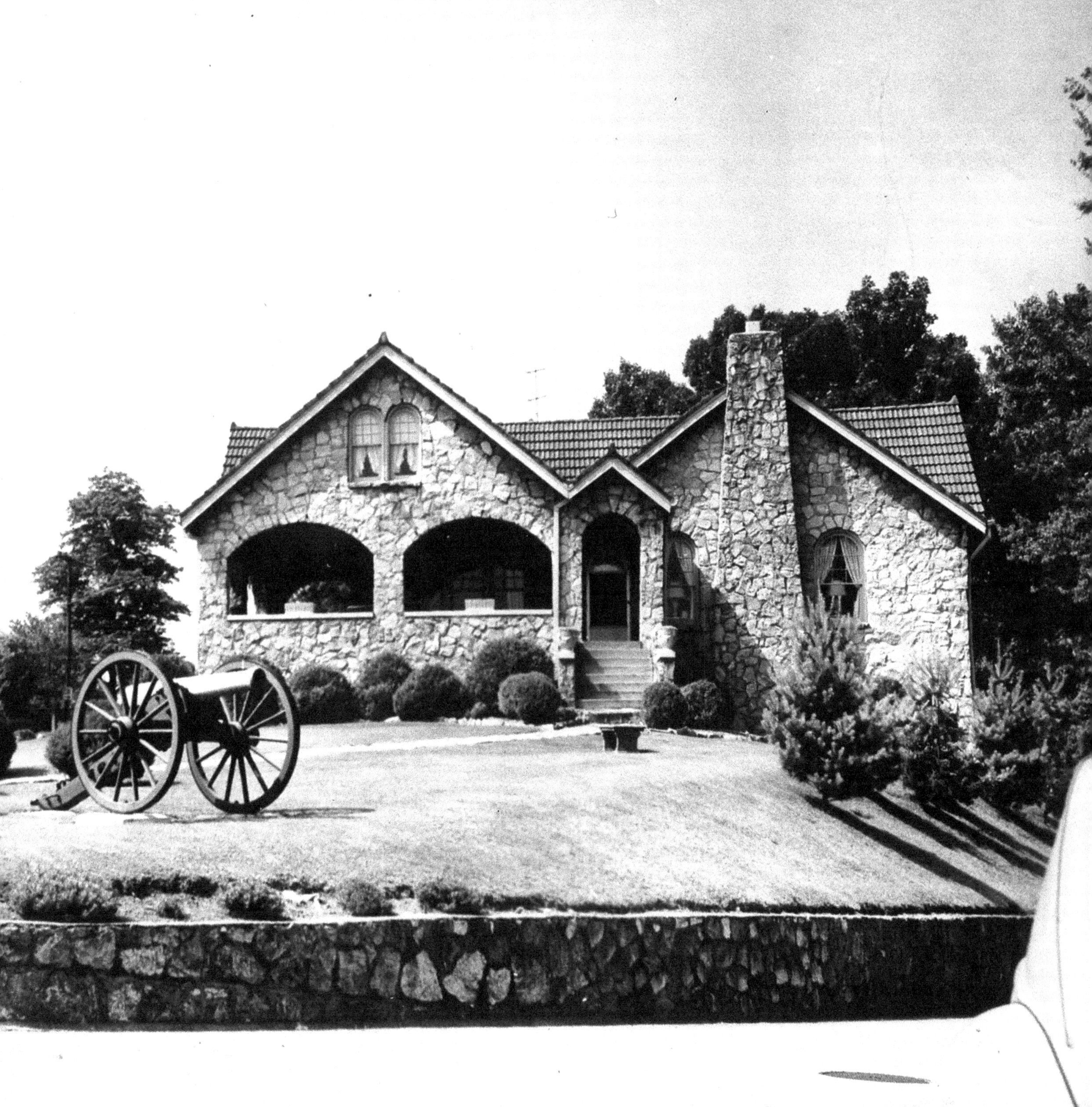

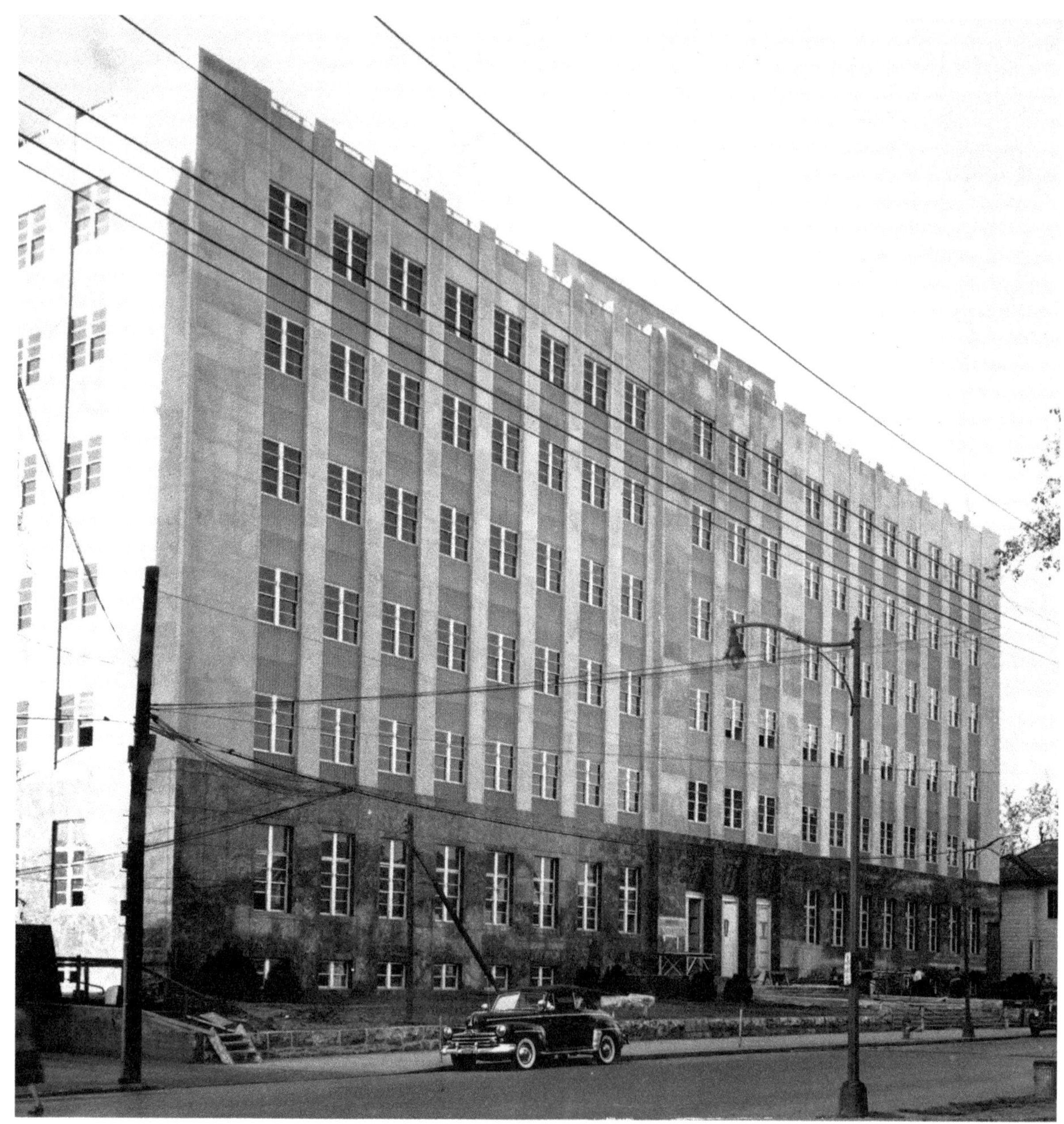

Following World War II, some residences were replaced with new construction. Completed in 1950, this impressive Art Moderne–style office building was built by the Interstate Life and Accident Insurance Company as its corporate headquarters on McCallie Avenue between the First Presbyterian Church and an older home visible on the right. Designed by R. H. Hunt and reaching six stories, it presently houses state government employees.

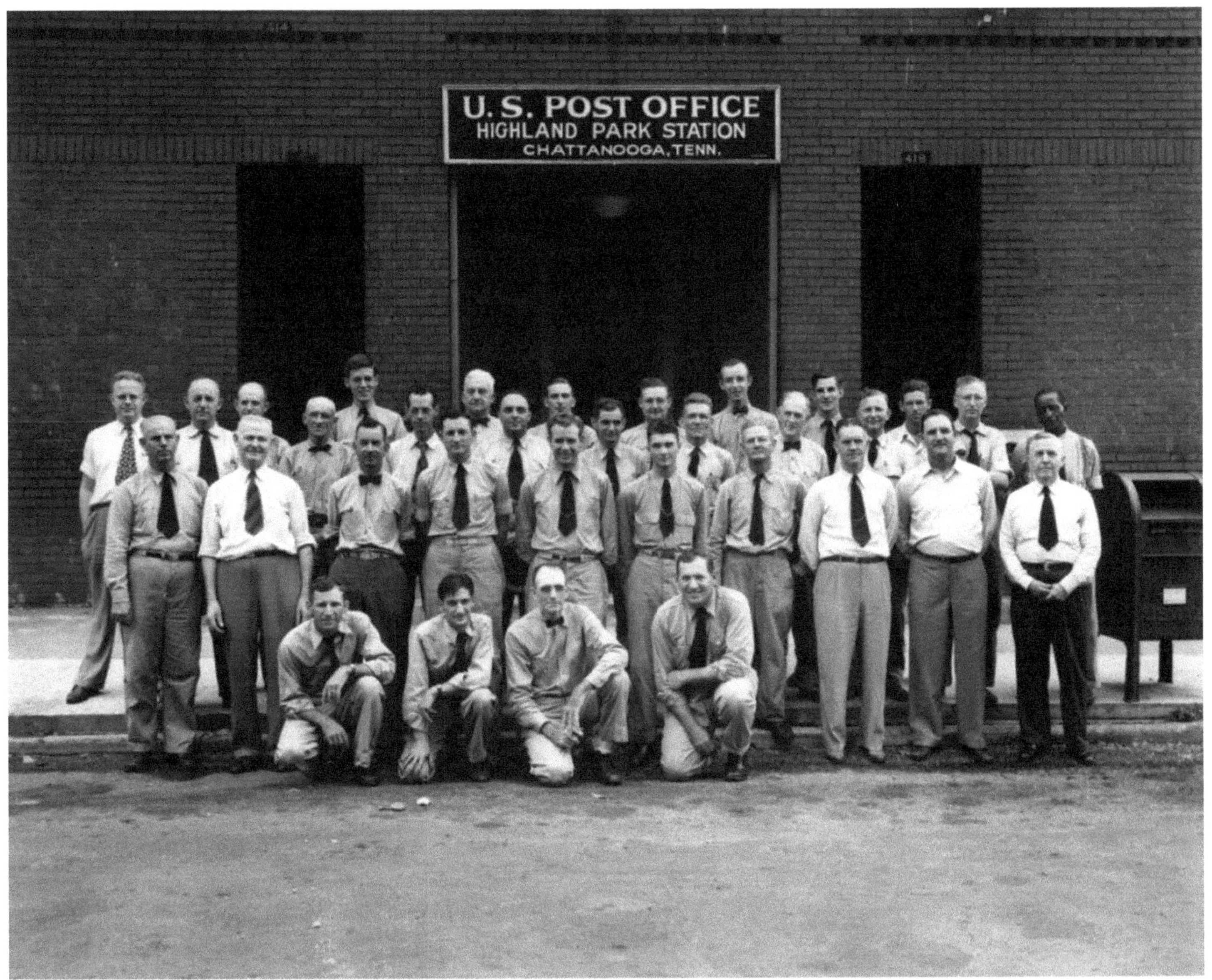

The U.S. Post Office staff at Highland Park Station pose for a group portrait around the turn of the decade. Highland Park and St. Elmo became Chattanooga's first two "suburbs" in the 1890s. Highland was built on high ground (hence the name), to eliminate the possibility of flooding. It was situated between two main east-west thoroughfares, Main Street (then Montgomery Street) and McCallie Avenue, the original road from town to Missionary Ridge.

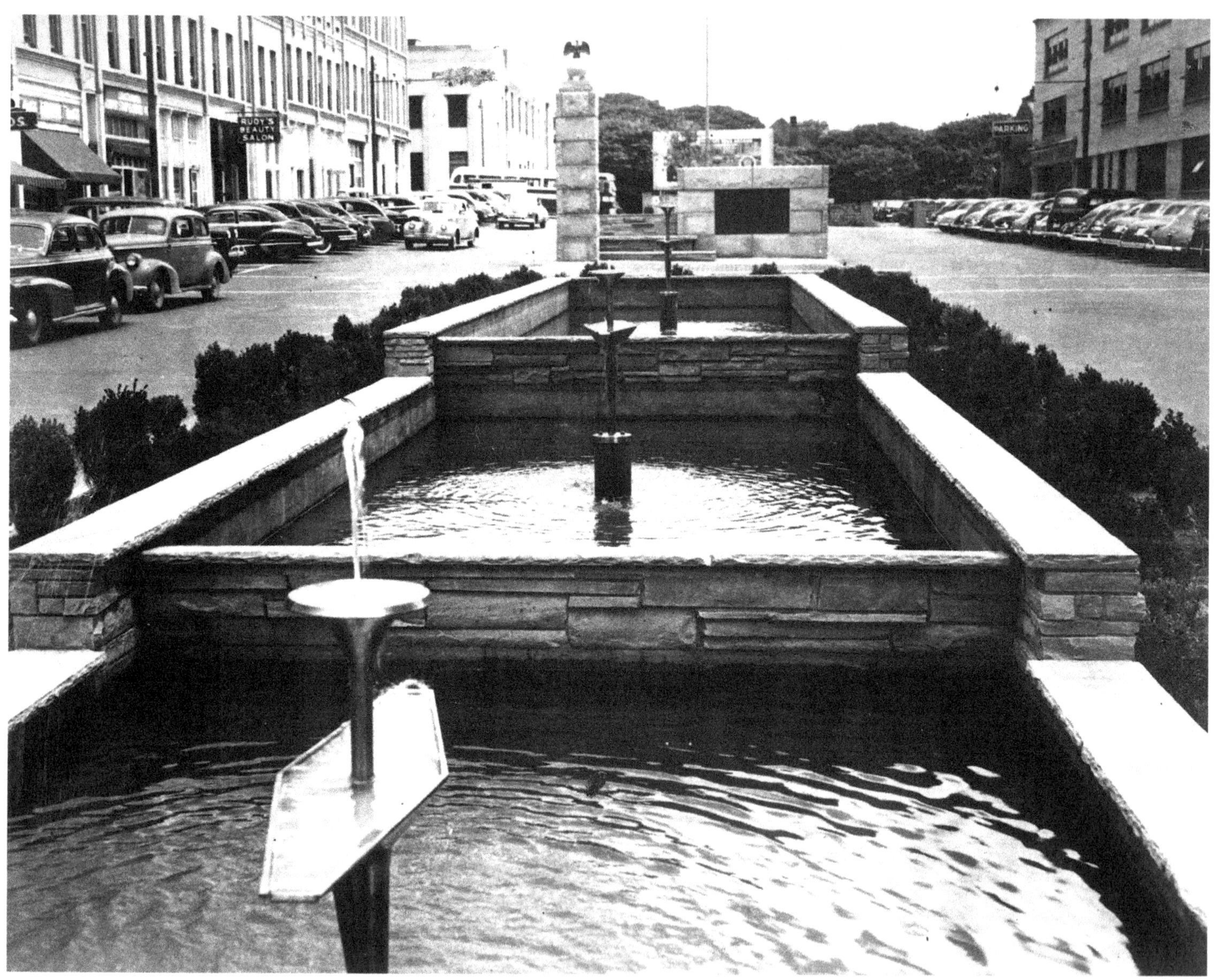

The Patten Parkway is an unusual one-block space off Georgia Avenue between Eighth and Ninth streets that once was home to a farmers' market. The water course and surrounding stonework memorialize local soldiers who fell in World War II. On February 22, 1950, the bronze tablet was unveiled in a ceremony by the mother of Joseph Whitehead, the first local soldier to perish in the war.

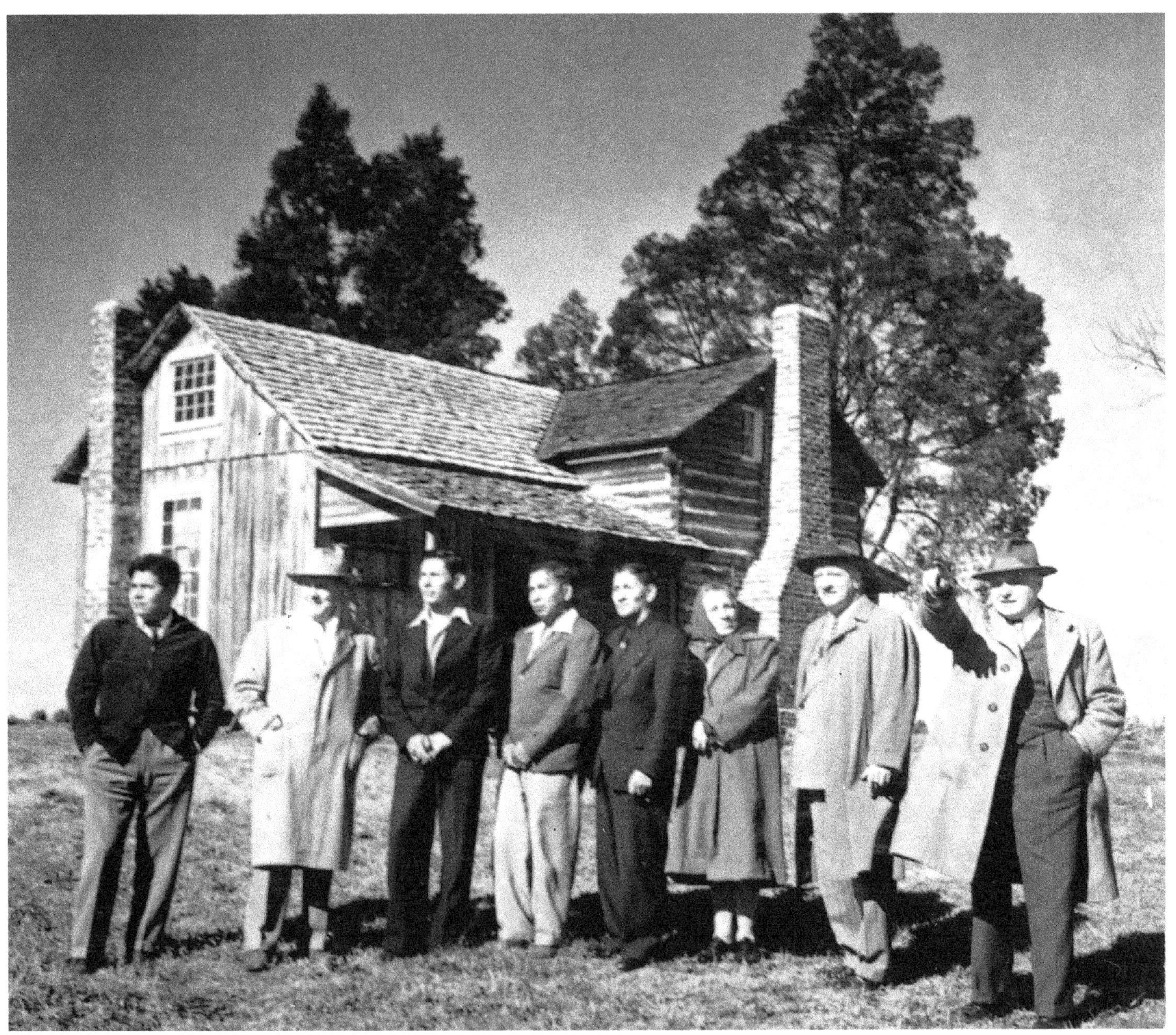

Spring Frog cabin stands on a hill at Audubon Acres (originally the Elise Chapin Wildlife Sanctuary) east of town near a branch of Chickamauga Creek. Constructed probably around 1800, the cabin was located near a settlement in the old Cherokee nation. Here a group of visitors from the North Carolina Cherokee reservation, including McKinley Ross, visit with the Chattanooga naturalist writer Robert Sparks Walker in 1950.

On a March day in 1950, an enormous crowd estimated at 20,000 people gathers on Market Street to witness the Chattanooga Shoe Shine Day Contest. A popular song, "The Chattanooga Shoe Shine Boy," was a big hit for country singer Red Foley and engendered the competition, which was won by 15-year-old Nathaniel (Bo) McCann, a student at Washington High School.

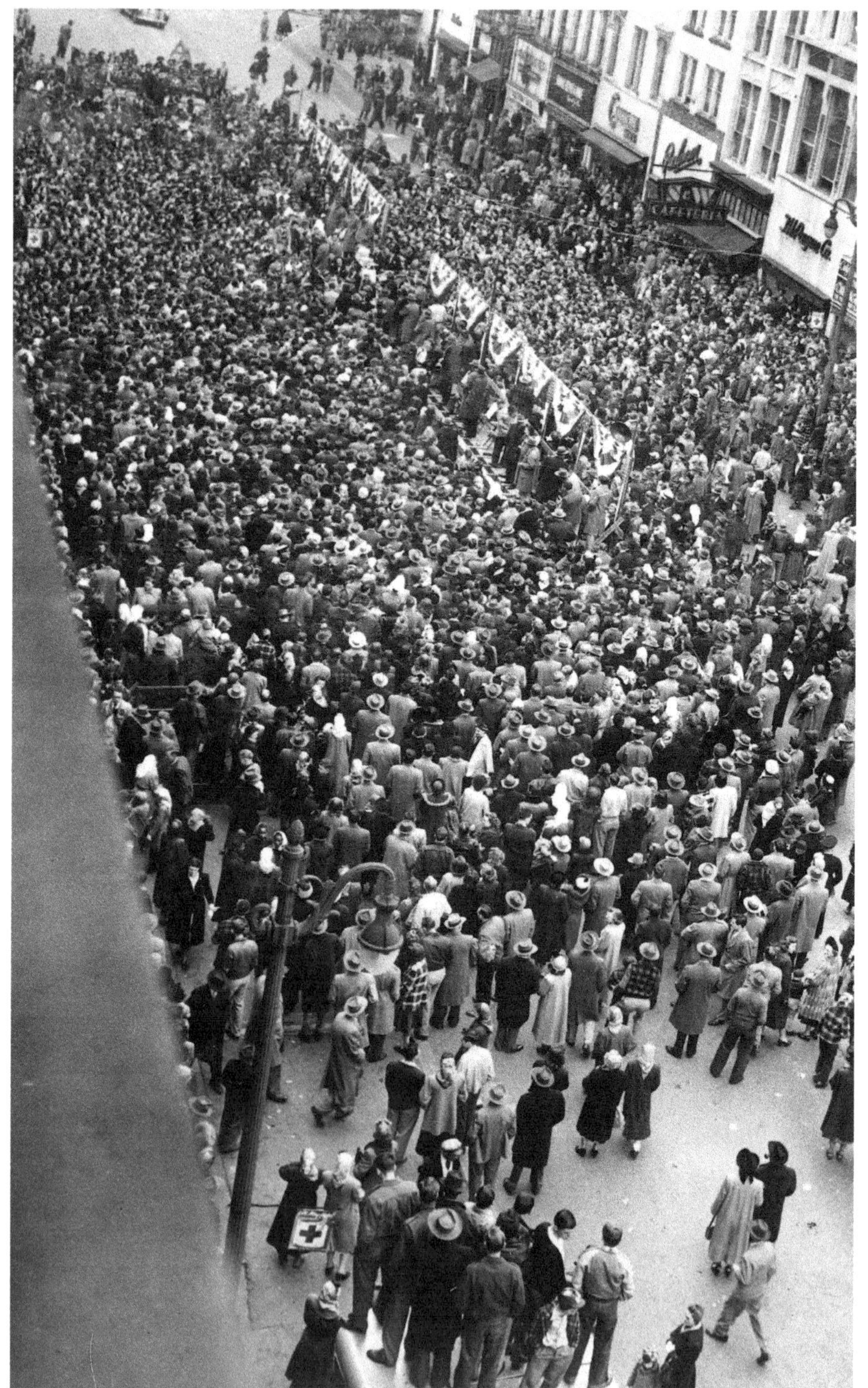

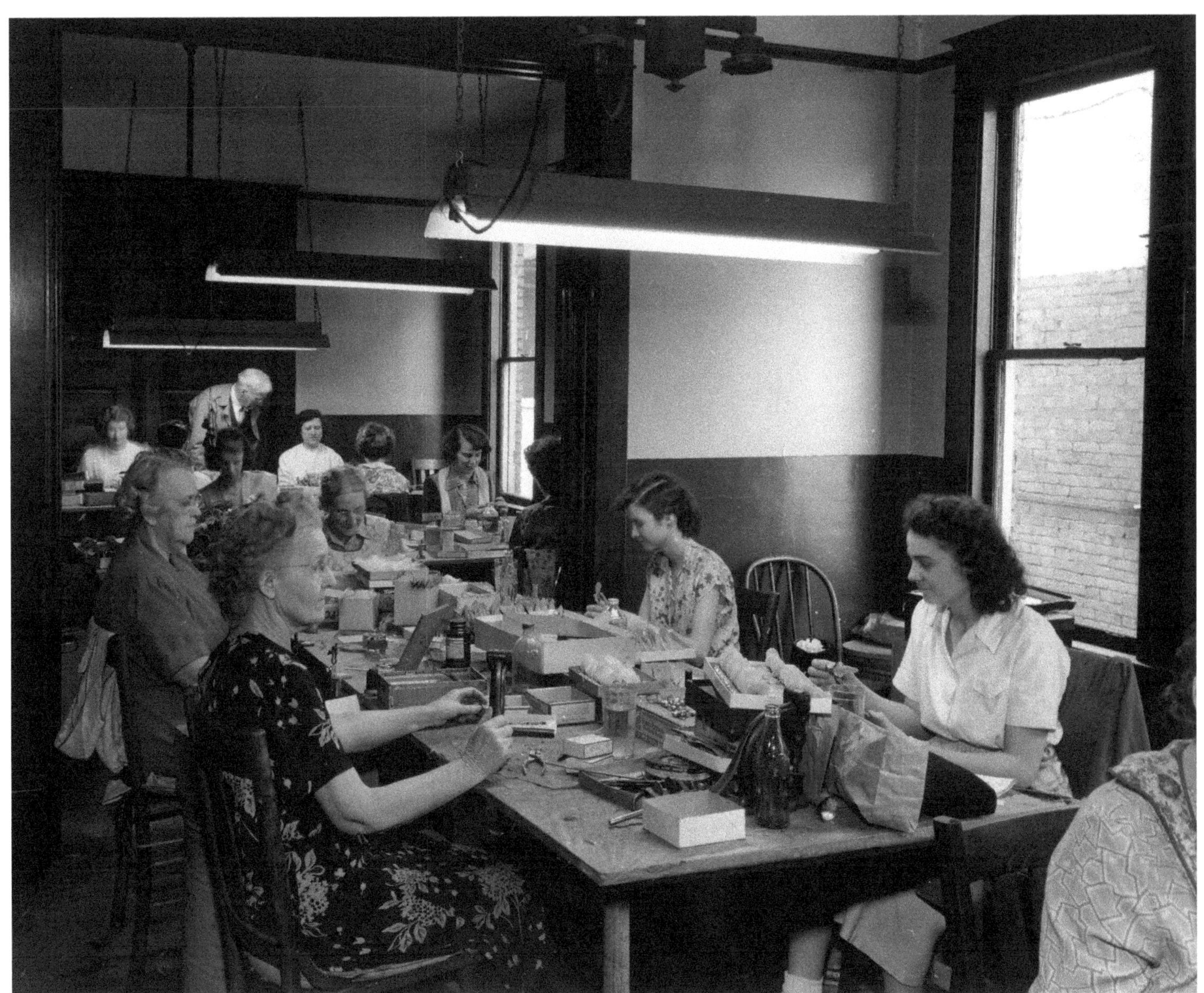

The art of fly fishing is well known, but the art of tying a fly may be underappreciated. Ernest H. Peckinpaugh began commercially producing fishing lures for southern sportsmen in the 1920s and by the 1940s could offer as many as 60 combinations and colors to those who cast in the countryside's many streams. Peckinpaugh can be seen in the back of the room supervising employees who in 1950 assiduously assemble the intricate lures.

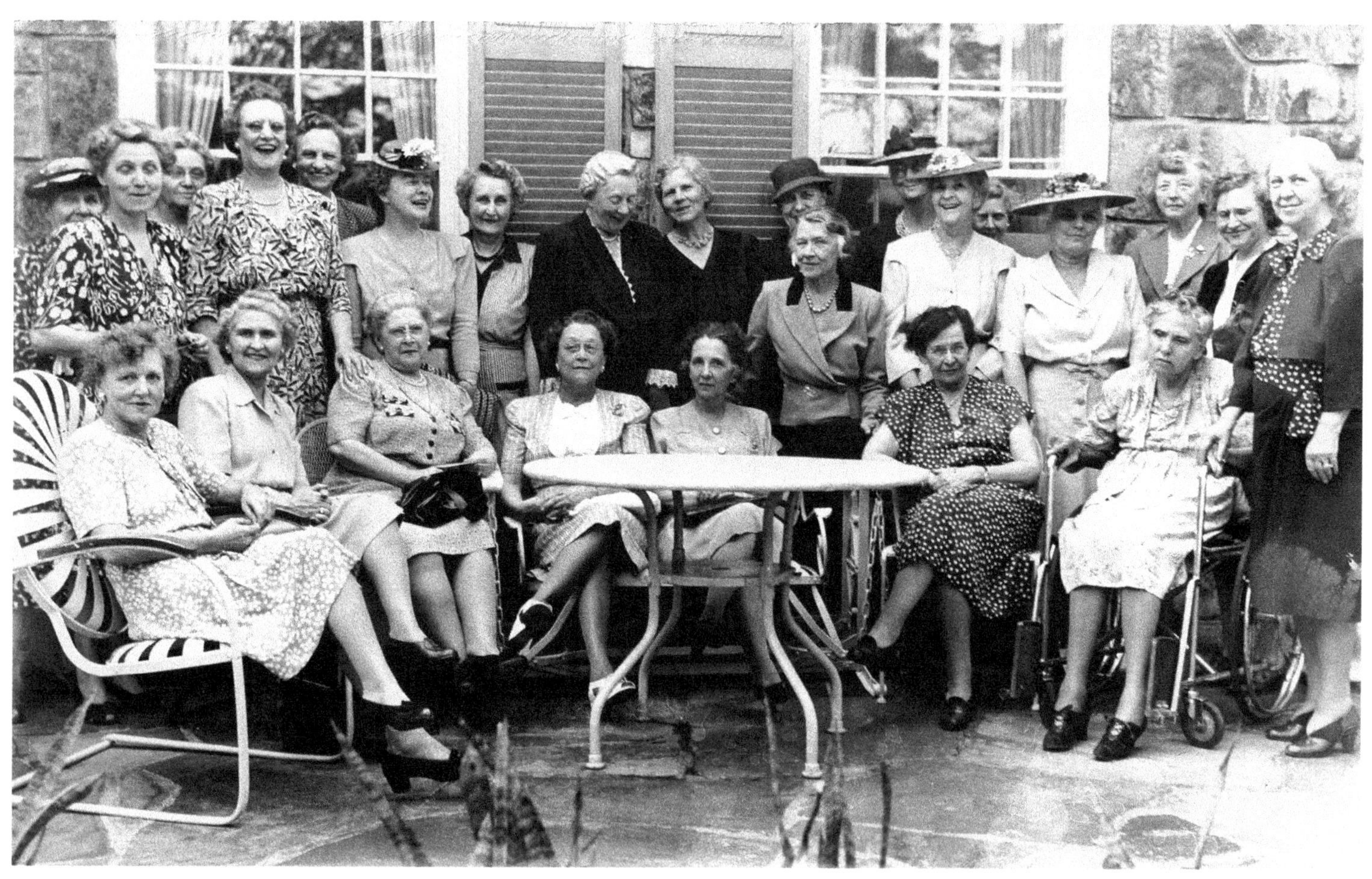

Women's clubs were a staple of polite society in the twentieth century, in Chattanooga as elsewhere. The 26 women in this photograph most likely form the Art Study Club organized in 1909. Believed to be in the photograph are Mrs. W. G. Oehmig, Jr., seated on the far left; Mrs. Garnet Carter (Frieda) in the wheelchair; and Mrs. James Finley (Cora) third from left in the back row. This image of club members was recorded in 1950.

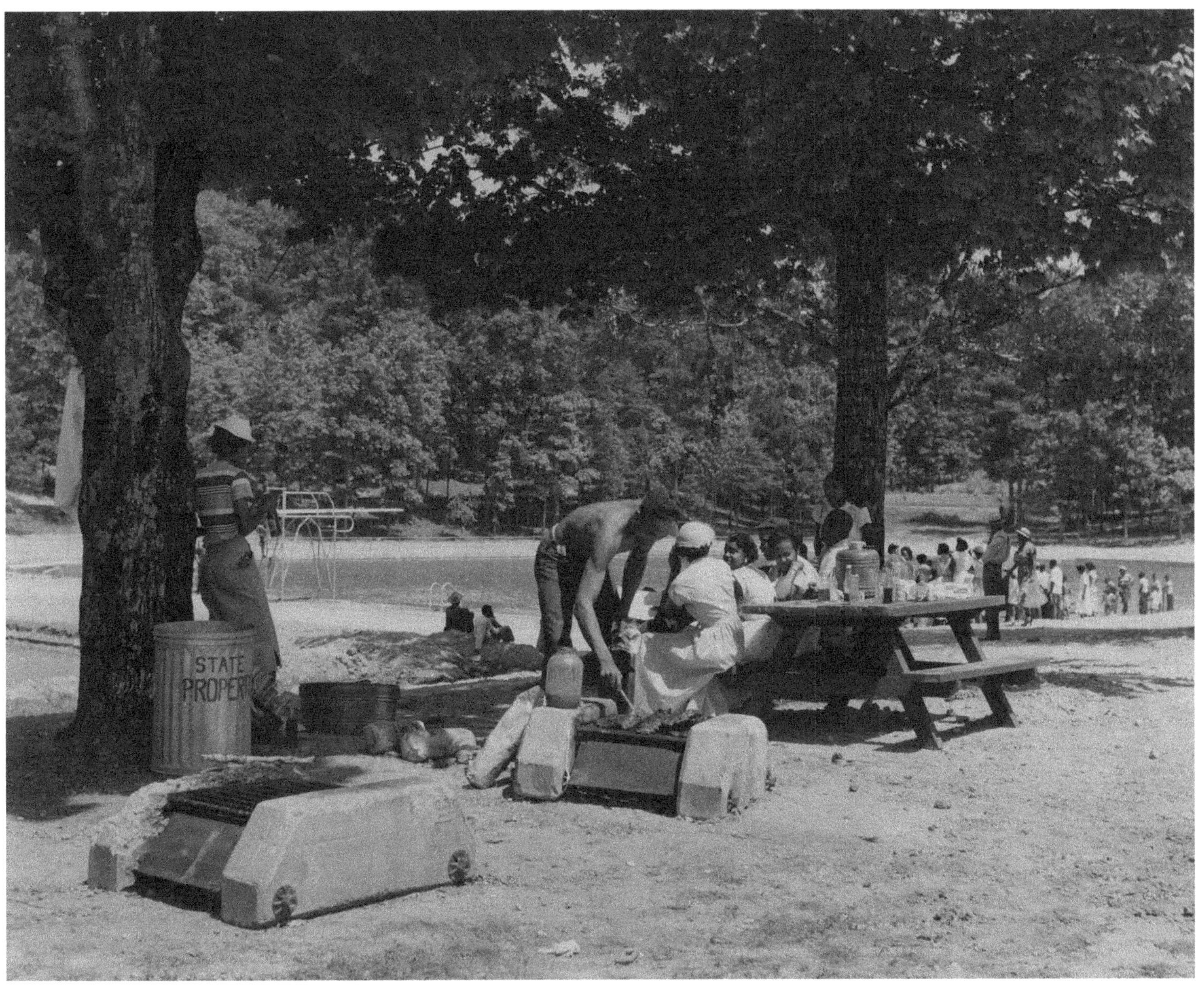

What's better than a summer day in July at the lake with sweet tea and ribs on the grill? For these Chattanoogans in 1950, the spot on the lake was Booker T. Washington Park, the only park blacks could frequent during the era of Jim Crow segregation laws in Tennessee. In the next decade, the public parks in Hamilton County would open to all citizens regardless of color.

Chattanooga's energy landscape was long dominated by electric power, courtesy of the Tennessee Valley Authority, but in 1950 another source of power—natural gas—made its appearance. On a hot August day in a ceremony at the Chattanooga High School, Tennessee governor Gordon Browning and Chattanooga Gas Company president Mike O'Lenic ignite a tall, flaming torch of natural gas to proclaim its availability.

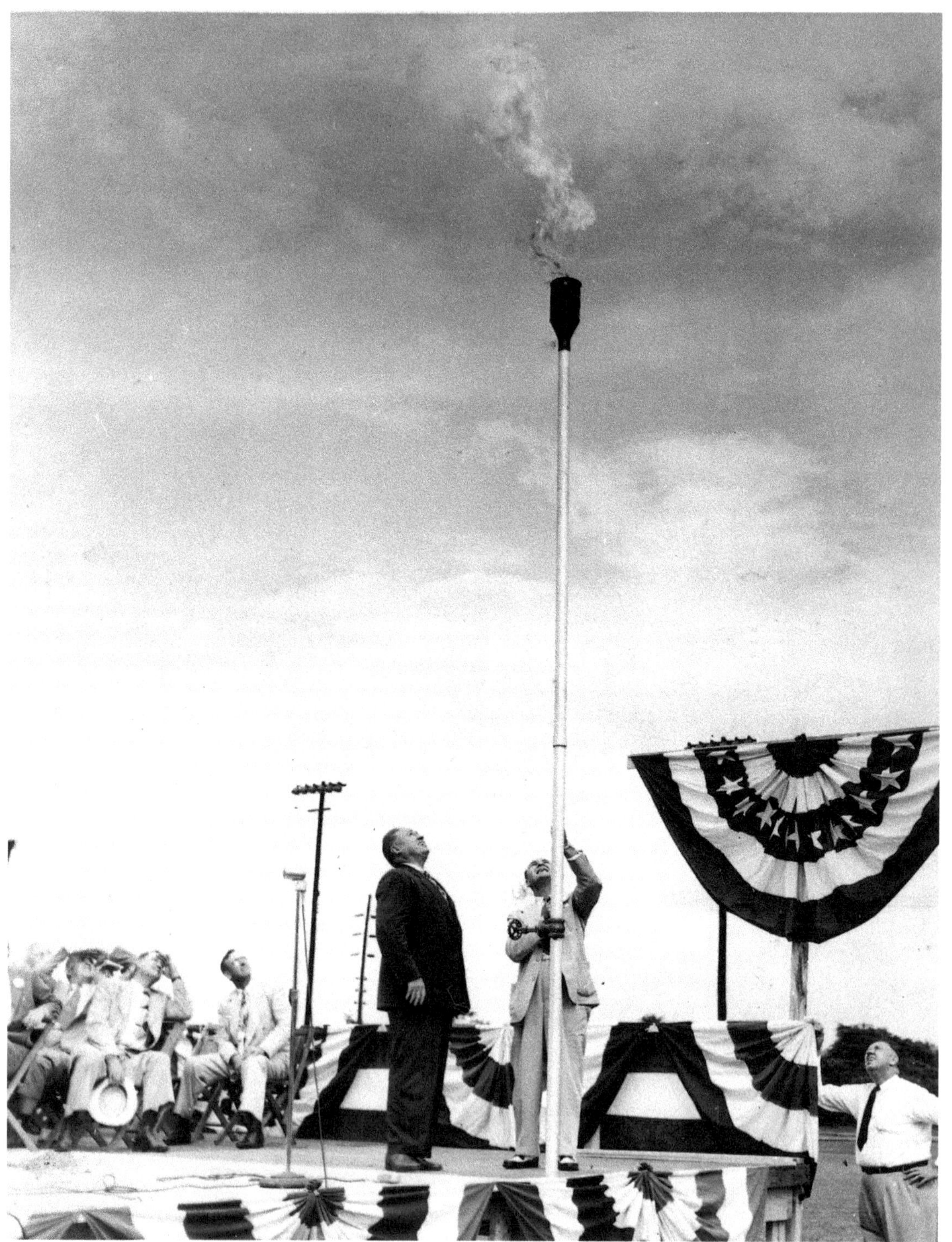

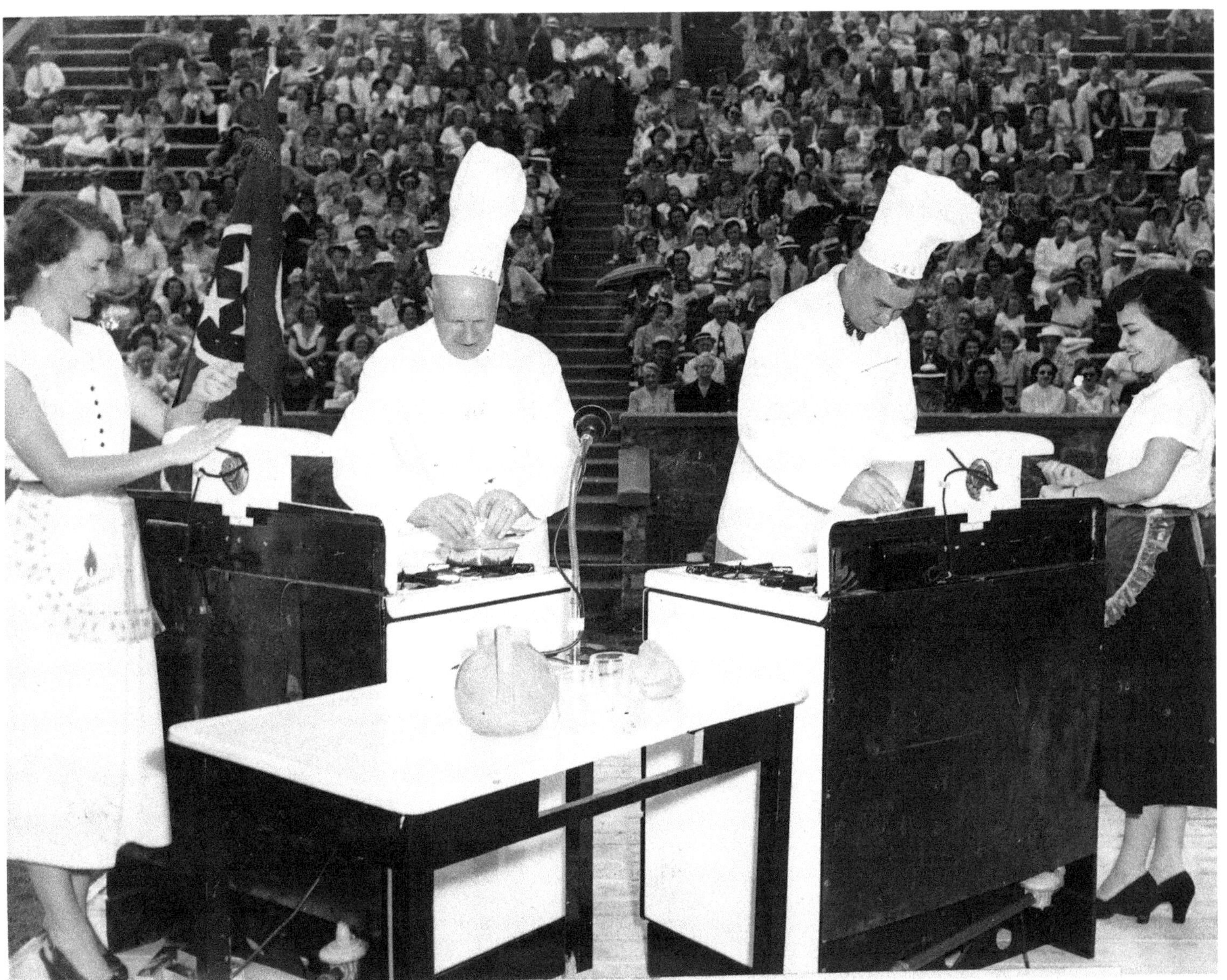

In August 1950, these two gentlemen in chef's hats are about to cook up something special with a stadium of spectators looking on. Chattanooga mayor Hugh Wasson and Hardwick Caldwell, the mayor of Lookout Mountain, demonstrate their prowess in the kitchen on a public stage in celebration of natural gas stoves, then being introduced to Chattanooga. Their aproned helpers are Lillian Roe to the left and Grace Morris to the right.

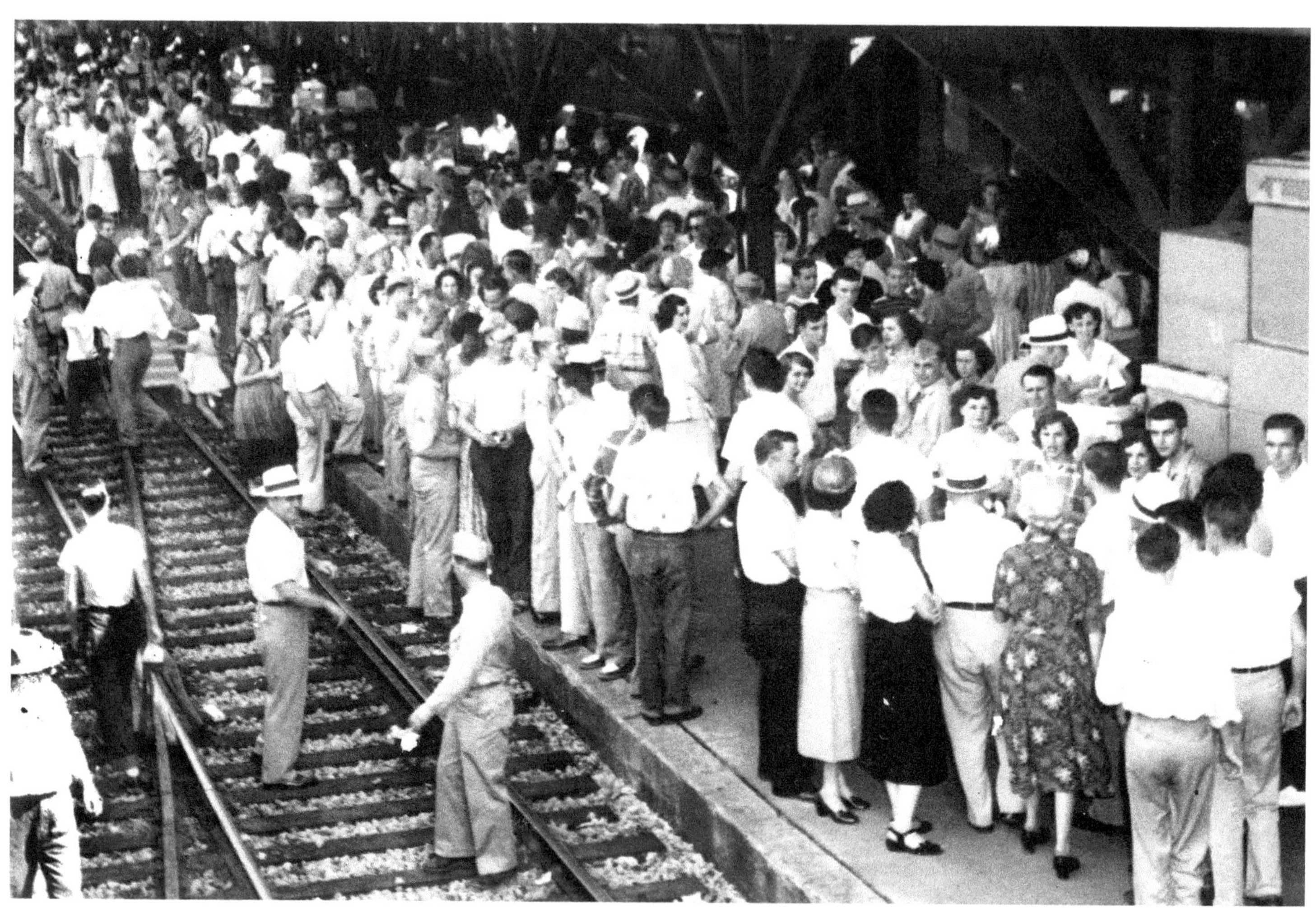

Crowds of well-wishers gather trackside in 1950 to give Chattanooga servicemen a big send-off. Animation in the groups of families and friends clearly implies the pride that citizens felt about their young men in uniform and the importance of the duty they would be called on to perform.

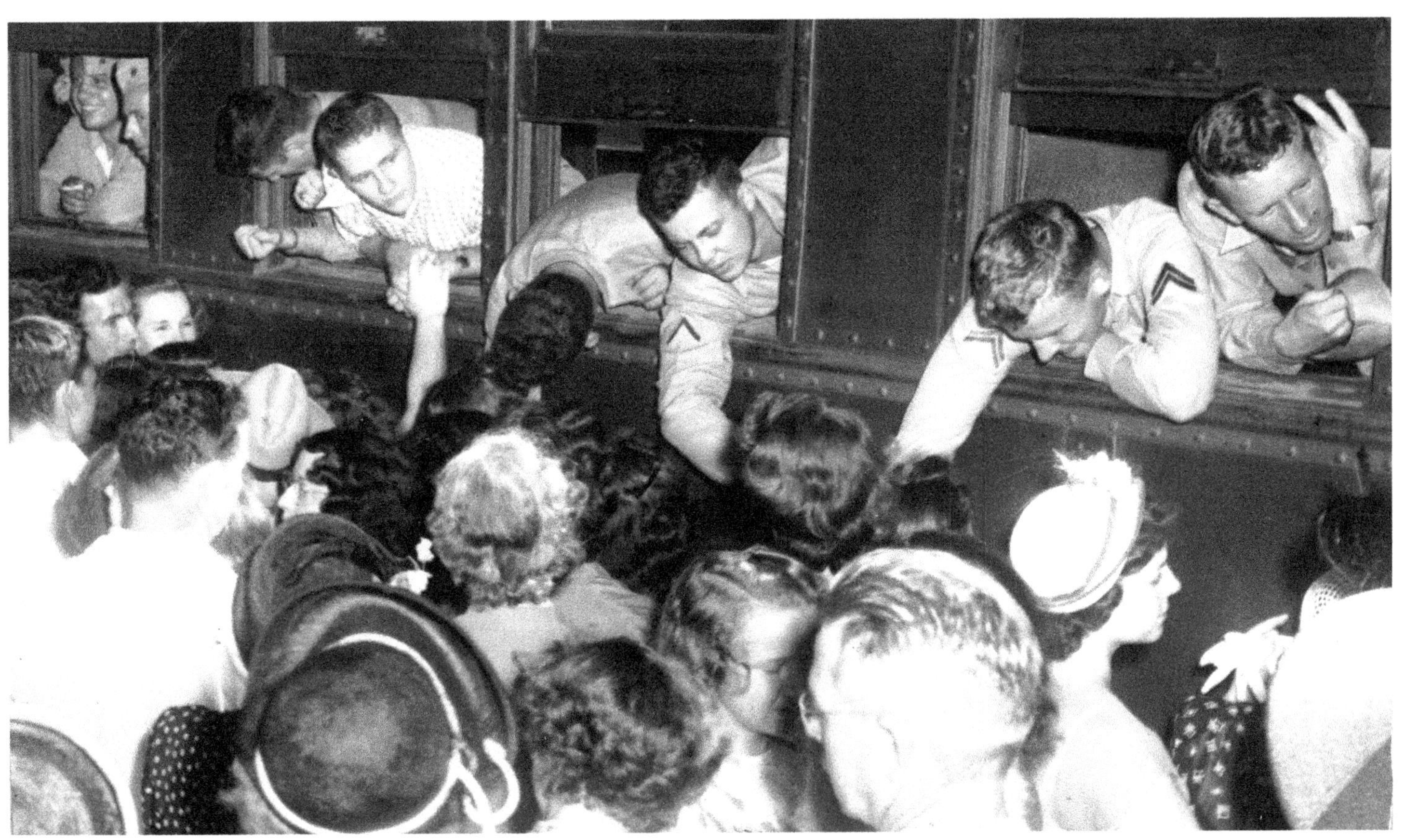

In the 1950s, the Cold War was a growing fact of life and the Korean War was in progress. Here young Marines lean out the windows of a train bound for Camp Pendleton, California, waving their last good-byes to loved ones and family members before taking the long journey cross-country and perhaps across the Pacific to the frontlines.

In 1950, Roy McDonald and a helper unveil a large portrait of the Baroness d' Erlanger, for whom Erlanger Hospital is named. The baroness's husband was the original benefactor of the hospital when he made the first contribution to the institution in 1889. Roy McDonald, primarily known as the publisher of the *Chattanooga News–Free Press,* was a mover and shaker in Chattanooga for decades.

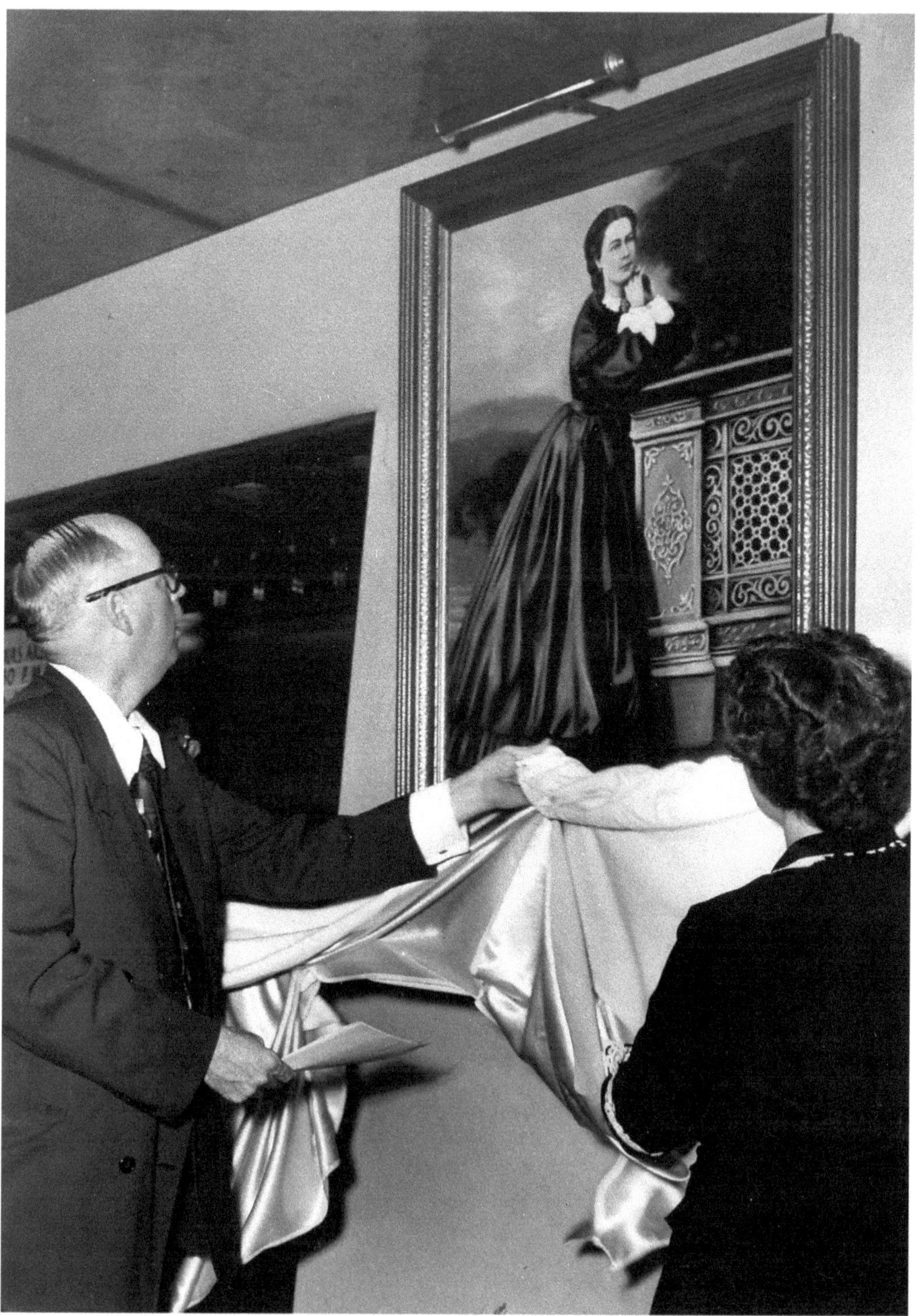

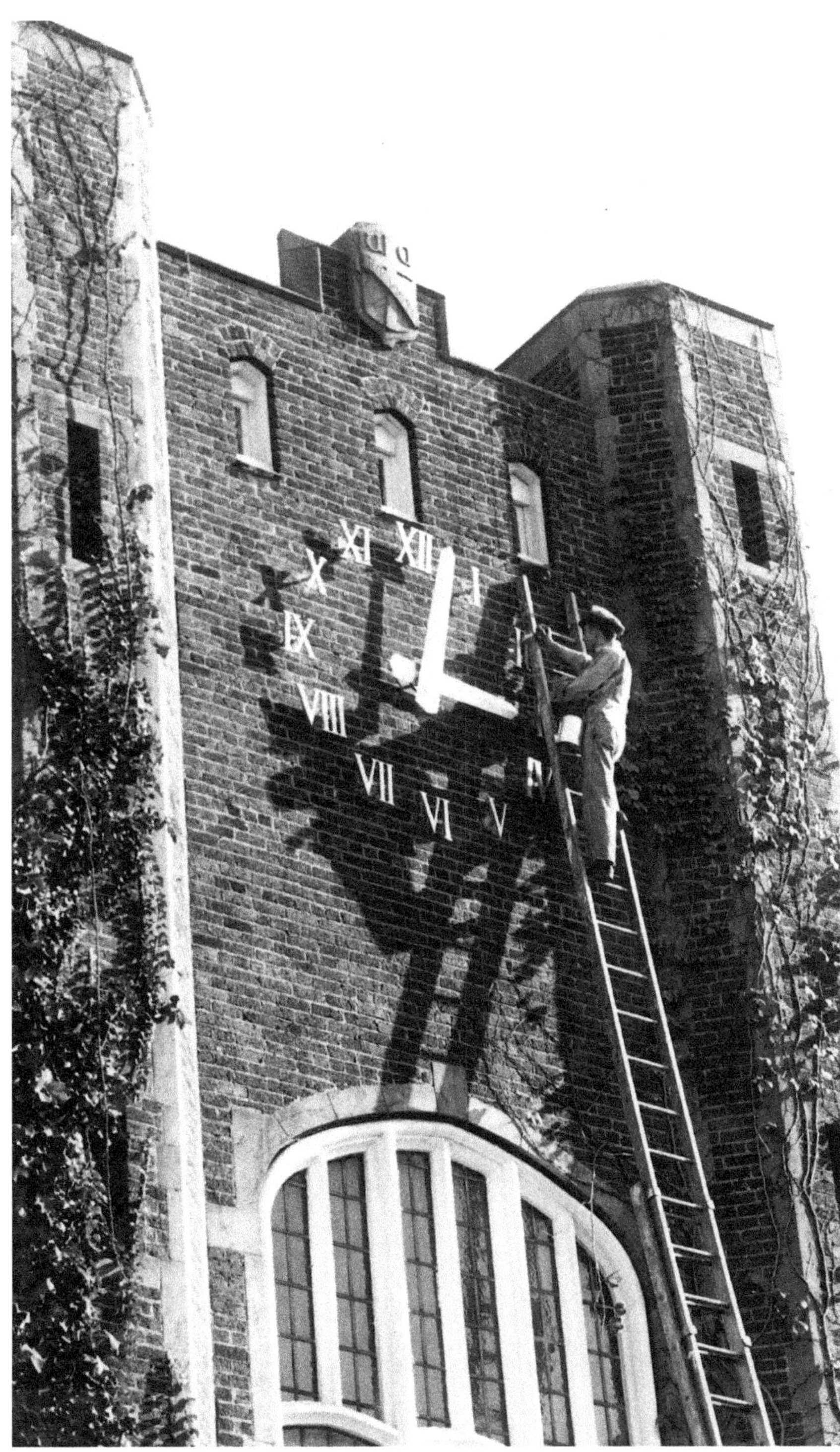

Three classes—of 1943, 1944, and 1945—at the University of Chattanooga joined hands in 1950 to make a gift to the school of this clock, which was mounted on Founders Hall. The electric clock was installed by Charles Wright, the maintenance superintendent, keeping students on time to class for years and reminding drivers on McCallie Avenue of the time of day.

Four uniformed men stand at attention while Nick Venza, the bugler, plays at a Victory Day ceremony on November 11, 1950. Stationed on Market Street are two Legionnaires, George Bessler and E. Mason Phillips, while color guards Gene Brown and Charles M. Blacker stand at present arms. The large office building behind the men is the Hamilton National Bank Building. At street level are W. T. Grant Company and Maclellan Stores Company Department Store.

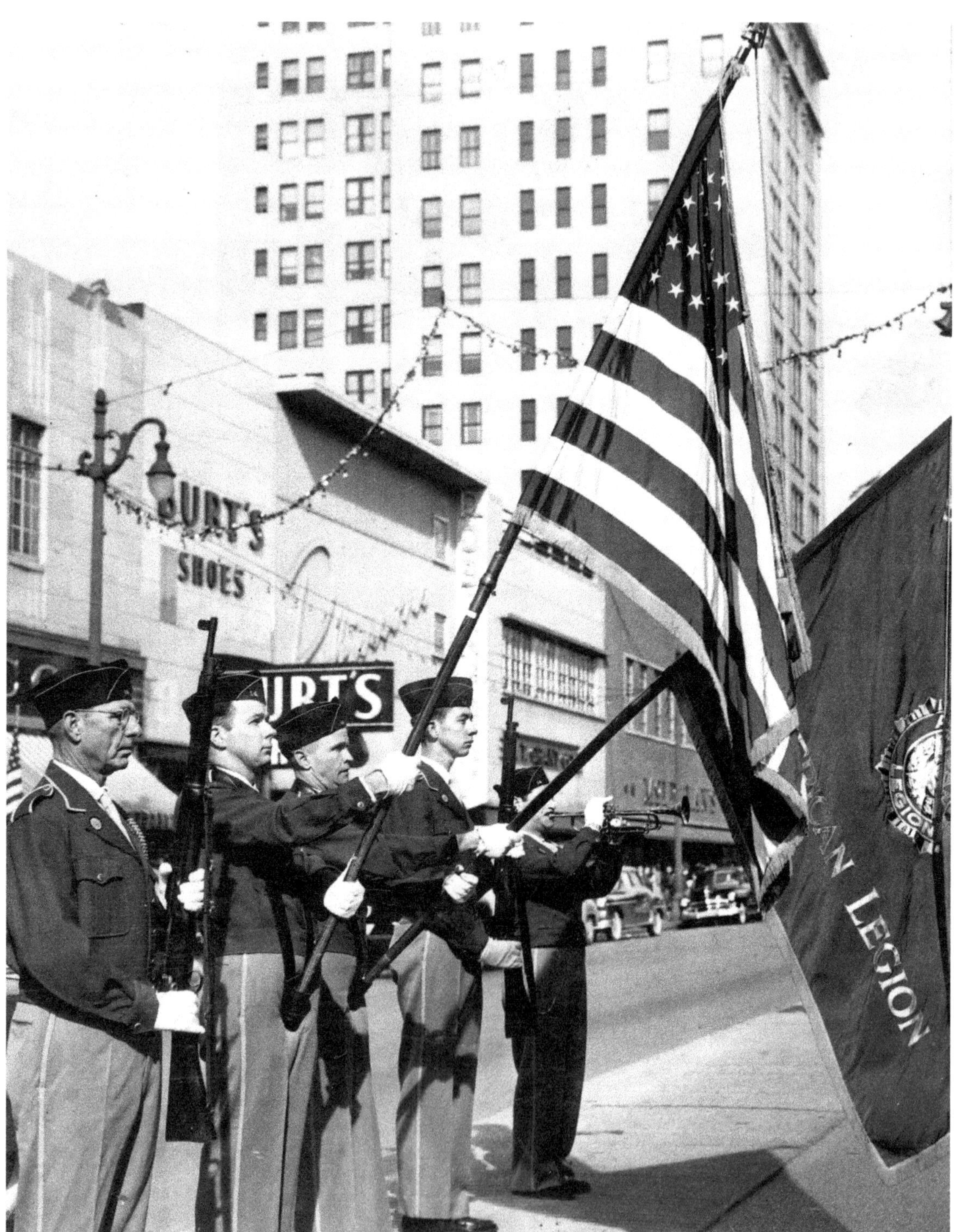

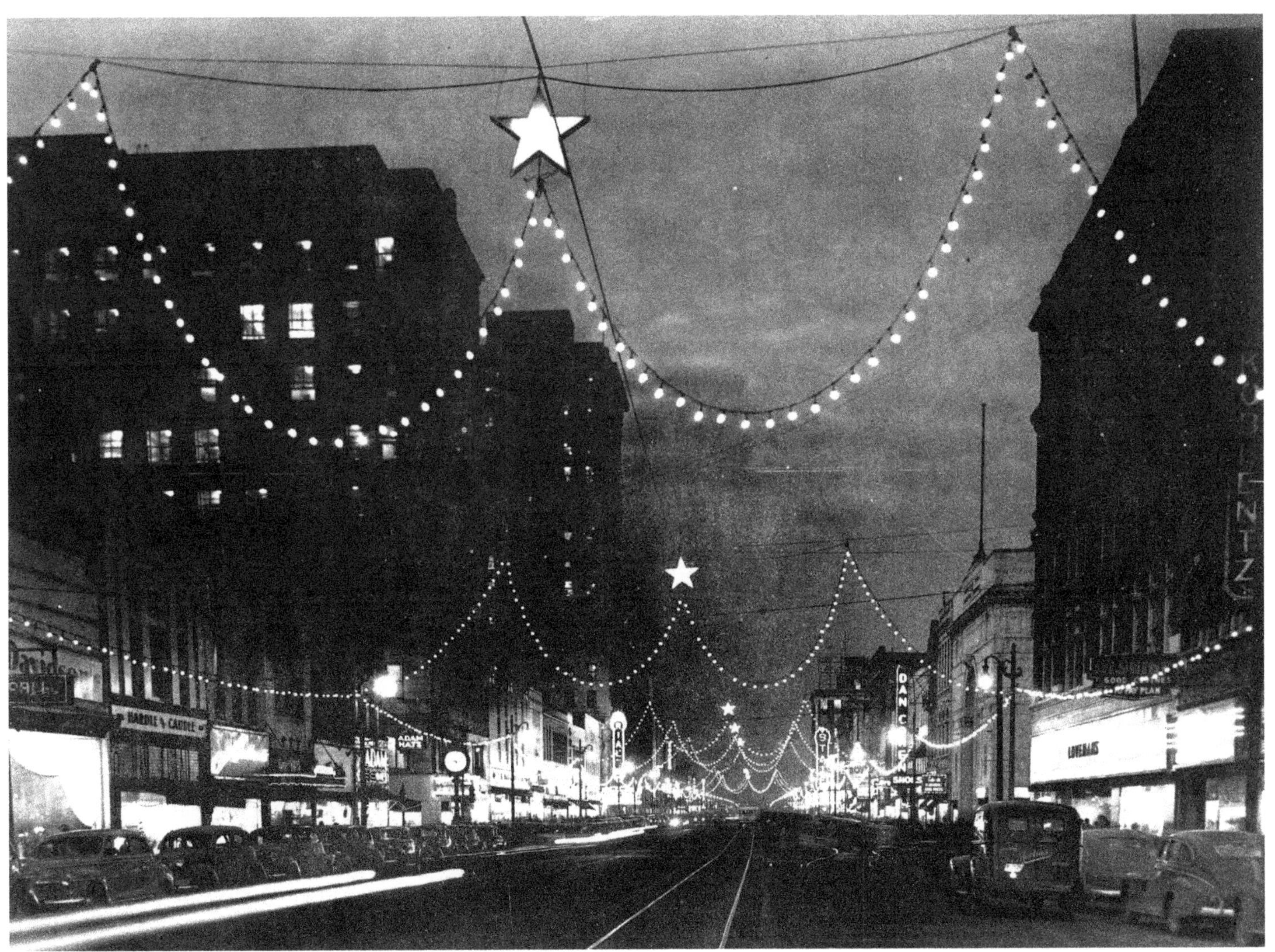

Christmas is a time of celebration and Market Street has seen decorations suspended across the thoroughfare for generations. The large stars have brightened many a wintry night sky, luring shoppers downtown after work during the evening hours to find that perfect gift for that certain someone. To the right stands Loveman's department store. Across the street, fine clothing was offered at Fulmer, Reeves, and Ware men's store and Hardie and Caudle's as well.

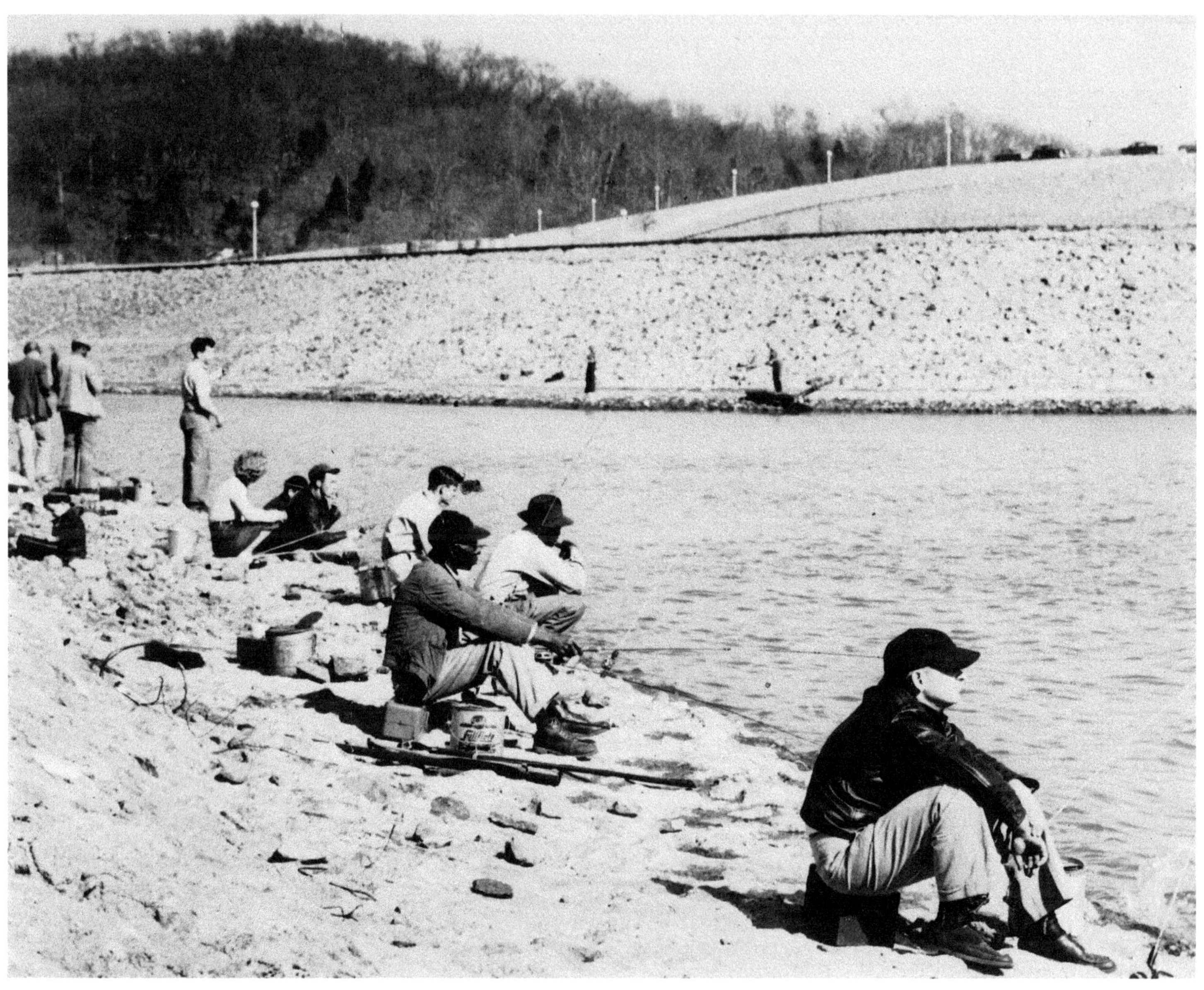

Any day the fish are biting is a good day to fish, and this photograph leaves the impression that this may be one of those days. Fishermen are lined up at the Chickamauga Lake inlet in 1951 near Chickamauga Dam, where periodic water releases keep things interesting for anglers. Nonetheless, these folks continue casting and waiting in a scene that is still common today.

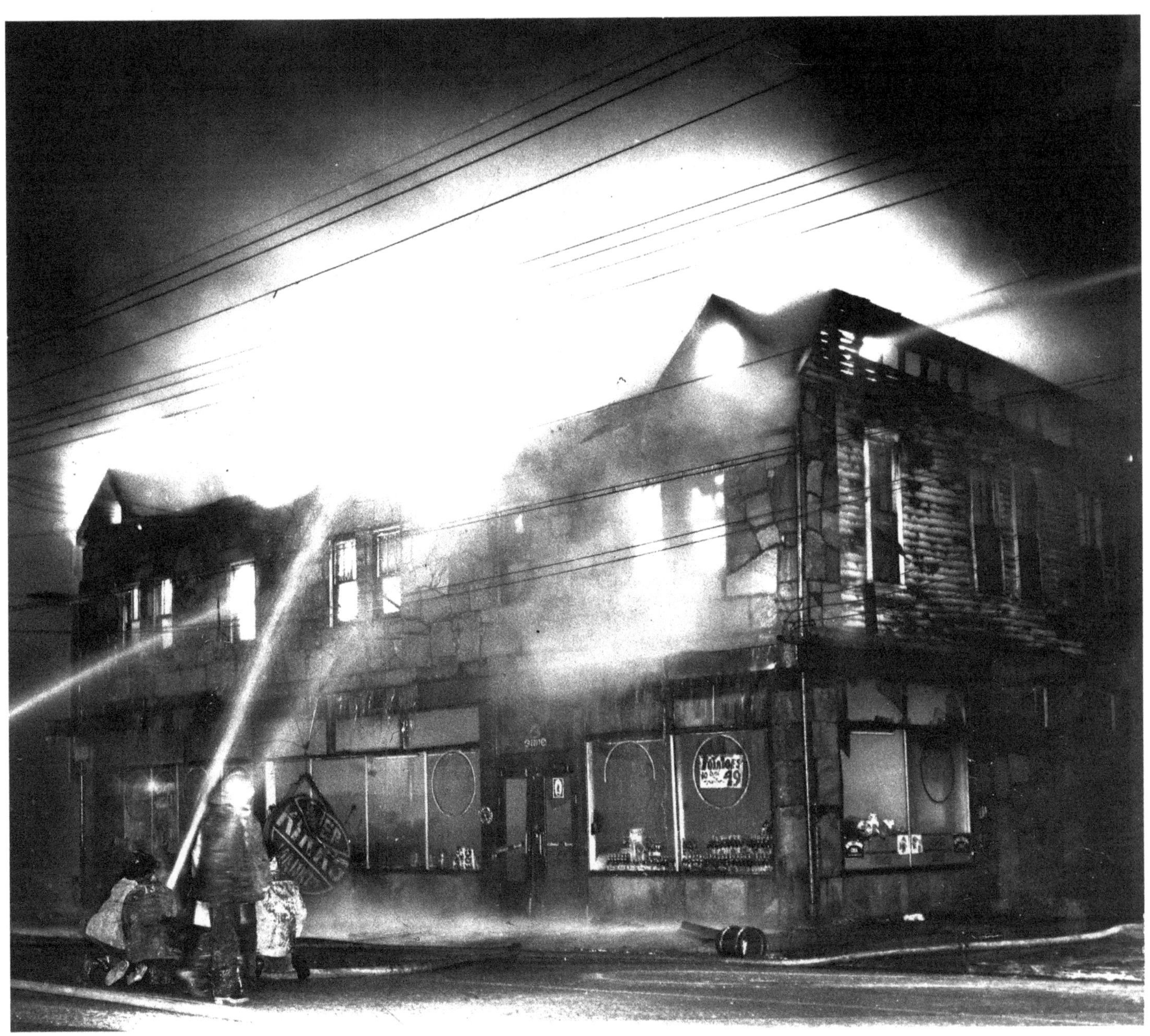

A raging fire illuminates the February night sky in 1951 as firemen work to control this intense blaze at Kirk's Supermarket at 2207 South Broad Street. Old clapboard buildings such as this one built of aged, dry wood could ignite quickly and succumb to flames in minutes. Unfortunately, David T. Bishop died in the fire, in one of the apartments upstairs.

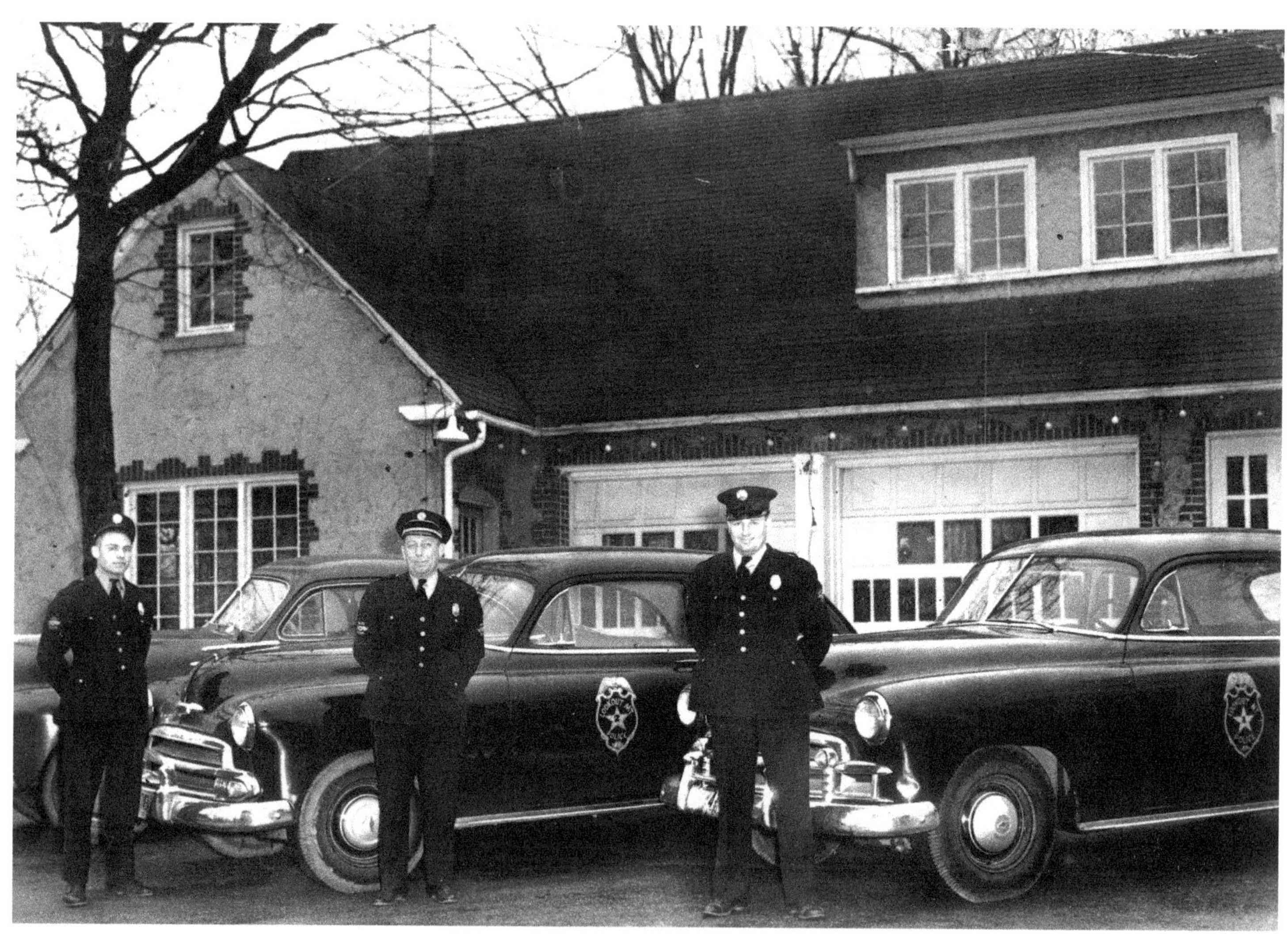

Proud policemen stand in front of their squad cars in 1951 at the town hall on Lookout Mountain. Though it is an integral part of Chattanooga and its history, Lookout Mountain is an incorporated town in Tennessee with its own police force and other services. Long a vibrant and important part of Chattanooga's economy, this town abuts the town of Lookout Mountain, Georgia, which sits right across the state line.

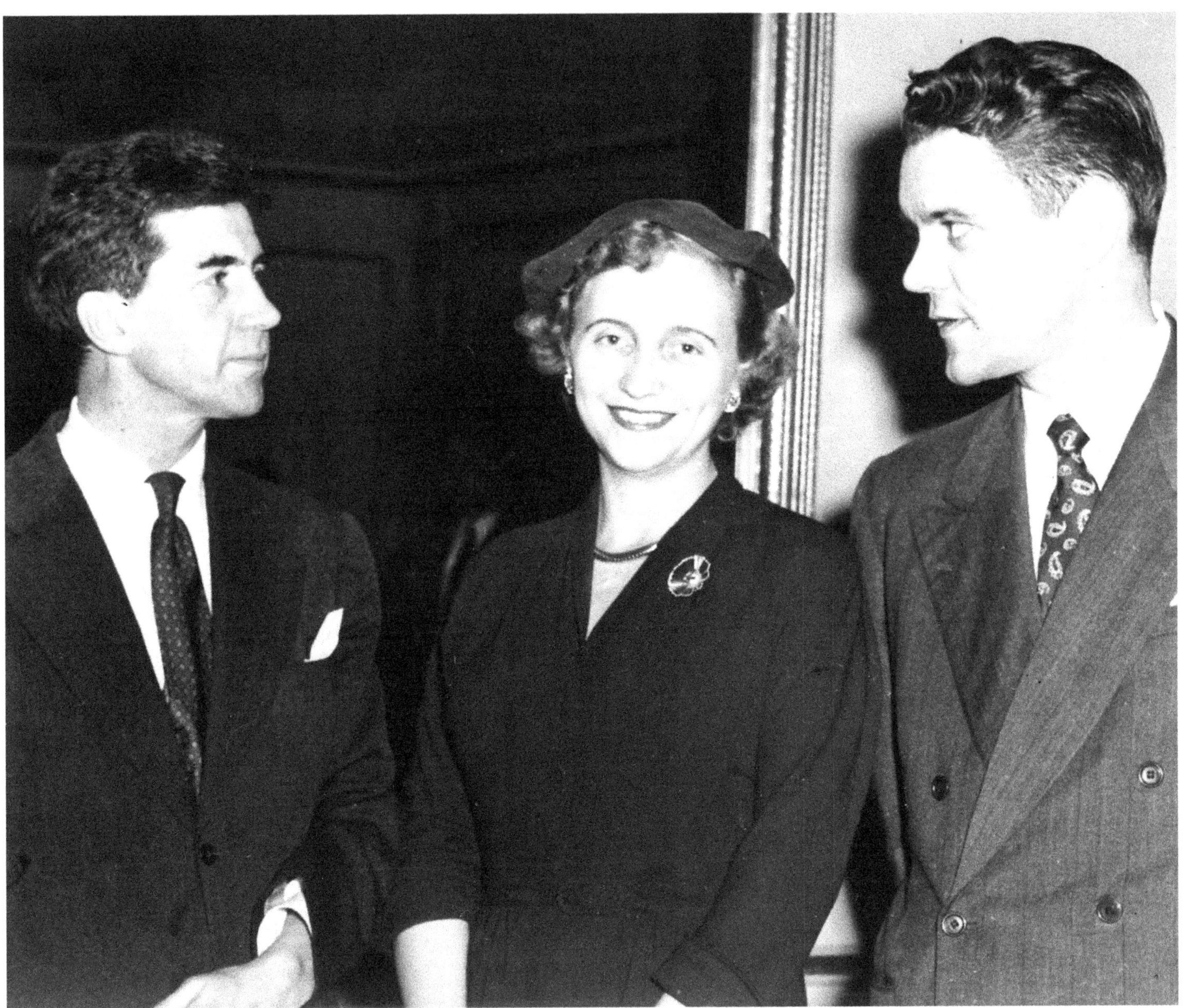

Margaret Truman, the daughter of President Harry S. Truman, pursued a professional singing career and appeared with the Chattanooga Symphony Orchestra on December 11, 1950. It was the same month that she received a tepid review from the *Washington Post* stating that she was "flat a good deal of the time." It infuriated her father. Here she stands with symphony conductor Joseph Hawthorne (left) and Shelby Brammer, president of the Philharmonic Association.

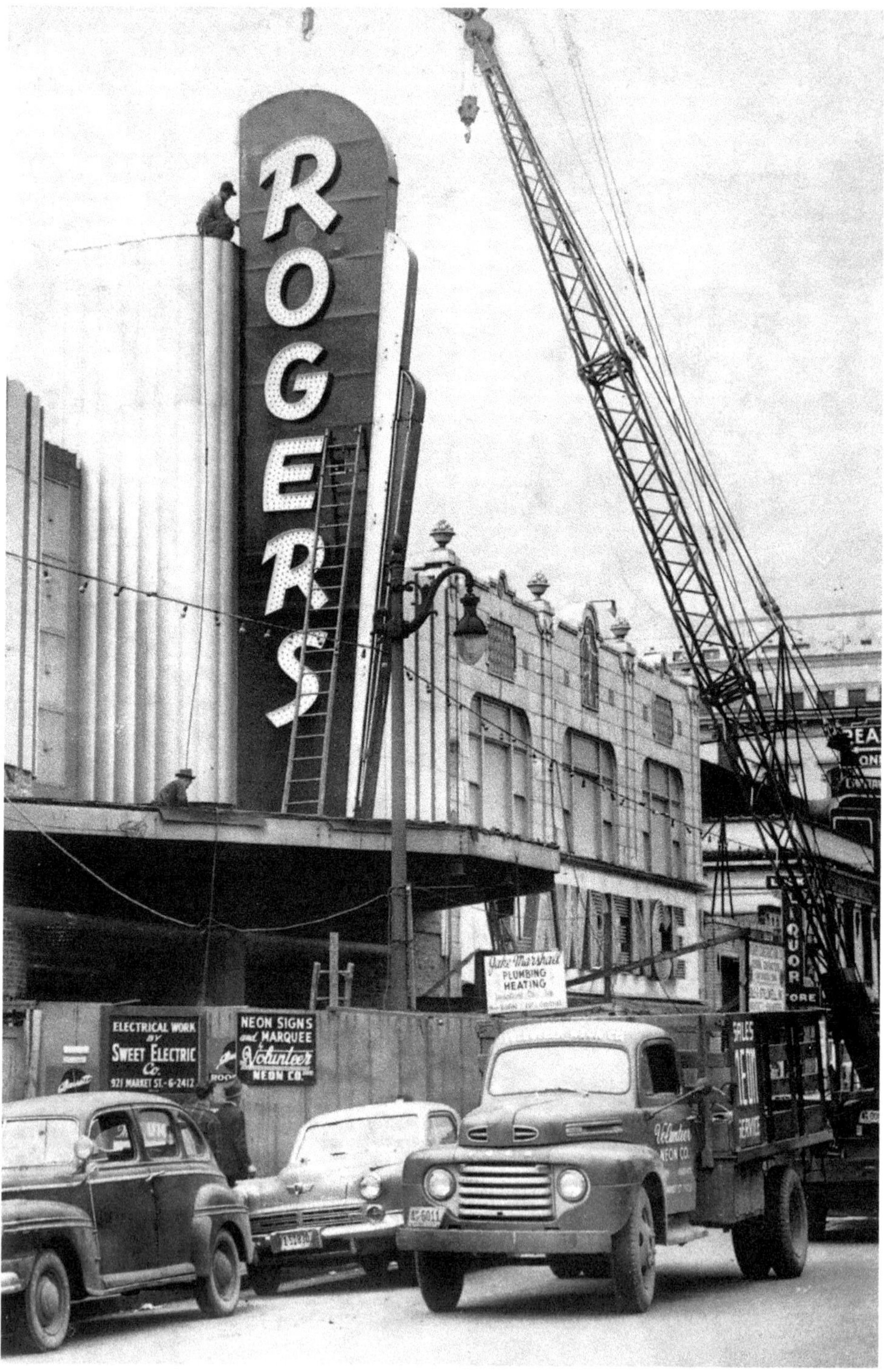

Downtown movie theaters were a fixture in American cities for decades beginning in the 1920s. In 1951, a new film palace was opening, named for local entertainment entrepreneur Emmett R. Rogers. Even though there were other movie houses nearby, the enormous popularity of westerns, crime dramas, and musicals in the 1950s made this new "picture show" a sure business bet, and succeed it did.

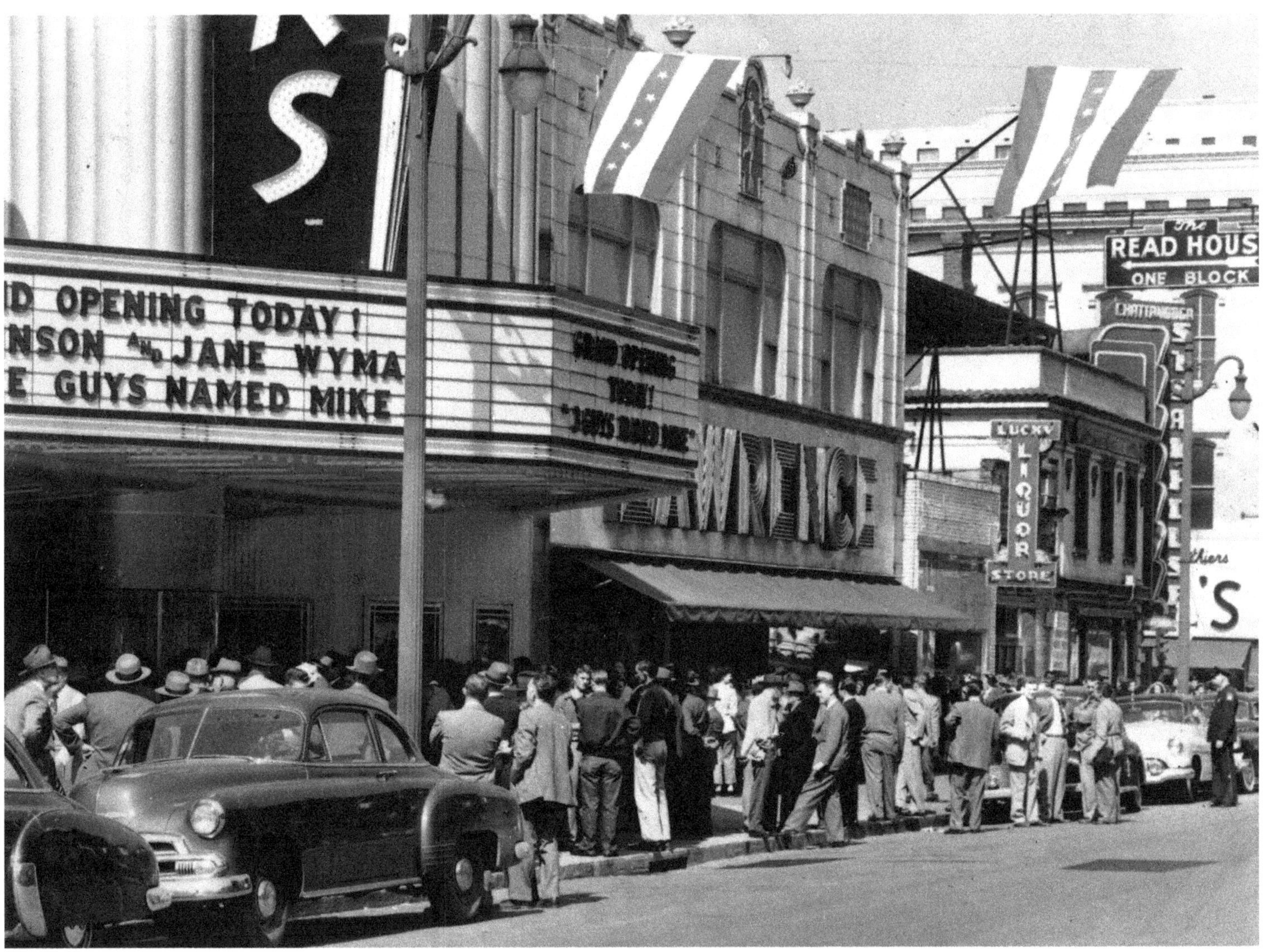

When the Rogers Theater opened in March 1951, it was no surprise that people showed up in droves. Larger and better appointed than the other local movie houses, it was the "newer and better" place to see a flick. It prospered for many years, but by the 1970s shopping malls with their suburban theaters were sapping the life out of downtown Chattanooga. The Rogers would close in 1976.

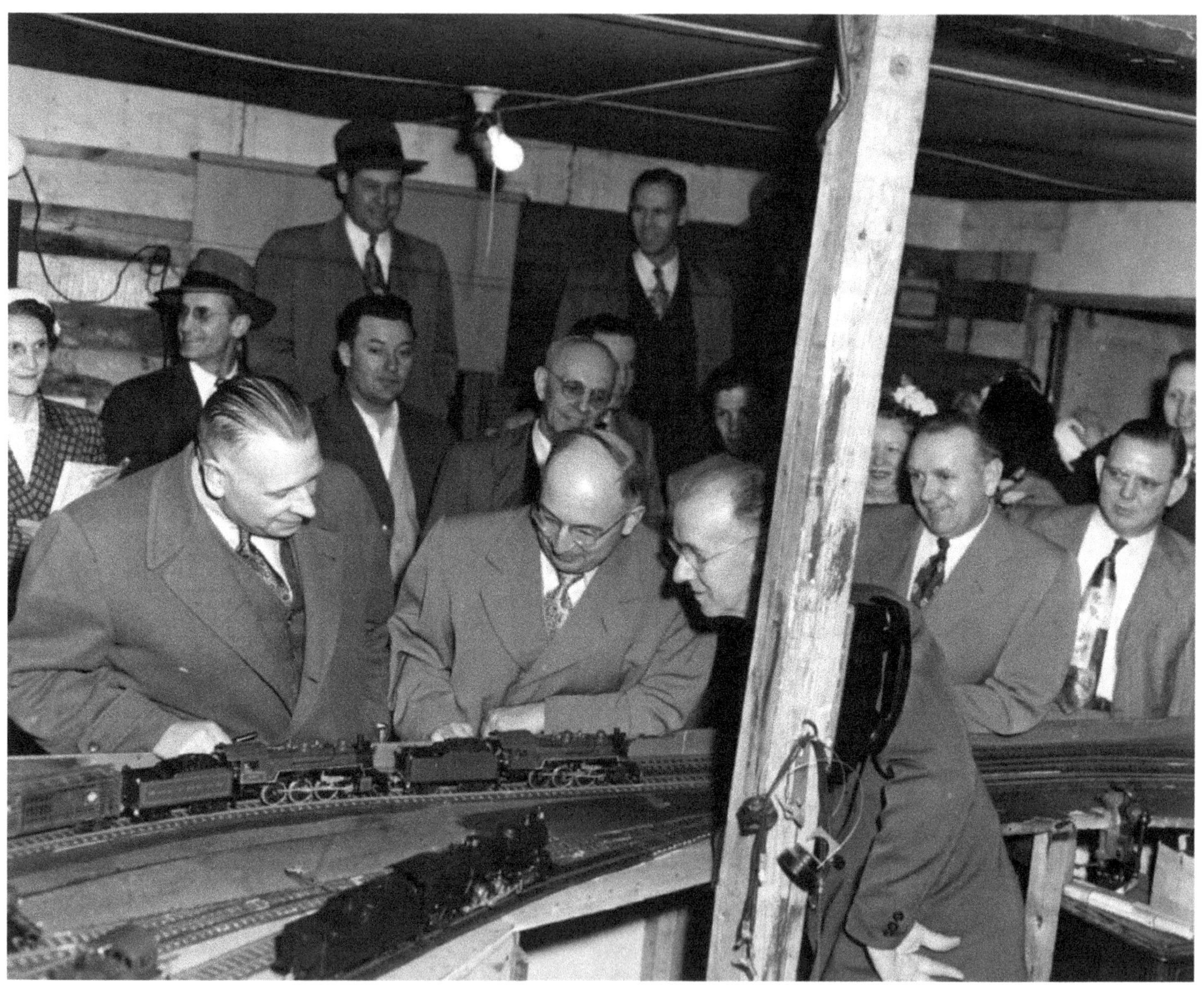

On Glass Street below Missionary Ridge, Thomas Cox and kin built a model railroad inside a real boxcar that Cox had installed behind the family home. When Mantua Metal Products executives got wind of the ambitious layout and that Cox had purchased their model of the *General,* a replica of the famous locomotive newly available to HO gauge modelers, they paid a promotional visit to the Cox & Lawson line. Here is the tour in progress.

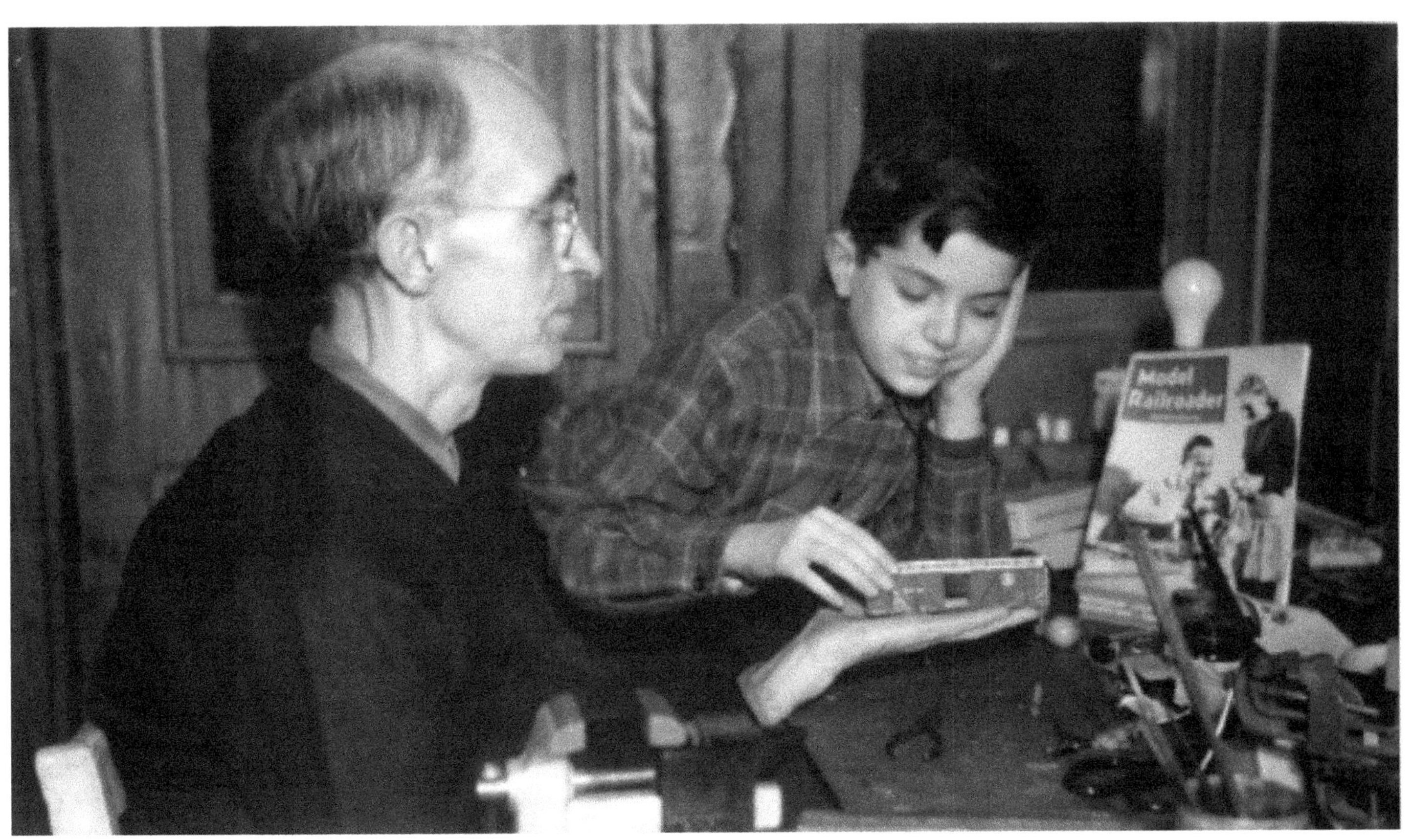

Homer Lawson and great-nephew Charles Cox display a model boxcar, on the assembly line at the Cox & Lawson railcar factory on Glass Street.

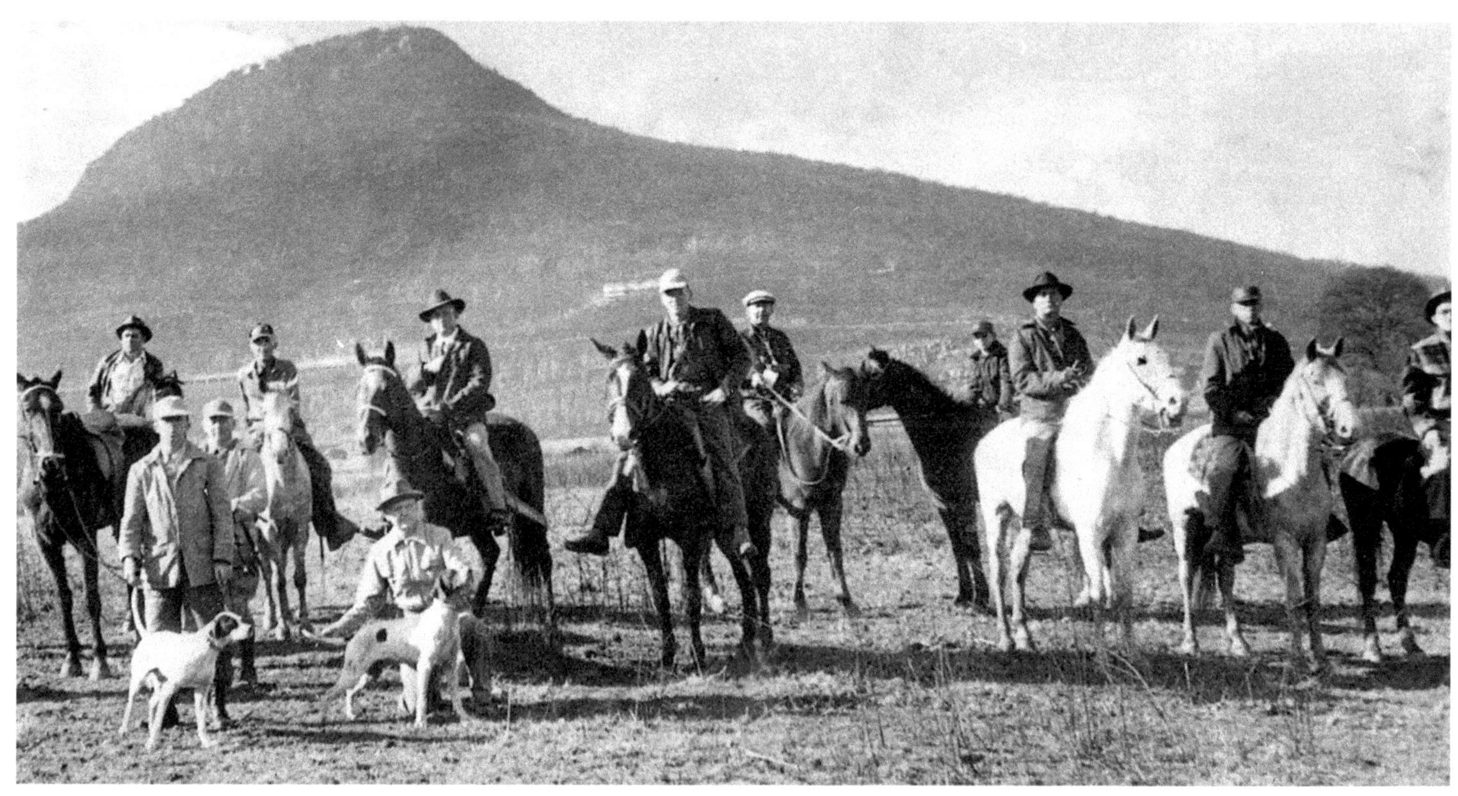

For those who like to hunt and fish, Chattanooga is the place to be. Moccasin Bend—across the river from Lookout Mountain—lends itself to both. Hunting tops the bill on this day in March 1951 as the Chattanooga Field Trial Association readies two dogs for the annual field-trial bird dog competition. Two canines with their trainers stand stiffly as the men on horseback alertly wait for the signal to begin.

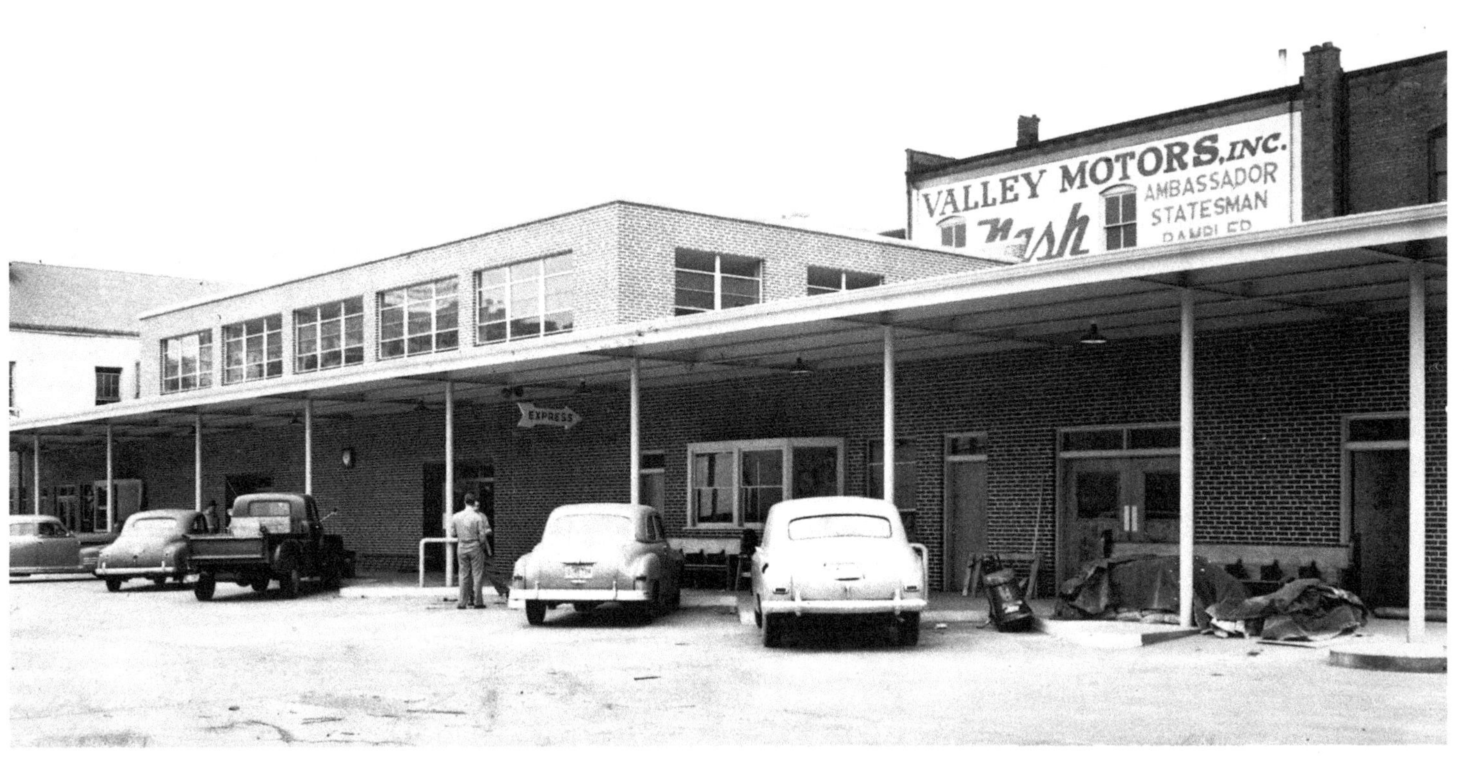

Riding the bus was something of a rite of passage for most people in the South, especially before families had more than one car or any car at all. The buses stopped at every town, and many of the passengers smoked. Every town had a bus station like this Greyhound station, which sat on Market Street between 9th and 10th until it was relocated in 1971.

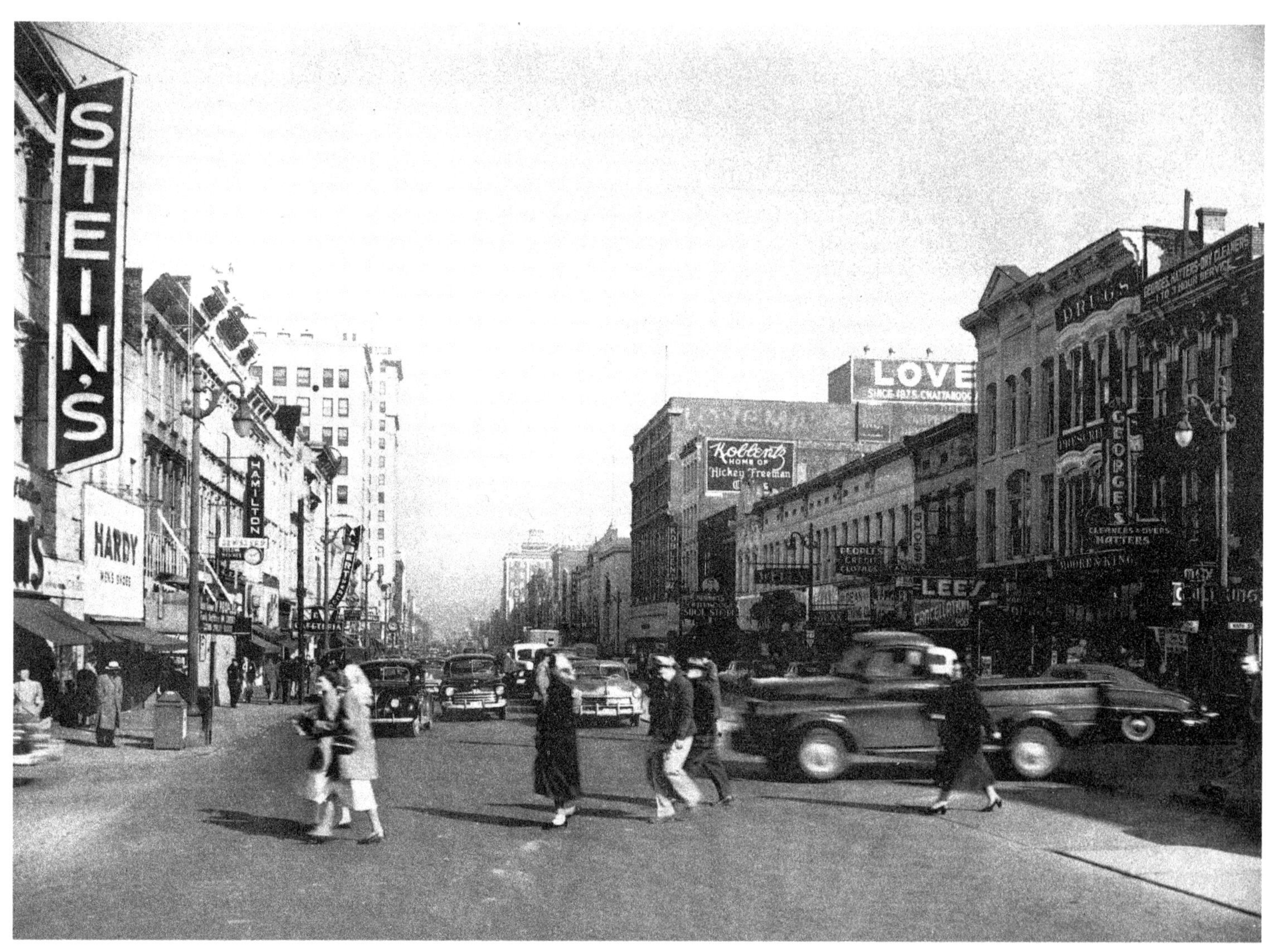

This image of Market Street faces north from Ninth Street, known today as Martin Luther King Drive. Pedestrians are crossing the busy thoroughfare in the morning in front of Stein's. To the right a block away is Loveman's department store, Chattanooga's finest for generations. People's Credit Clothes, Koblentz's, and George's Cleaners were some of the many stores that were clustered in this part of downtown in 1951.

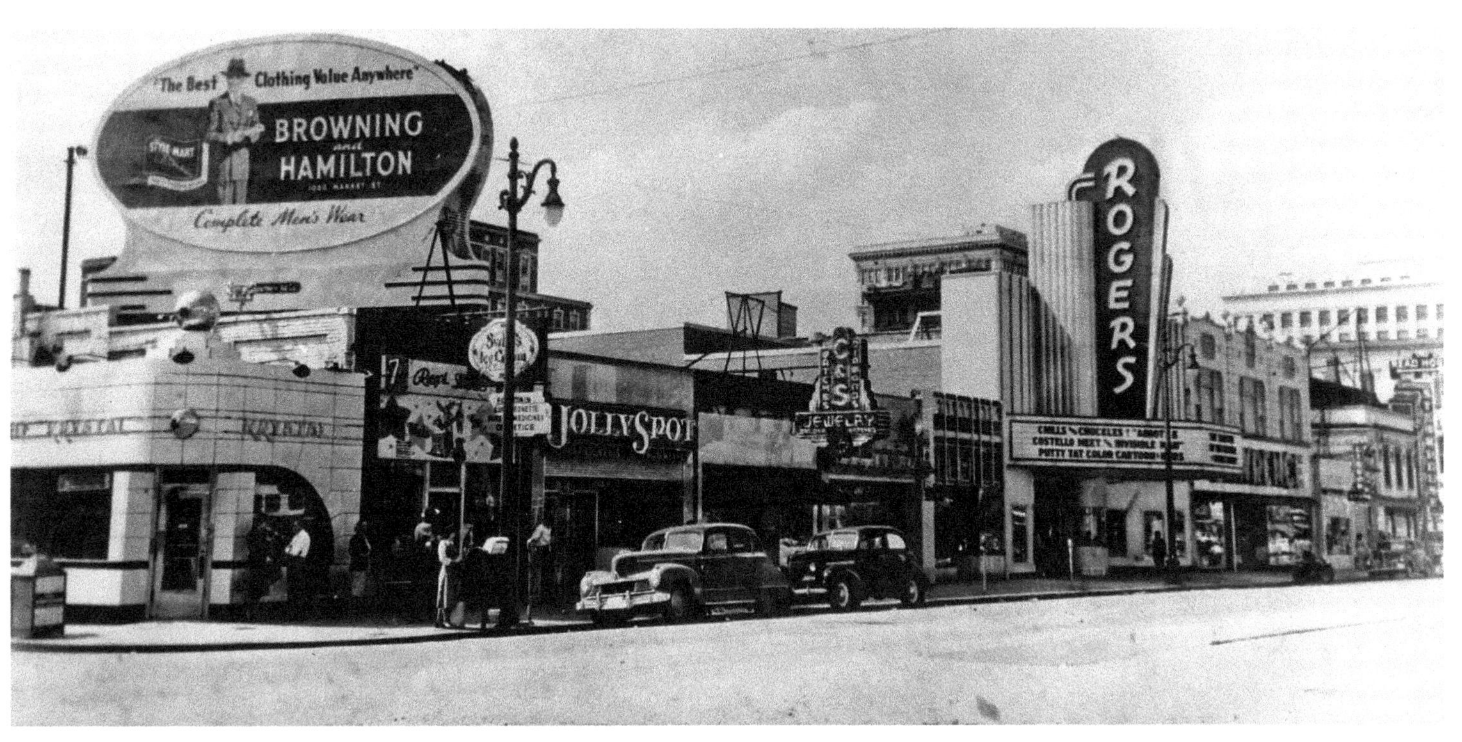

The Rogers Theater block was bounded by Market, Broad, Ninth, and Tenth streets and was the property of the state of Georgia dating back to the first rail line from Atlanta in the 1840s. Pictured here in 1951 are several businesses, among them the successful Chattanooga hamburger company, Krystal, founded by Rody Davenport in the city in 1932. The building housing the very first Krystal, at Seventh and Cherry streets, still stands, but the block shown here would eventually lose patrons to suburban neighborhoods. Today this land is a public park.

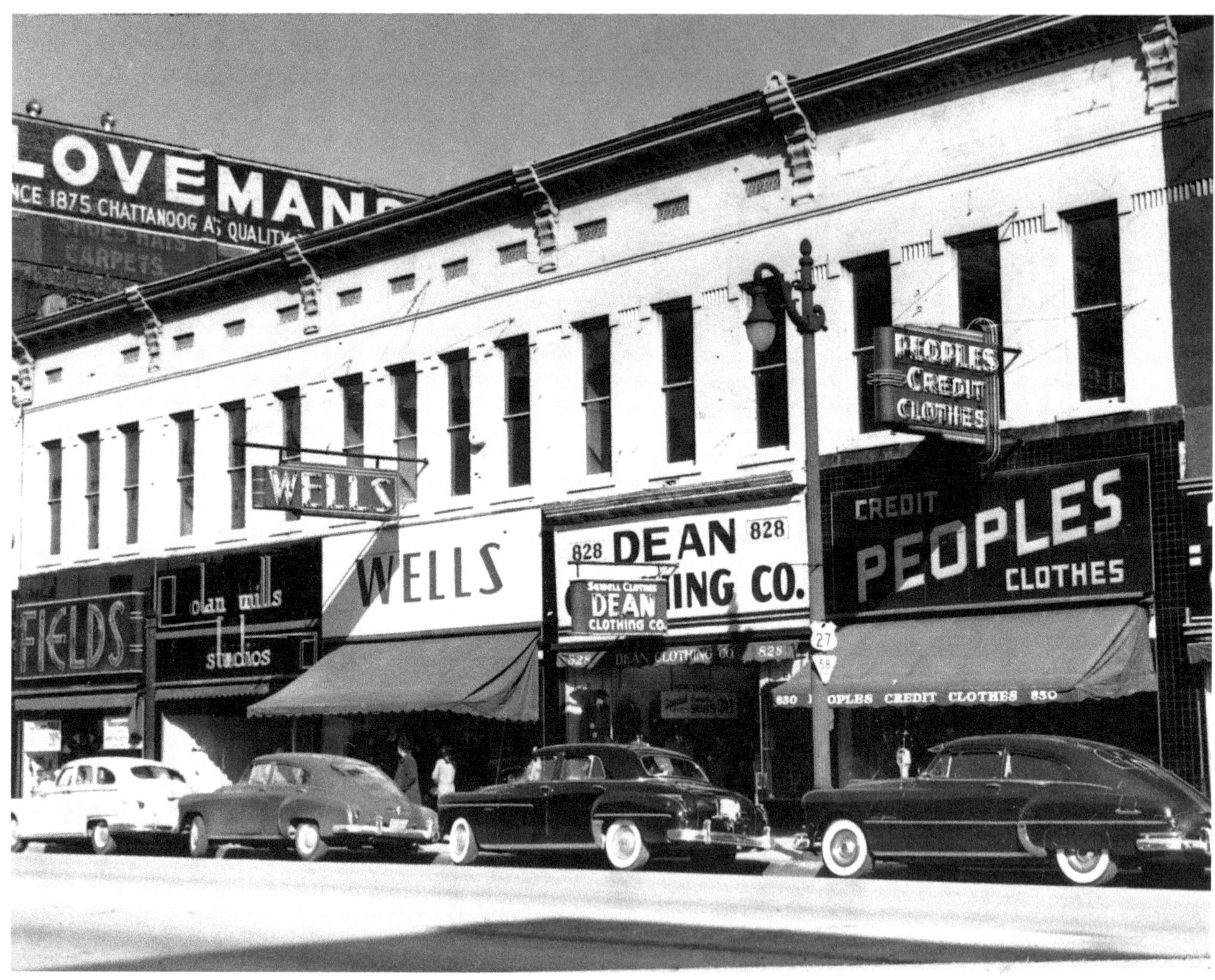

Market Street in the 1950s was a thriving economic thoroughfare. Situated near the elegant Loveman's department store, these businesses saw a lot of foot traffic. To the left is Olan Mills Studios, a photographic enterprise that would become a Chattanooga success story. Started by Olan Mills and his wife, Mary, in 1932 as a traveling photographic service in the region, the company grew to become one of the largest portrait studios in the South, specializing in church and school group portraiture.

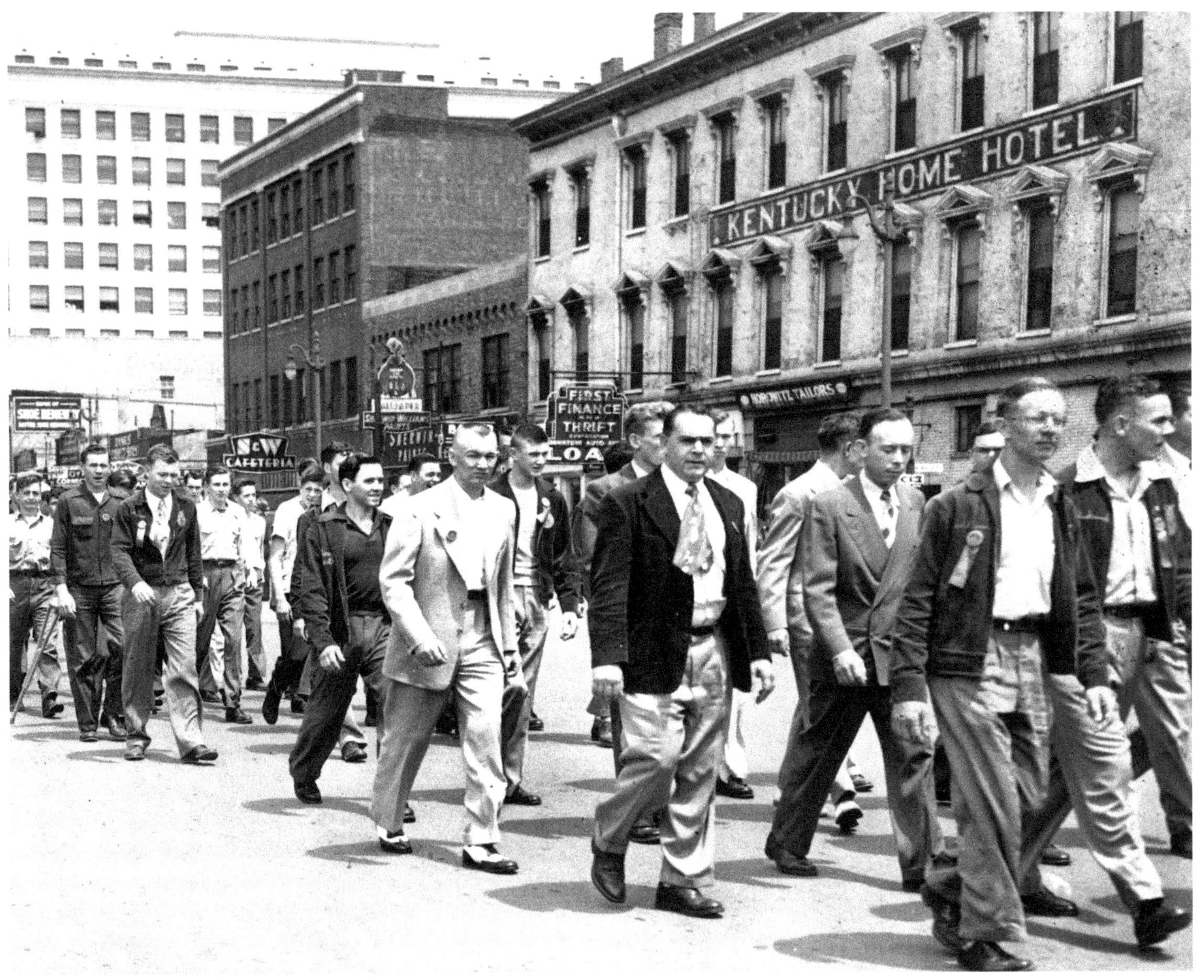

Tennessee is one of the country's key agricultural states, and in April 1951 Chattanooga hosted the Tennessee Division of the Future Farmers of America convention. These young men and their mentors paraded down Broad Street on April 27 past the Kentucky Home Hotel close to the Read House. The youngsters look chipper here, but the small farmer in America would begin passing into history by the 1960s, a casualty of expensive machinery and pesticides, skyrocketing land values, government regulation, and the advantages of economies of scale.

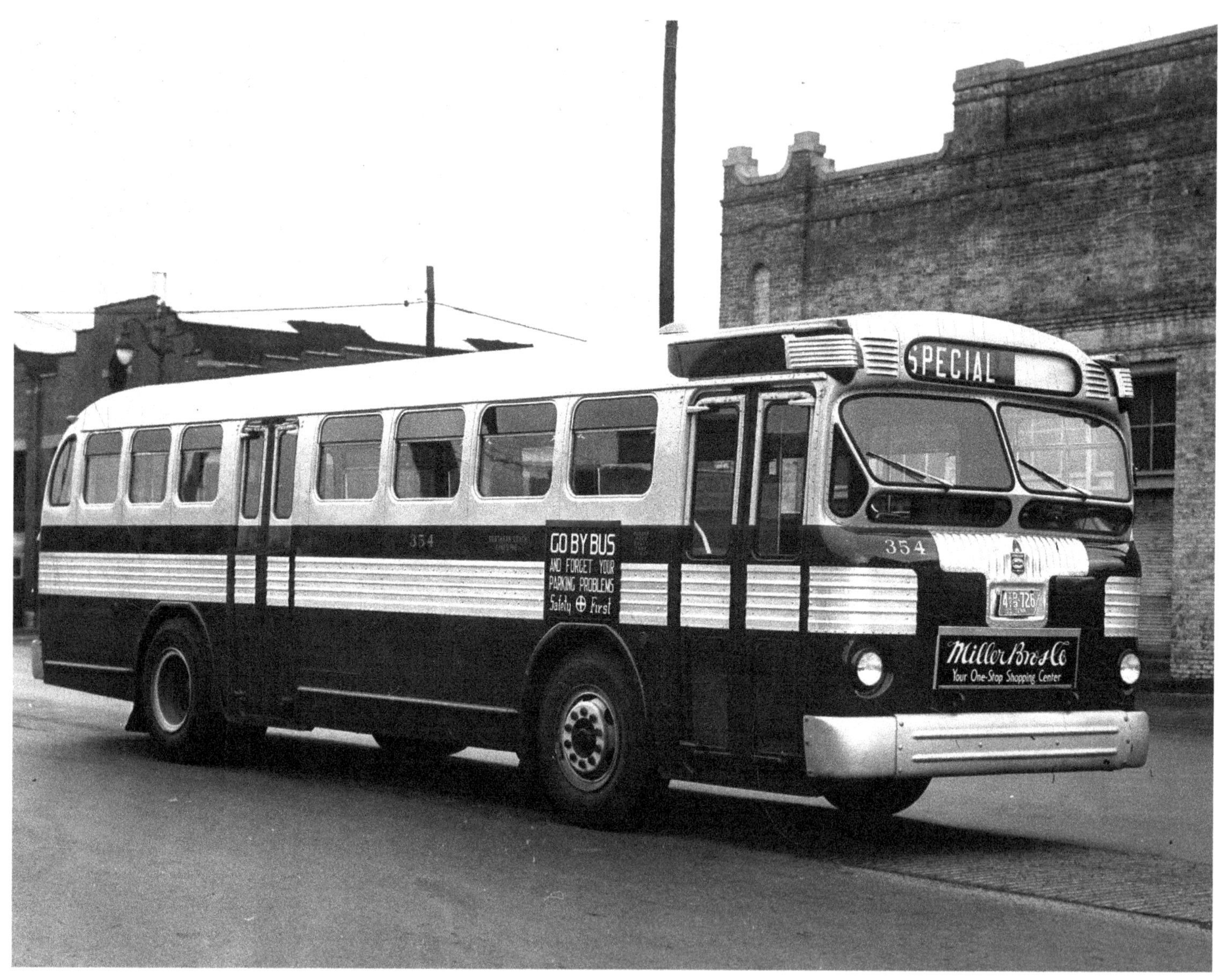

Alongside the larger national bus lines were smaller regional carriers that thrived serving small towns and wayside communities in the South. The Southern Coach Lines is pictured here on Broad Street near the "car barn" that serviced city buses in Chattanooga. The advertisement on the front is for Miller Brothers department store, a large establishment and chief rival to Loveman's in 1951.

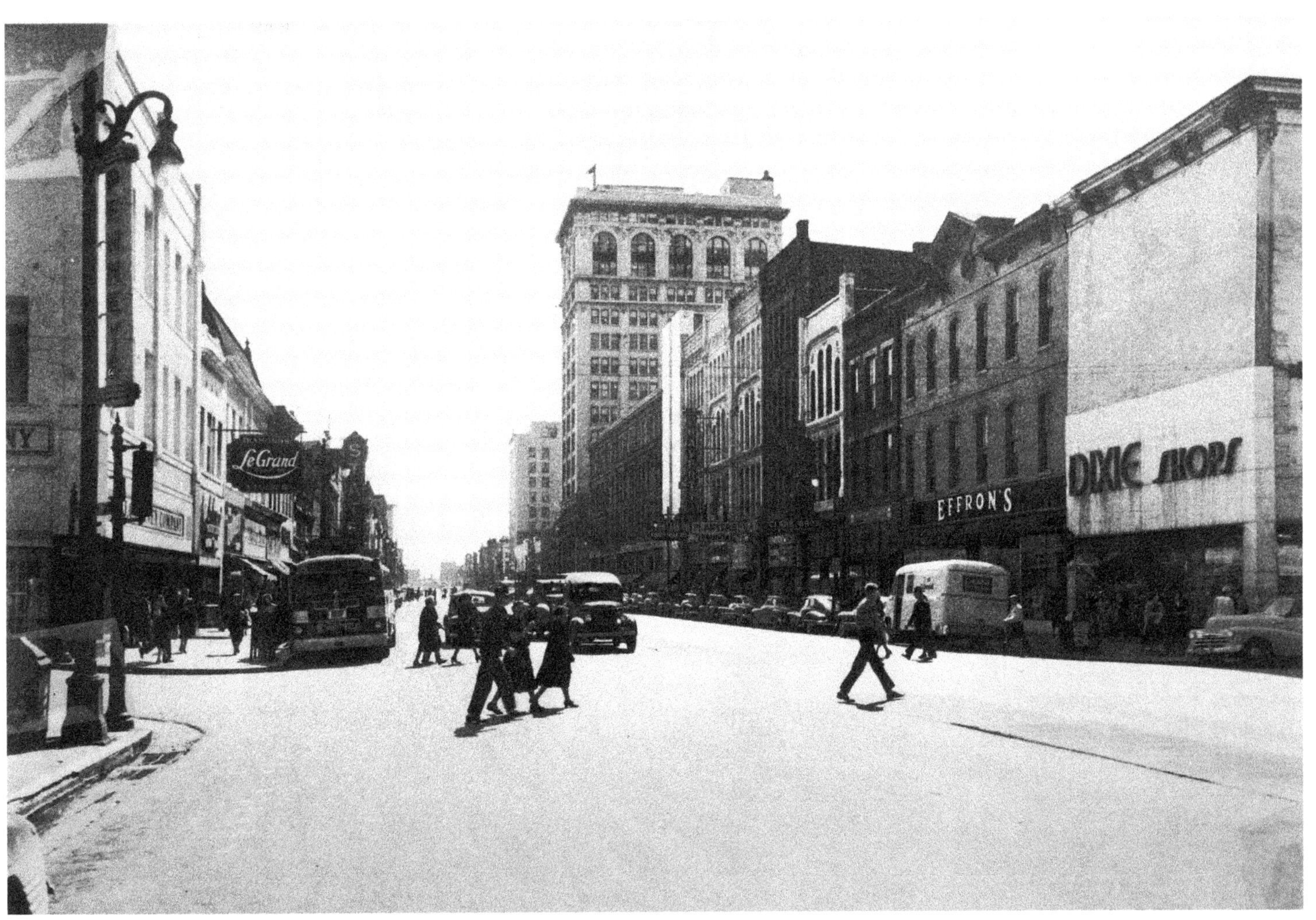

This view south on Market Street from Sixth Street shows the density of retail shopping that was downtown Chattanooga in the 1950s. Shops like Effron's and the Dixie Shop served the needs of shoppers, as did Penney's (today's JCPenney) department store. At left in the distance is the vertical sign for the State Theater, a local movie house in 1951.

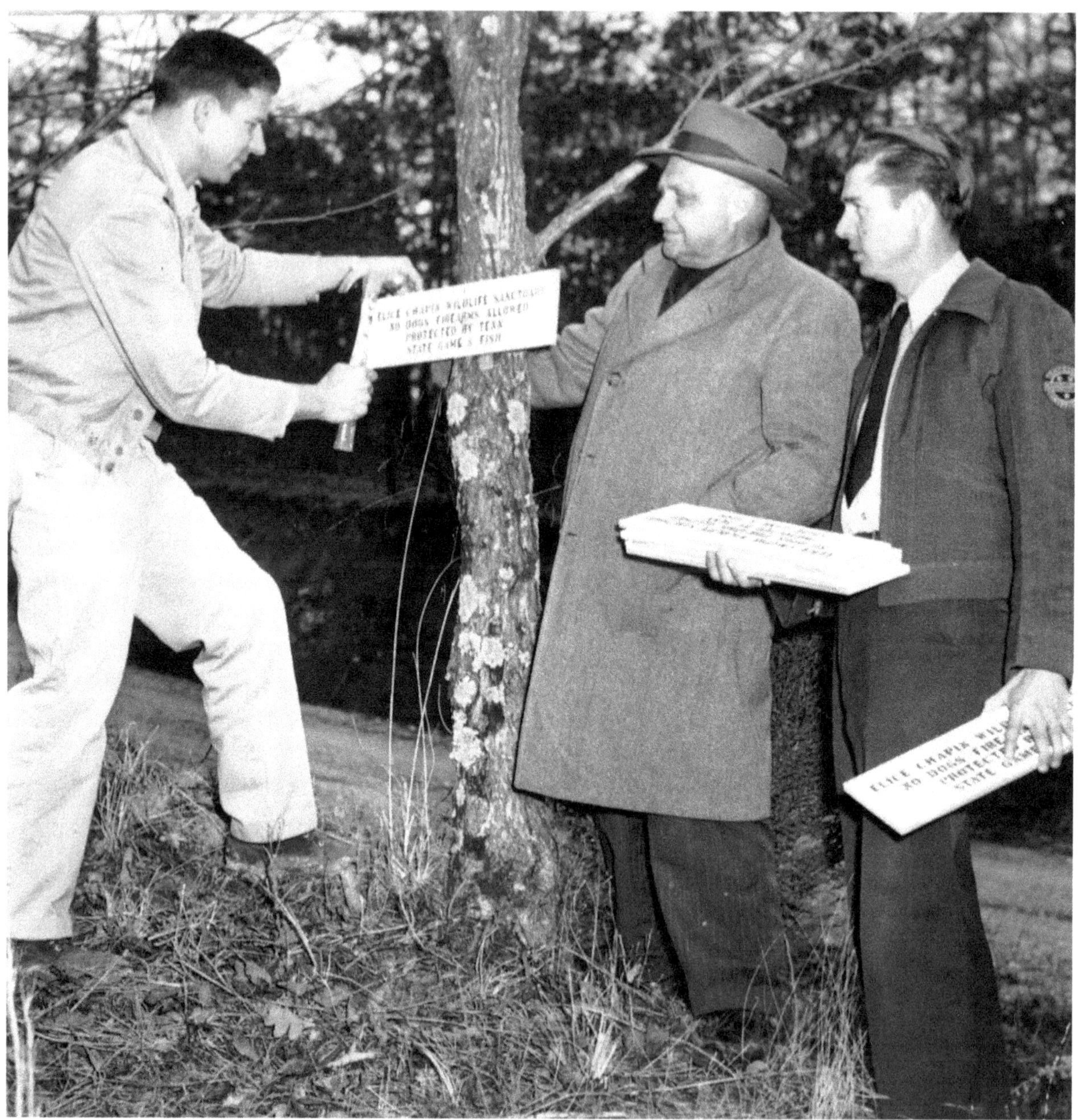

Making certain that the message is clear, these men are posting multiple "no hunting" signs in the Elise Chapin Wildlife Sanctuary in 1951. The man in the middle, naturalist Robert Walker Sparks, watches as one of the signs is nailed to a tree. The preserve was and continues to be a beautiful retreat from the surrounding world. Helping Sparks are E. L. Boyd and Martin Clark.

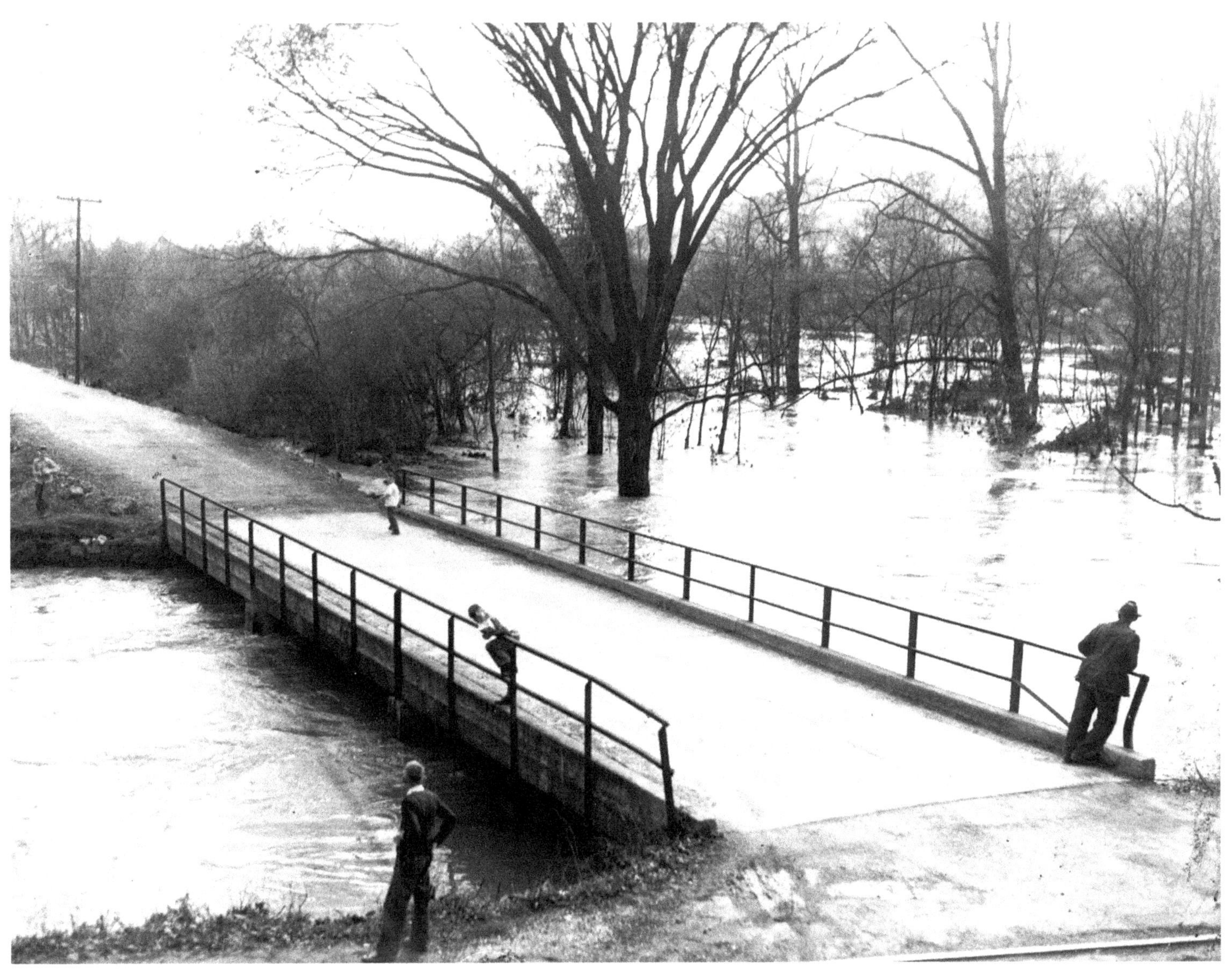

Flooding remains a fact of life in the Tennessee Valley, especially during the rainy springtime. In neighborhoods around town, wide, fast-flowing creeks can be a real problem. Low-lying areas in Brainerd and Alton Park can experience serious water damage, particularly when the ground becomes saturated and the rain keeps coming. Here in 1951, onlookers watch the rushing water at the Burnt Mill Bridge in St. Elmo near the Georgia line.

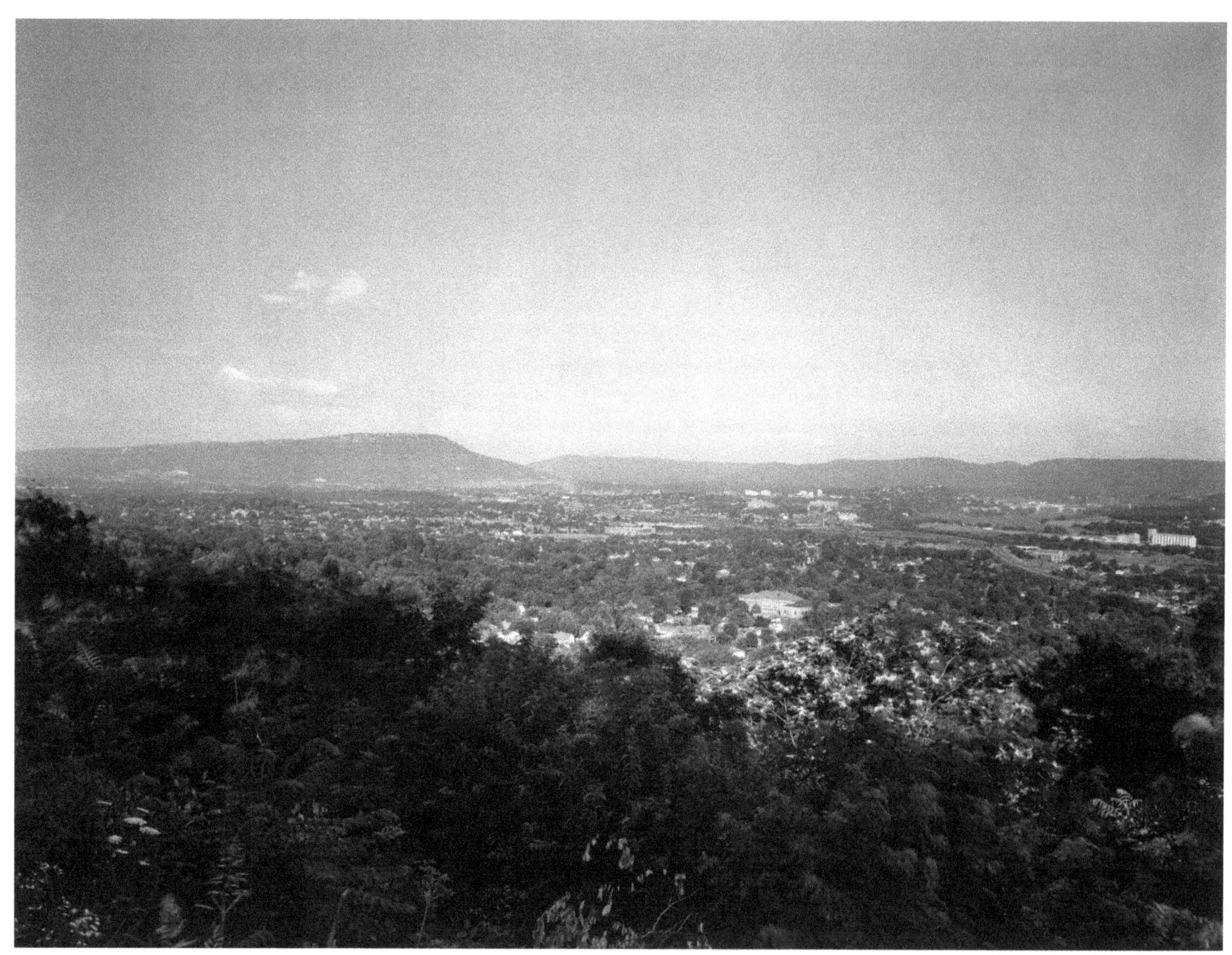

Chattanooga is located in a verdant Tennessee River valley surrounded by ridges and mountains in the southern Appalachian region. This morning view of the city in June 1952 was taken from Missionary Ridge on the eastern side of town facing west toward Lookout Mountain, visible to the left with its distinctive brow. At center is Raccoon Mountain and farther to the right lies Signal Mountain.

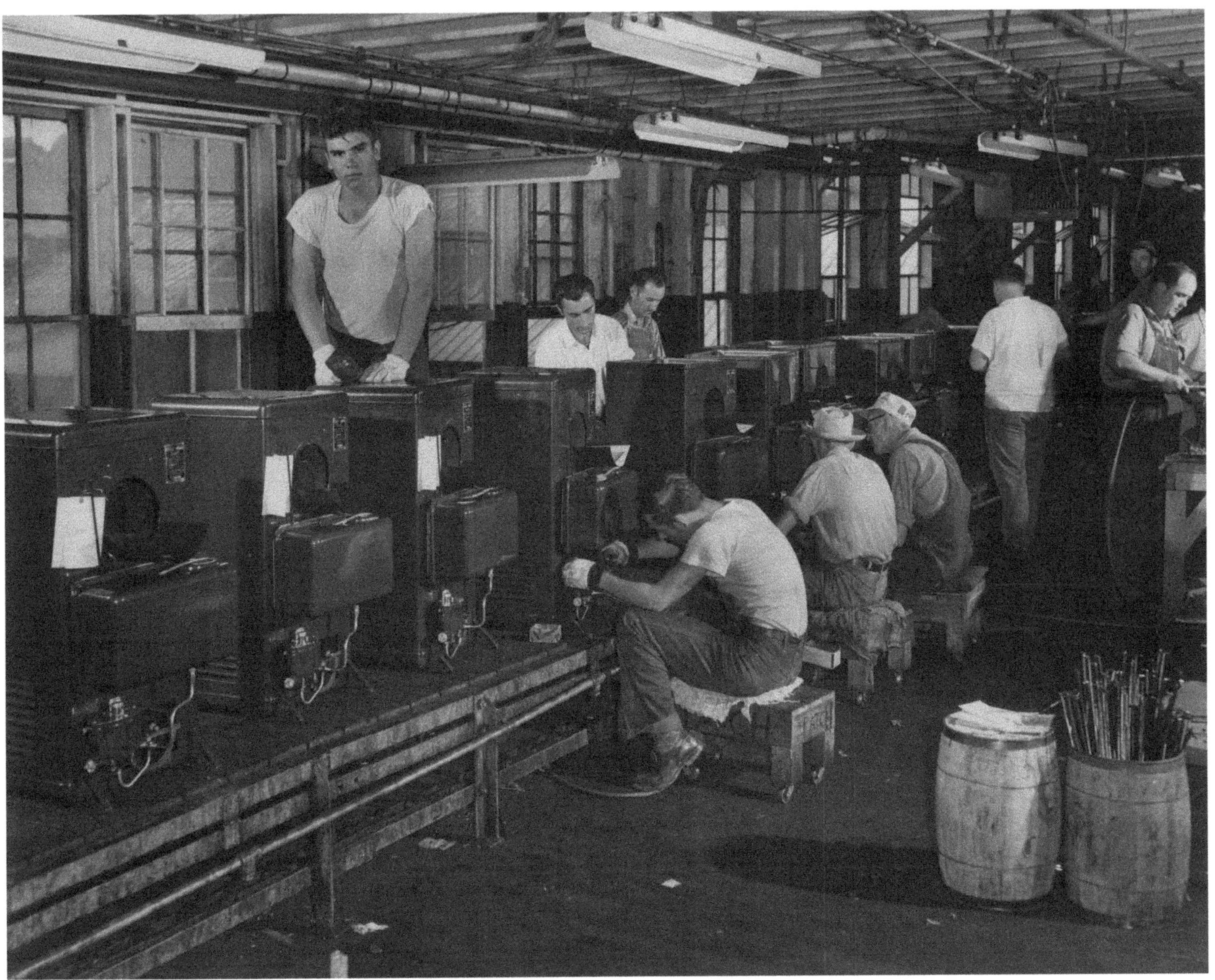

A young, well-muscled worker pauses from his work to gaze at the camera. This group of men were employed by the Cavalier Corporation, a company that would grow successful in the production of vending machines. These employees appear to be intent on adjusting the gas feed line assemblies necessary to the proper functioning of new stoves moving slowly down the assembly line.

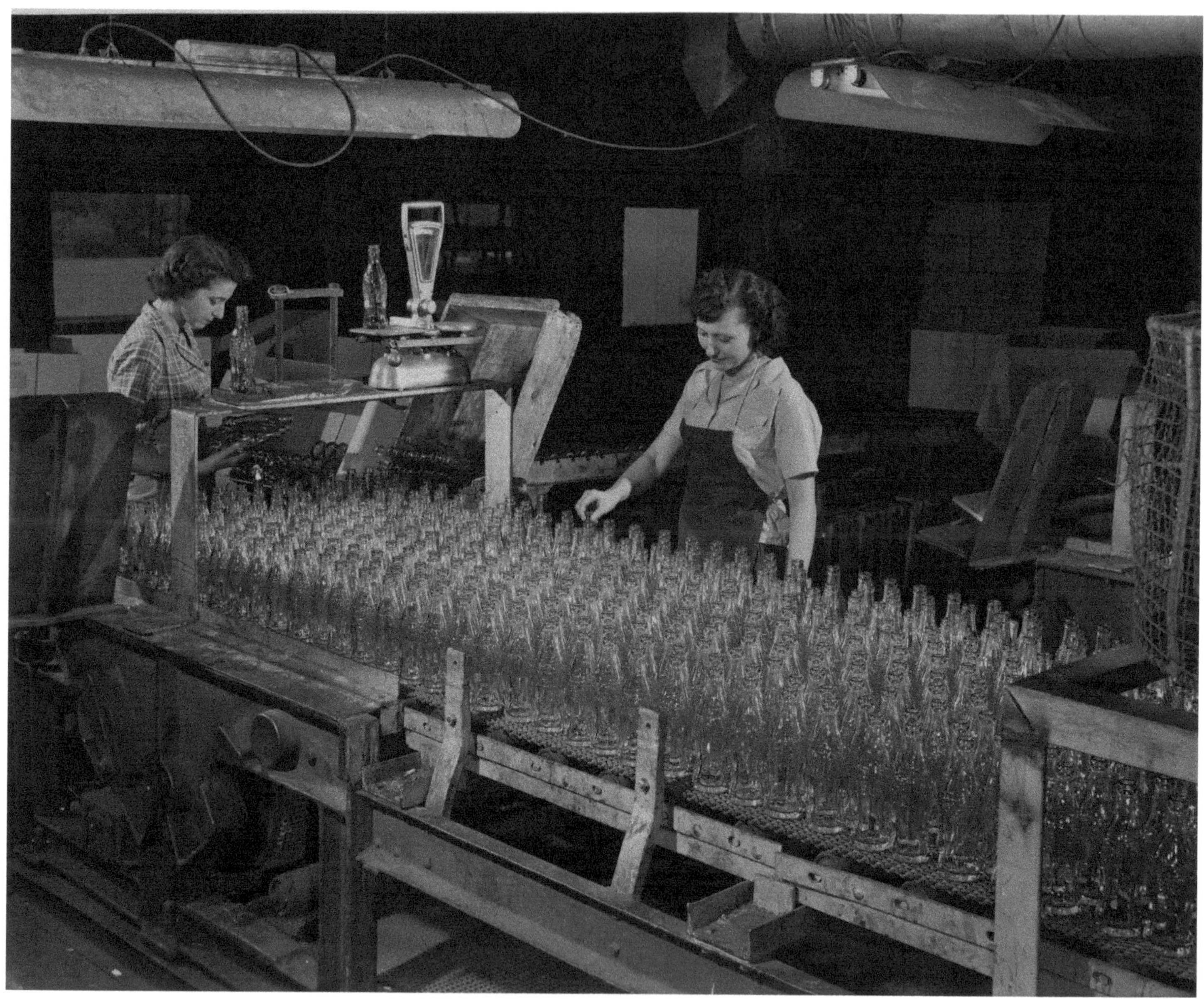

Coca-Cola and Chattanooga share a long history, beginning in 1899 when two Chattanooga gentlemen secured the rights to bottle the soft drink from the maker of Coke, Asa Candler in Atlanta. Bottling operations began immediately and plants like Chattanooga Glass Company became part of that production. Here in 1952, employees in aprons check the quality of new glass bottles, both visually and with simple weights and measures equipment.

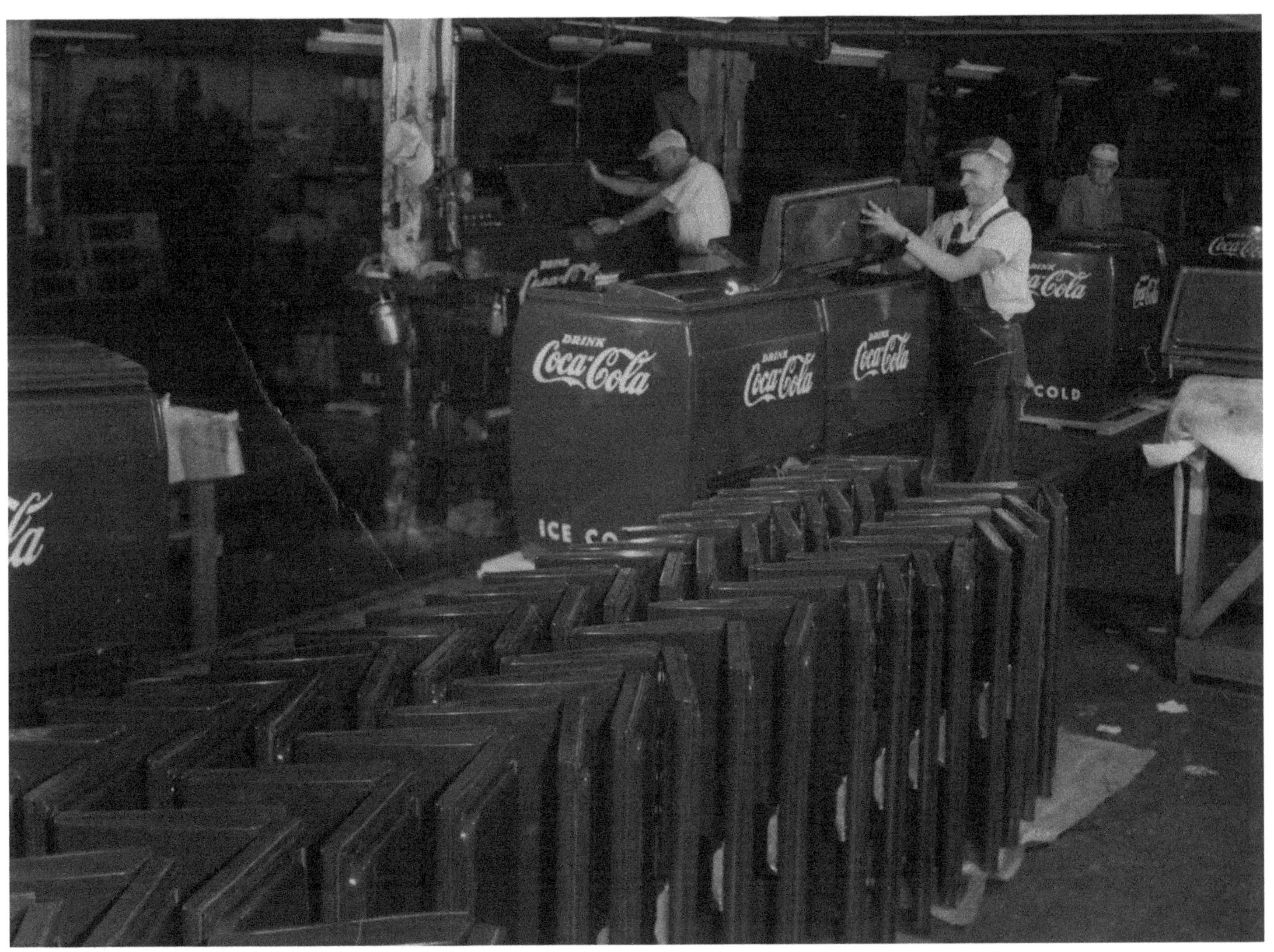

Another Chattanooga connection to Coca-Cola involves the Cavalier Corporation. Originally a furniture factory in the late 1800s, Cavalier in the early days of the twentieth century produced simple refrigeration units, commonly known as "ice boxes." When an order came to the company to make a container to keep Coca-Colas cold, Cavalier created what we know as vending machines. Their success was immediate, profitable, and long-lived.

Before the days of hairnets and plastic gloves, production work at food factories was a "hands-on" experience. Food laws were simpler and many of the facilities were only minimally air-conditioned. In this photograph from 1952, workers at the Brock Candy Company chat as they work both sides of a conveyor belt, where delicious, chocolate-covered cherries are being undercoated with tasty chocolate.

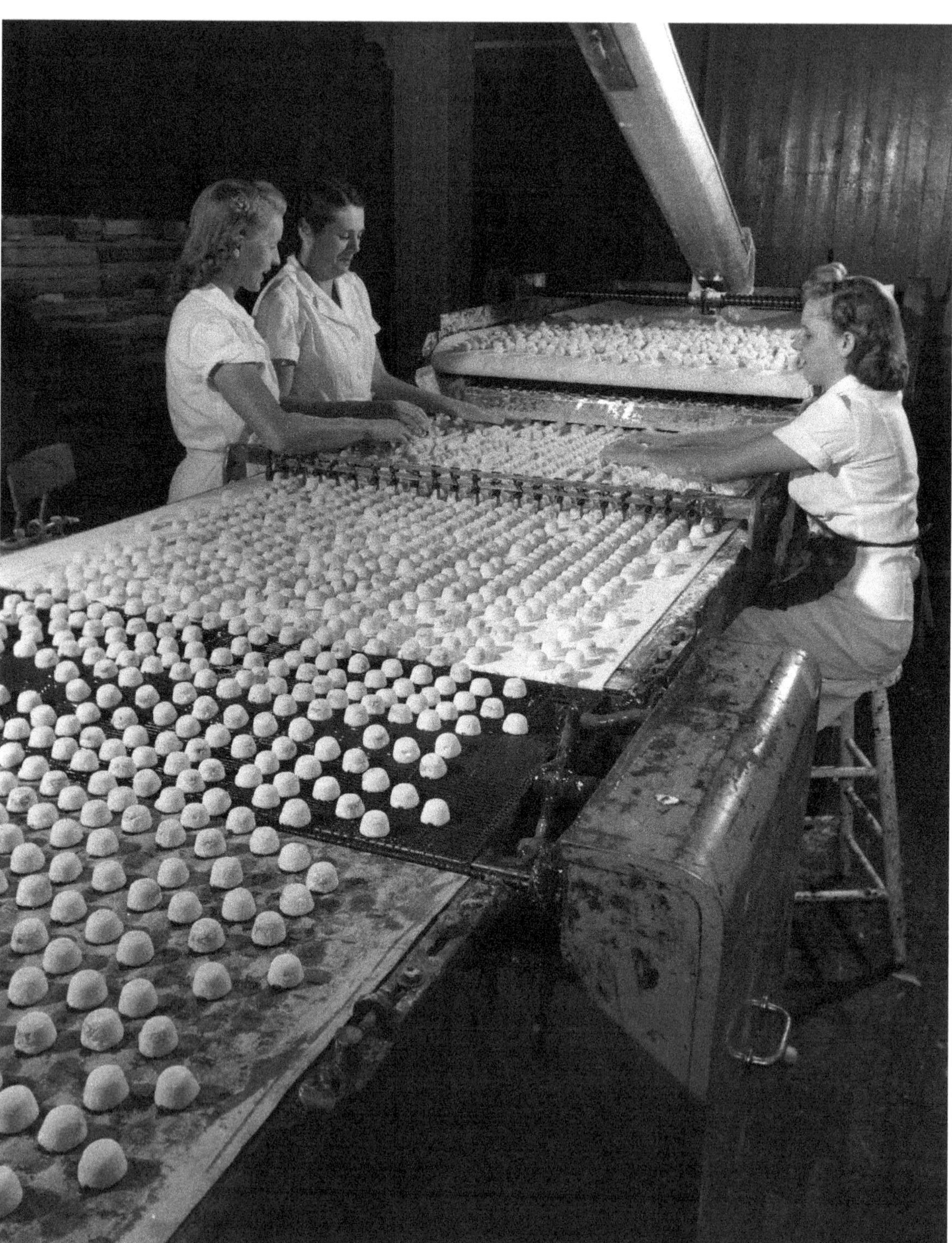

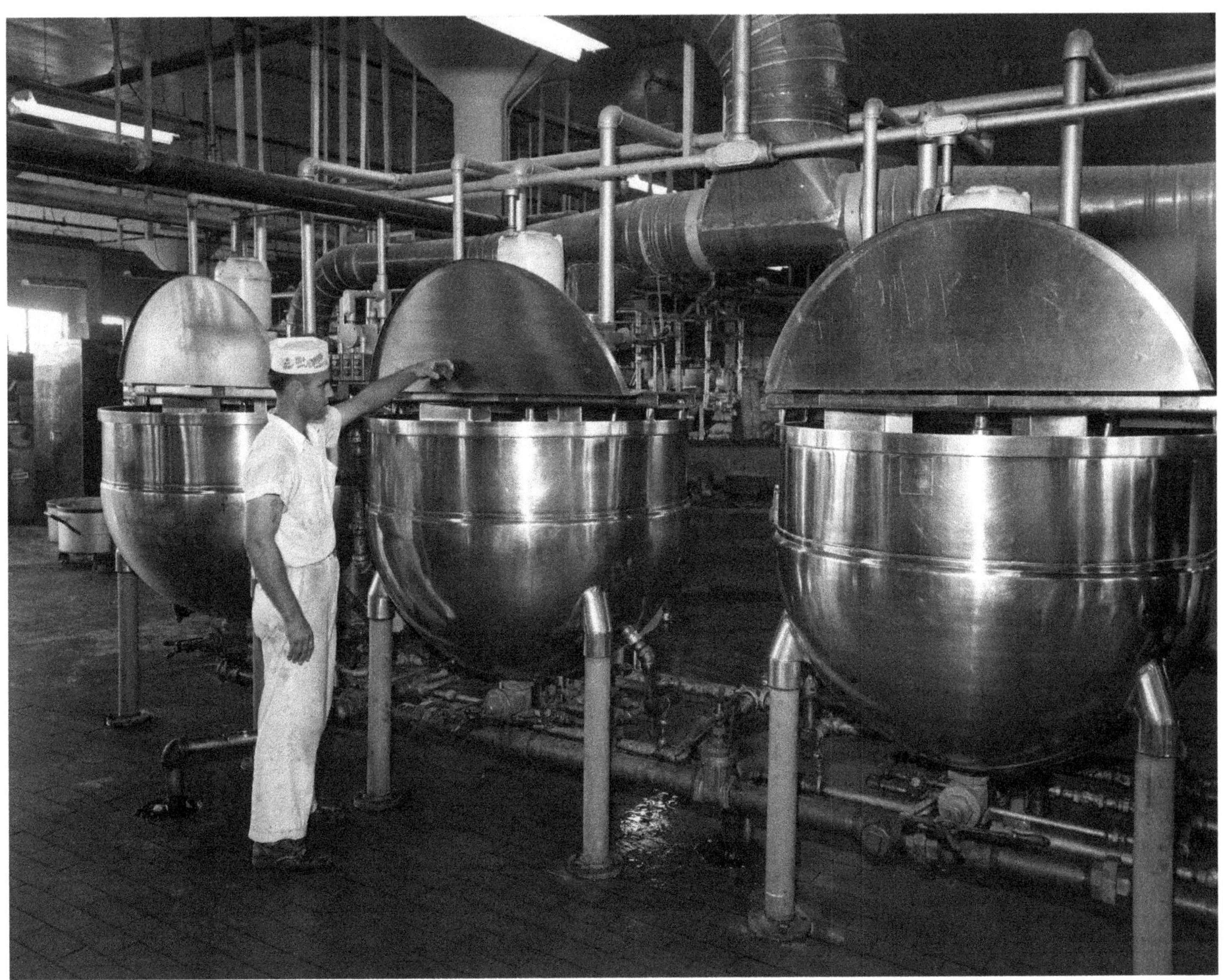

William Brock, a successful entrepreneur, began his candy business in the early 1900s. By the 1950s, the syrup that was cooking in these vats was coating hundreds of thousands of pieces of candy shipped all over the country. A prominent citizen, Brock served a partial term in the U.S. Senate. His son, William (Bill) Brock III, became a local congressman and Tennessee senator in the 1960s and 1970s.

Mrs. Wanda Sloan looks as happy as someone picking the winning lottery number out of a giant jar. She does have her hands on some really sweet stuff, which we all know as jellybeans. Actually, the rounded metal drum is a polisher used to smooth and shine the candies to give them that extra eye appeal.

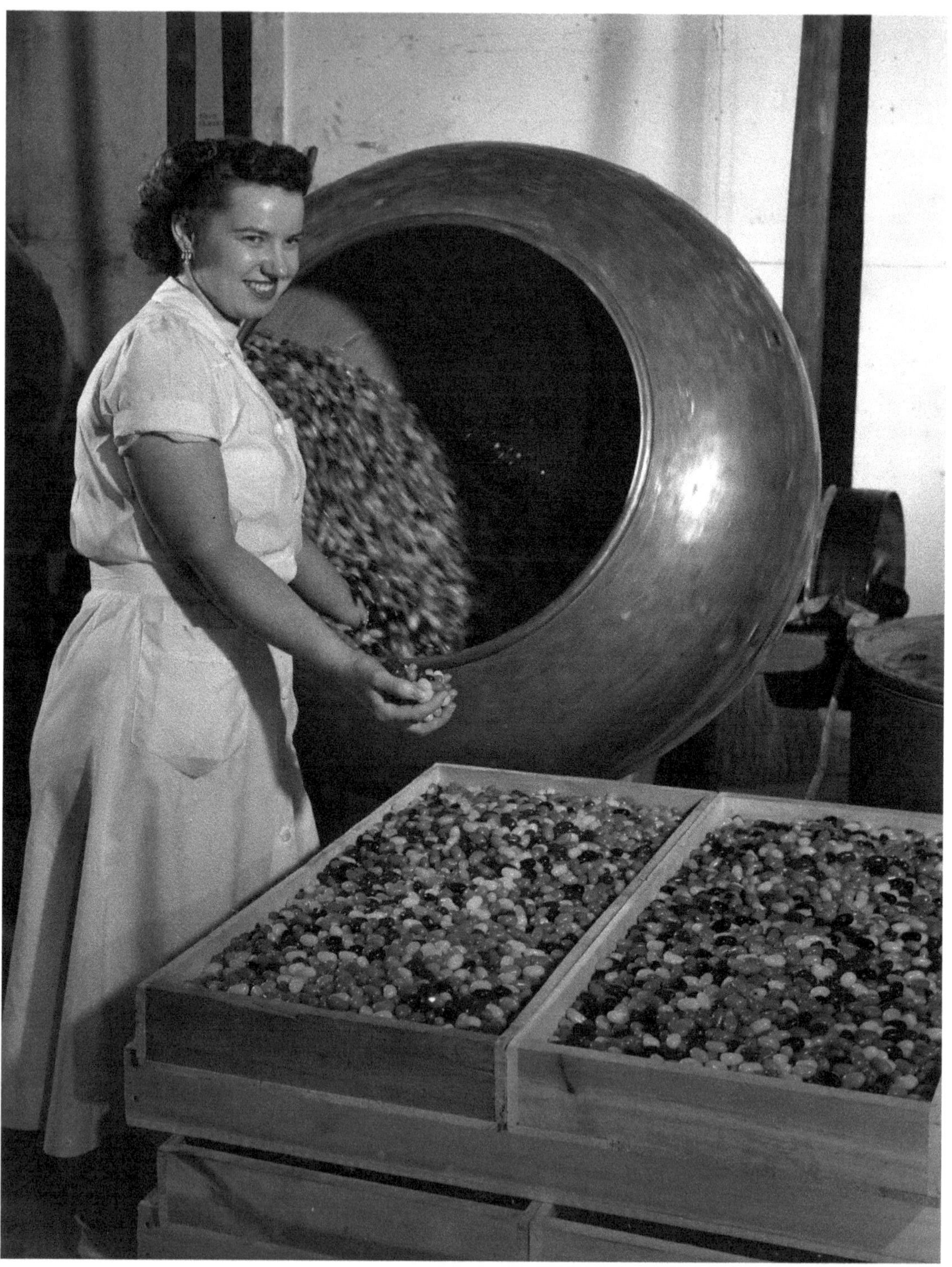

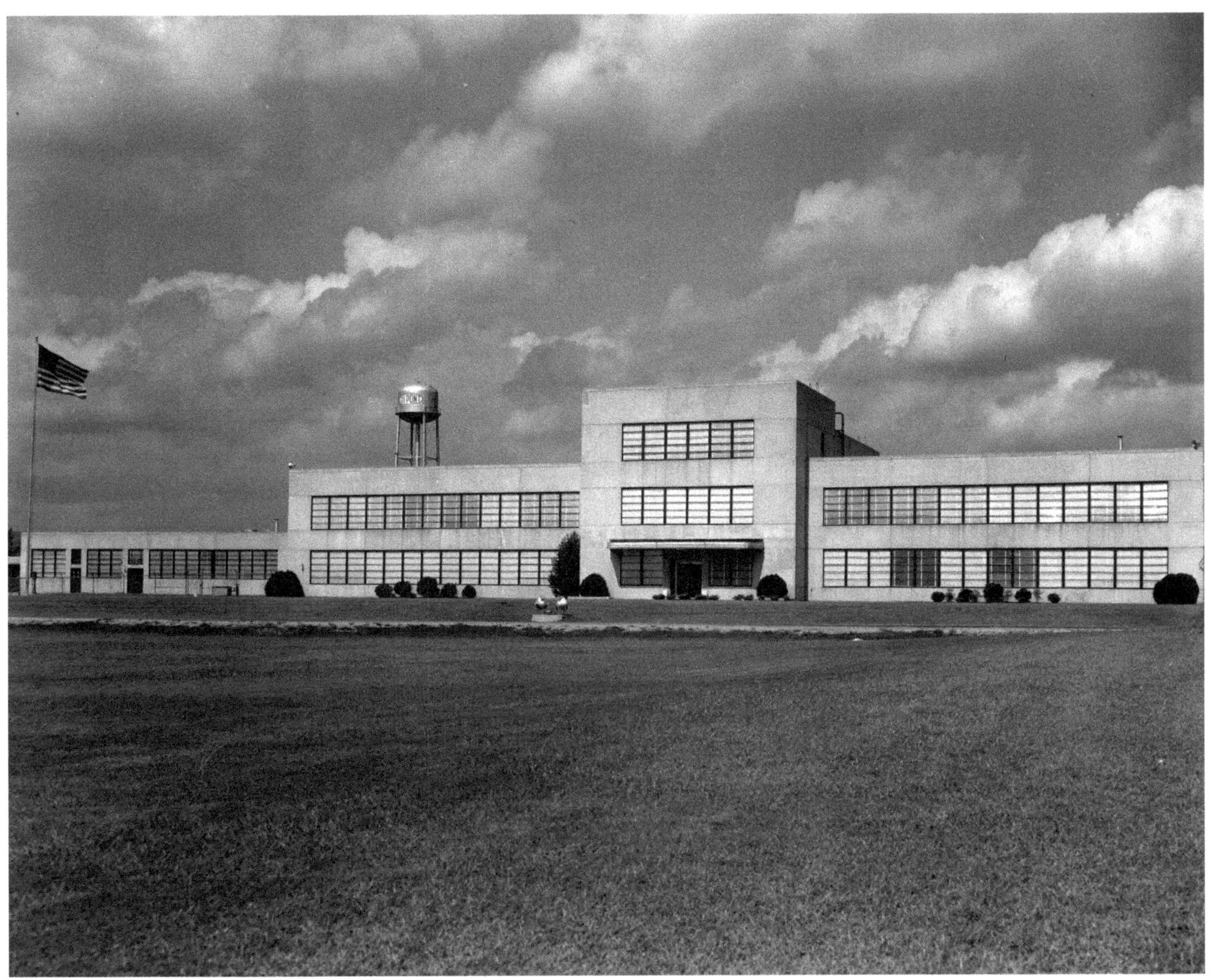

Though its cool, Bauhaus exterior speaks of corporate anonymity here in 1952, the E. I. du Pont de Nemours plant was anything but unimpressive when it was built in Chattanooga near the Chickamauga Dam. The plant was a major investment in the city. In 1948, it began running shifts around the clock, and with its emphasis on producing nylon represented a new aspect of manufacturing that had eluded Chattanooga up to this time.

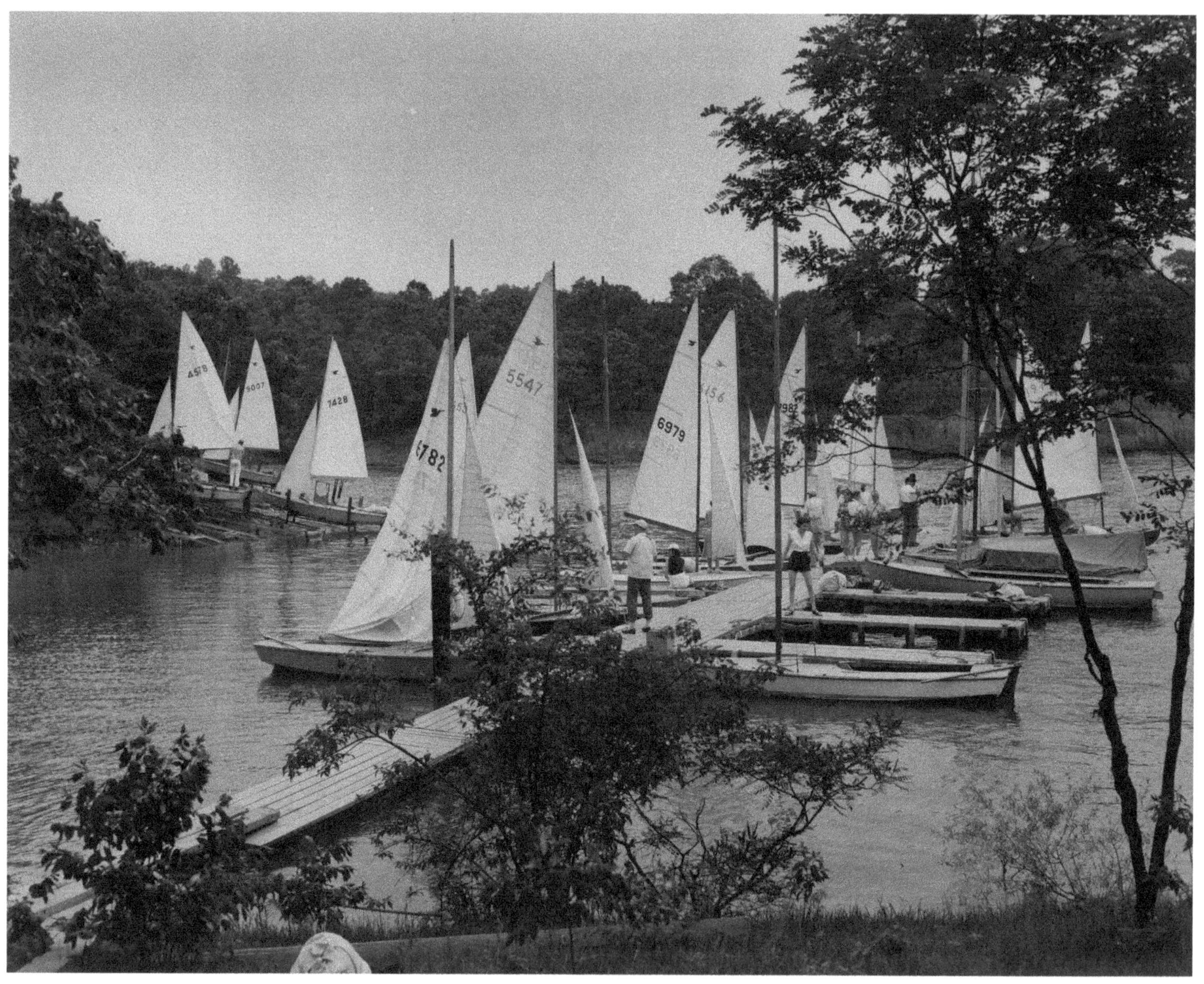

When Chickamauga Dam was completed in 1940, it accomplished several important objectives. One of course was the production of electricity through harnessing the Tennessee River, which dropped against and spun the dam's powerful turbines. Another was the creation of a lake behind the dam, which gave local folks the chance to swim, ski, or sail, as this 1953 photograph of the Privateer Yacht Club on Chickamauga Lake illustrates.

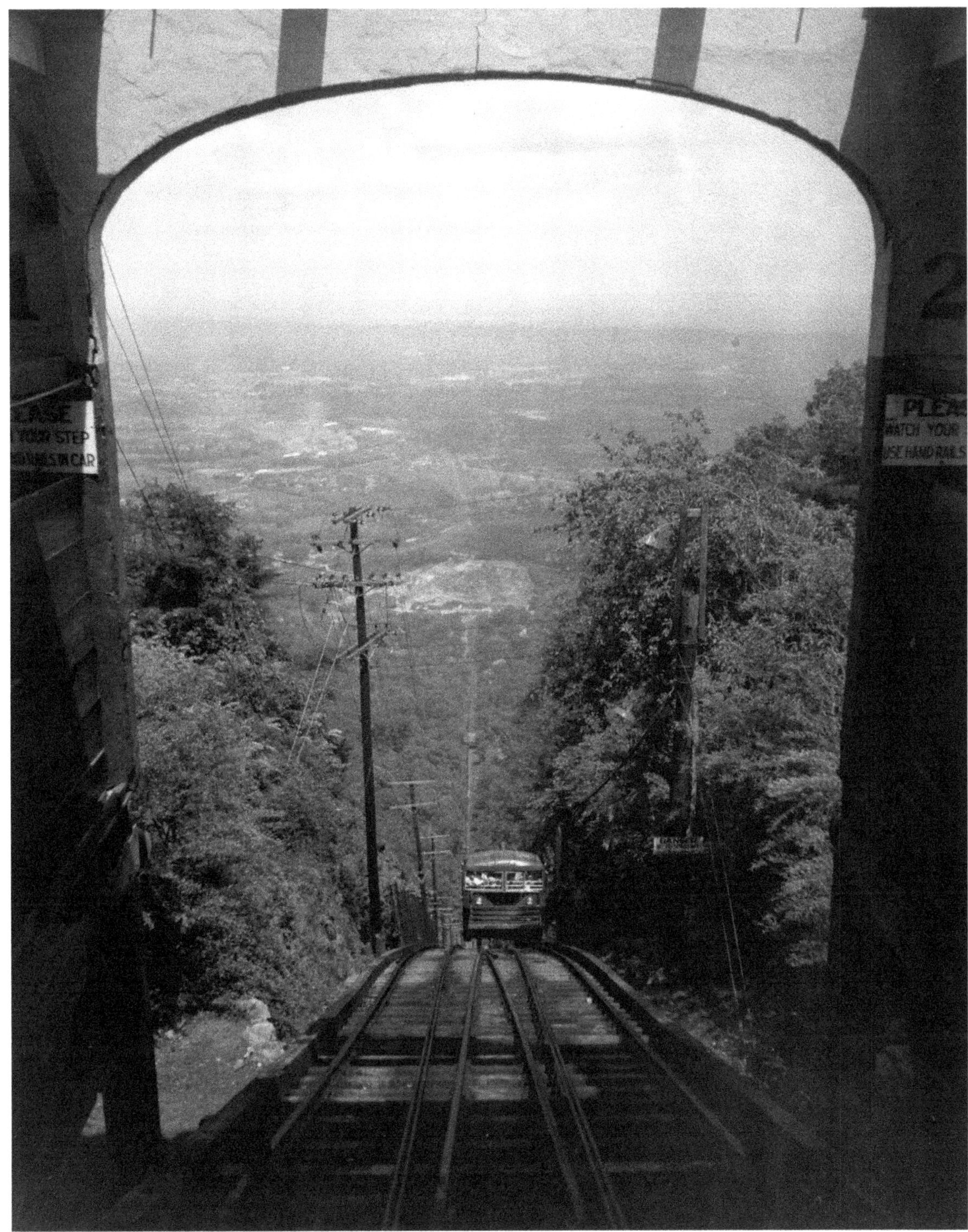

This breathtaking 1953 view from the upper station of the Lookout Mountain Incline Railway conveys the distance the cable cars must travel to make the steep ascent and descent of "America's most amazing mile." The cars reach a maximum angle of 72 degrees, one of the steepest in the world. The rail line, built in 1895, was actually the second railway constructed up the famous mountain and was originally known as Incline no. 2. In the early days, the lines were relied on by residents traveling between the mountain and downtown Chattanooga.

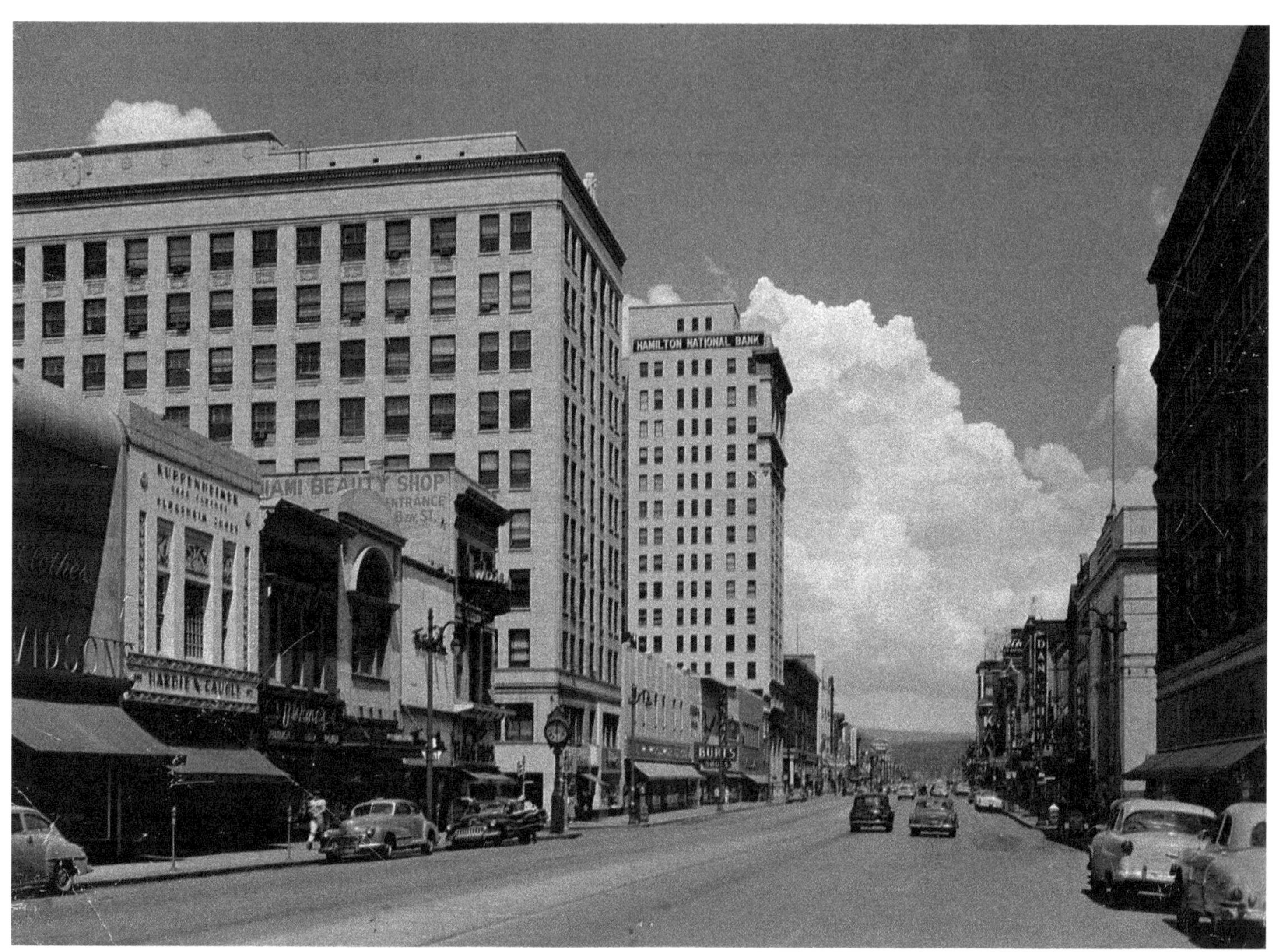

This 1953 view along Market Street facing north from Eighth Street is dominated by two handsome commercial structures: the Chattanooga Bank Building on the left and the Hamilton National Bank Building a block away, also to the left. From this vantage point today, one would see the first building under renovation and the second enclosed in a dark, steel sheath as home to First Tennessee Bank.

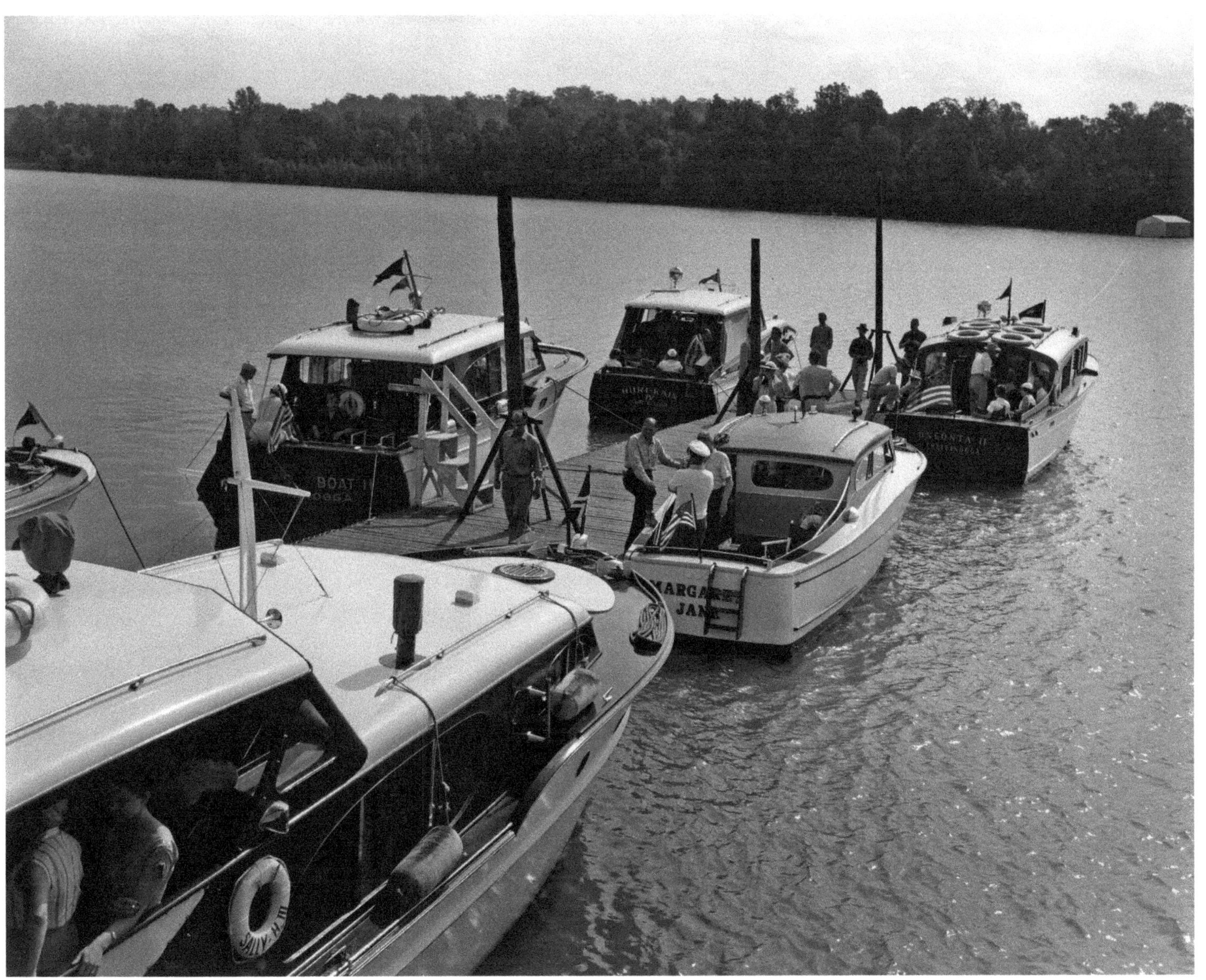

Travel writers are constantly drawn to Tennessee, for many reasons—southern food, old-time music, and the state's natural beauty primary among them. And it seems the state's numerous waterways always figure in their descriptions. These newspaper journalists are cruising the river to Watts Bar Resort Village in 1953 after a visit to the Chattanooga area and a brief stop at the Chattanooga Rod and Gun Club on the lake.

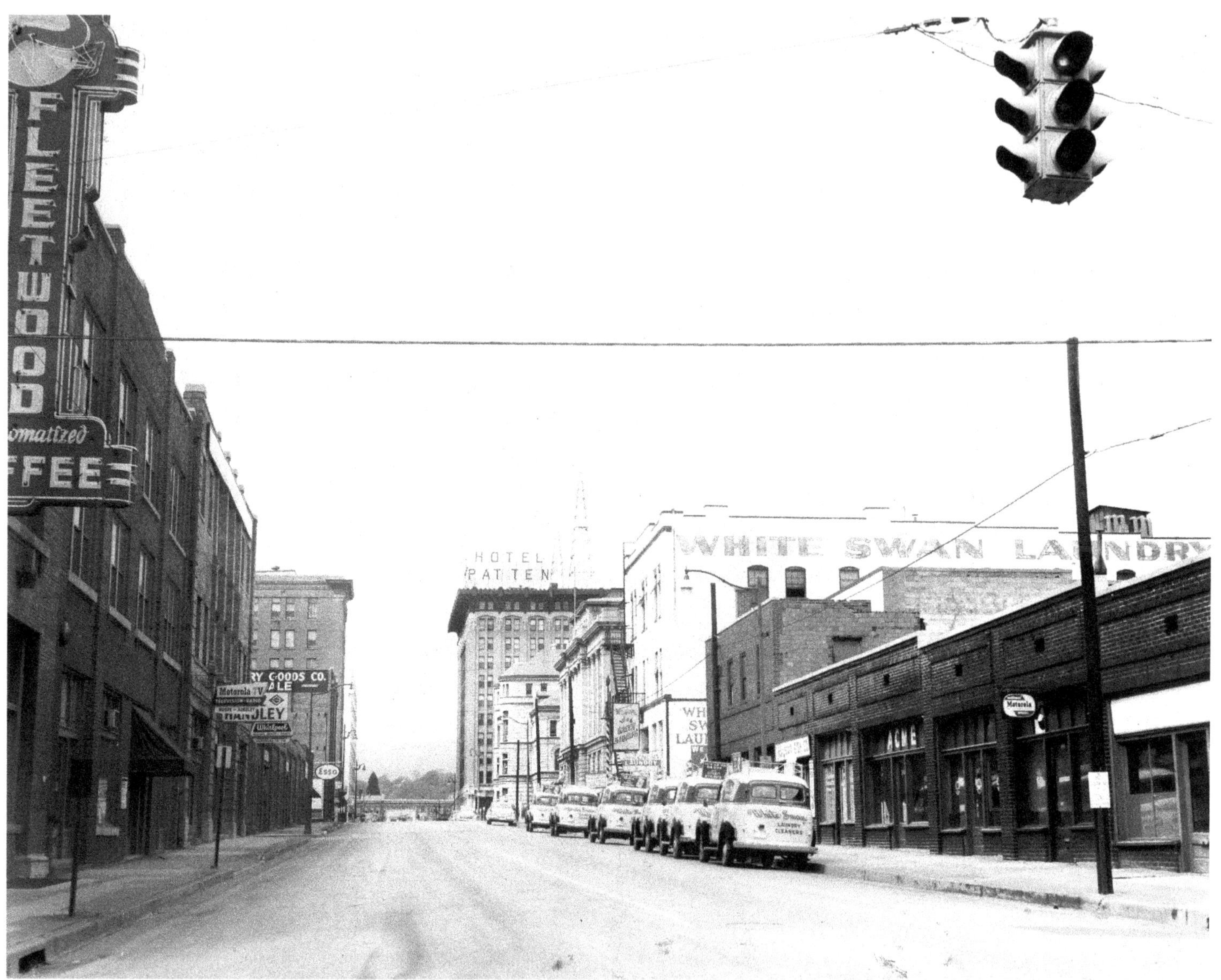

A prominent sign for Fleetwood Coffee looms large on Eleventh Street around 1954 in this view westward. Nearby rail lines facilitated the shipment of goods for both manufacturers and merchants. Down the street to the right is the Municipal Building with its columns, the Custom House, and last the Hotel Patten, built in 1908. Across the street from the hotel is the Pound Building, built by hotel and newspaper proprietor J. B. Pound.

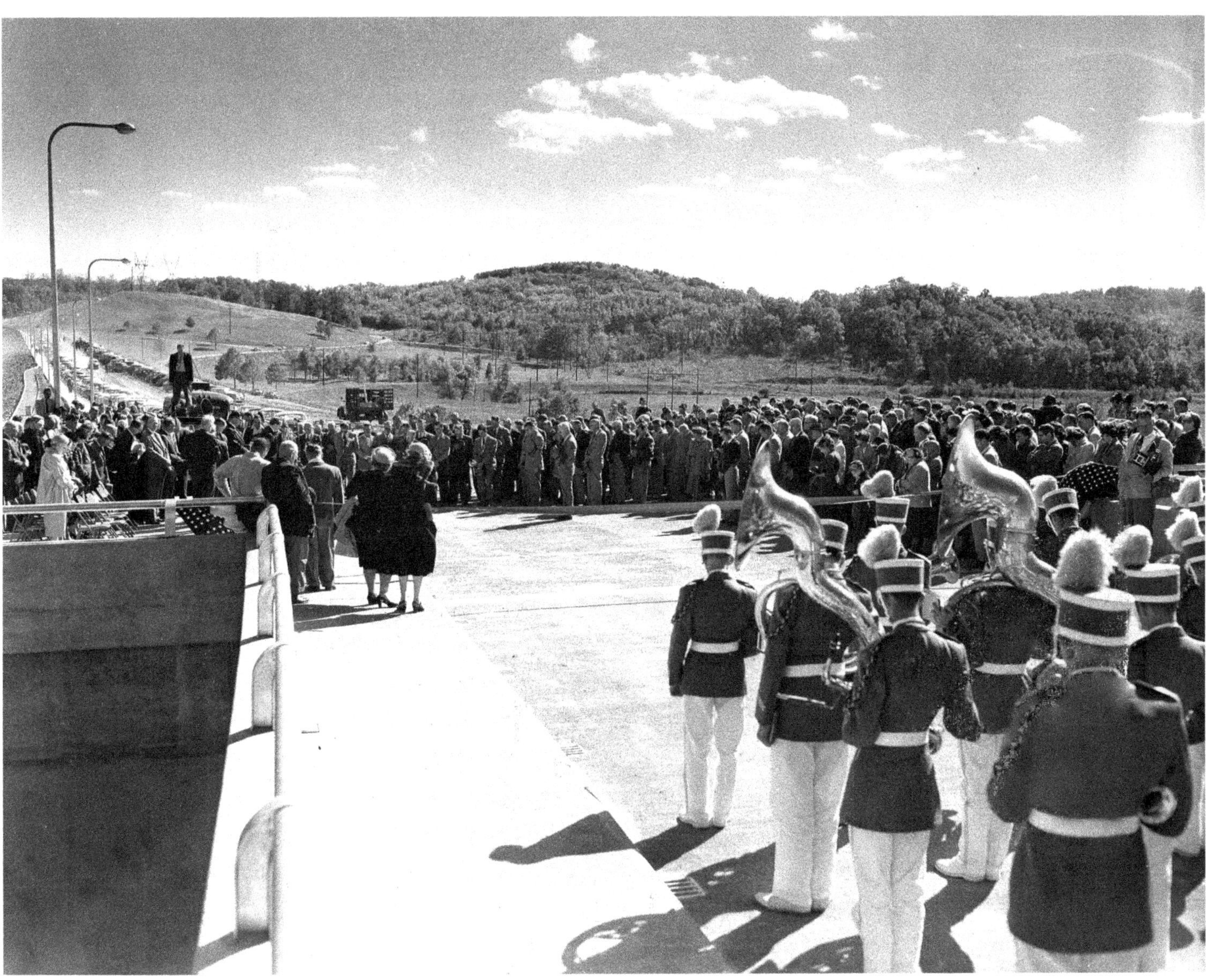

The completion of TVA's Chickamauga Dam in 1940 was a landmark event in the city, attended by no less than President Franklin Roosevelt, who had created TVA in 1933. By the 1950s, it was obvious from Chattanooga's growth that a bridge was needed across the dam to carry automobile traffic. In 1955, the vehicular bridge was dedicated with all appropriate fanfare as the Wilkes T. Thrasher Bridge, in honor of a prominent, local judge.

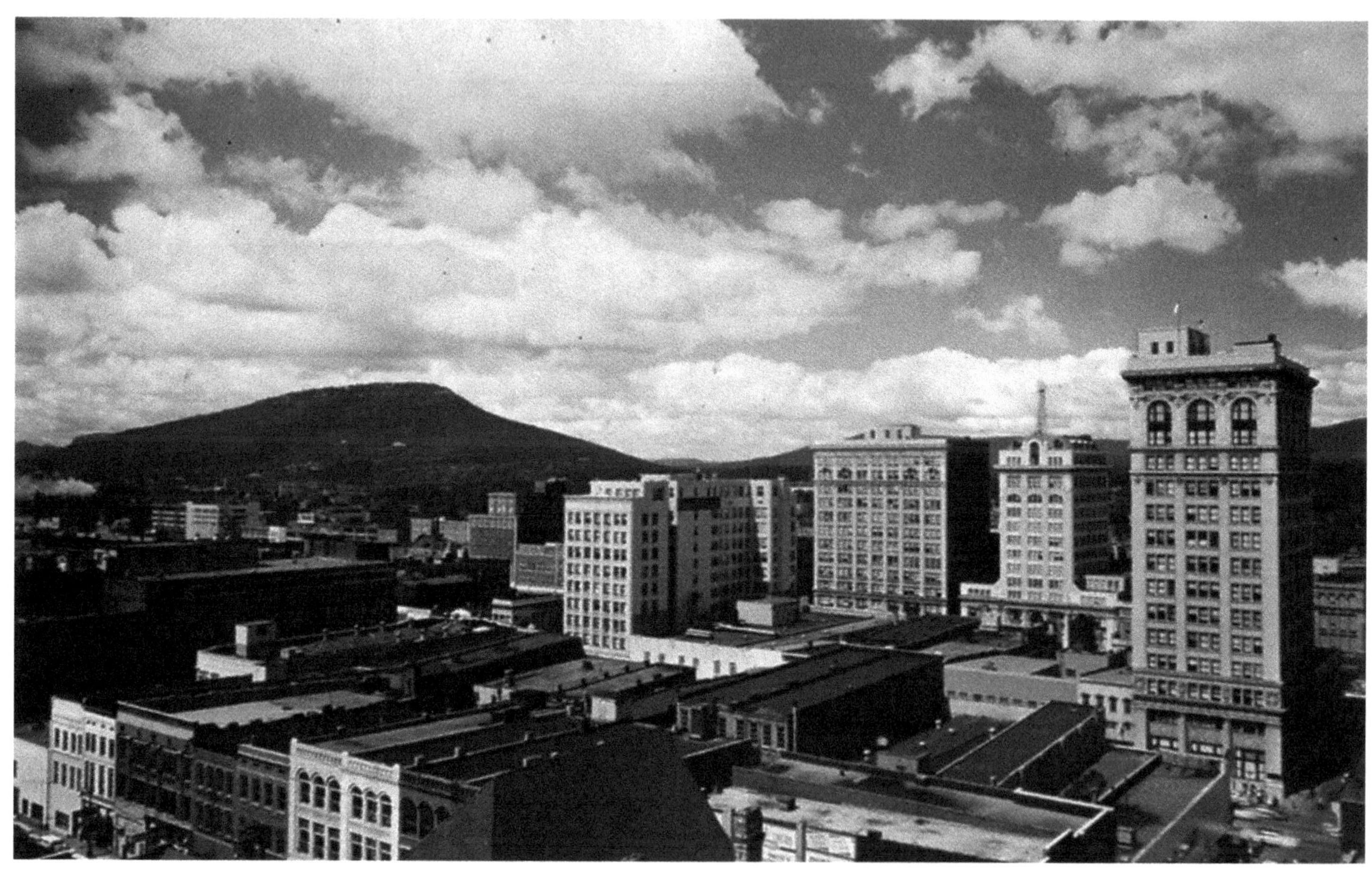

This photograph from 1955 shows why Chattanooga is often referred to as the Scenic City. With a moderately sized downtown and picturesque Lookout Mountain presiding over it, the city has many of the resources and amenities of a larger town, but the ease and pleasantness of a smaller town. This view shows the Maclellan Building to the right and the Hamilton National Bank Building to the far right.

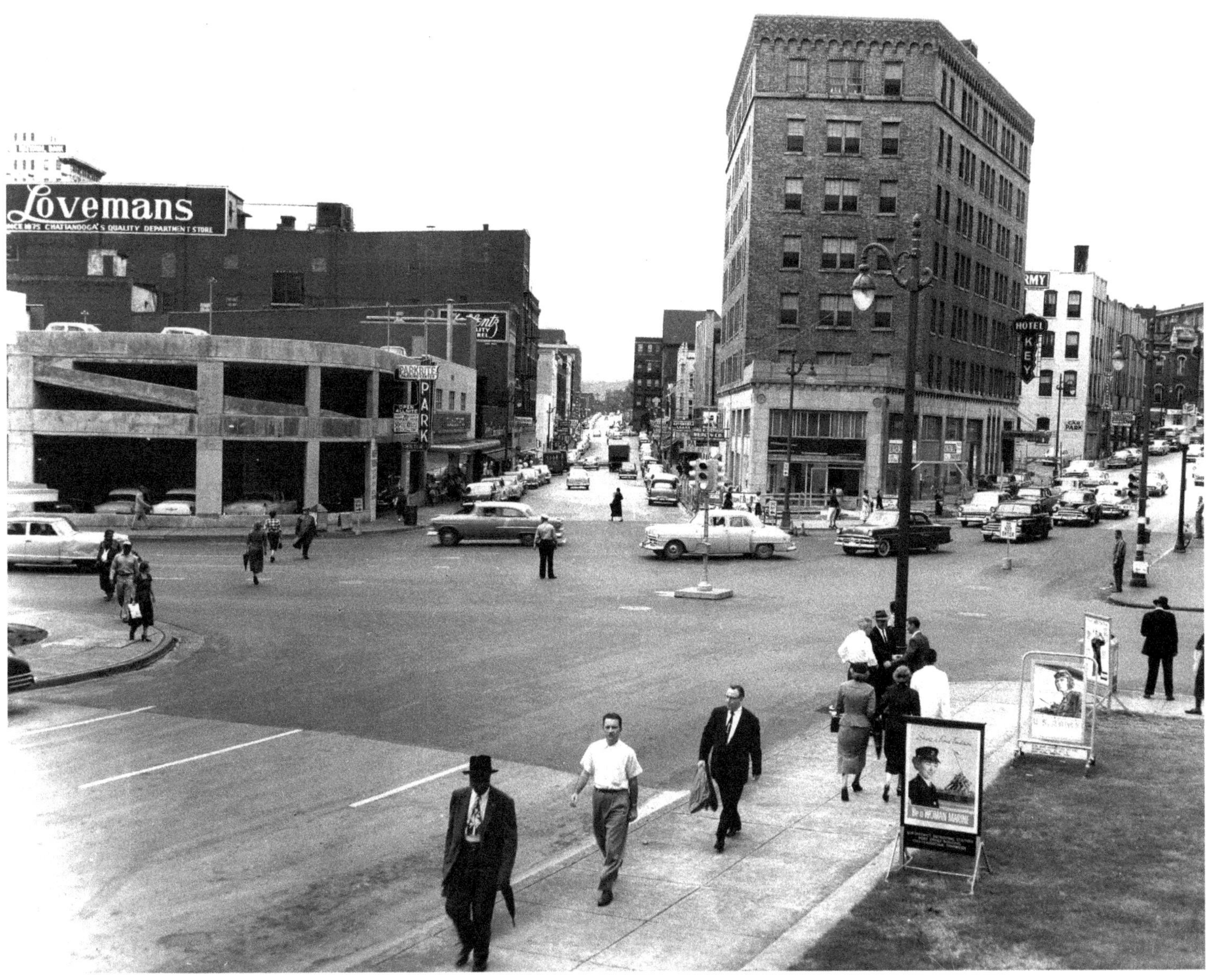

Here in 1956, the Hotel Key is prominent at right as pedestrians go about their daily business. Cherry Street extends into the distance at center, and evidence of the general ugliness creeping into American cities during these years is embodied in the concrete parking garage at left. Large posters recruiting for the armed forces dot the grassy lawn of the U.S. Post Office.

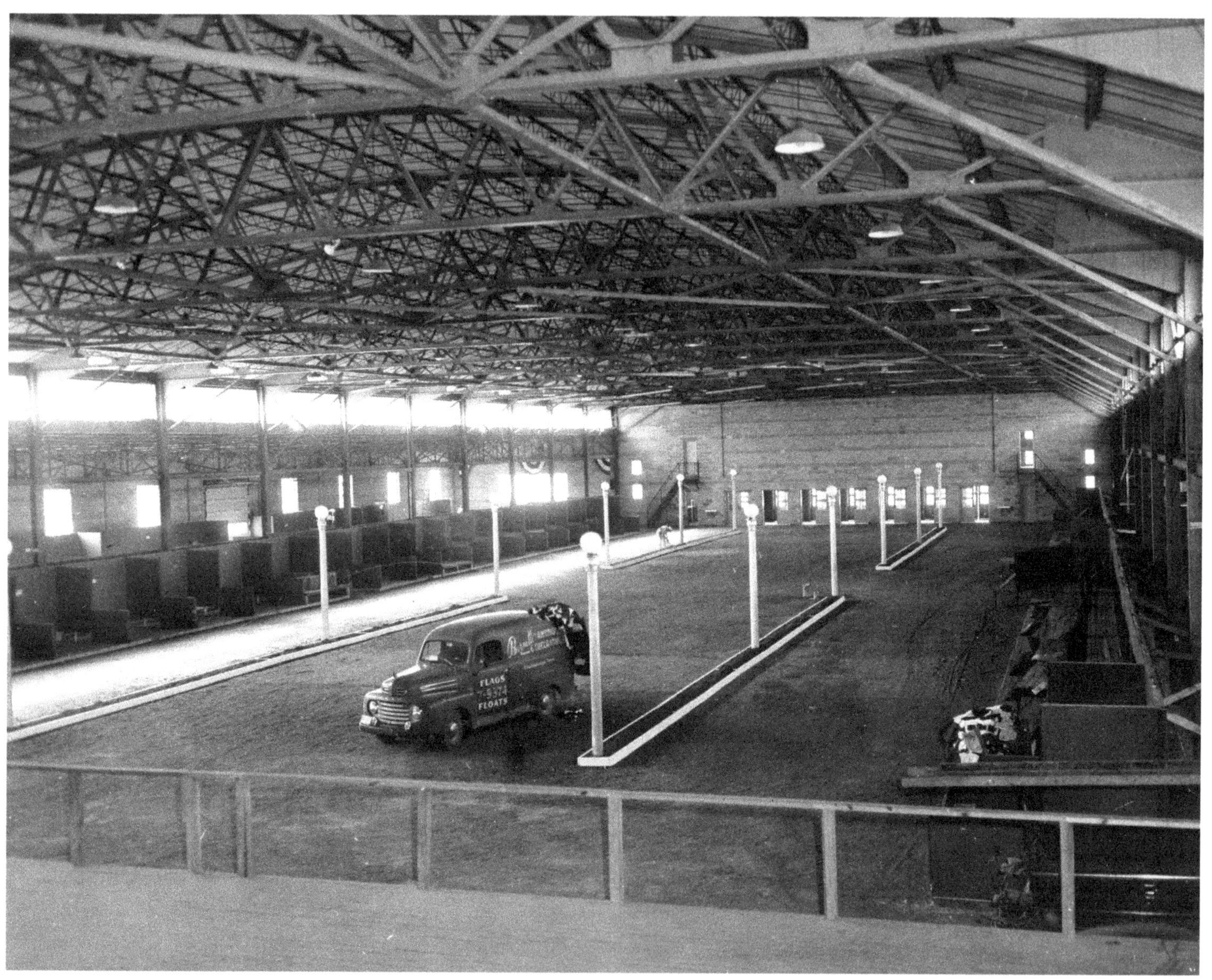

Warner Park is the oldest municipal park in the city, located east of downtown near Engel Stadium and the National Cemetery. The park's field house was originally built to hold crowds for a popular series of revivals by the Billy Graham Crusade in 1953. On the building's floor, a panel truck with lettering that reads "Burnette's Awning and Decorating" is parked here in 1955, suggesting that the groundwork for an event is being installed.

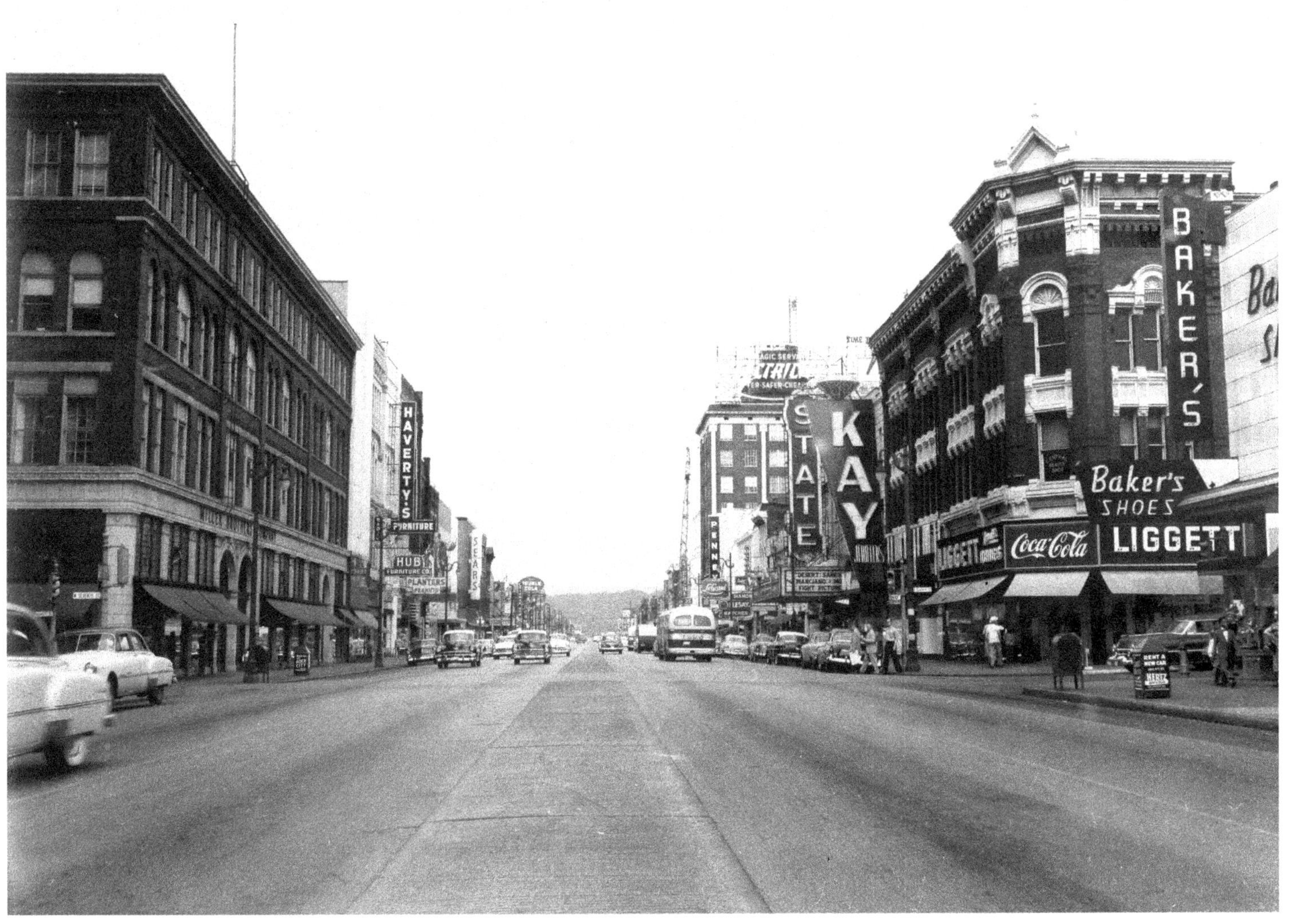

At the corner of Market Street and Seventh Street stands (to the right) one of Chattanooga's oldest intact structures, the Central Block building. Built in 1883 and fronted with intricate brickwork, it has been home to several businesses, including Liggett's drugstore, seen here with the prominent Coca-Cola sign above the front door. This view was recorded in 1955.

Effron's was a stylish shop that opened in 1920 on Market Street. Like many businesses in downtown Chattanooga housed in older nineteenth-century buildings, Effron's felt the need to modernize its appearance. By the mid-fifties, modern facades like the one in the photograph were sweeping the nation. With its minimalist, rectangular form and bright surface quality, the store's new front achieved the look.

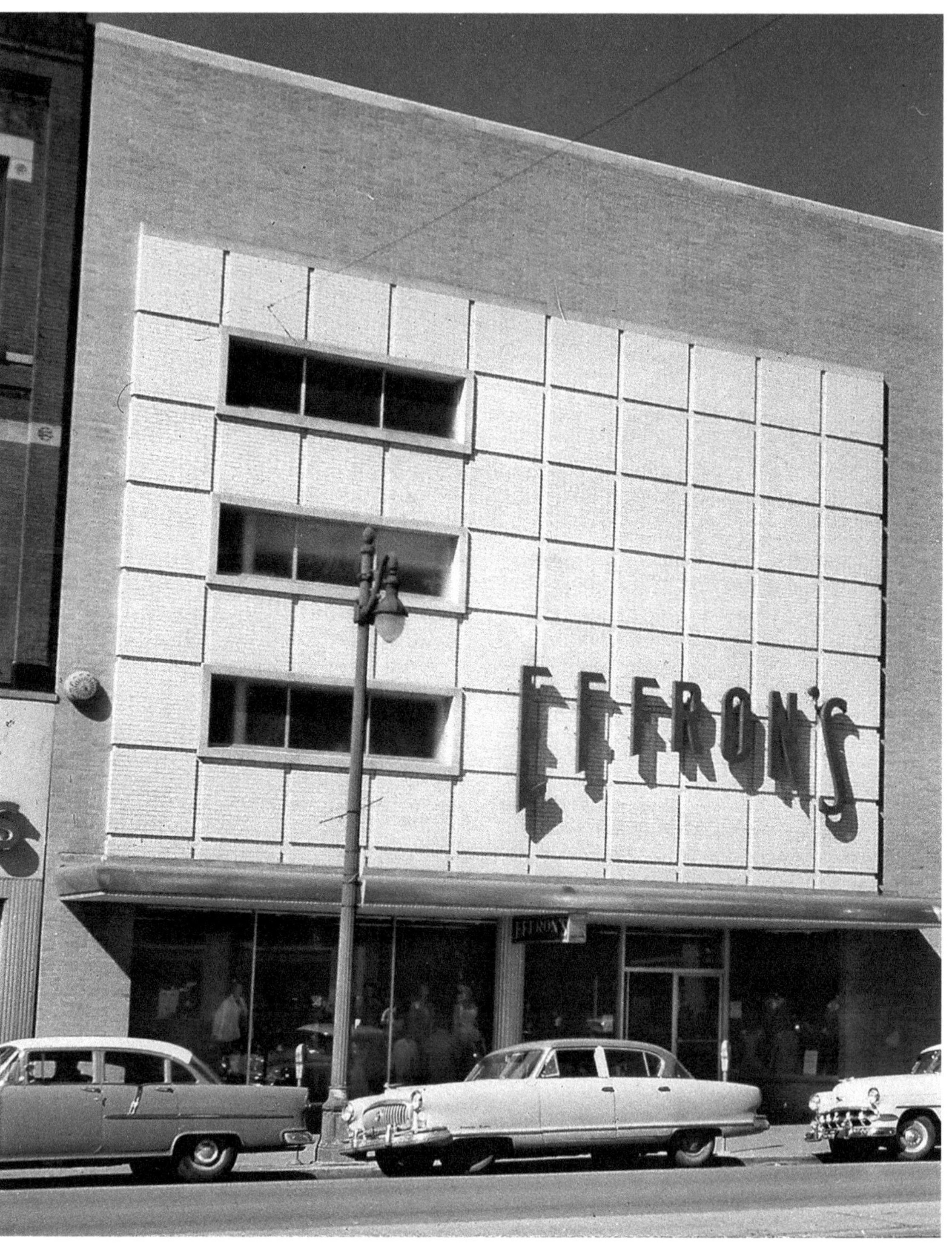

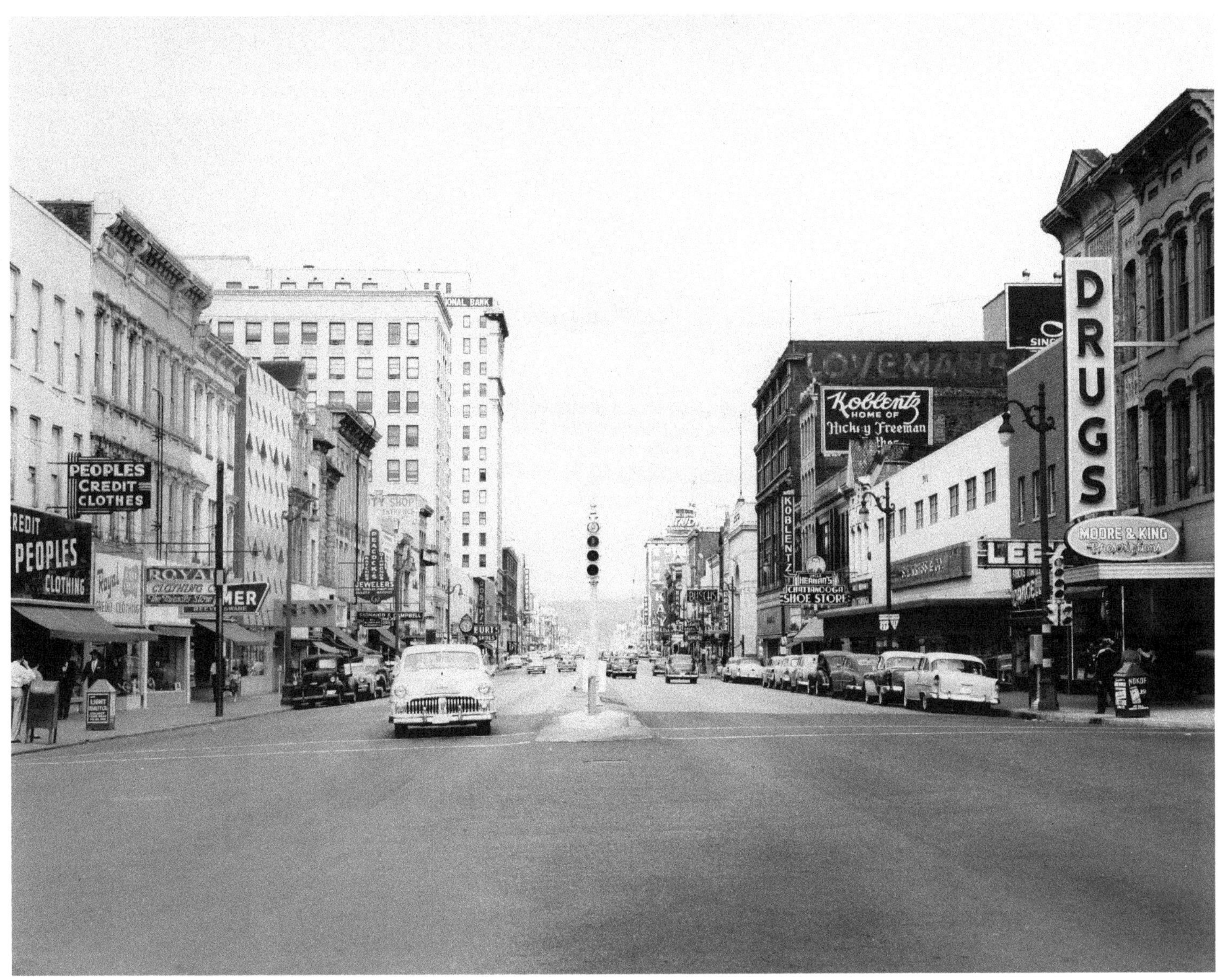

A classic 1950s automobile grill stares straight ahead while the driver waits at a red light at Ninth and Market streets in 1955. The block between Ninth and Eighth streets was home to several of Chattanooga's fine clothiers, among them Fulmer, Reeves, and Ware, and several shoe stores such as Burt's and Chattanooga Shoes. The S&W Cafeteria, a southern eatery, was always busy, and an S. H. Kress's five-and-dime was available for sundries.

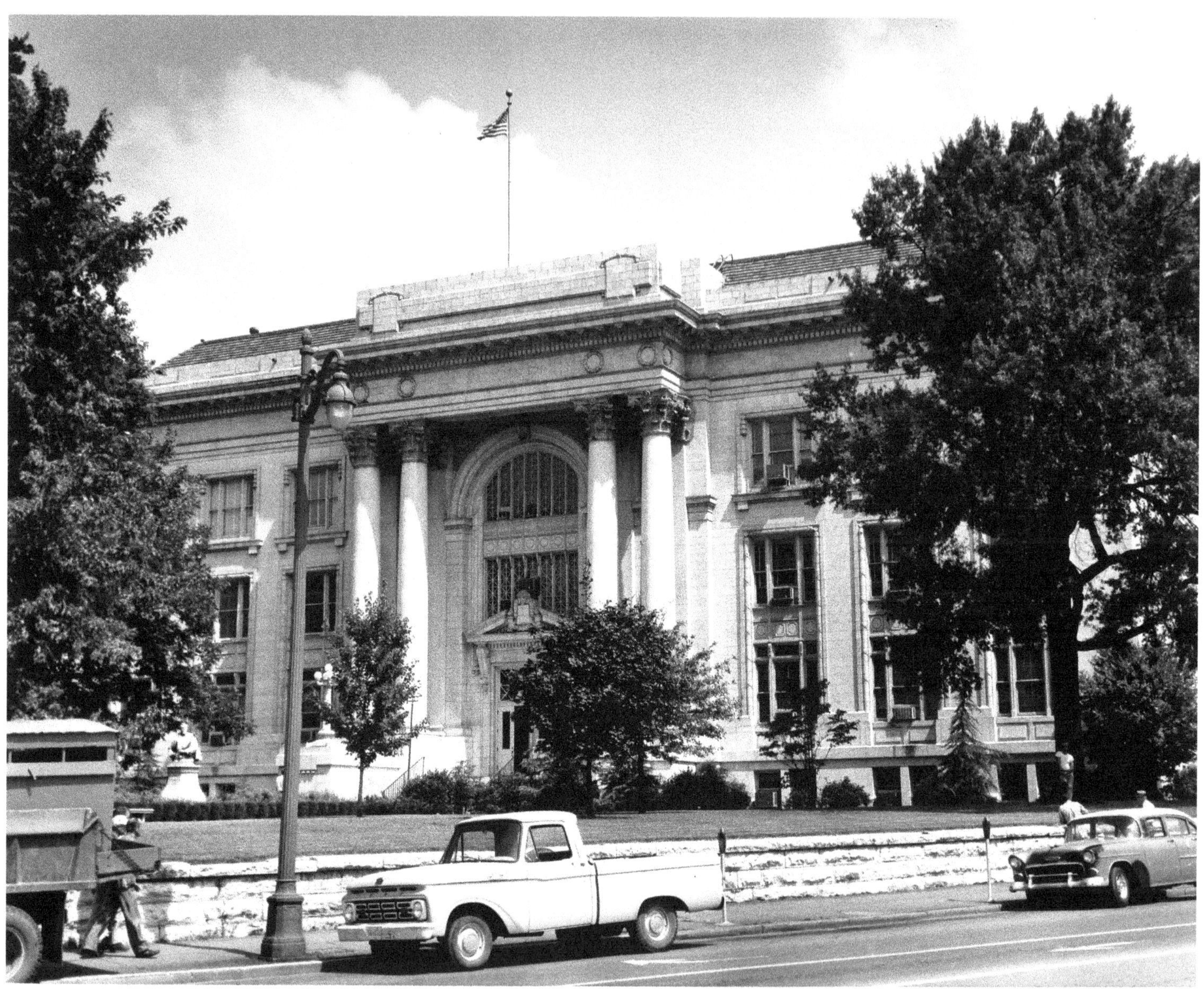

The handsome Hamilton County Courthouse stands on a high hill on Georgia Avenue. Designed by the noted, local architect R. H. Hunt, it is a striking example of municipal architecture with its columns, arched window above the entry, and detailed, Tennessee marble facade. Constructed in 1913 after the former courthouse was struck by lightning and burned to the ground, the courthouse looks out on the grounds and a statue of Confederate general A. P. Stewart.

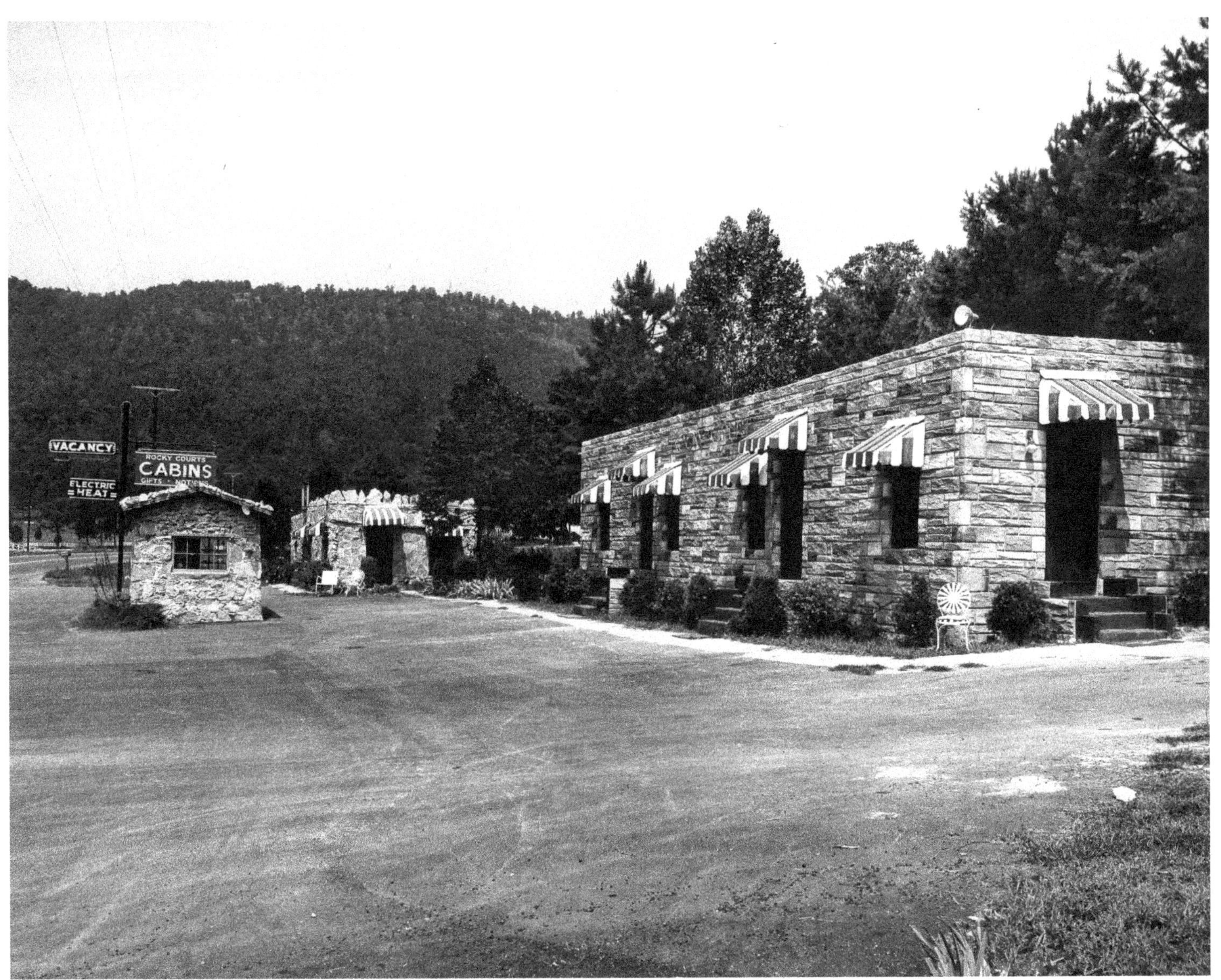

Before the era of today's national chain hotels, roadside inns varied in style from town to town. Small, homey affairs like the Rocky Courts Cabins, with their clean, cut-stone exteriors, awnings, and simple accommodations, fit well with the mountain terrain around them. These sorts of "tourist courts" were numerous along roads like the Dixie Highway, a national north-south artery organized in and running through Chattanooga. This view of the Rocky Courts was recorded around 1955.

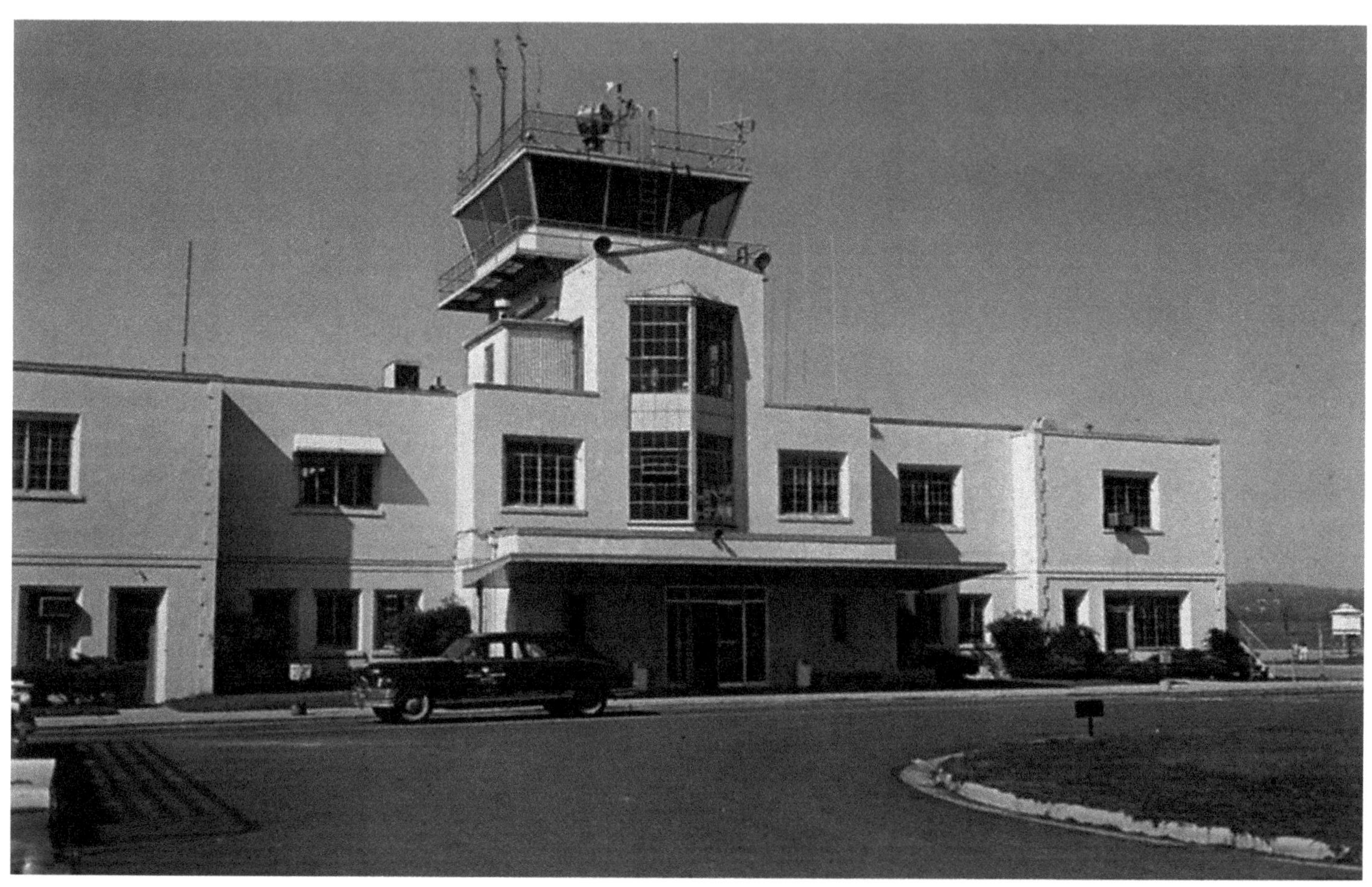

Public fascination with stunt flights and the possibilities of commercial aviation was, by the 1920s, bearing fruit in the construction of airfields across the nation. Chattanooga was determined to be part of the aeronautical age and to that end constructed the original terminal for Lovell Field in 1930, about five miles east of town on approximately 1,000 acres of land. The tower was built in 1942 and the airport has grown steadily ever since. This image shows the tower as it looked around 1955.

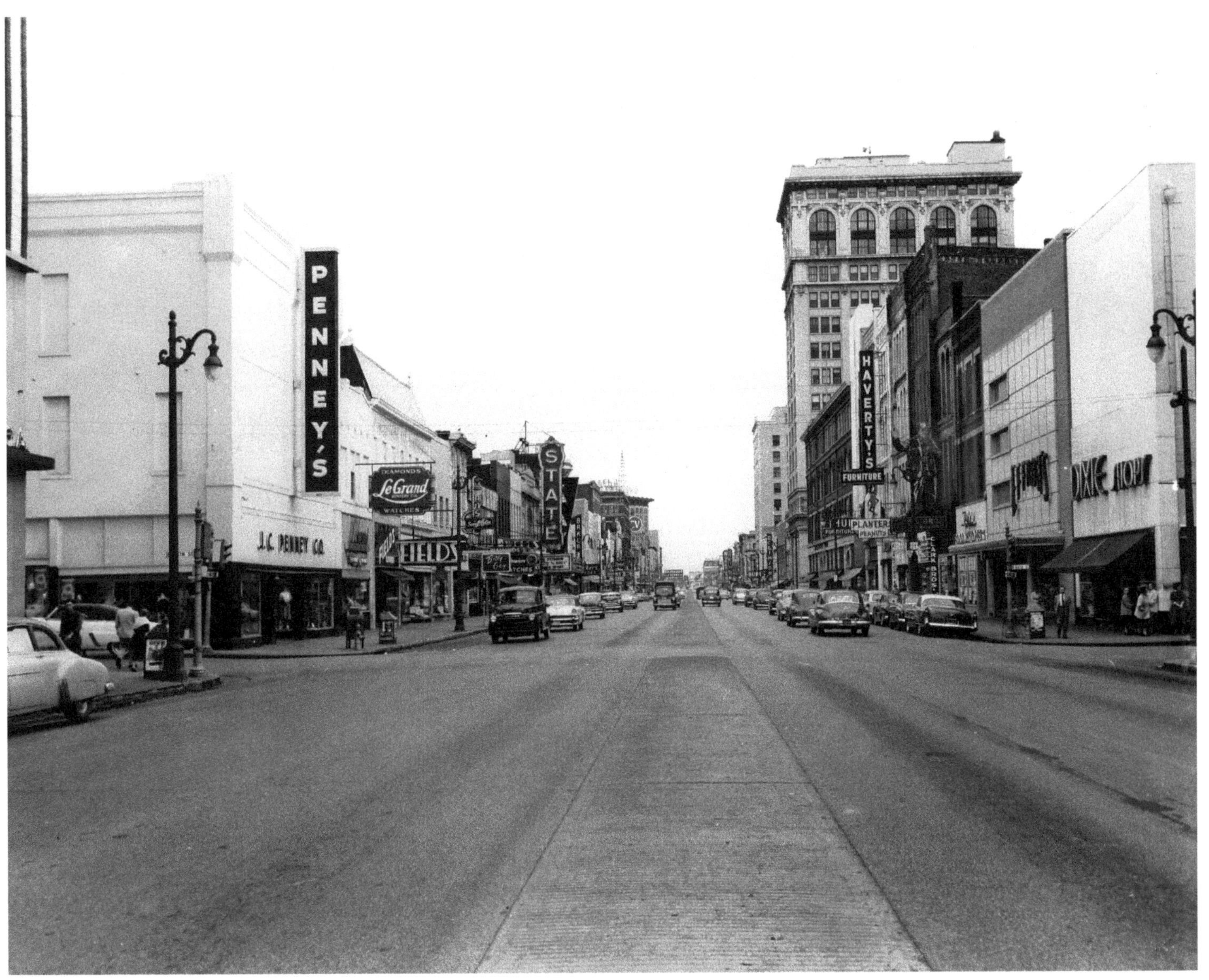

A busy day on Market Street in 1955 reveals the variety of businesses that were thriving downtown. Besides the corner J. C. Penney's, there was the popular State Theater, probably showing a western. To the right were the tall Hamilton National Bank Building, Haverty's furniture store, Effron's, and the Dixie Shop. Overhead traffic lights were absent from the street; instead, they were situated on corner posts.

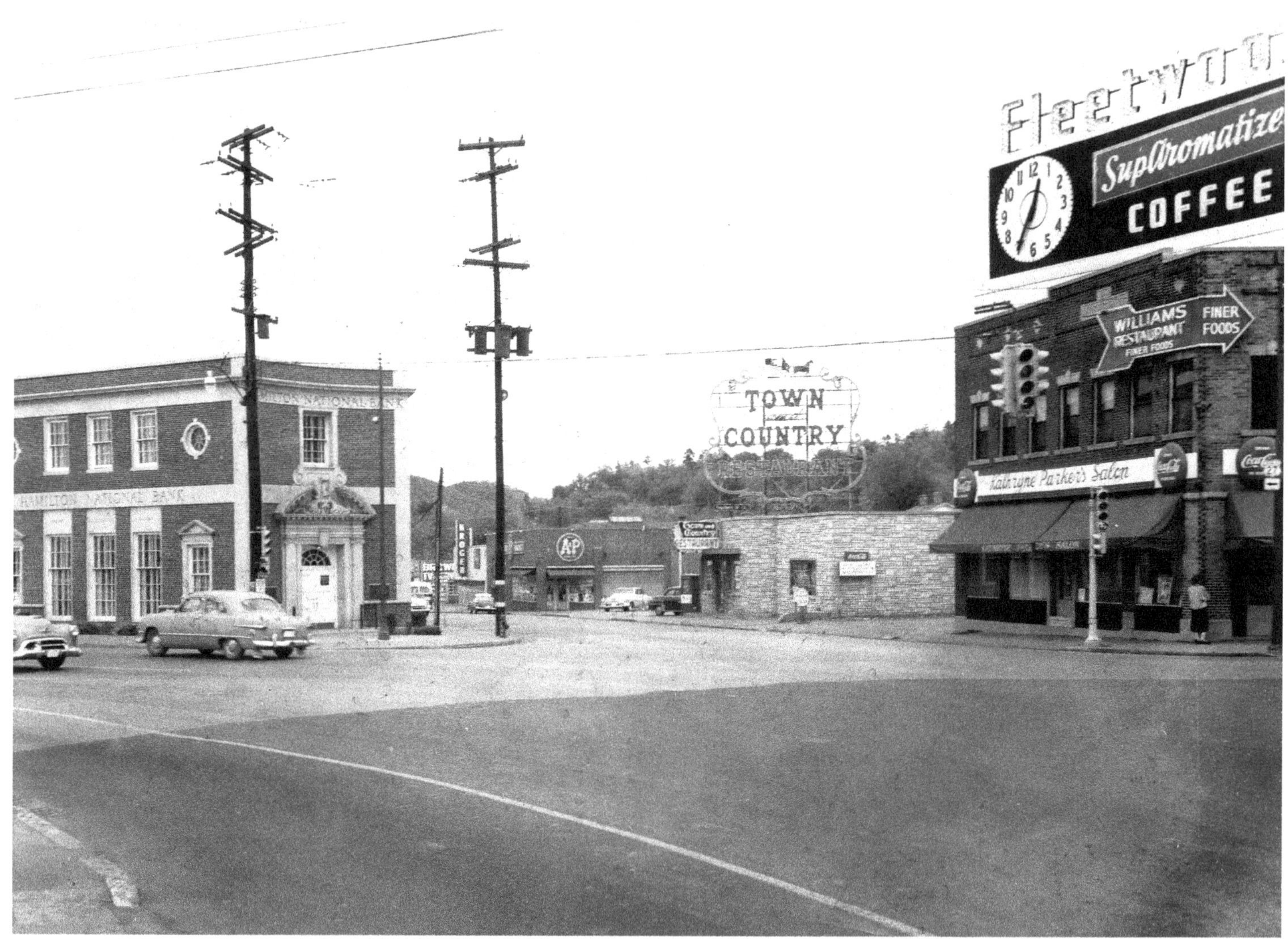

One of the city's most beloved restaurants, the Town and Country Restaurant was located near the intersection of Cherokee Boulevard and North Market Street here in the Hill City neighborhood. Run by the Hall family for 50 years, the restaurant was famous for fried chicken and greens and a warm, familial atmosphere. A stop for many travelers, the establishment was easily identified by its tall, elegant neon sign of a horse and carriage.

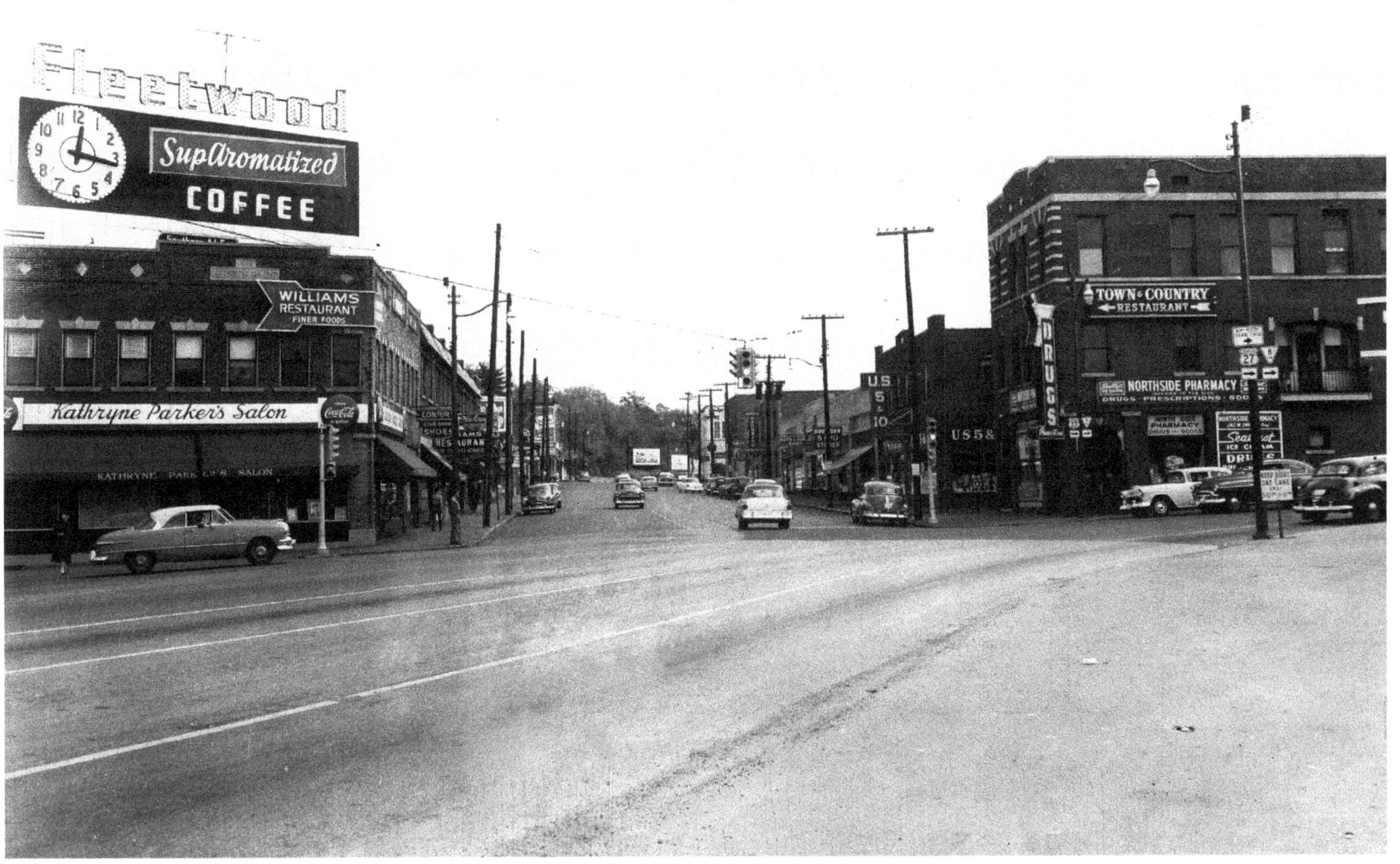

The clock above Frazier Avenue says it's lunchtime here in 1955, maybe even time for a "suparomatized" cup of Fleetwood Coffee, Chattanooga's hometown choice. This view looking east at the intersection of North Market Street is crowded with signs for restaurants, a beauty shop, and a 5 and 10. Some of the buildings to the left would be demolished, but the businesses to the right are still a busy spot in the Hill City neighborhood today.

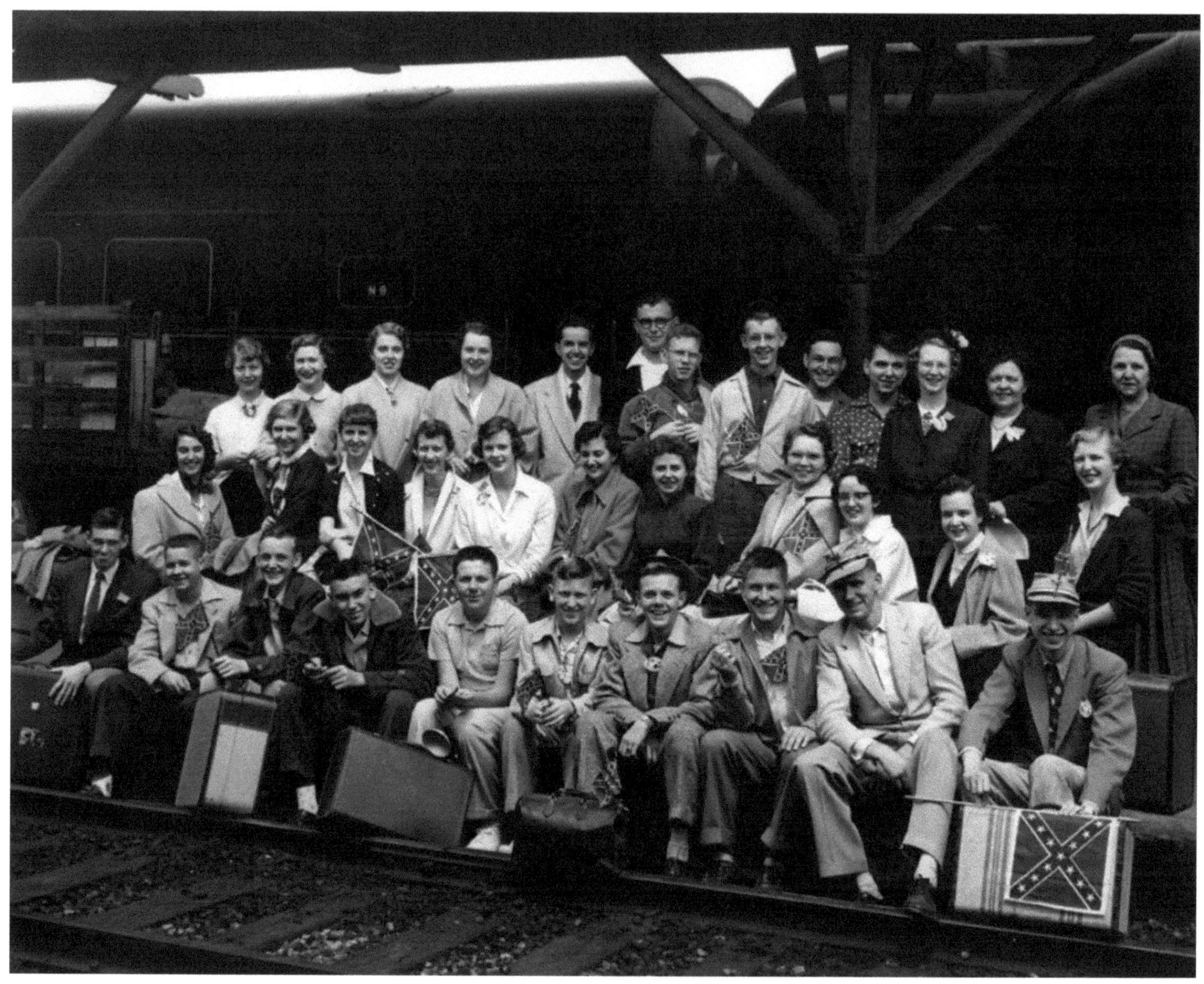

Members and friends of Eunice Kerr's art club at Chattanooga City High School are all smiles as they prepare to embark from Terminal Station around 1955. Destinations for the club's excursions included New Orleans, New York, and Washington, D.C. In the 1950s, emblems of the Confederacy, including the Confederate flags seen here, were popular among many youth as a means to appreciating their southern identity. Not yet part of the daily news, political divides and racial turmoil were issues for another, less carefree day.

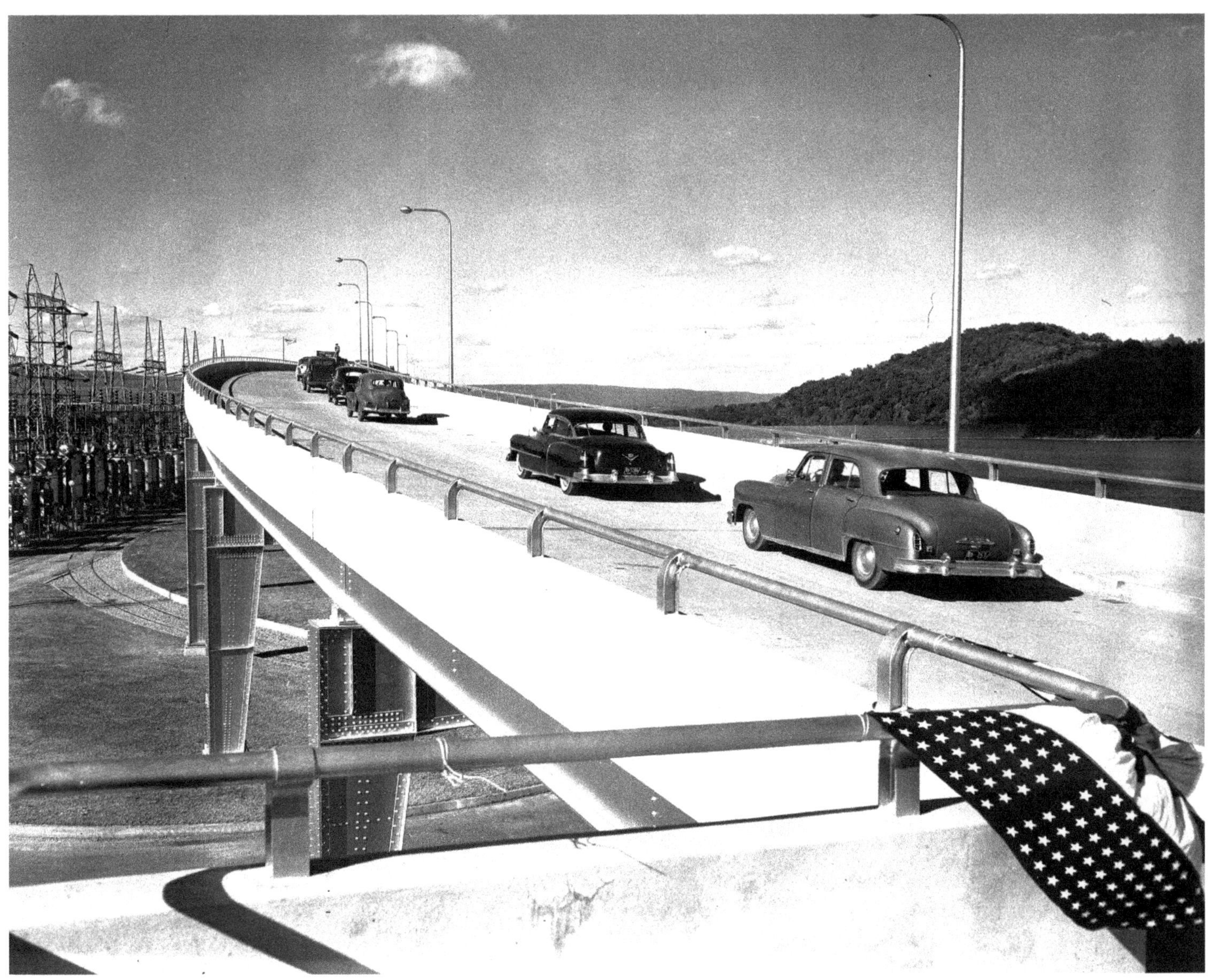

Automobiles stream across the new Wilkes T. Thrasher Bridge over Chickamauga Dam in 1955. The flag bunting in the foreground and the clean, white road indicate that this may be the day the bridge opened to the public. The fact that the cars are all moving the same direction turns the image slightly surreal. The completion of this span crossing the river spurred development of the entire Hixson area.

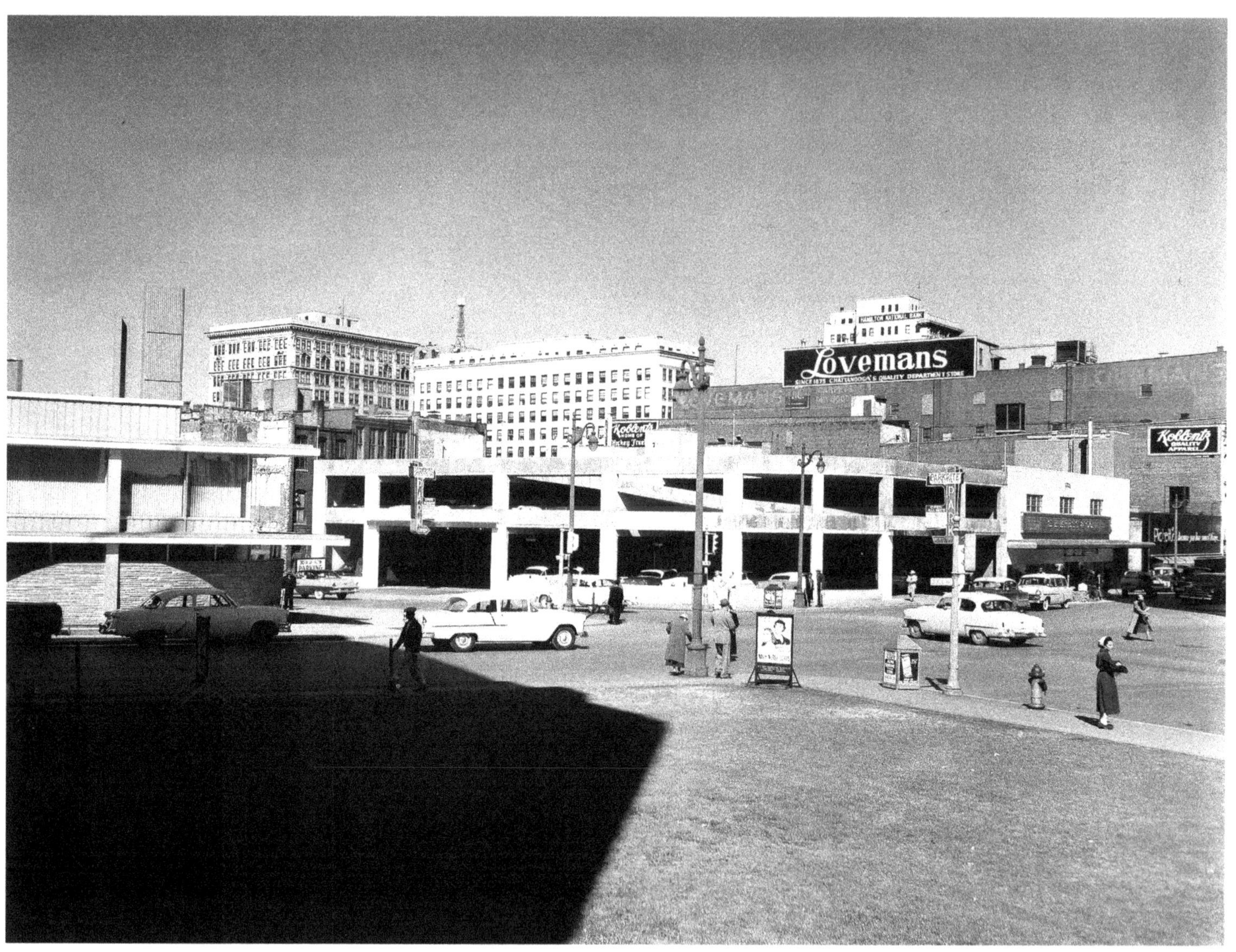

In 1956, morning traffic passes through the intersection of Georgia Avenue and Ninth Street, now known as Martin Luther King Boulevard. The name was changed in 1982 by the city council at the request of the African-American community in Chattanooga. Ninth Street or the "Big Nine" was the thoroughfare where black businesses, restaurants, churches, and newspapers were centered earlier in the twentieth century.

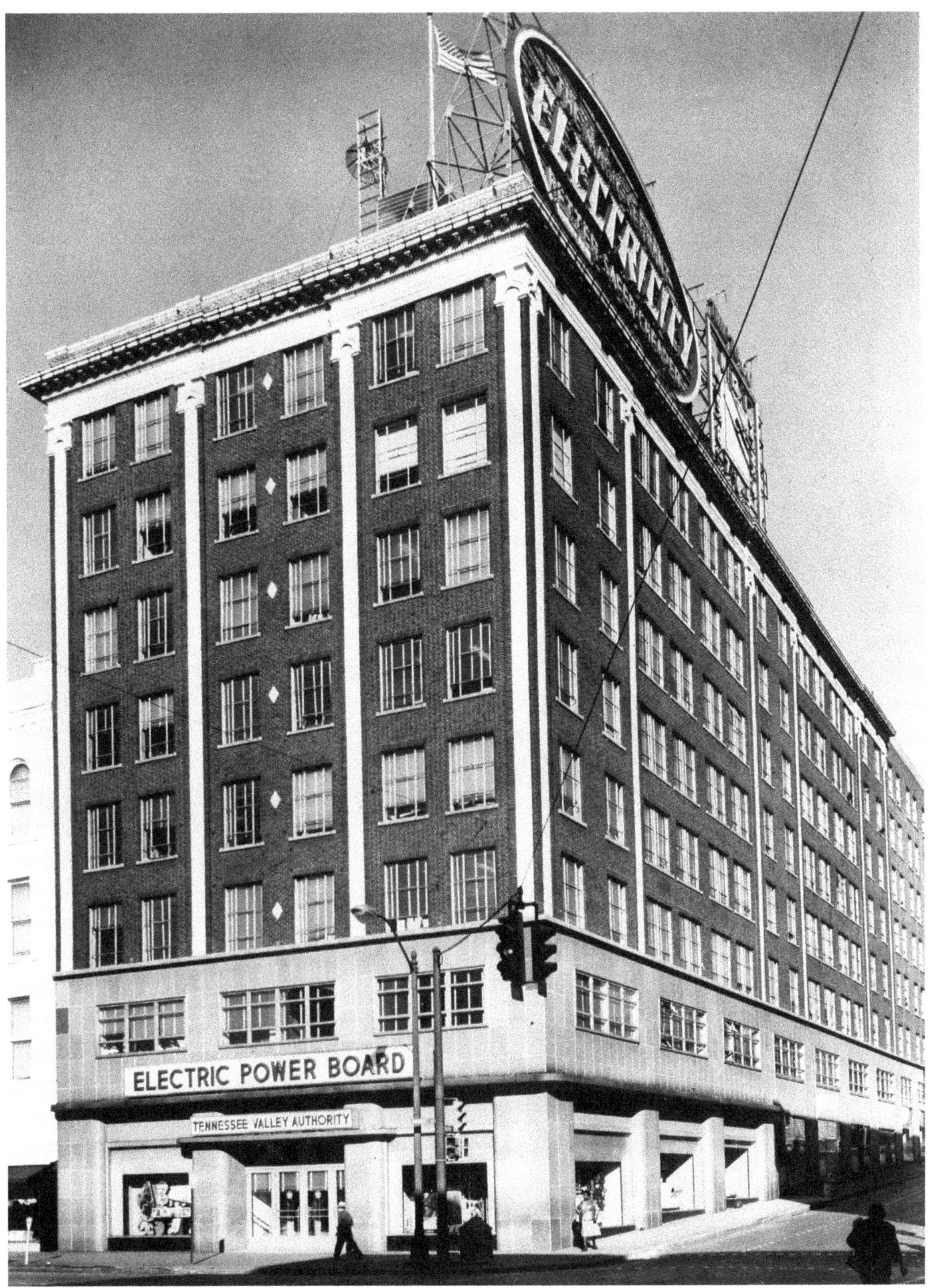

This fine, eight-story example of commercial architecture stood on the corner of Sixth and Market streets for decades before succumbing to the wrecking ball in 2008. Long the home of the Electric Power Board—or EPB as it is known in this era of abbreviations—it sported a spectacularly large, oval-shaped sign on its roof that shown throughout the city at night. It is seen here around 1958.

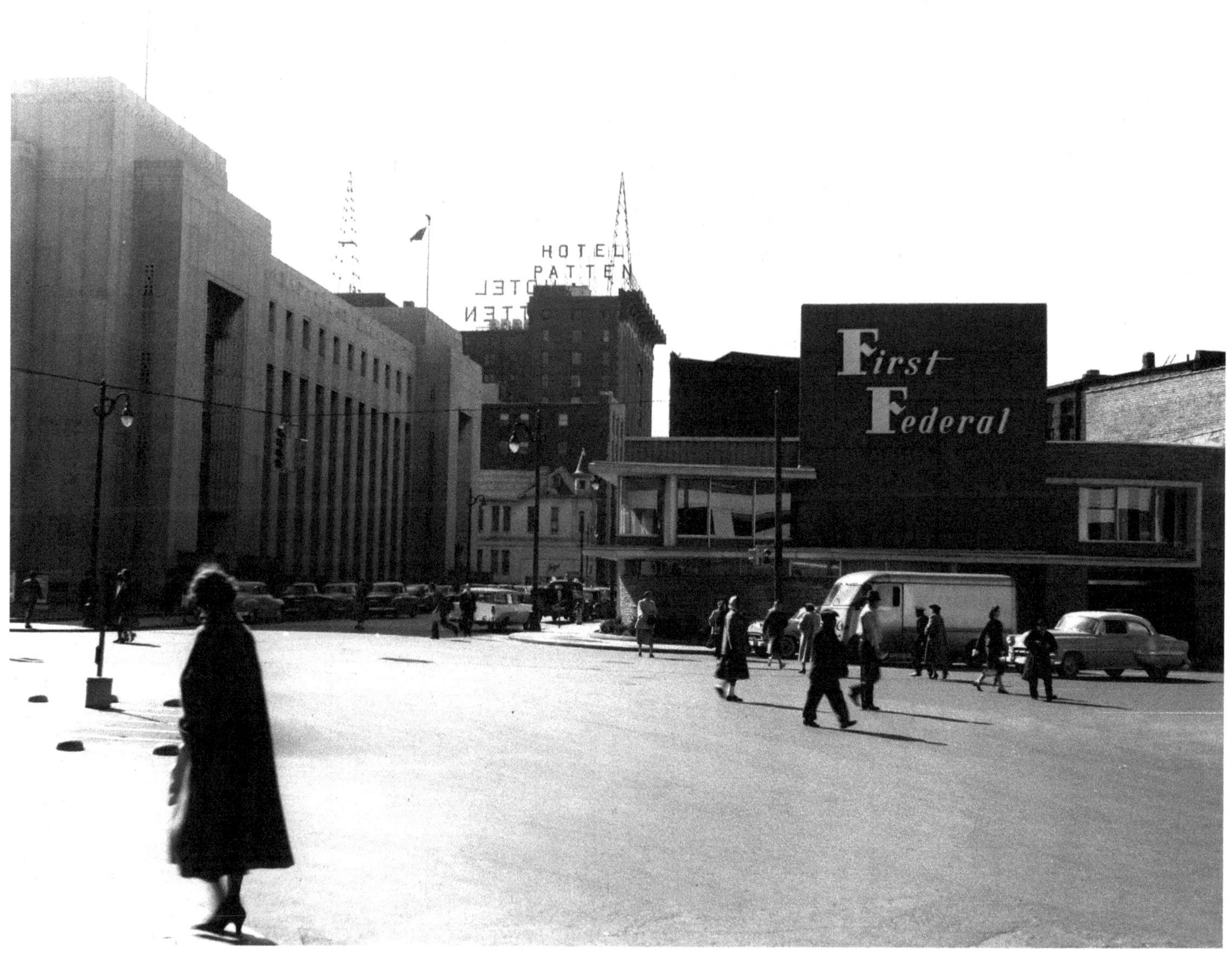

The gleaming, Art Moderne United States Post Office presides over Georgia Avenue on a workday morning in 1956. Built by Reuben Harrison Hunt, and known today as the Joel W. Solomon Federal Building, it opened in 1933 and houses several courtrooms as well as a stunning Works Progress Administration mural. In the distance is the Hotel Patten on Eleventh Street with its radio antenna beaming news and entertainment across the valley.

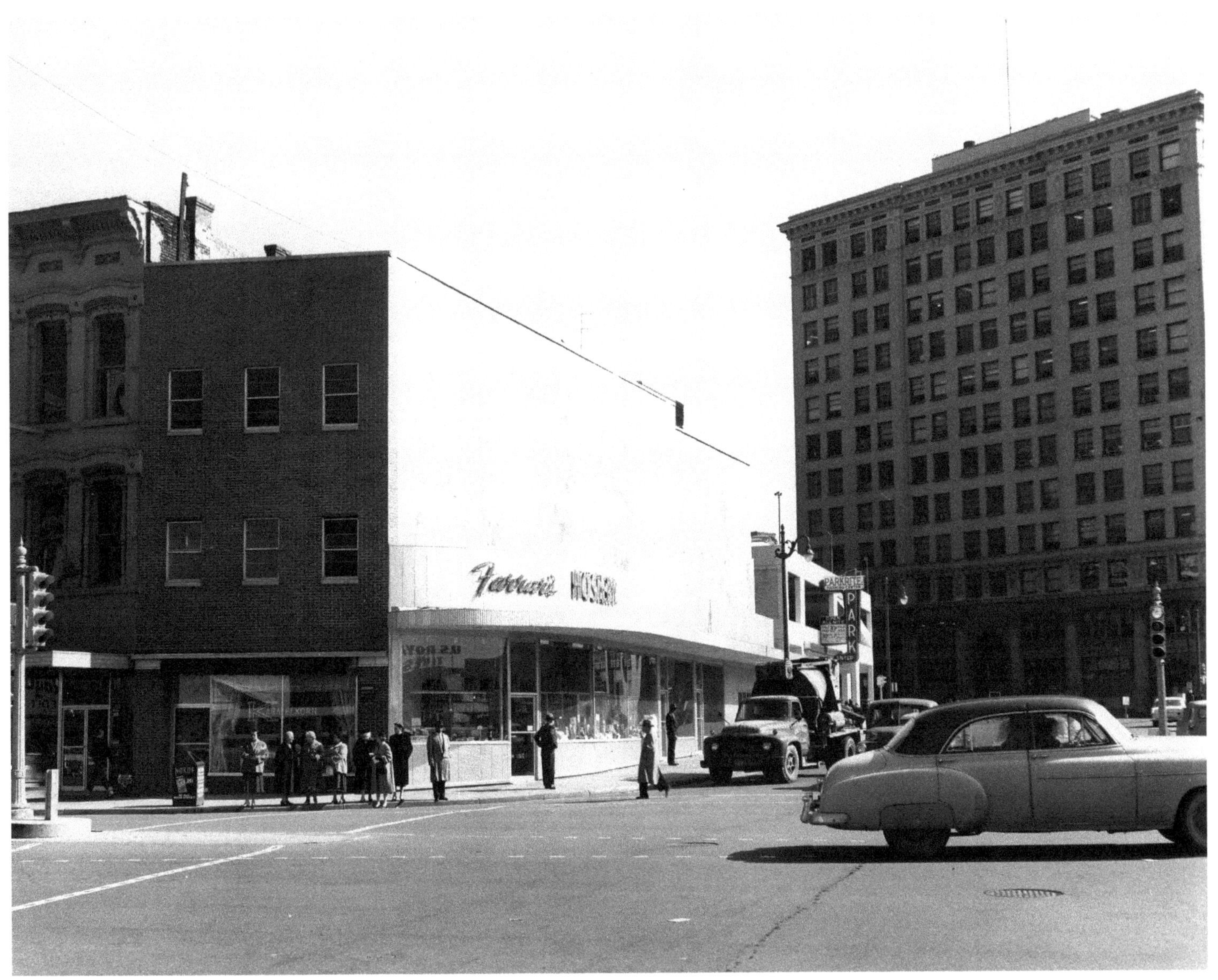

It is hard to believe that there once were shops specializing in stockings and socks, but that was the business of Farrar's Hosiery store on the corner of Market and Ninth streets. Next door was the Karmelkorn Kandy Shop, selling sugary wares no doubt. Looming over these smaller enterprises was the Volunteer State Life Insurance Building on Georgia Avenue.

Sam O'Neil owned a livestock company and later a stockyard in Chattanooga. The Sam O'Neil Horse and Mule Barn was located on St. Elmo Avenue near Lookout Mountain and the scene of regular auctions. Here around 1956, two mules are brought forth and folks are welcome to bid. Without a doubt buyers and onlookers are having a good time, and will as long as they behave themselves and remember the rules: No Profanity and No Drinking.

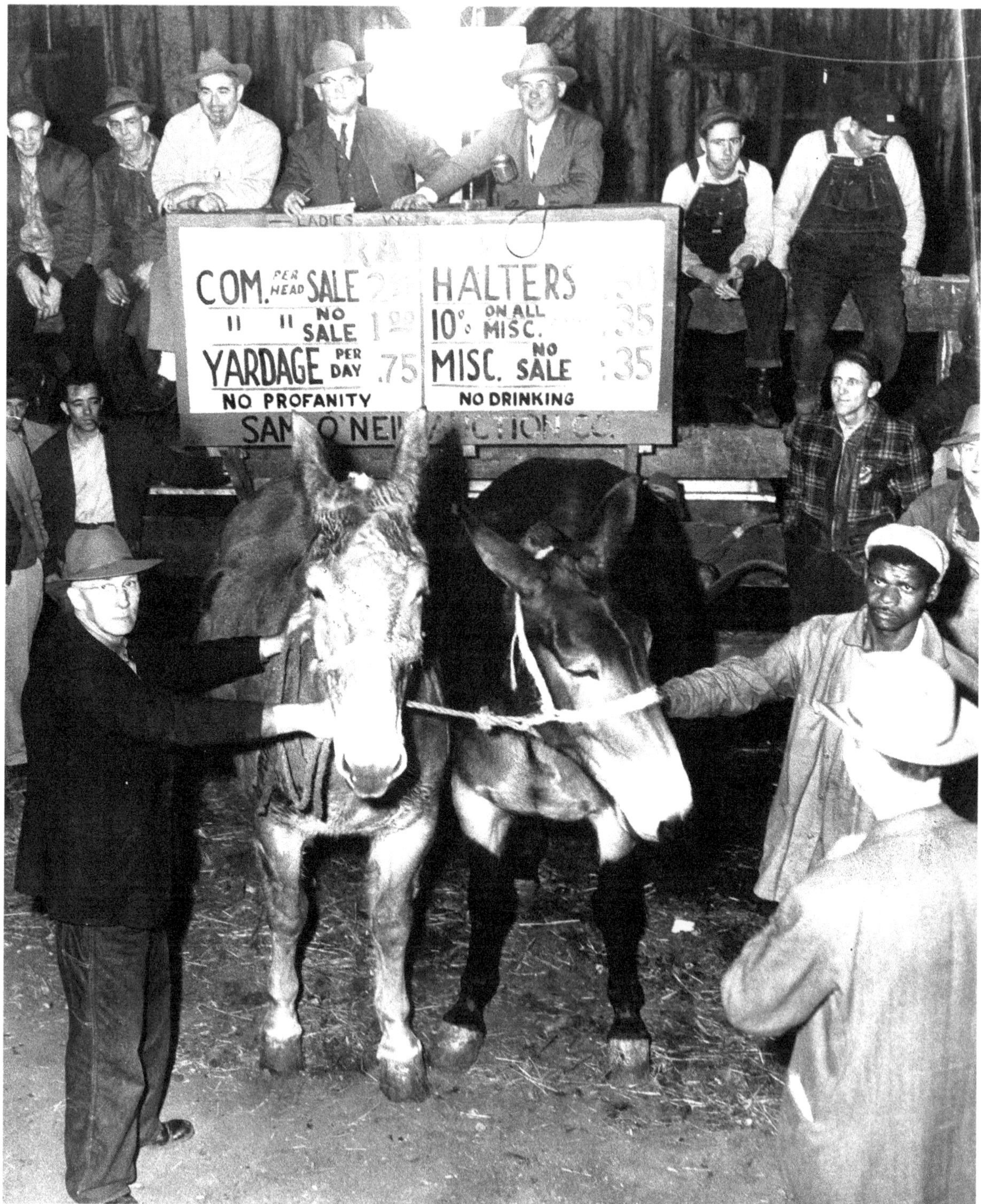

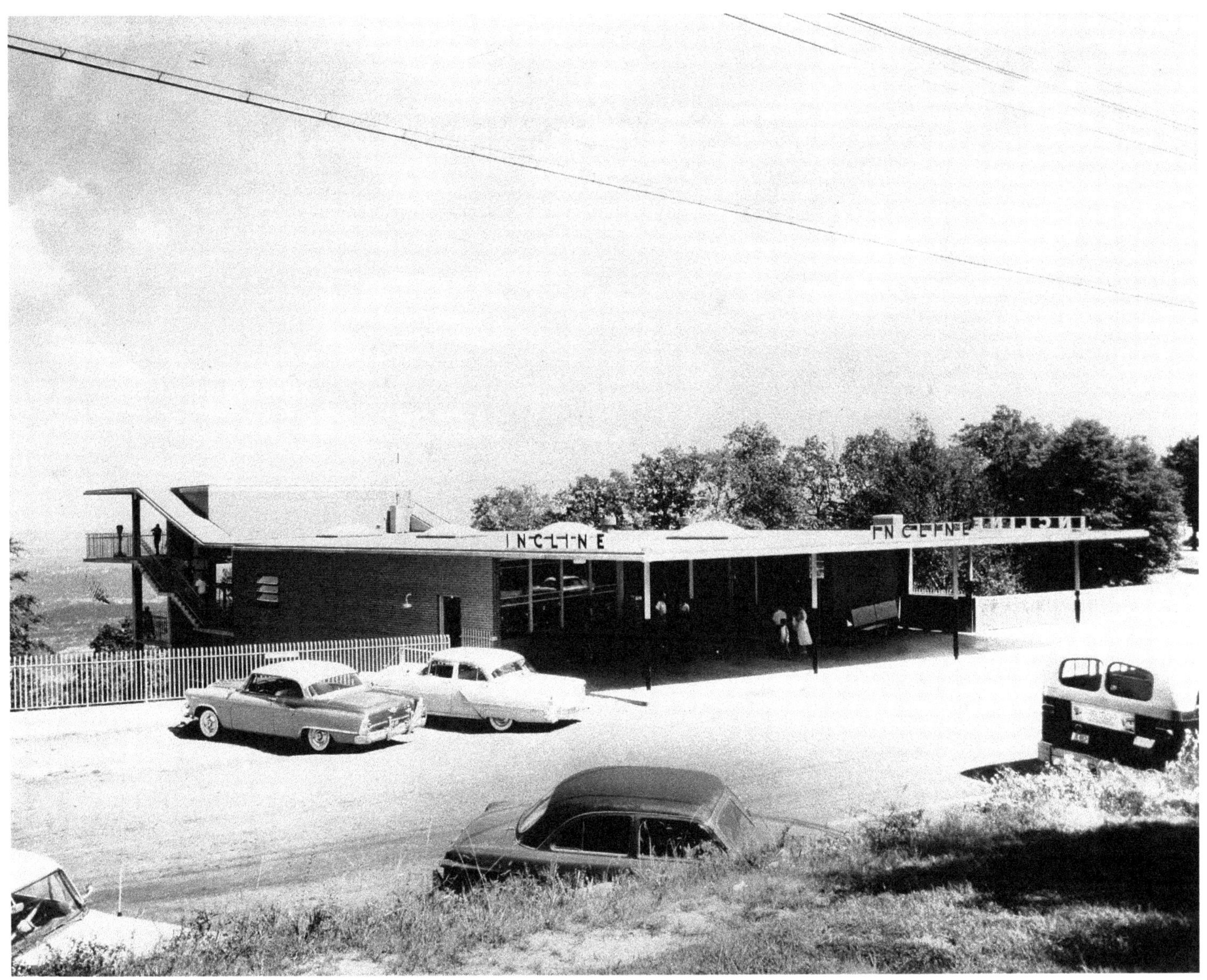

The Lookout Mountain Incline Railway has a ticket station of old, red brick at the bottom and a wider, newer departure point at the top. The original station at the crest burned; the current station boasts platforms with large, coin-operated binoculars for viewing the Chattanooga valley. For souvenir hunters, keepsakes like key chains and coffee mugs abound, along with an endless array of T-shirts to bear witness to one's travels. This is a view of the station at the top as it appeared in 1956.

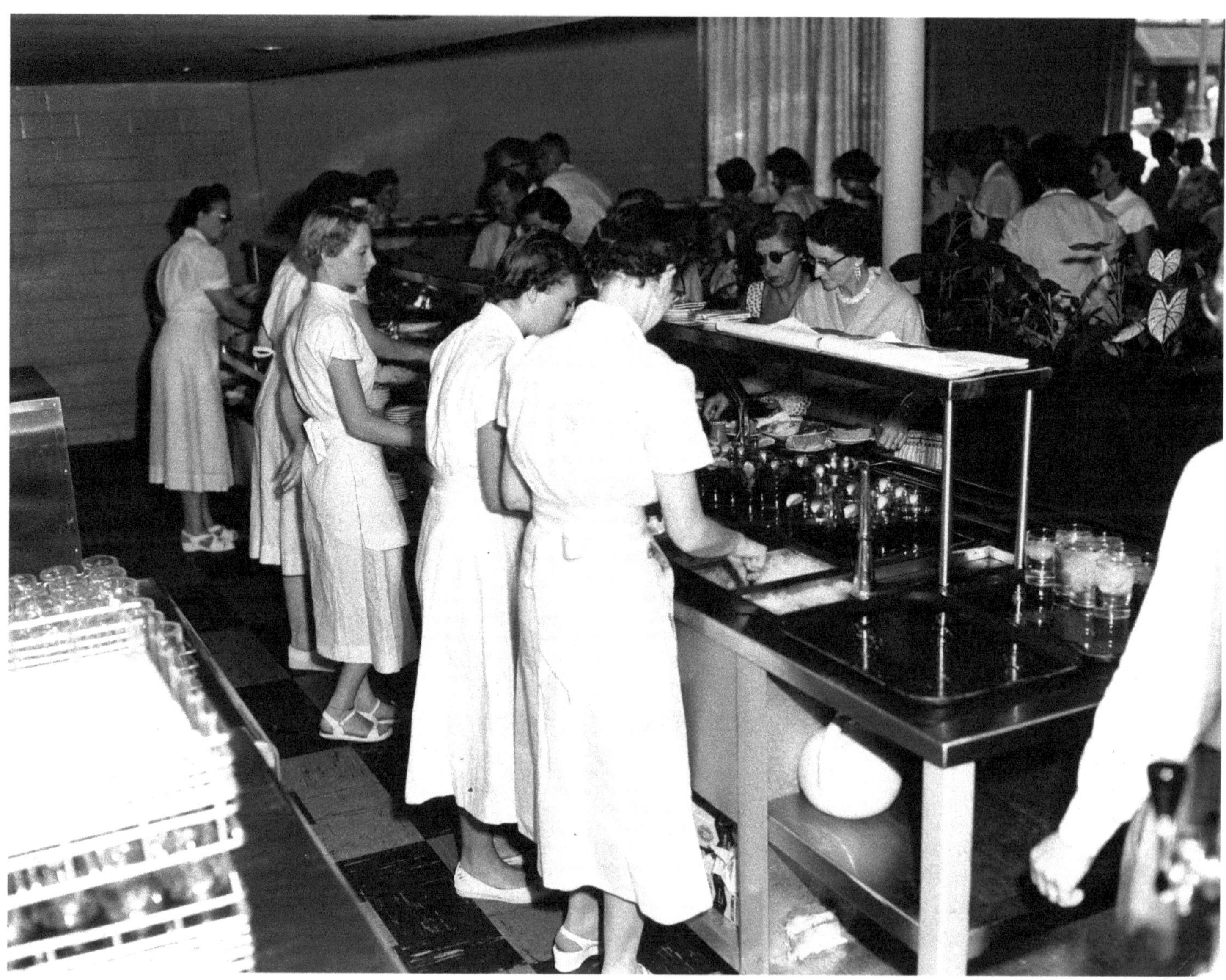

White-clad servers keep the food fresh and hot for the hungry patrons at the Home Plate Cafeteria around 1956. Opened in 1928 in the era of Babe Ruth, the Home Plate served classic southern fried chicken and steamed table vegetables to local folks for decades. Located at Cherry and Seventh streets across from the original Krystal Restaurant, it was one of several cafeterias downtown until it closed in 1987.

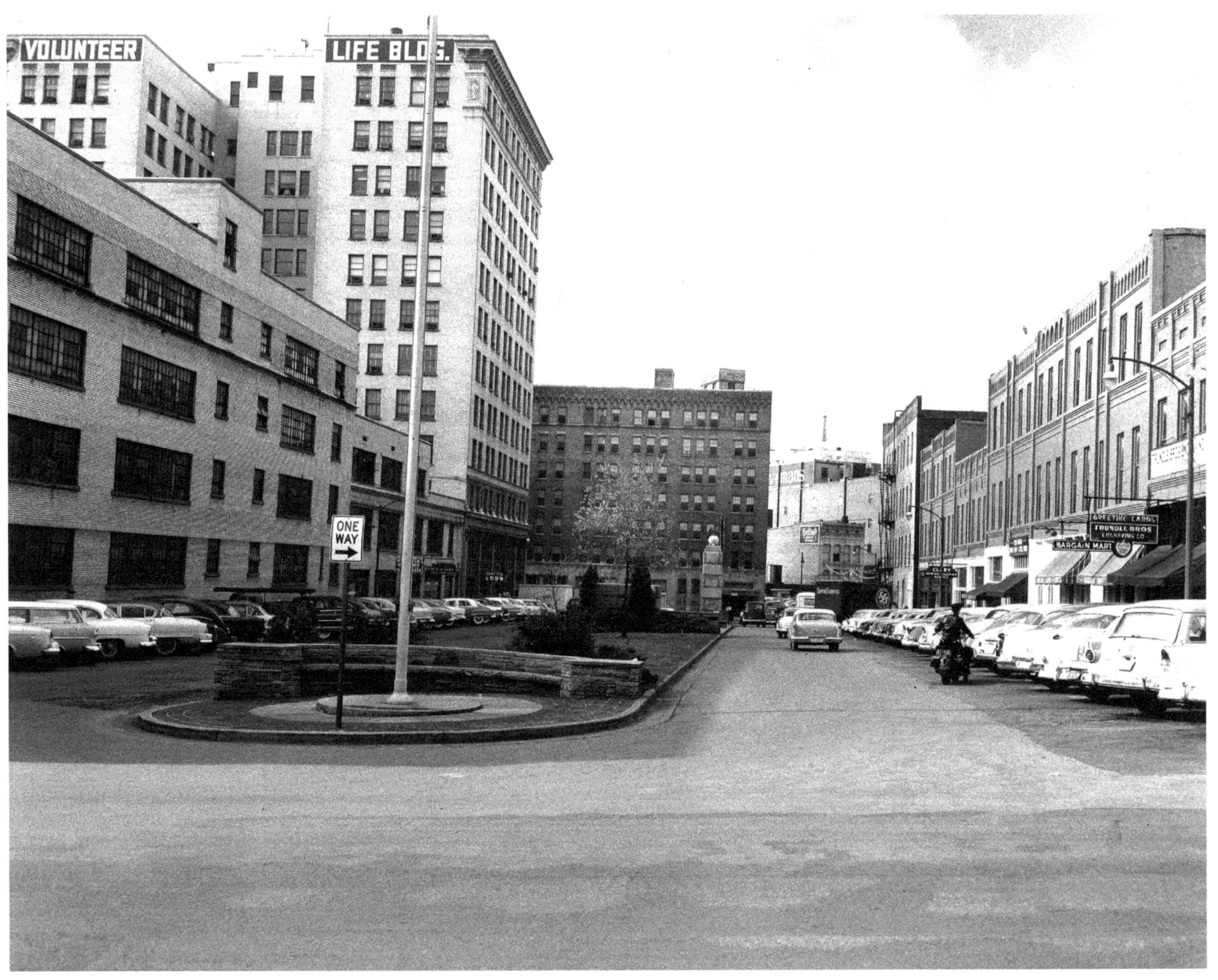

This view of the Patten Parkway facing west depicts the Volunteer Life Insurance Building to the left. It was founded by Z. C. Patten, for whom the park is named. The park was originally the site of a successful fresh produce market built in the late 1880s, until it was torn down in 1942, a casualty of "indoor" grocery stores. Following World War II, the land was designated as a memorial park for Chattanooga veterans. This is the view in 1956.

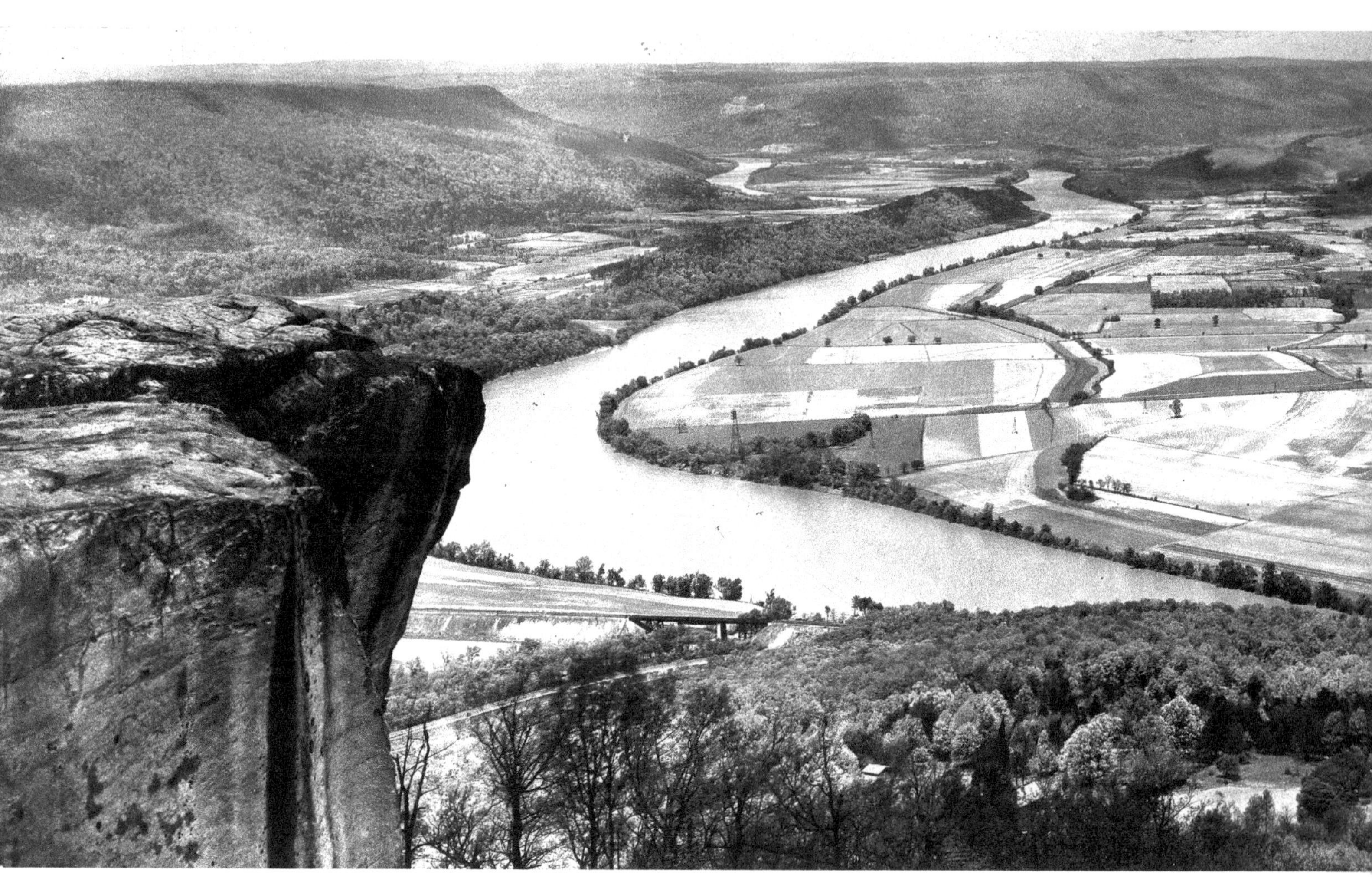

This long, sweeping turn in the Tennessee River is part of the magnificent panorama visible from Lookout Mountain. Known as Moccasin Bend for its foot-like shape, the land has been inhabited for what archaeologists believe is thousands of years. During the Civil War, Union artillery lobbed cannon balls toward the Confederate soldiers on the mountain. Recently a portion of the Bend has been designated as federal park land in perpetuity.

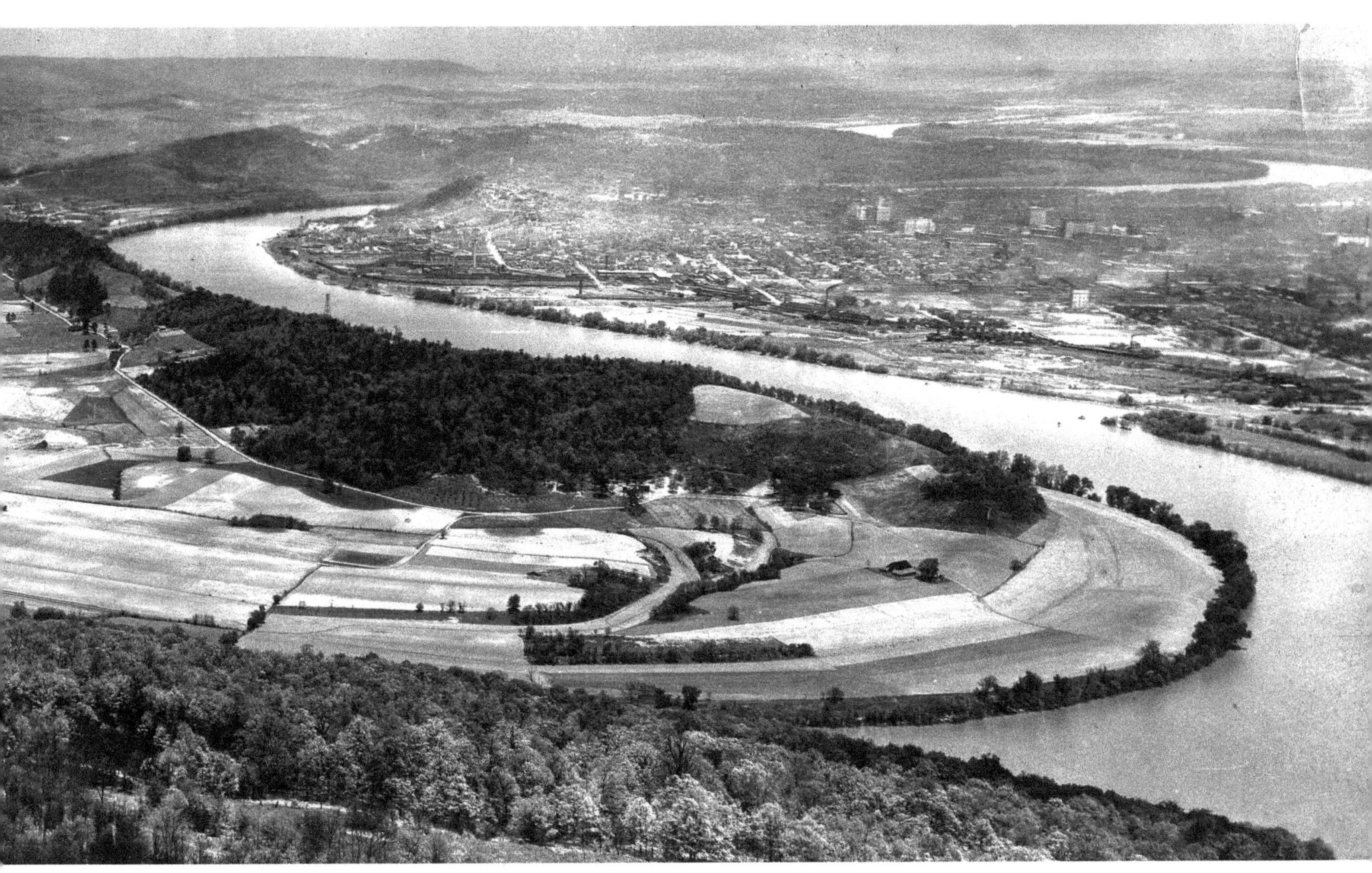

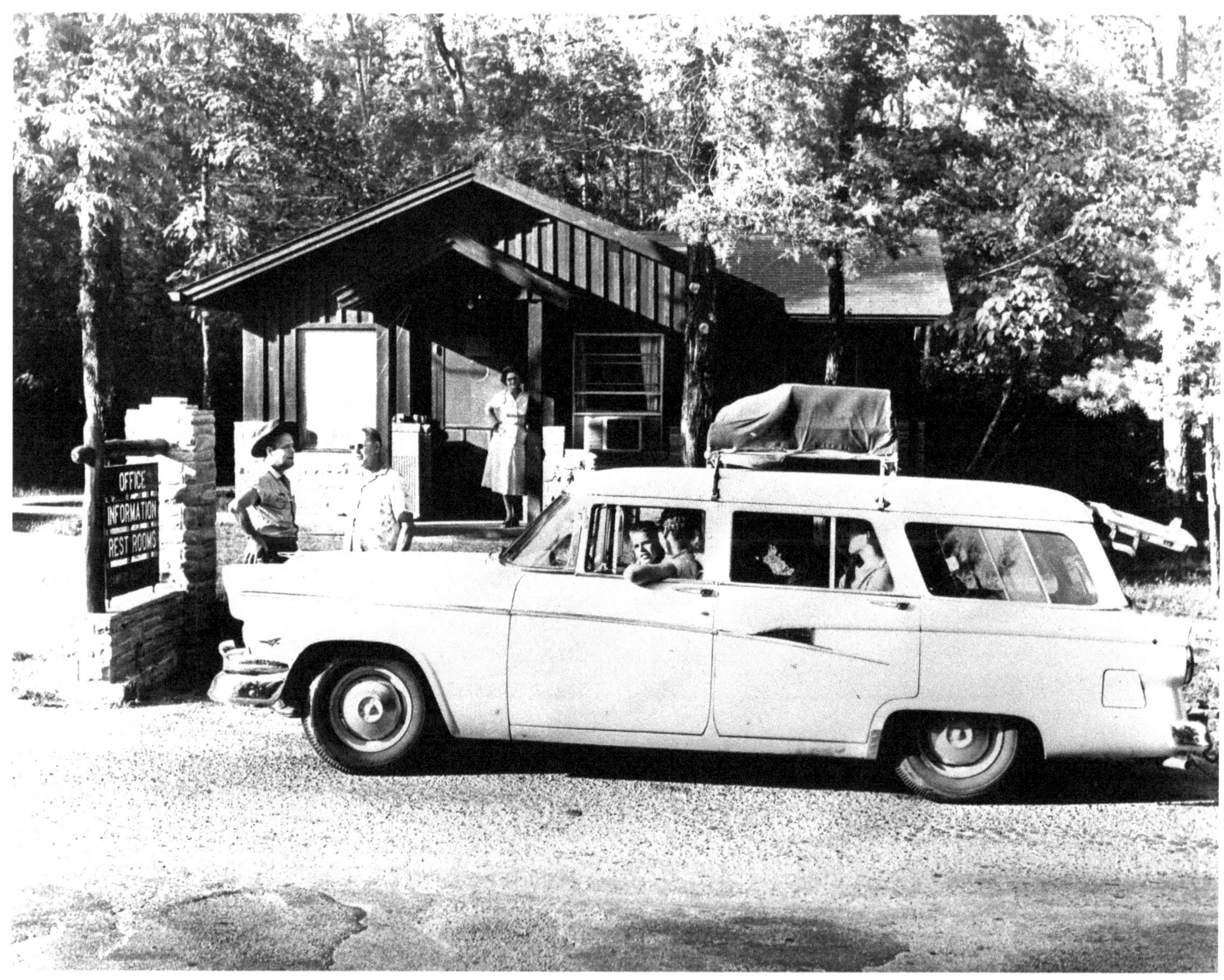

Remember summer vacations in which you were packed into the car and on the road forever? If you had a father who loved to camp and your family had a station wagon, you probably do. These travelers have stopped at the information center at the Harrison Bay State Park in 1956 to talk to a ranger about a camping spot. Completed in 1940, the park is on Chickamauga Lake north of town.

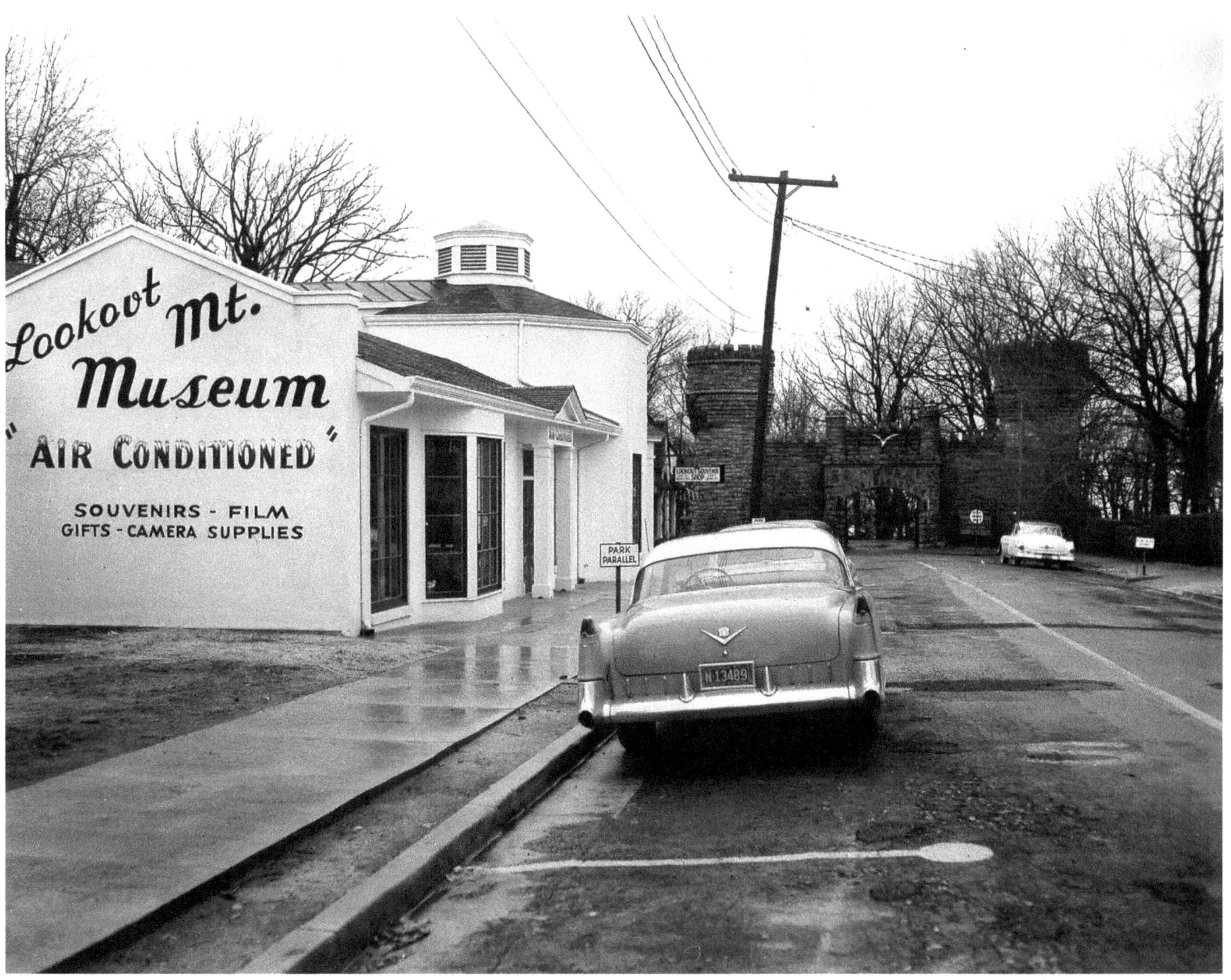

Tourists have come to Lookout Mountain for generations to explore Civil War history at Point Park, the entrance to which is visible in the distance. Nearby some version of the Lookout Mountain Museum has stood for decades. In the 1950s, when the summer vacation was becoming an institution, cars were cooled by rolling down the windows. So it makes sense that the lure of an "air conditioned" building was a real attraction in the hot months of July and August.

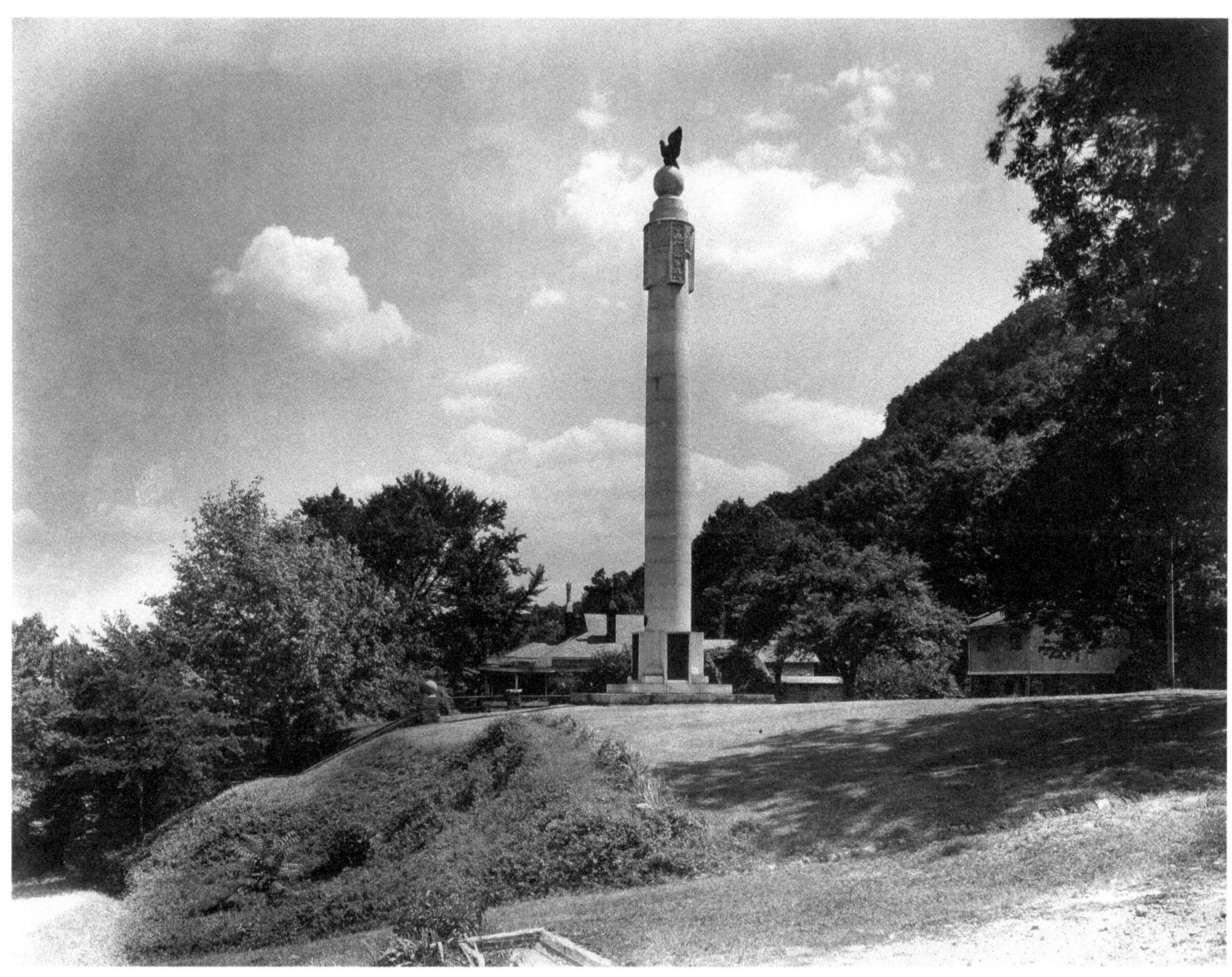

The Ohio monument on Cravens Terrace on the side of Lookout Mountain commemorates an intrepid assault by Union troops. Charging from the valley below on November 24, 1863, the Ohioans confronted a sizable force of Confederates on this small clearing at the Cravens House and pushed them up the mountain, thereby establishing a position for the Federals that would enable them to drive the Southerners off the crest.

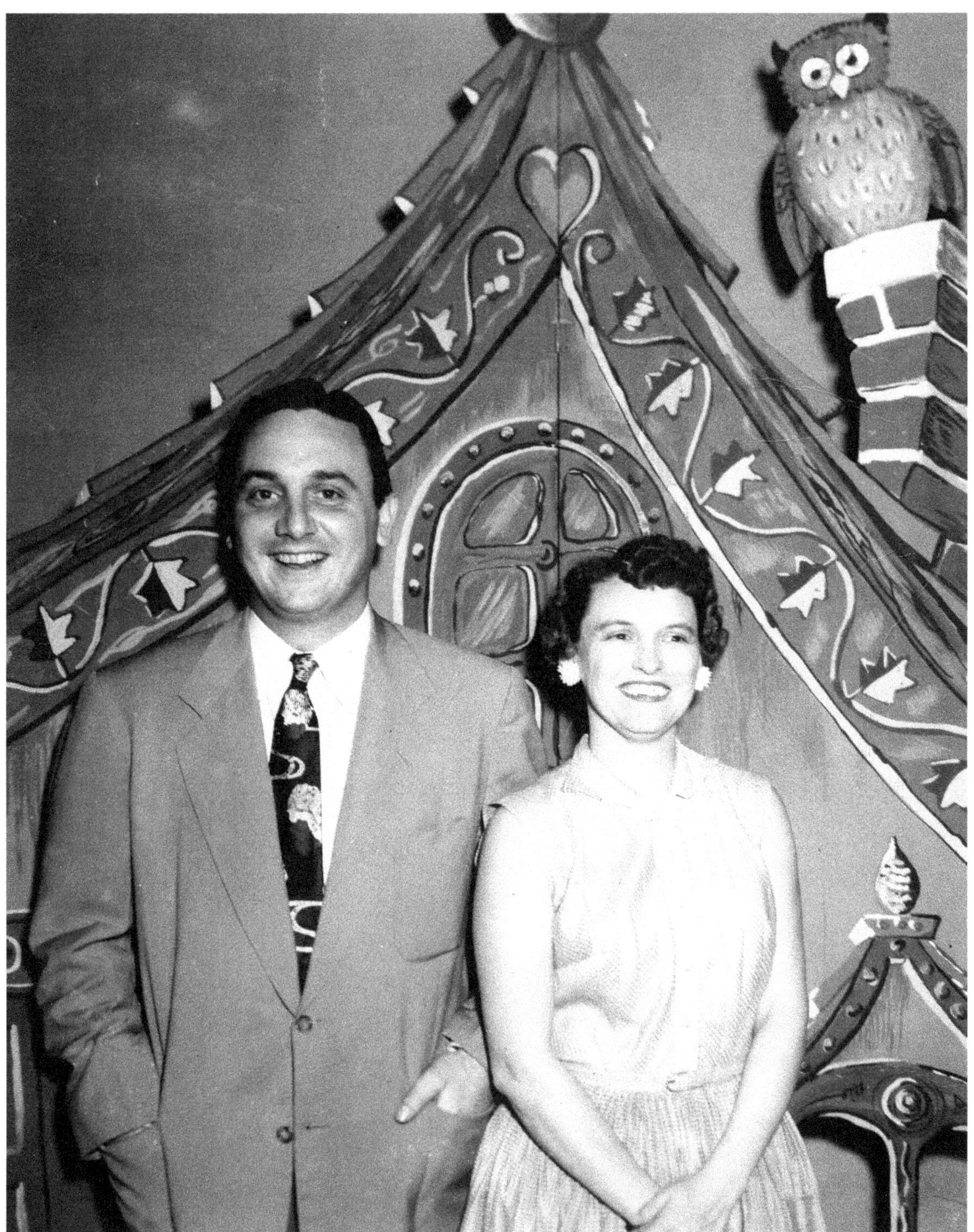

The staging of early television shows relied directly on theatrical stage sets, as this giant house with an owl coming out of the chimney demonstrates. *Chickaroonie* on WDEF-TV may have been Chattanooga's most popular children's show in the 1950s, with Warren Herring and Mildred McCune serving as hosts, telling stories, talking to stuffed animals, and giving gentle instruction to afternoon viewers. They are seen here in 1956.

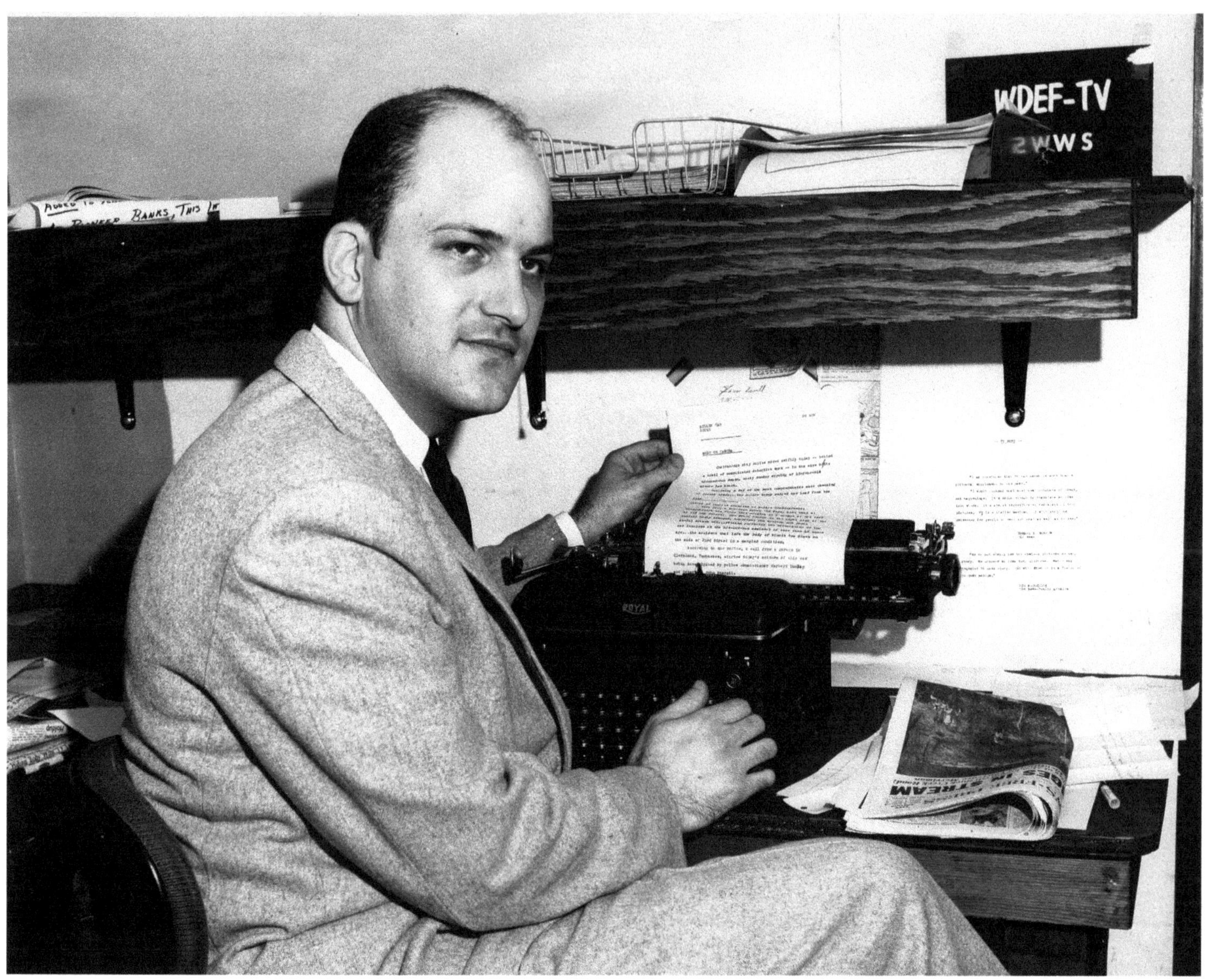

Mort Lloyd was a well-liked and long-running television newscaster first on WDEF-TV, where he is shown here around 1956, and then for WRCB-TV. Known for his thoughtful style of reporting and resonant, rich voice, Lloyd resigned his position to run for Congress in 1974. In the middle of a spirited election on a trip to Manchester, Tennessee, his propeller plane crashed, ending his life tragically.

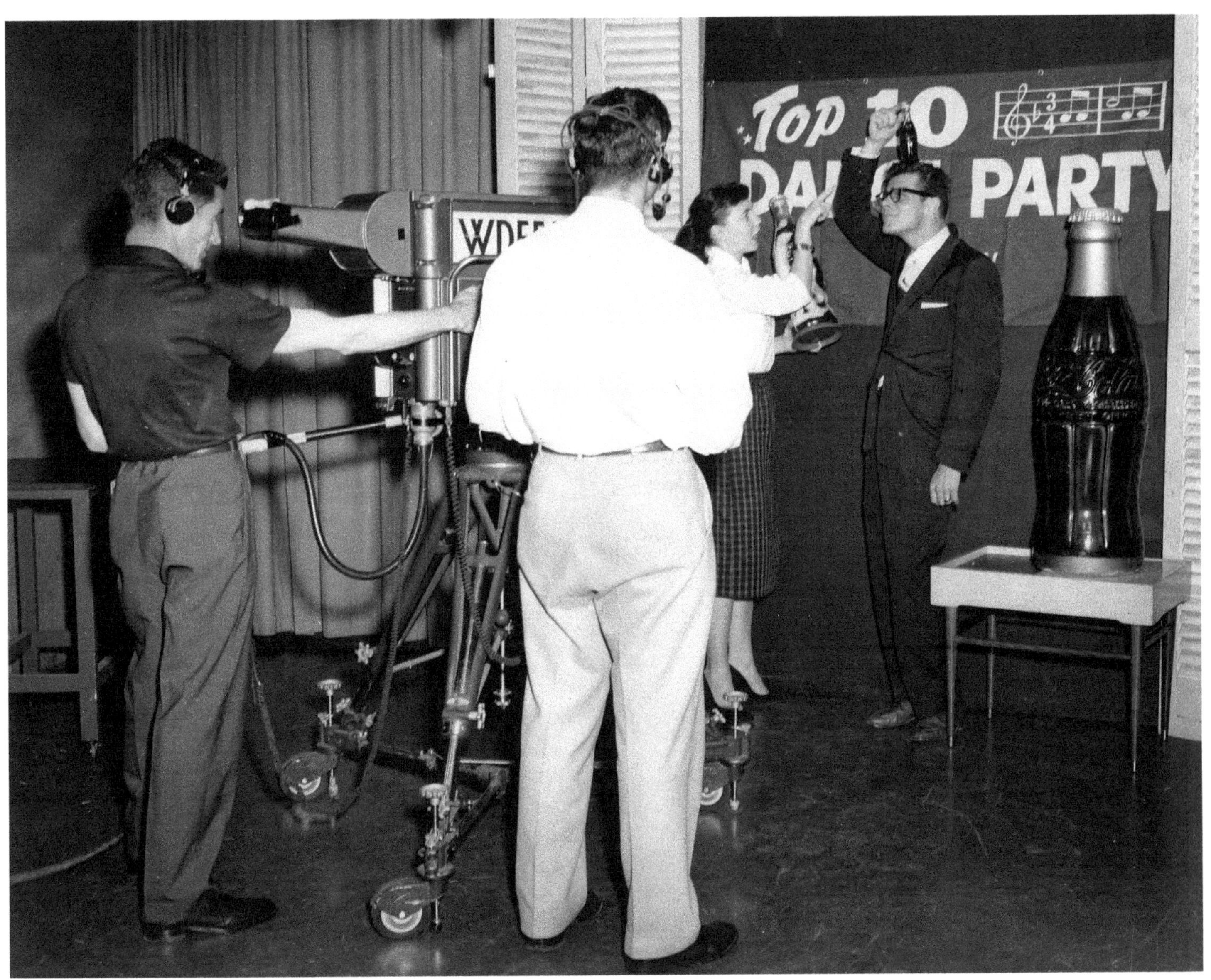

With only a few props, a television host has to do anything he can to liven up the show. Pete Griffin is doing his Coca-Cola balancing act on *Top 10 Dance Party* around 1957. And so it went on the WDEF-TV program, with Barbara Delaney Hofer and Pete Griffin, as they played the hits in the early days of rock 'n' roll. The two cameramen are identified as Andy Jonse and Don Turner.

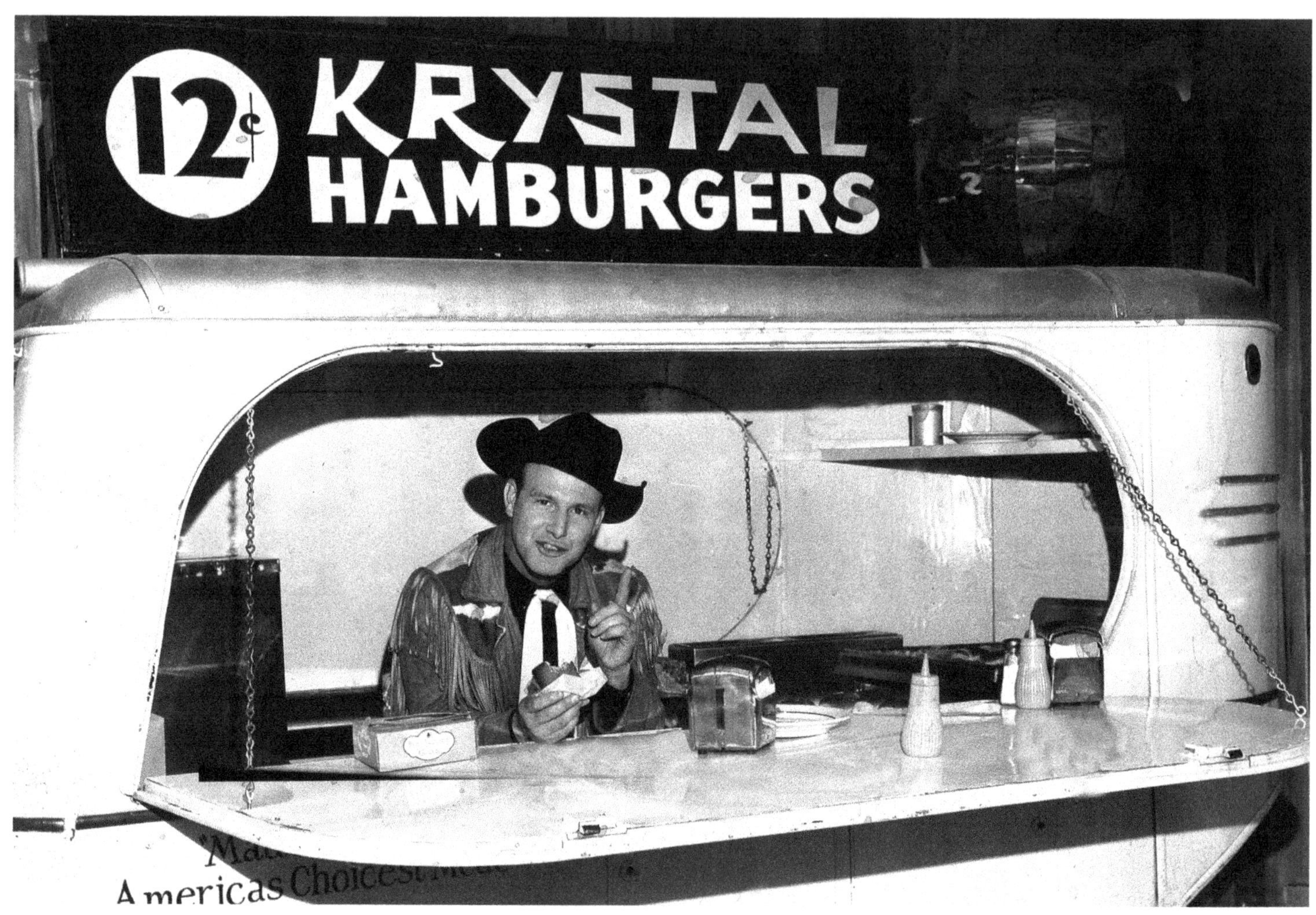

Television in the early days had much more local programming and creativity than it does today. For children in Chattanooga, one of the most popular shows was *The Bob Brandy Show* on WTVC. Bob and his wife, Ingrid, were the hosts and featured games, cartoons, and their horse, Rebel, quite often before a live audience of schoolchildren. Here in 1958, Bob pontificates about that tasty Chattanooga original, the Krystal hamburger.

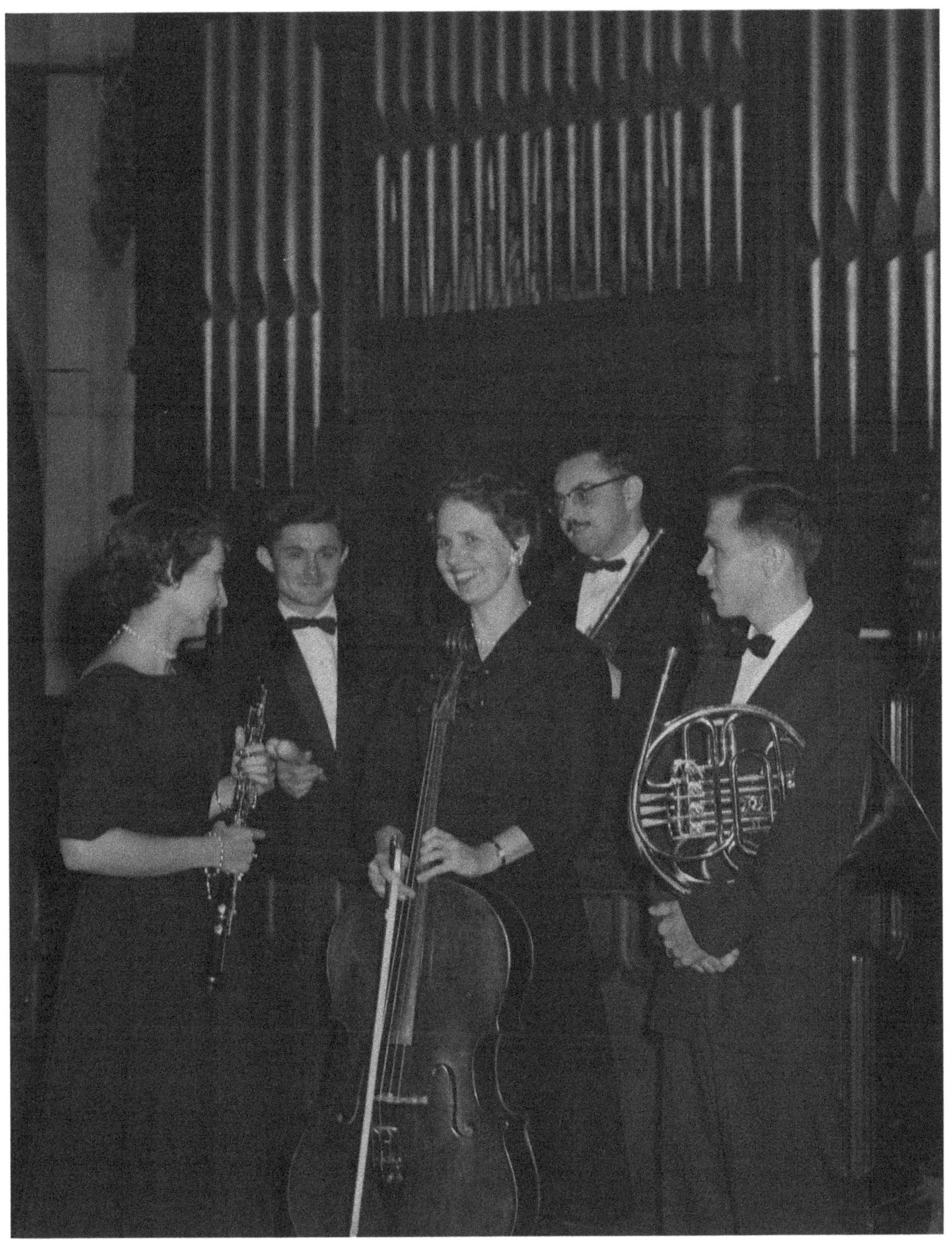

Members of the Chattanooga Symphony Orchestra, representing the string, woodwind, and brass sections, chat in front of some large organ pipes at the University of the South in Sewanee, Tennessee, in 1957. They are part of a summer music camp that began on Monteagle Mountain the same year. The CSO has been a bedrock part of the city's cultural heart for decades, delivering beautiful, absorbing music continuously since 1933.

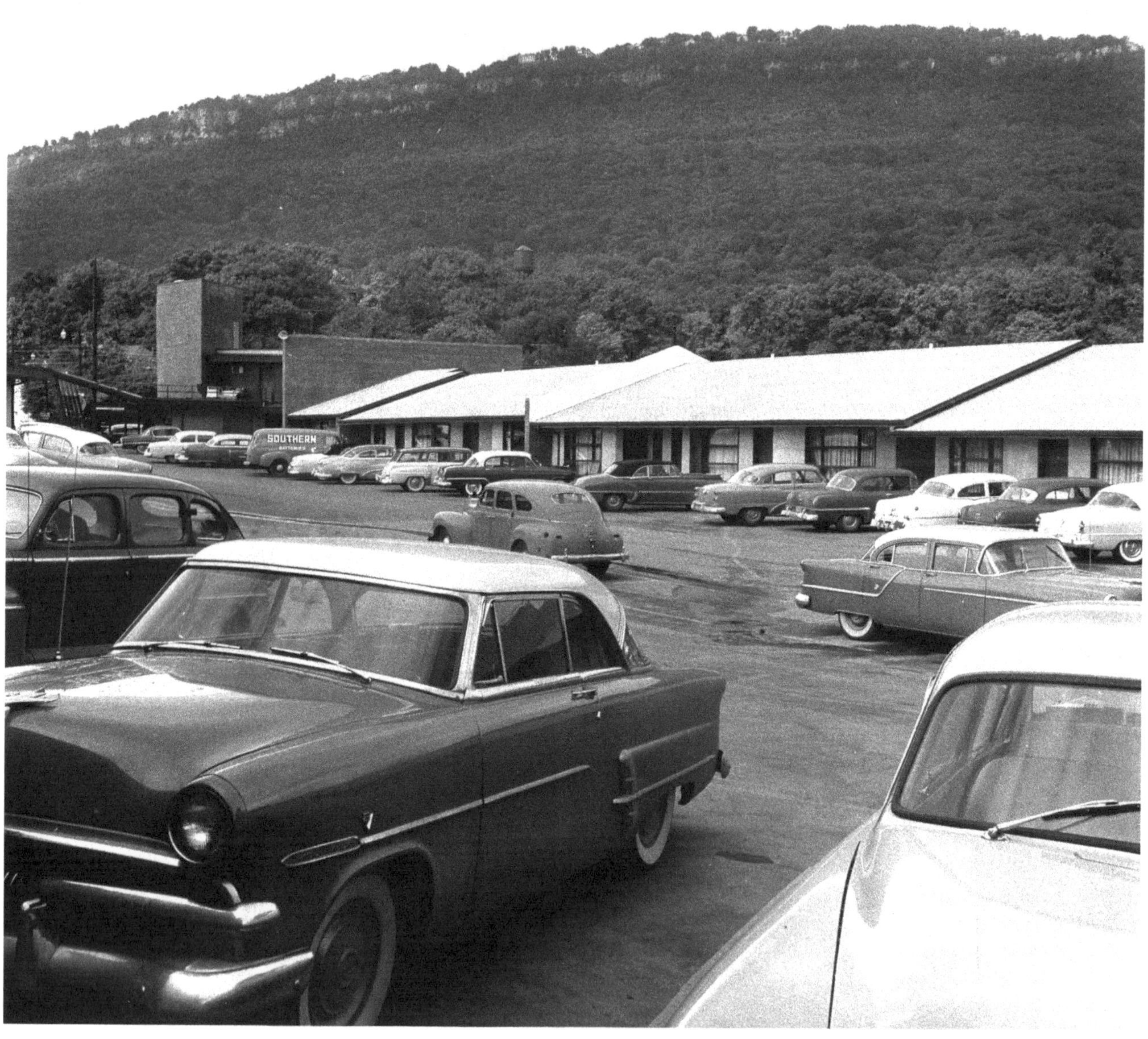

Chattanooga has two main streets, Market Street and Broad Street, which from the earliest days forward have run between the Tennessee River in the heart of downtown and south toward Lookout Mountain. Broad Street once sported several motels, such as the Drake Motor Court, which stood at the foot of the mountain and offered clean sheets and a quiet night for motorists traveling on U.S. Highway 41. This is a view in 1957.

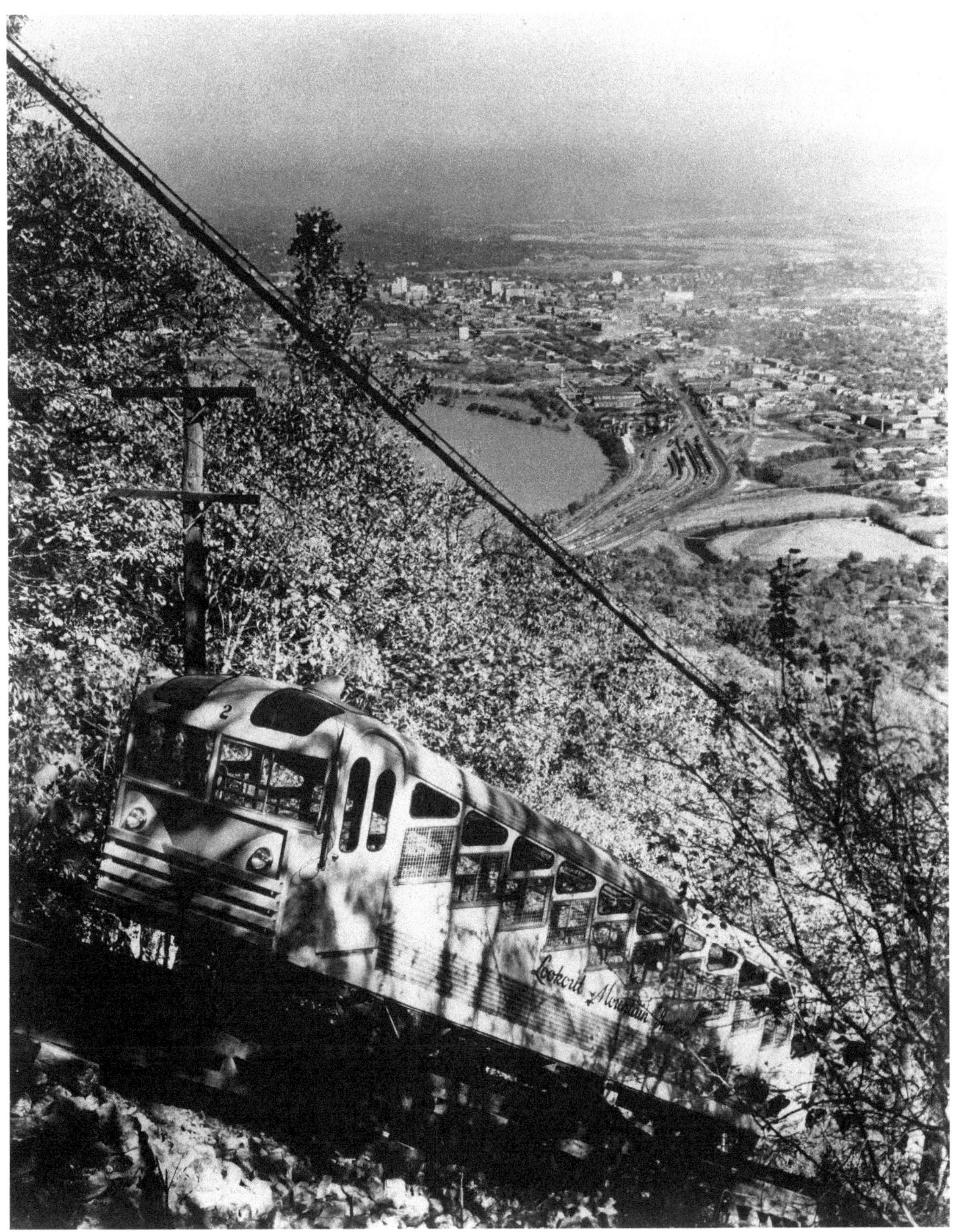

The slow ascent of the cable cars up the slope of Lookout Mountain intrigues some people, but makes others nervous, especially since the nature of the steel rope is at times to "slip" or lurch a few feet. For people living on the mountain, there have been times when the Incline was a godsend. During some treacherous ice storms, when the two mountain highways were impassable, the rail was the only way down. Here in 1957, one of the cars is near the summit.

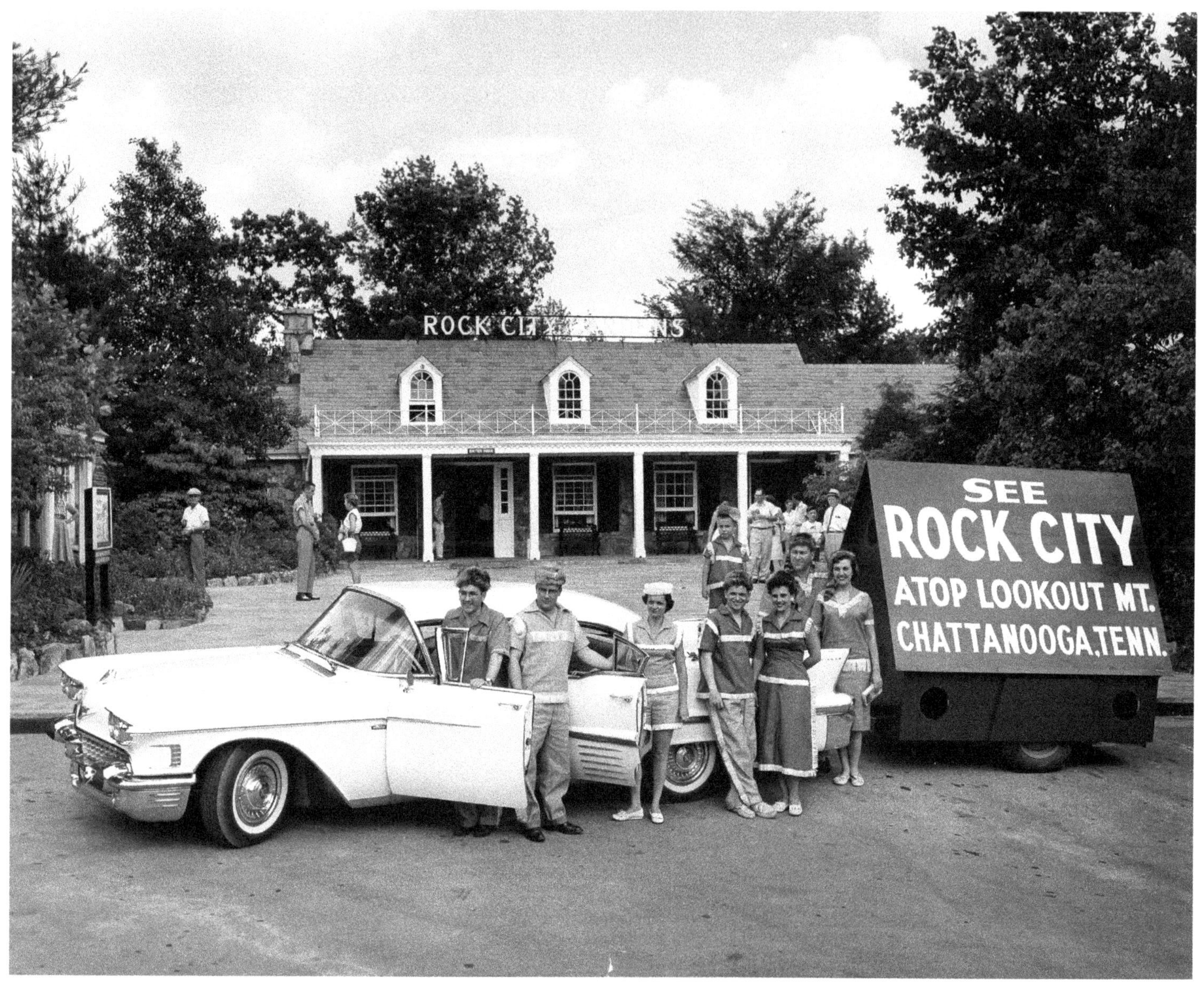

Rock City has always promoted itself in novel ways, first with huge signs painted on barn roofs and later by selling painted birdhouses with the "See Rock City" slogan. This eye-catching ad has a classic 1950s Cadillac with large fins to take it around the valley for all to see. Here in 1957, the coonskin caps suggest that the Davy Crockett craze was in vogue.

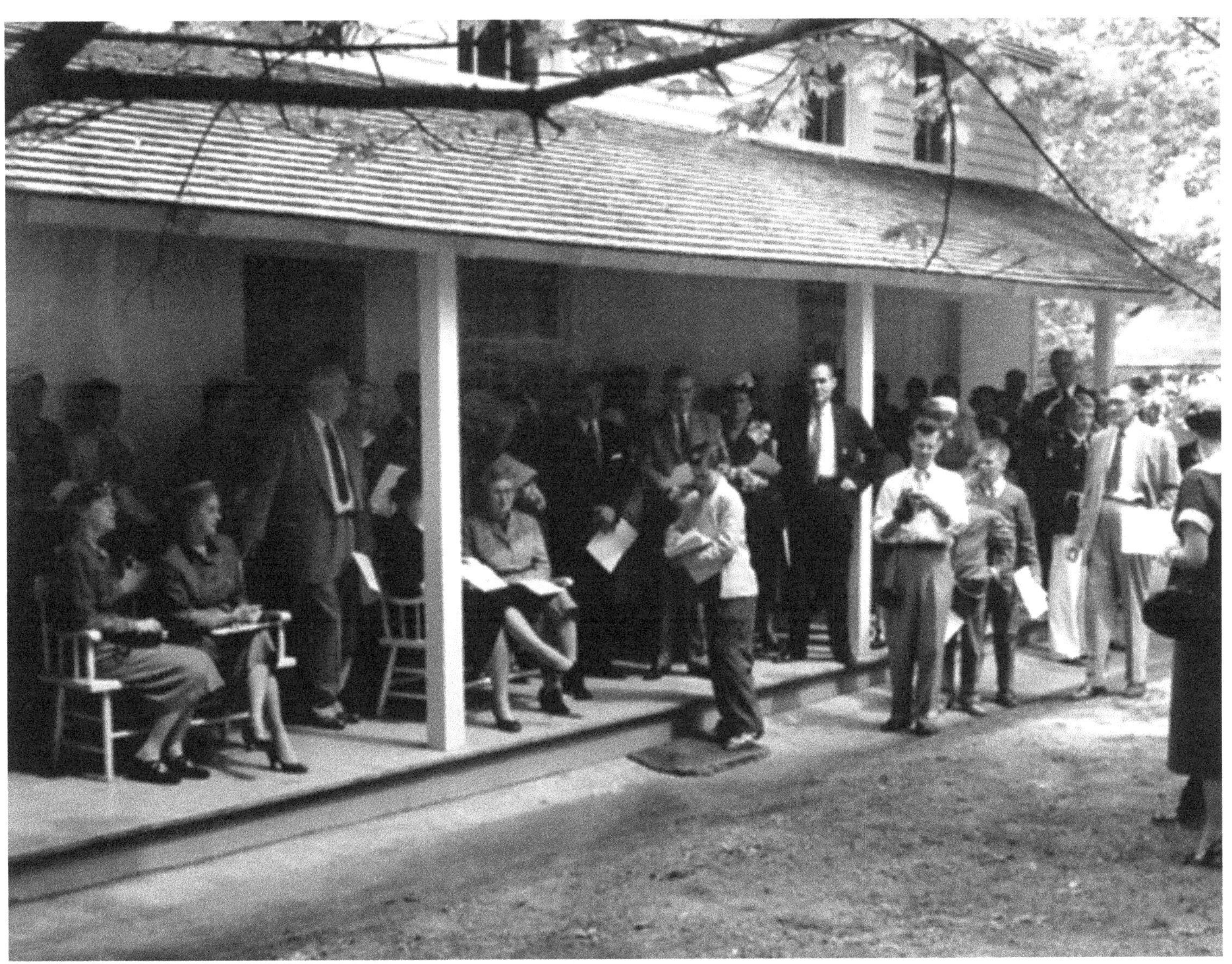

The crowd milling around the porch of the Robert Cravens House on April 21, 1957, has gathered for the dedication of the restored structure. Robert Cravens was an iron master who created a furnace on the Tennessee River bluffs before the Civil War. His house, the site of a critical fight during the Battle above the Clouds on Lookout Mountain, was renovated by a local group of citizens and opened to the public.

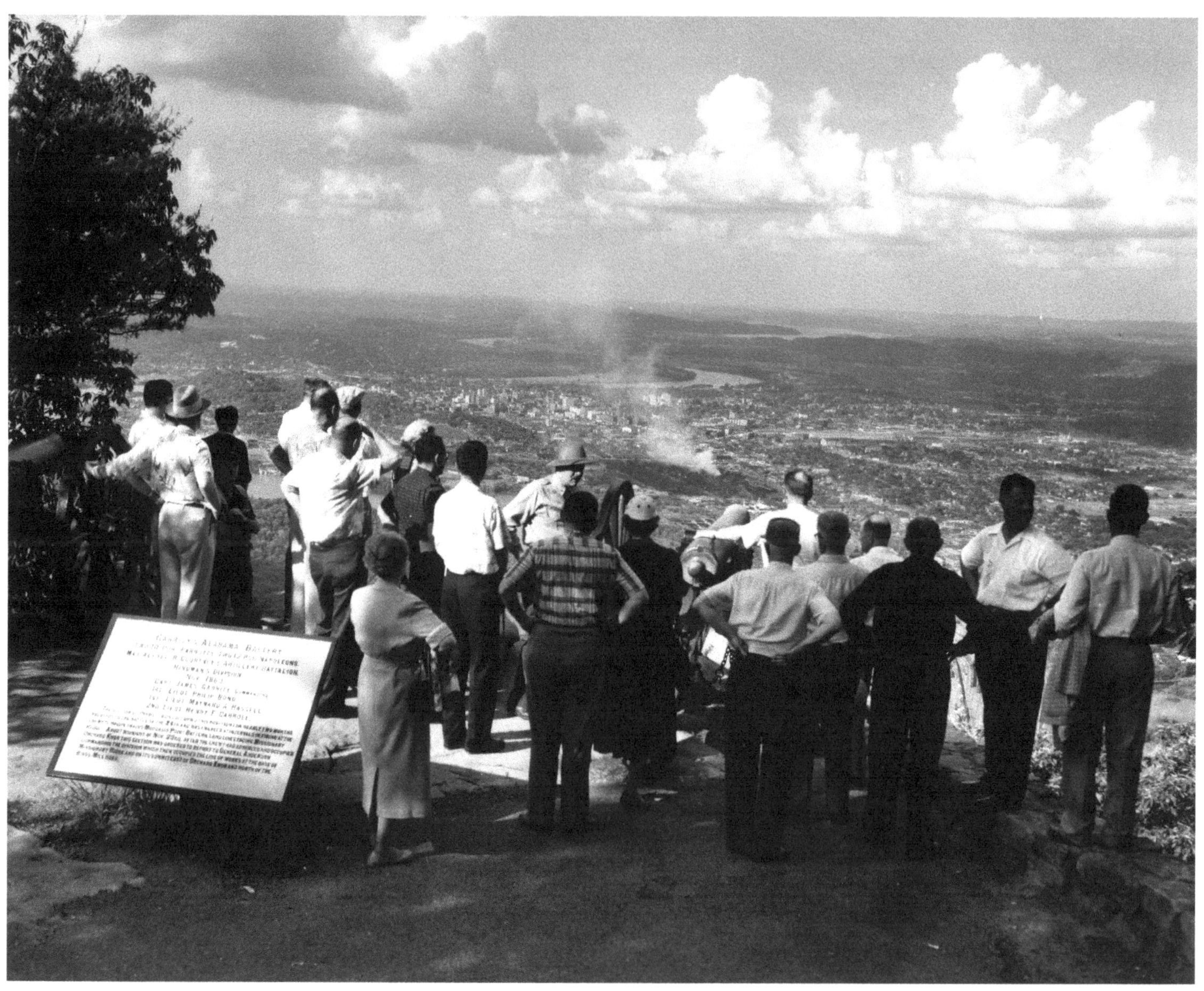

In 1957, a ranger in a pith helmet at Point Park on Lookout Mountain explains the course of battle that unfolded in November 1863 when Federal troops fought to break out of Chattanooga. The unparalleled panorama of the valley allows the viewer to see and clearly imagine the positions of the Rebels on Missionary Ridge, the placement of troops by the Union, and the route taken to develop the Cracker line for reinforcements.

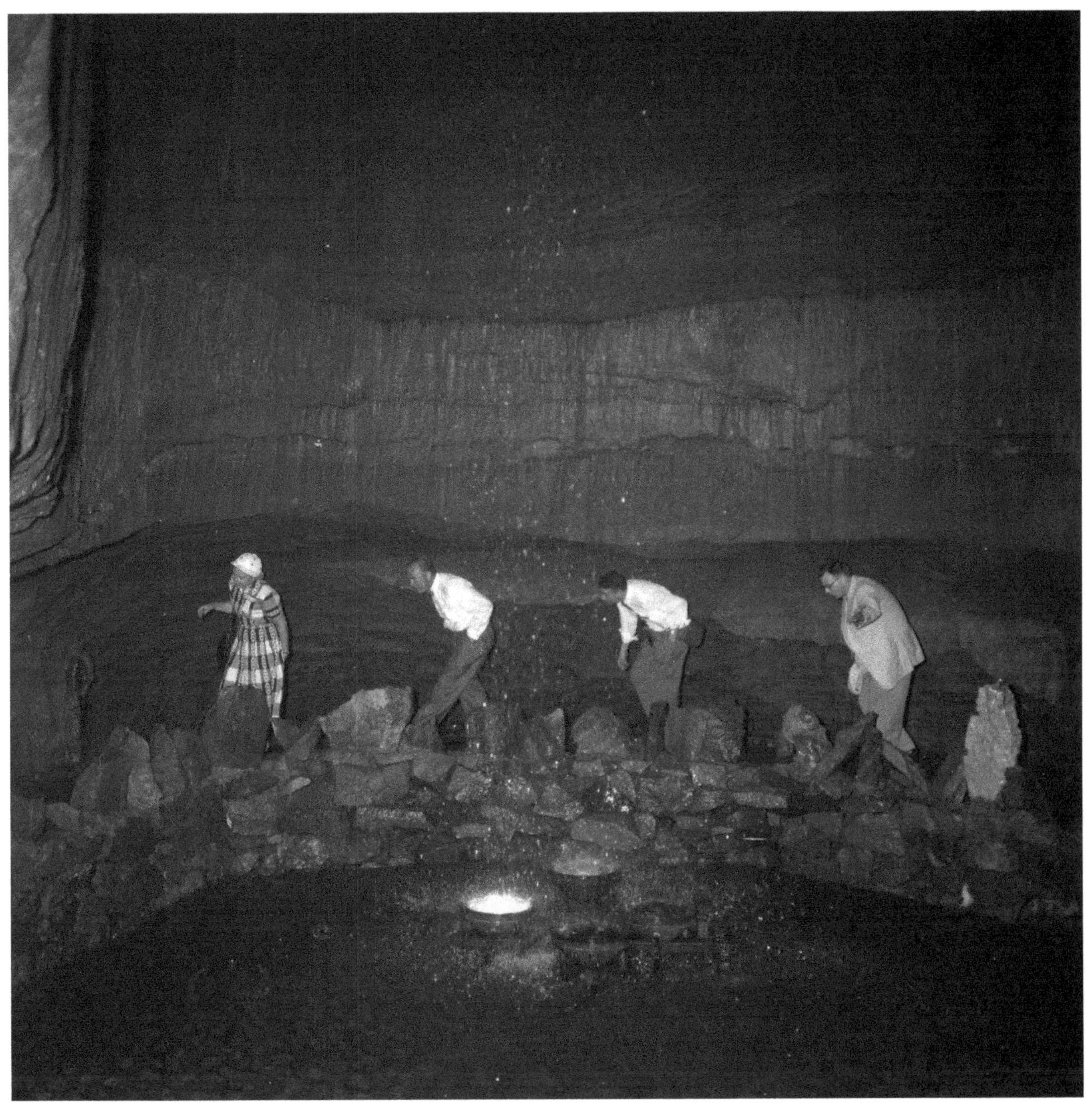

A group of journalists creep around the waterfalls to keep from getting wet inside Ruby Falls on the "See Tennessee Tour" in May 1957. The cave was discovered by Leo Lambert in 1928. After drilling for months, his group of spelunkers descended more than 200 feet into the cave and crawled around for 17 hours, fascinated with the astounding falls they had discovered inside the earth.

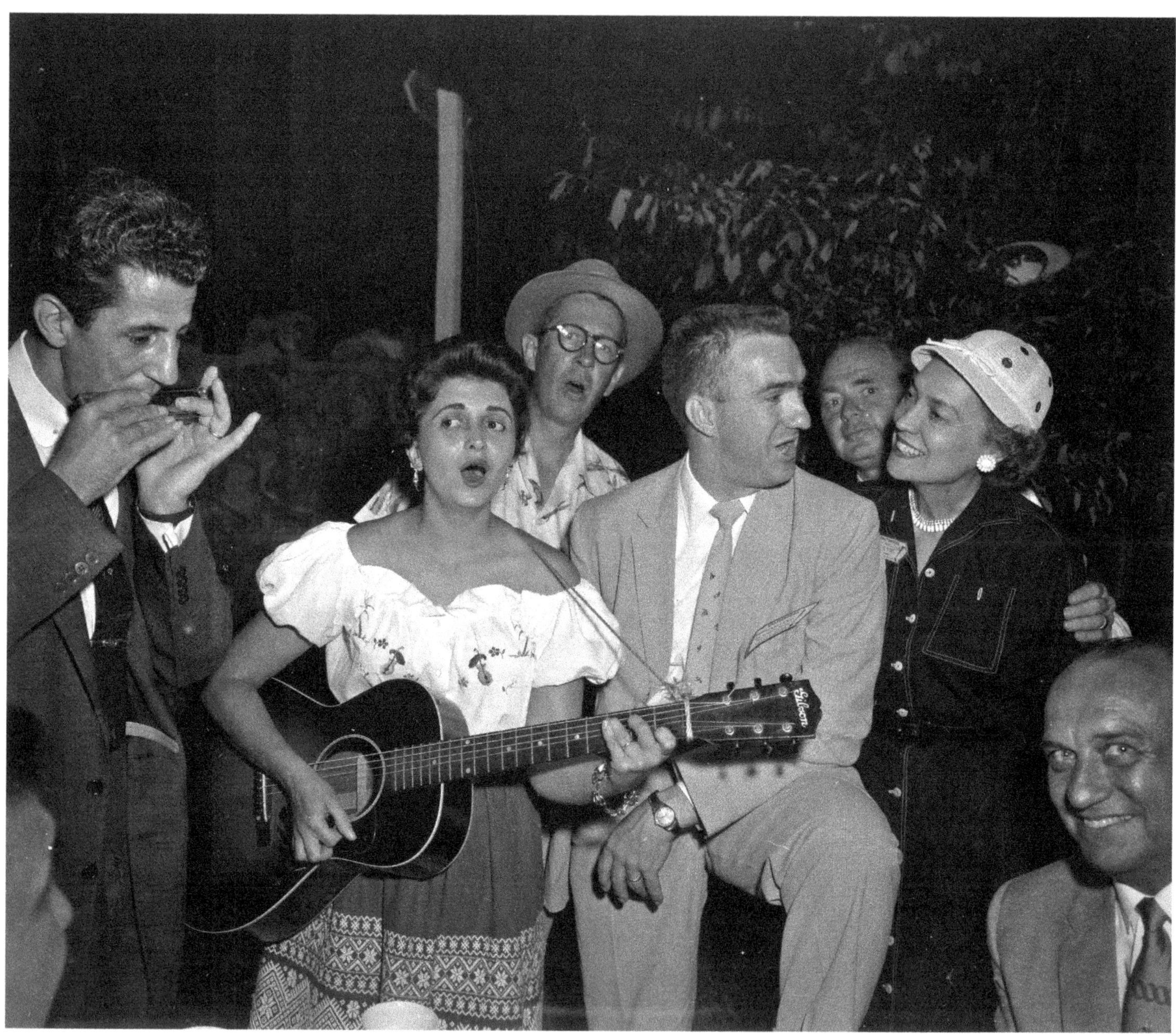

Tennessee is known for its country music and that includes Chattanooga. These folks seem a little too dressy to be country pickers, although the Gibson flat-top guitar would fit right in with that style. Nonetheless, in the 1950s the vast majority of southerners had roots in the countryside. The harmonica, played by the fellow at left, though seldom heard in country music recordings, was often heard in pick-up sessions and during stage performances.

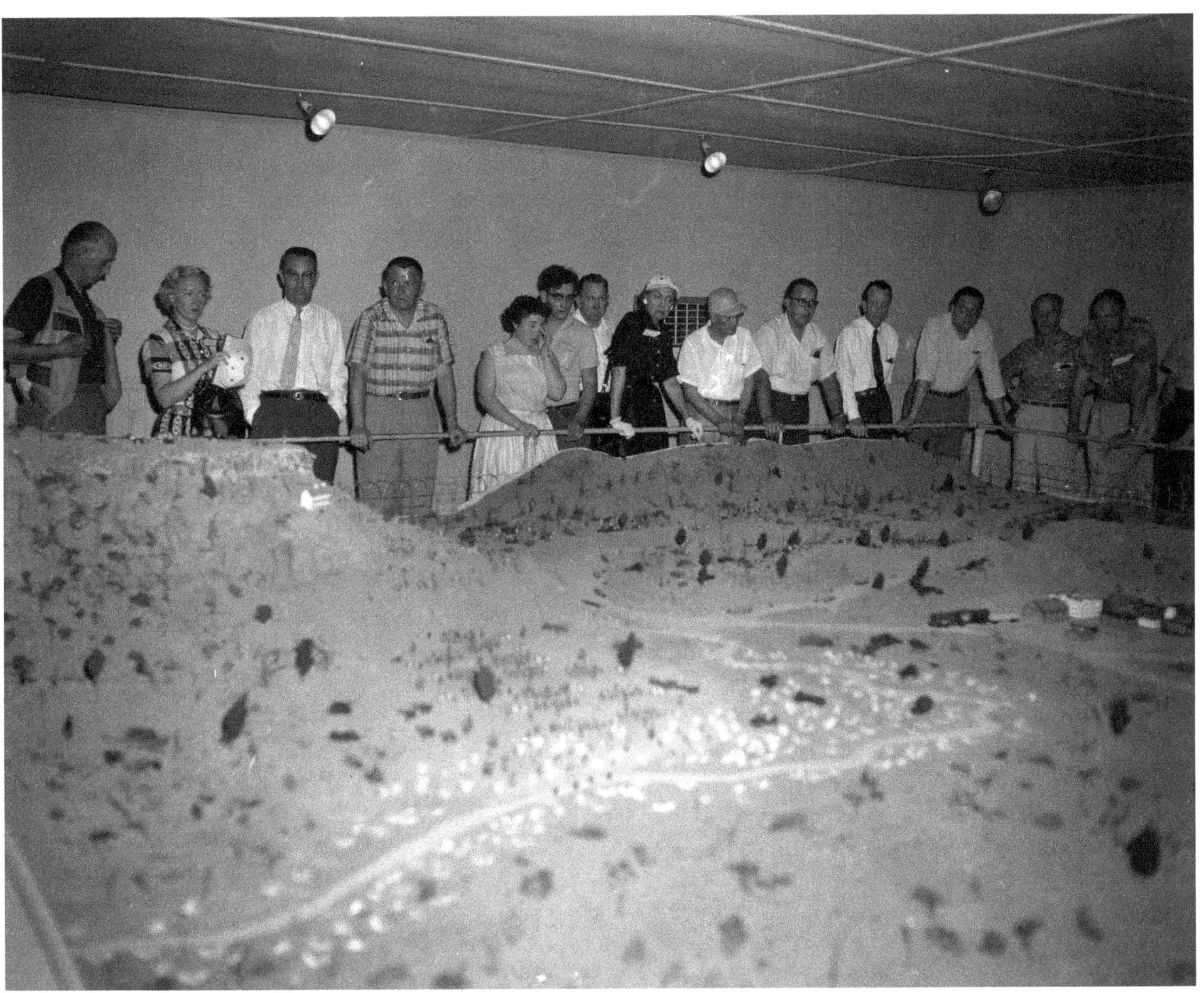

The memory of the Civil War is kept alive in a number of ways, and one of Chattanooga's creations toward this end was the Confederama—an indoor geographical re-creation of the Chattanooga valley during the siege of 1863. The huge, three-dimensional display was covered with metal soldiers and cannons that lit up and were accompanied with sounds and a recording that told in dramatic fashion of the historic struggle. Visitors in 1957 tour the unfolding conflict.

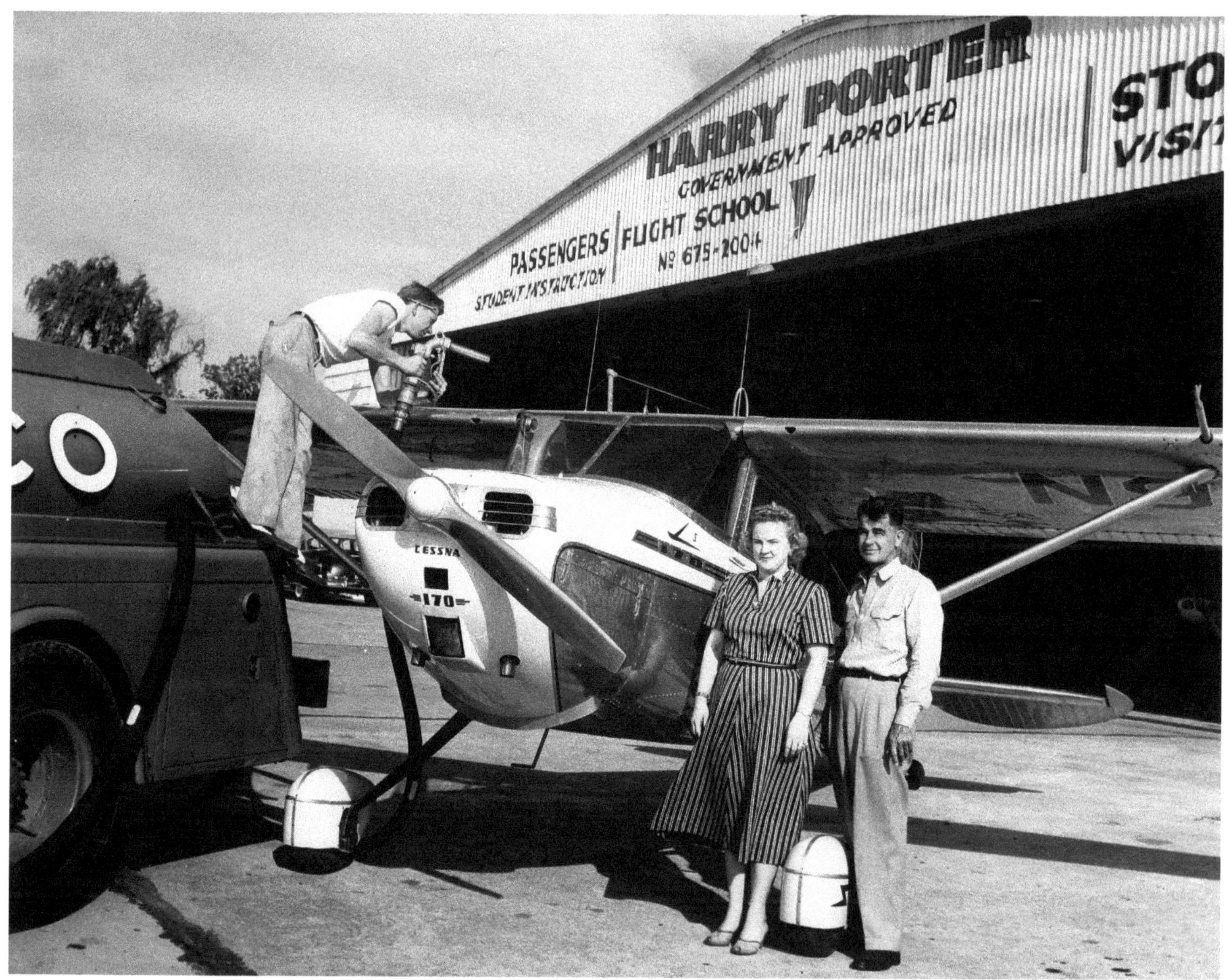

Harry Porter was something of a legend in aviation in the South. Stationed at Chattanooga's Lovell Field, he first took to the air in 1923 during the heyday of independent pilots and stunt fliers. Later he ran a flying school at the airport and trained pilots for World War II. His career lasted an astonishing 64 years, and at age 90 he was officially recognized as the oldest active pilot in the nation. A plane is being fueled at the school here in 1958.

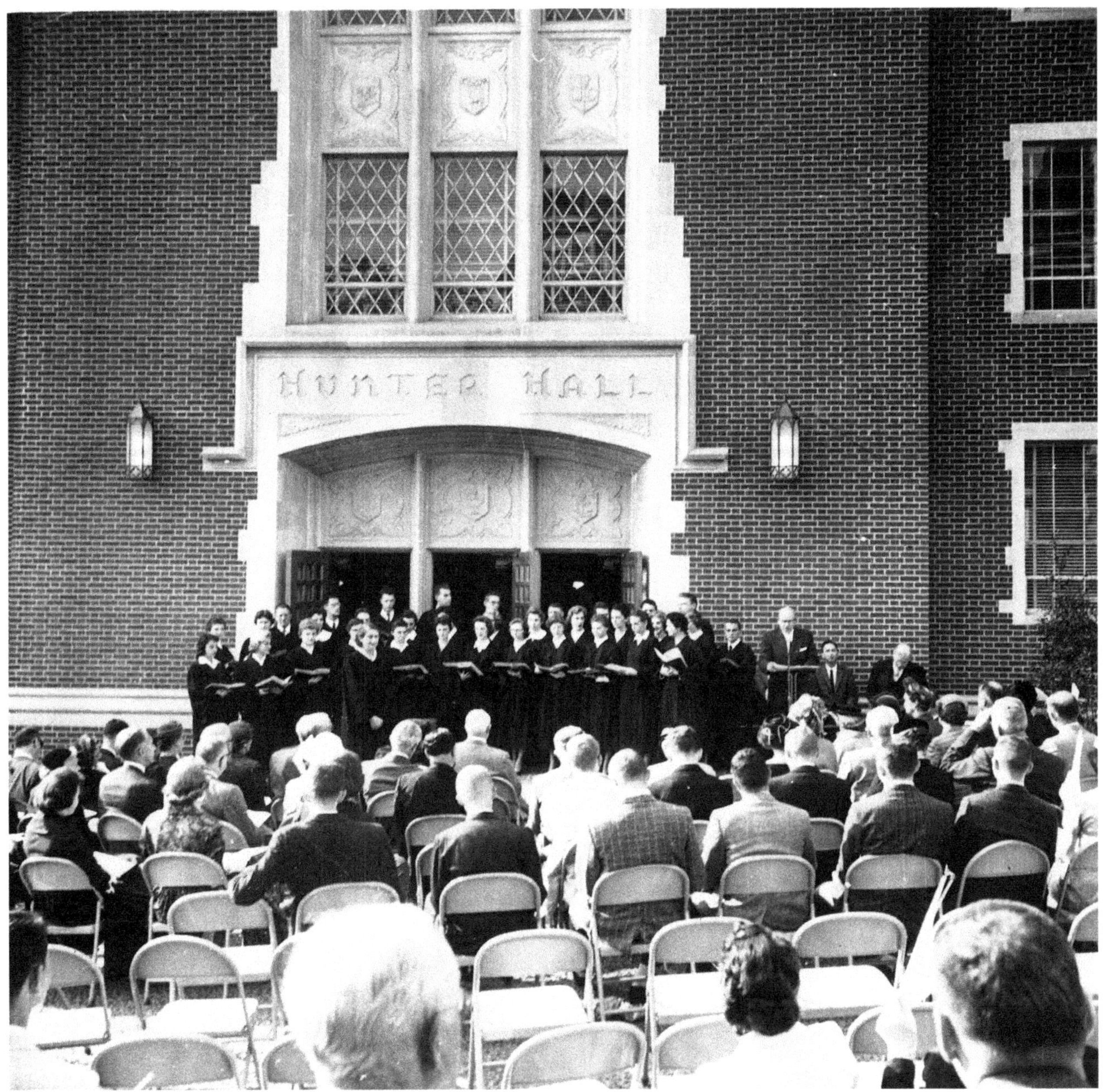

The University of Chattanooga choir stands in front of Hunter Hall in the fall of 1958 while a speaker makes remarks at what appears to be a dedication service. The hall was named for Chattanooga Coca-Cola Bottling magnate George Thomas Hunter and displays classical "university Gothic" architecture—diamond pane windows, the bas relief above the doorway, and intricate Flemish bond brickwork.

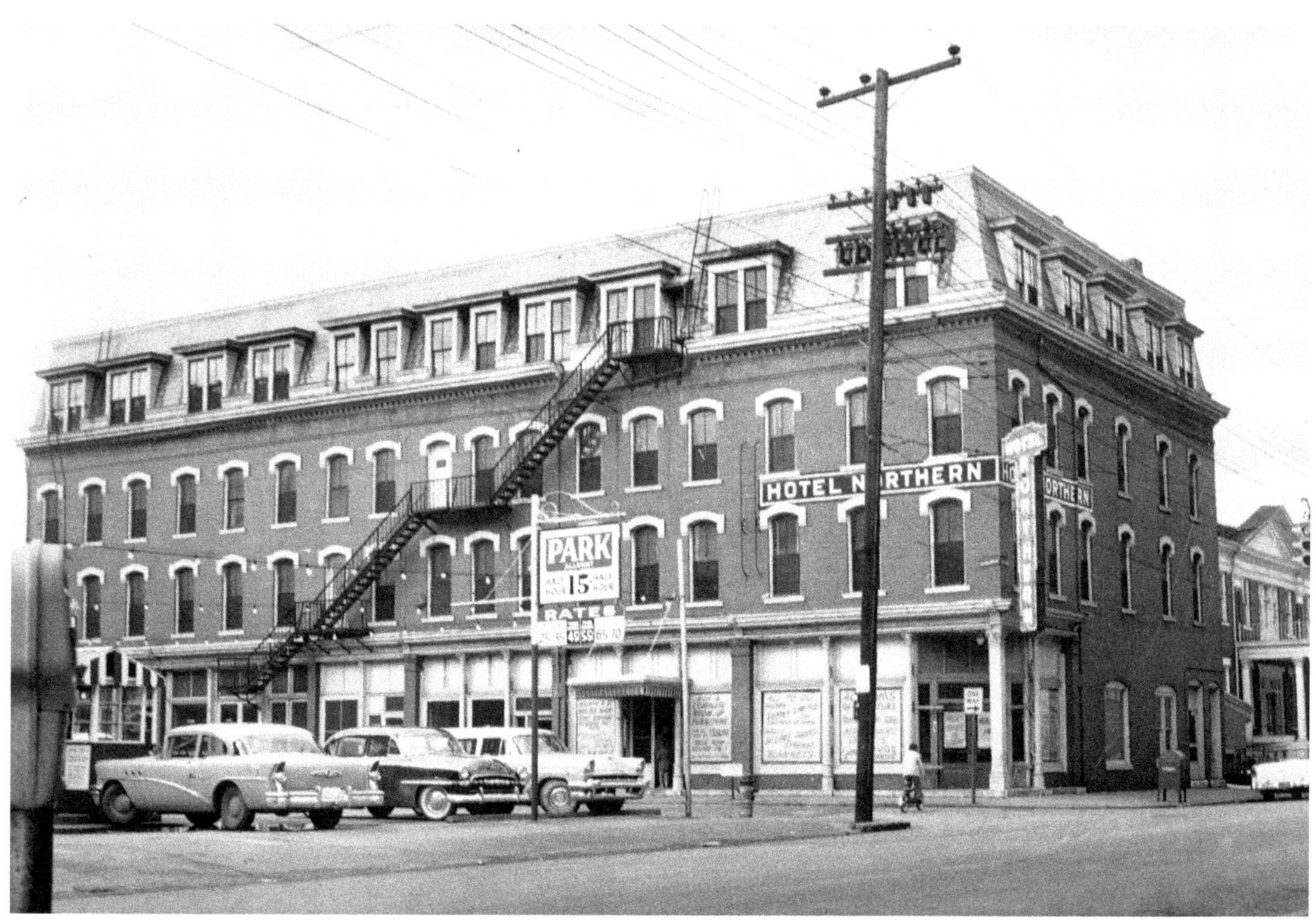

When Chattanooga's first railroad entered town it terminated on Ninth Street. The area around that site was fertile territory to establish a hotel, and it is not surprising to find the Hotel Northern located at Eighth and Chestnut streets. The brick guest house with its modified mansard roof was constructed in 1886 and originally featured a turkish bath and a tailor's shop. It was demolished in 1958, not long after this image was recorded.

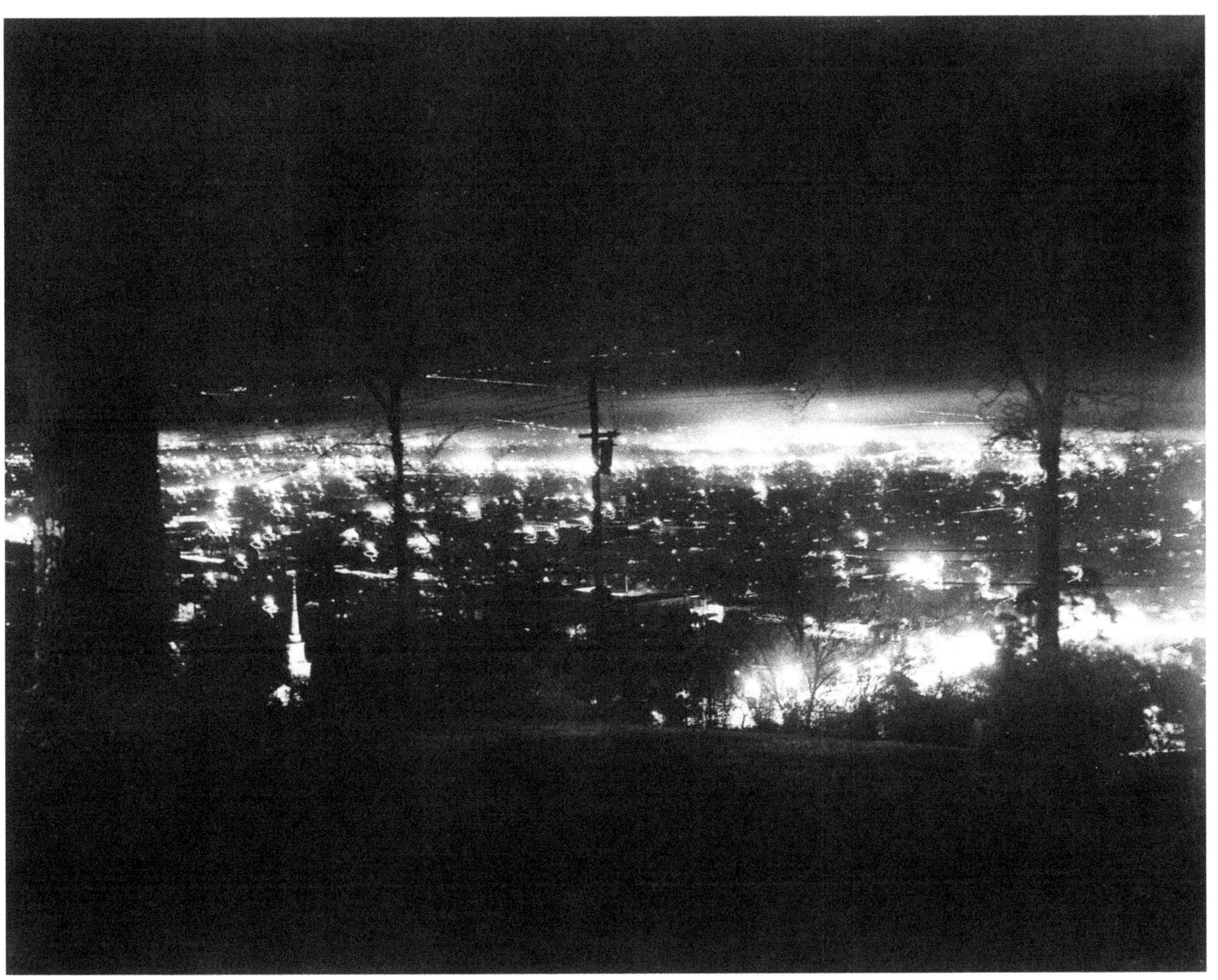

One of the city's attractions is its beautiful vistas from the ridges and mountains. No less impressive are the scenes at night when the streets, stores, and houses twinkle and glow in the evening air. Before the Tennessee Valley Authority built dams that produced electricity en masse in the 1930s, evening lights were nothing compared to what is visible in this view from Missionary Ridge in 1958.

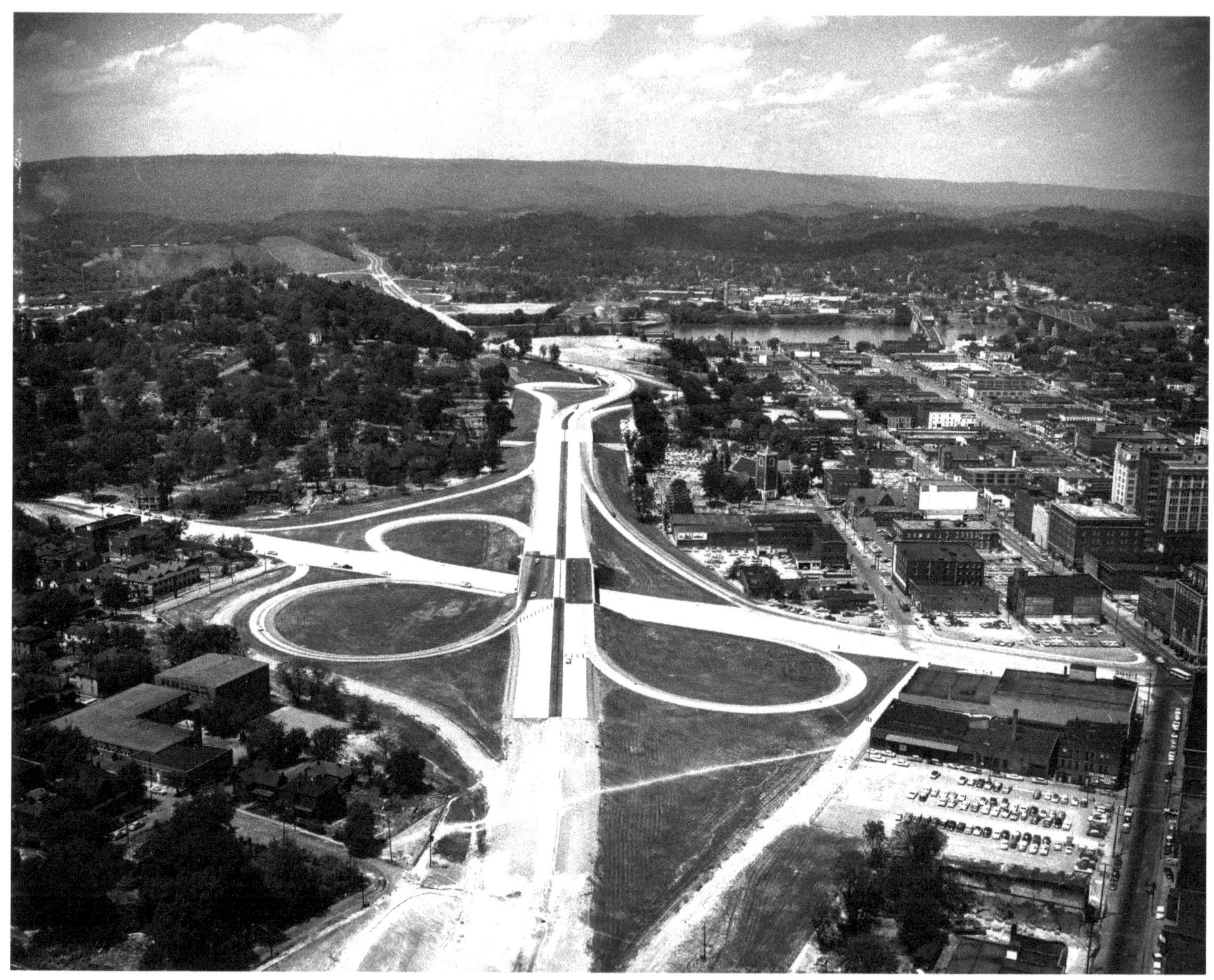

In the 1950s and 1960s, national interstate highways were built at a feverish pitch all across the United States. In Chattanooga and other cities, the government program advanced as a part of Urban Renewal, and highways were usually routed through poorer, black neighborhoods. This newly built downtown interchange at Ninth Street shows the scraping and paving of the old West side residential neighborhood undertaken to complete U.S. Highway 27.

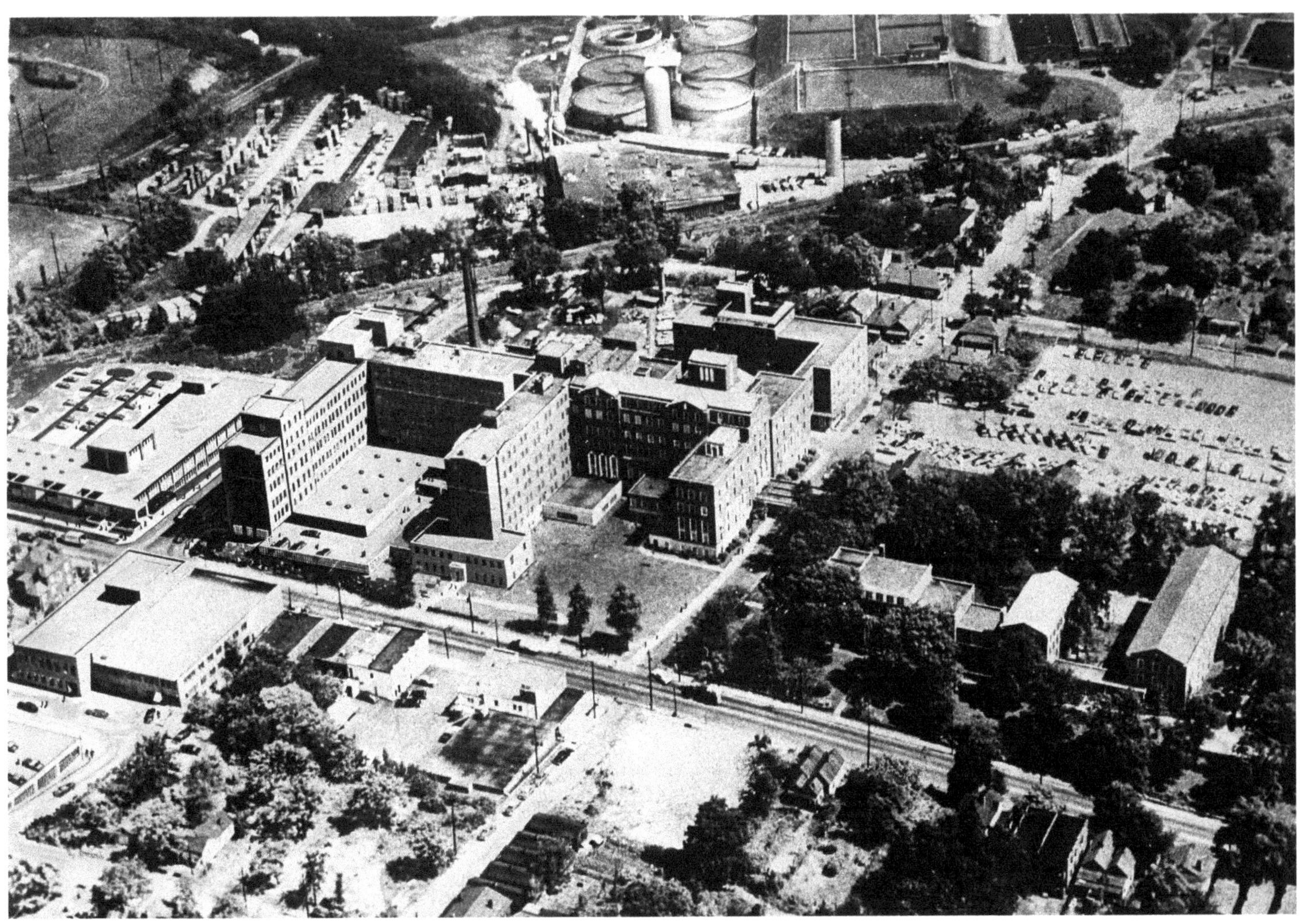

This 1959 aerial view of the Erlanger Hospital complex on East Third Street shows the original building and the wings that were added over the decades. Chattanooga's oldest hospital, dedicated to health care for residents regardless of income, would later expand to the right and left of what is visible here. An academic teaching hospital for a century, Erlanger today includes the T. C. Thompson Children's Hospital and functions as a regional trauma center.

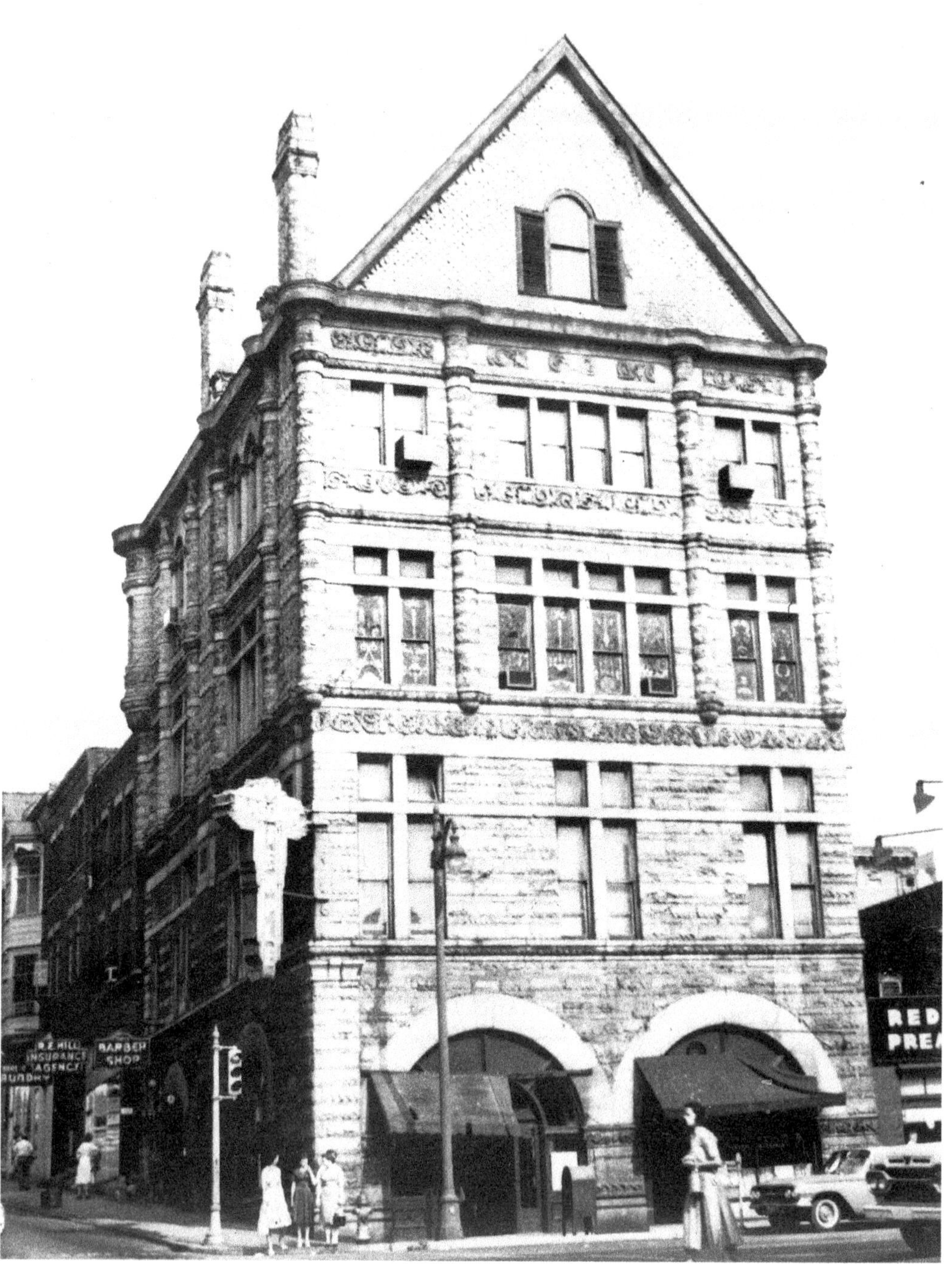

This solid Romanesque structure anchoring the corner of Cherry and Seventh streets was a fixture in the city for 70 years. Completed in 1890 it was home to the Mountain City Club, but by 1899 had become the domicile of the Masons. With its ground floor arches and finely cut and fitted block stone facade, the Masonic hall was an impressive architectural statement until its demise in 1960. The building is seen here around 1959.

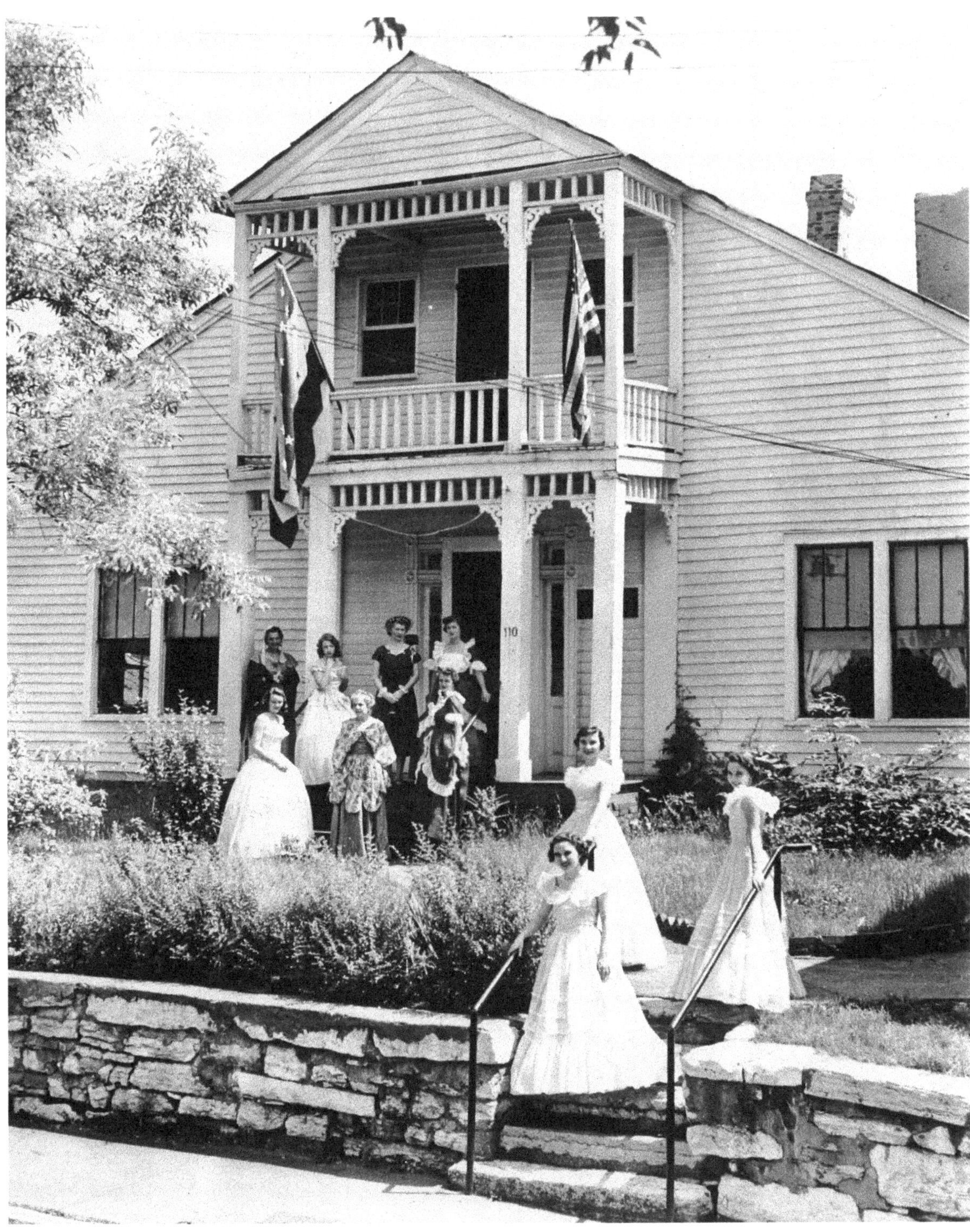

The Old South has long been a source of fascination for Chattanoogans, and these ladies are right in the spirit of things around 1959, dressed in period fashion hoopskirts. They may be preparing for the annual Cotton Ball, which remains an ongoing tradition. The gabled house behind them is believed to have been commandeered by General Ulysses S. Grant to serve as his headquarters during the siege of Chattanooga.

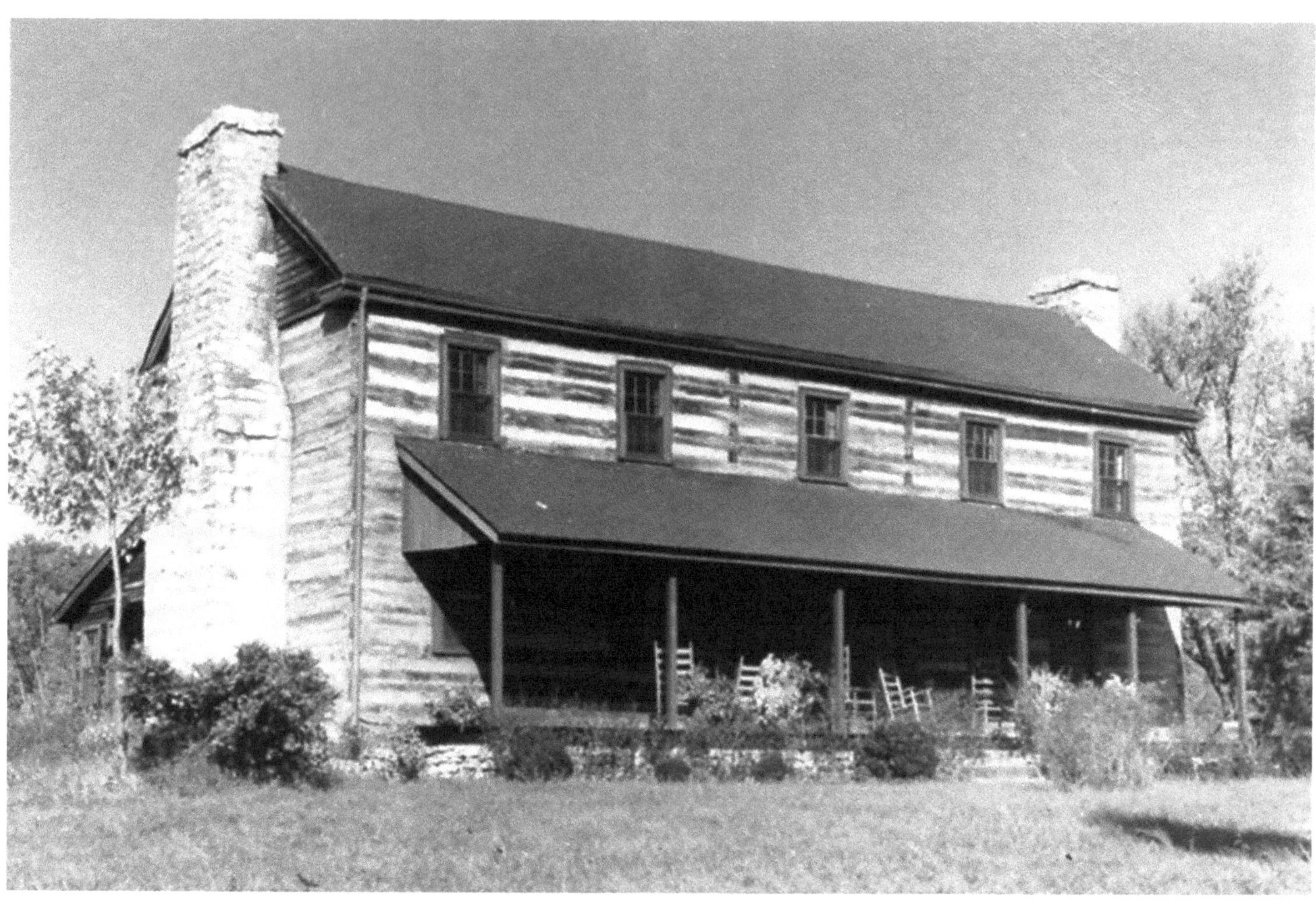

Brown's Tavern lies on the river near the Great Trading Path at Lookout Mountain. Considered Hamilton County's oldest house, the inn was constructed in 1803 by Casper Vaught for John Brown, a Cherokee Indian who operated a riverboat landing there as well as a mill, and a ferry downstream. John Brown was prominent in his community and after the removal to Oklahoma, was elected Principal Chief of the Cherokee Nation West. This is the house as it appeared in 1959.

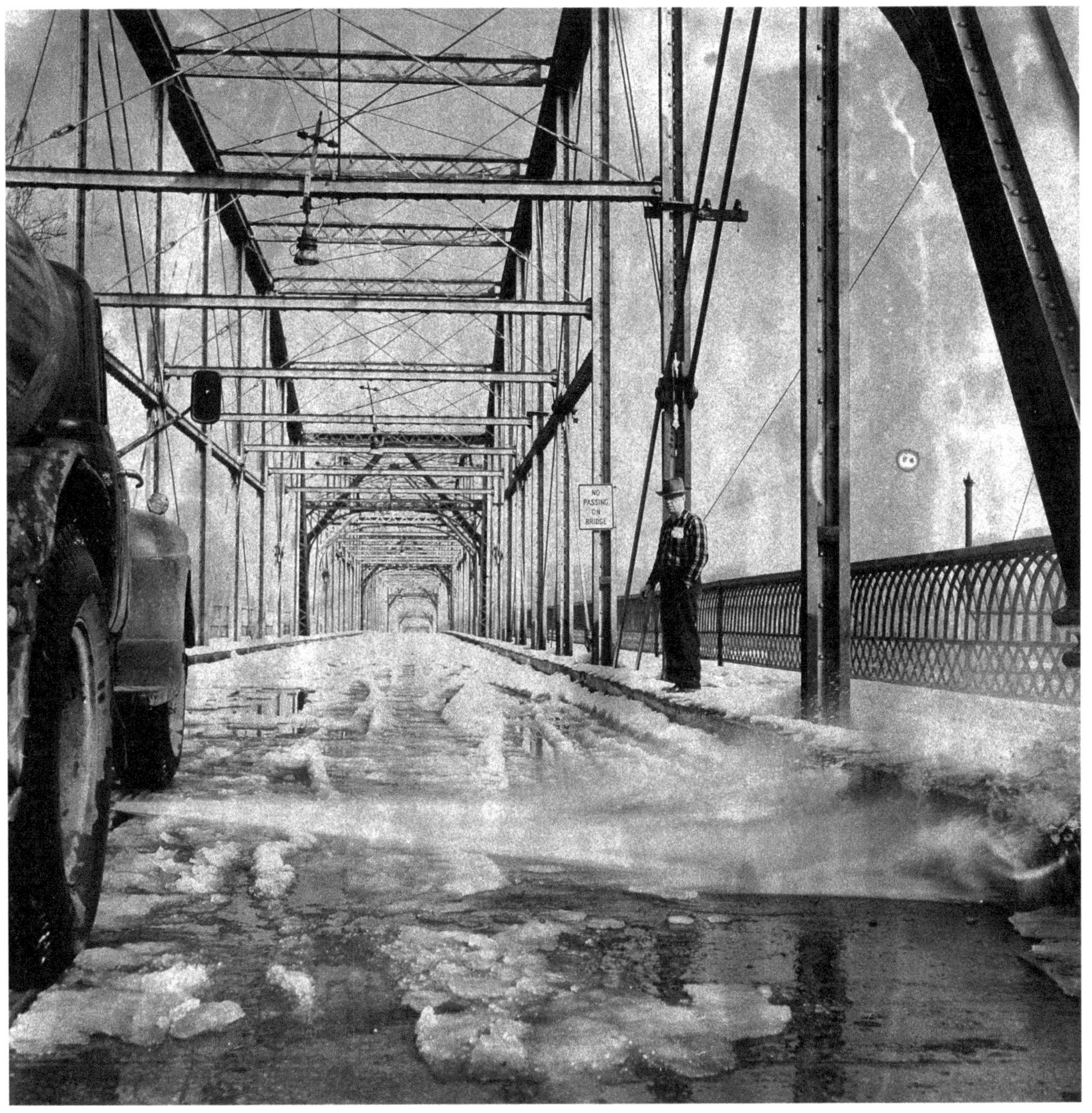

Snow comes occasionally to the valley, but ice is really the more difficult winter affliction. Ice can form quickly and cling stubbornly to structures like the Walnut Street Bridge, as it did here in February 1960. On the right, the lean gentleman in the hat is James Templeton, Assistant Superintendent of Public Works, who watches the progress of a service truck as it melts the cold stuff from Chattanooga's oldest bridge.

To say that Luther Masingill is the voice of Chattanooga is an understatement. The WDEF radio personality, known simply as "Luther," has been a morning show fixture since 1941 when he was discovered by baseball owner Joe Engel. He is a legendary finder of lost pets for forlorn owners and recently the recipient of an official acclamation by the Tennessee legislature for his long public service. Luther is seen here broadcasting around 1959.

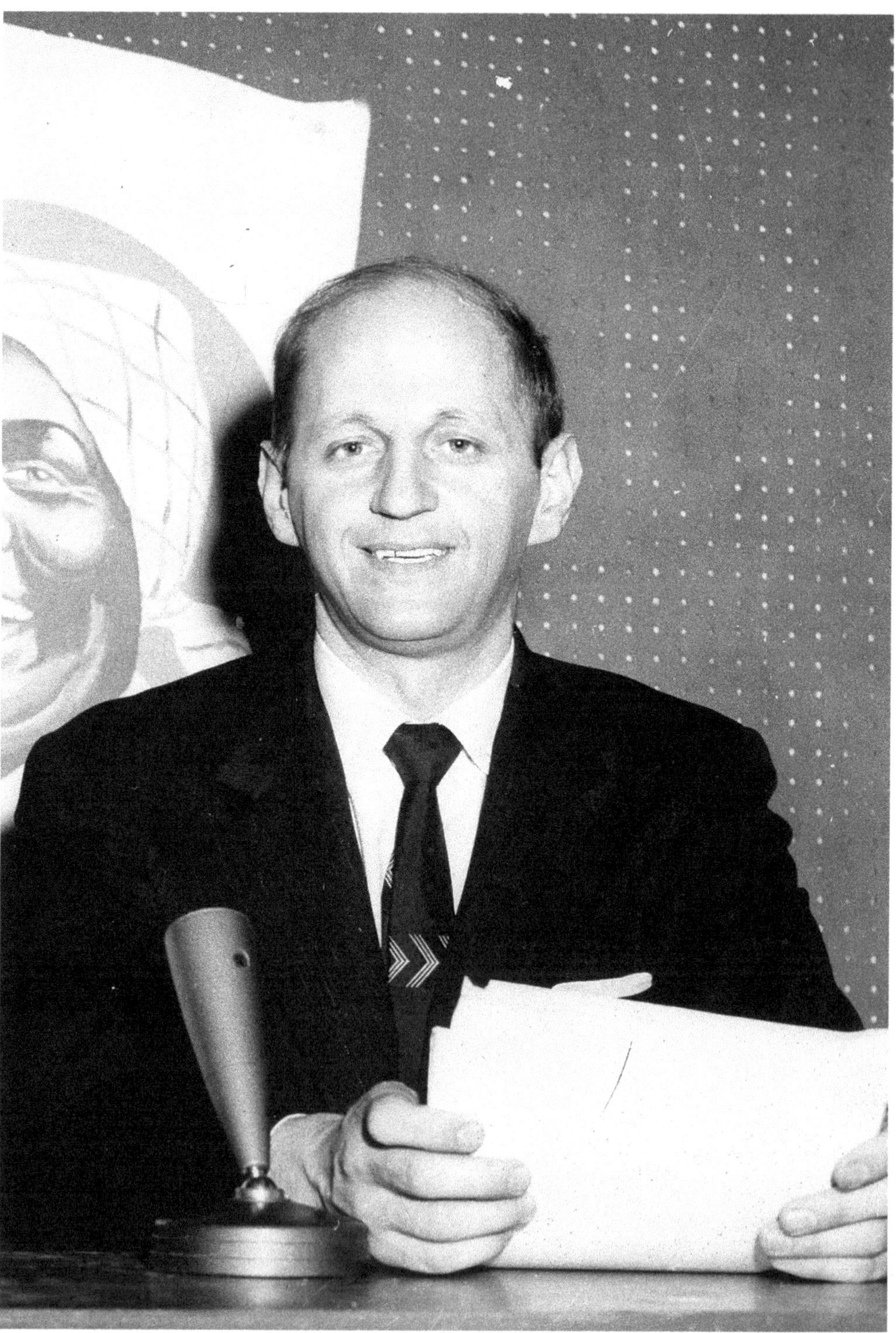

Challenges and a Choo Choo

(1960–1969)

What is generally known as "the sixties" broke late in this traditional southern town. But the challenges of modern urban life were unmistakable. In February 1960, a group of high school students, essentially on their own, decided to stage sit-ins at local department stores in downtown Chattanooga to the surprise of black and white leaders alike. And to everyone's credit, violence of any magnitude was averted. Desegregation of public accommodations and public schools became paramount as the city moved ahead with racial integration. Perhaps this was one reason the city was nationally acclaimed as an All-American City in 1963 to the delight of civic leaders.

In the local economy, Chattanooga held fast to its industrial base, but decades and decades of pollution-spewing smokestacks were beginning to be a real problem. The air sometimes stank, and hazy, grimy days were not unusual. On smoggy days, automobiles frequently turned on their headlights in the daytime. In 1969, Walter Cronkite proclaimed on the national evening news that Chattanooga, Tennessee, had officially been designated "the dirtiest city in America" by the U.S. Health, Education, and Welfare Department. The embarrassment was profound. A combination of industrial pollutants coupled with tricky temperature inversions had created an intolerable situation.

On the lighter side, Mayor Ralph Kelley and a "gang" of officials diverted a rail car as a political prank, snatching the famed locomotive the *General* from Georgia and bringing it back to Chattanooga in an effort to keep the historic engine in the city. The city's popular minor league baseball team, the Chattanooga Lookouts, brought home the Southern Association title in 1961. Play at Engel Stadium had been a tradition since 1930, but in a few years minor league play would expire, a victim of televised baseball and racial problems. In 1964 national attention focused on the city when the infamous labor leader Jimmy Hoffa was convicted in the federal courthouse on Georgia Avenue for jury tampering. A young man, Samuel L. Jackson, was attending Riverside High School on East Third Street and practicing trumpet and French horn on his way to becoming one of America's iconic movie actors on the silver screen. And a longtime institution, the University of Chattanooga, donned a new identity as the University of Tennessee at Chattanooga.

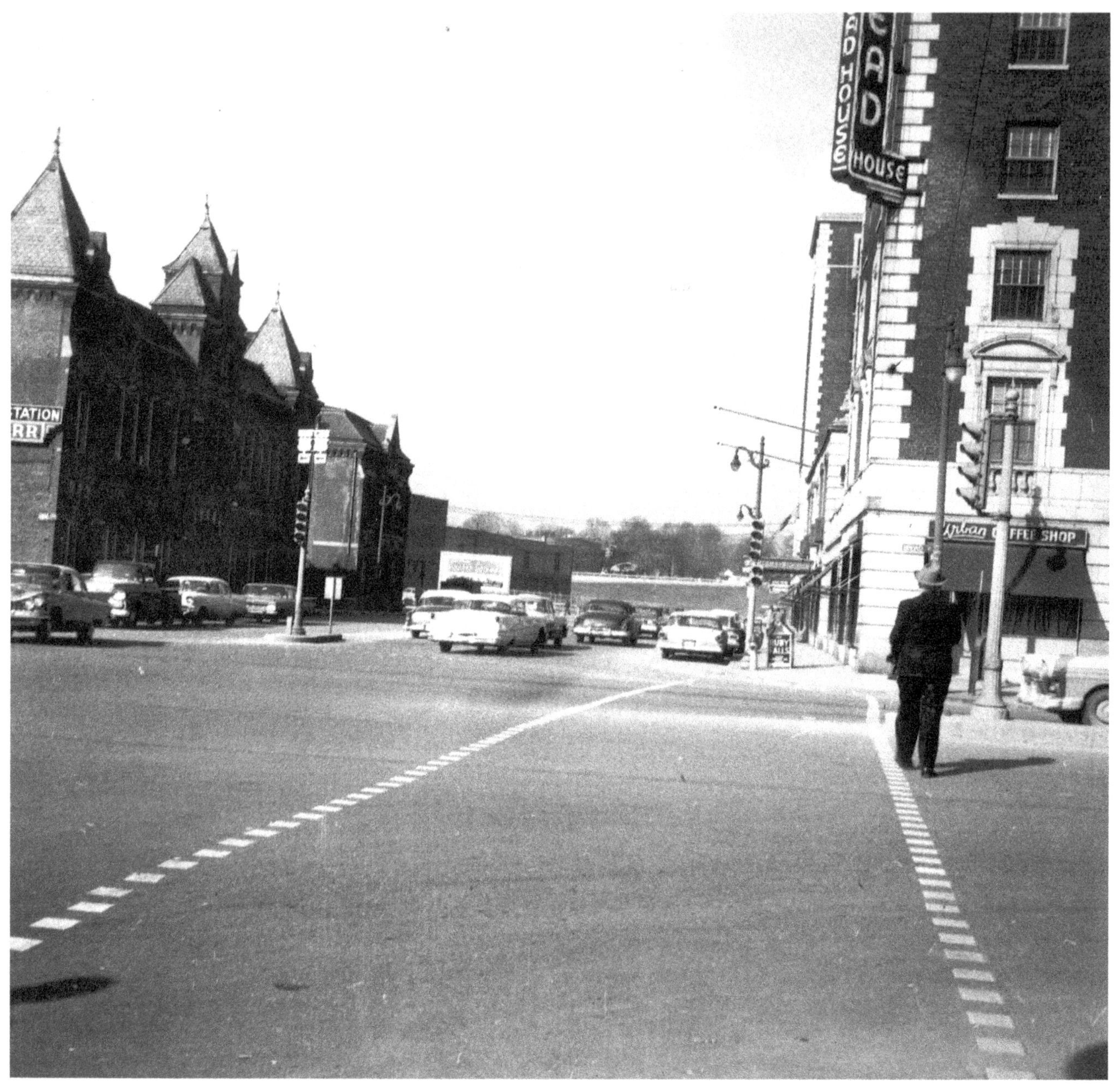

A gentleman crosses the street in front of the Read House in 1960. Across from the hotel stands the Union Depot, completed in 1881 to accommodate the busy passenger trains that came through the city on an hourly basis. The Read House (originally the Crutchfield House) was specifically built on this spot to take advantage of the first rail line laid into Chattanooga from Atlanta.

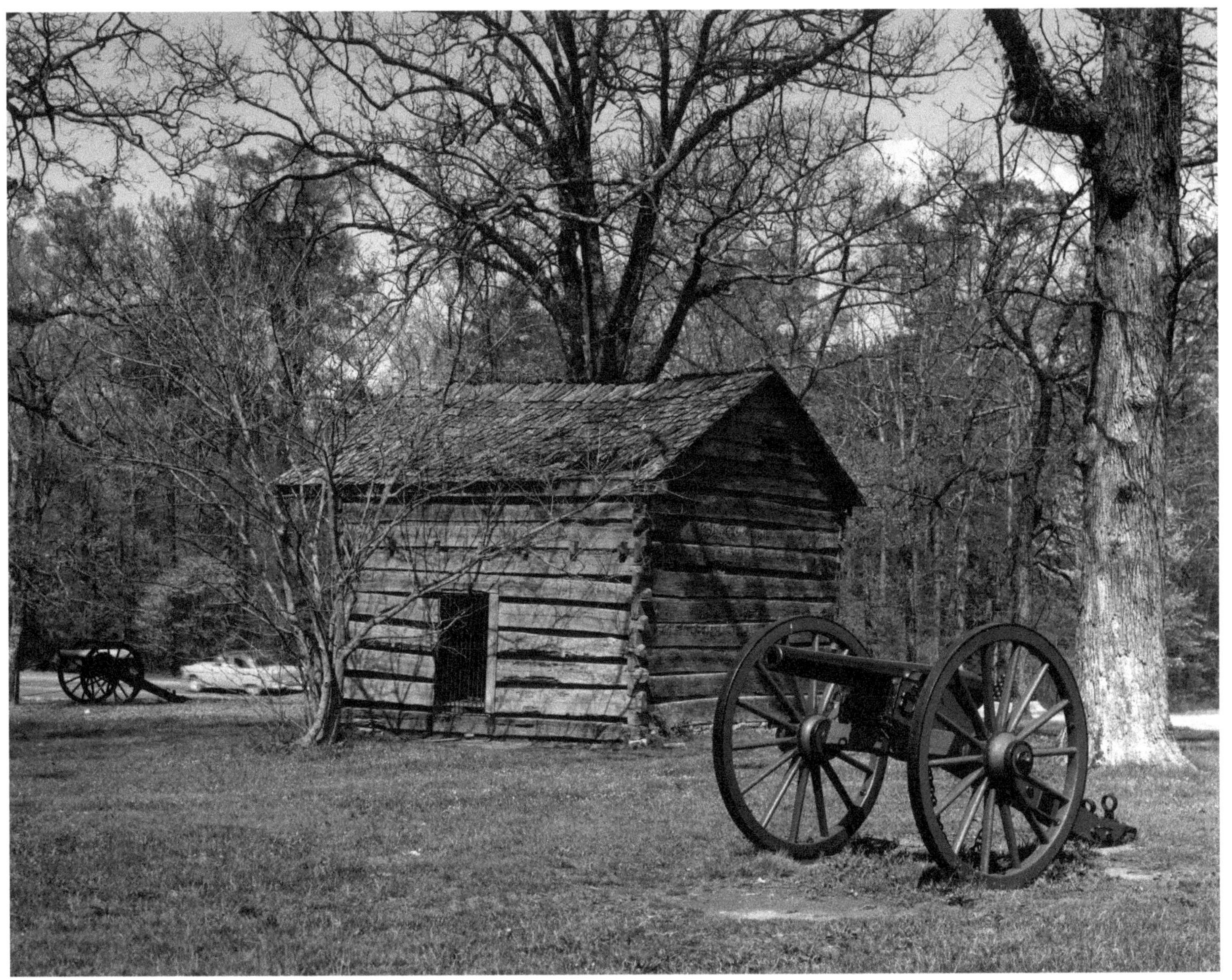

This dark cannon sits in front of the Brotherton House at the Chickamauga and Chattanooga National Military Park in 1960. The Brotherton family had moved here in 1860, only to find Union troops swarming around their home in September 1863. The family hid in a ditch while the fighting raged. It was here that Longstreet's troops charged through a gap in the Union line, turning the battle into a disaster for the North.

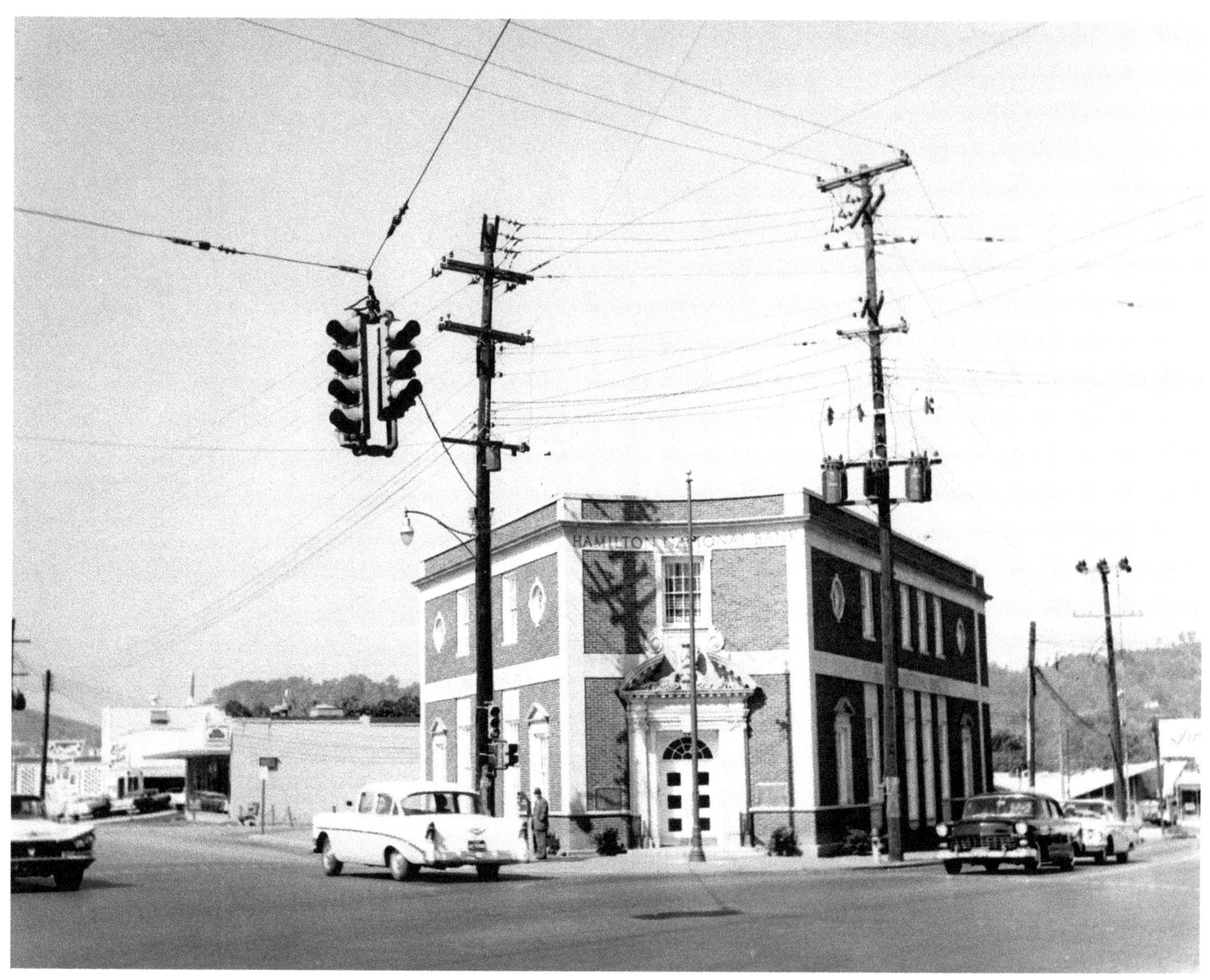

This truncated two-story bank building with its concave, clipped corner stands facing the Market Street Bridge in North Chattanooga and is something of a landmark for travelers around the city. Once a branch of the Hamilton National Bank, it now houses First Tennessee deposits and is an active part of the revival that the "North Shore" area has undergone in the last decade.

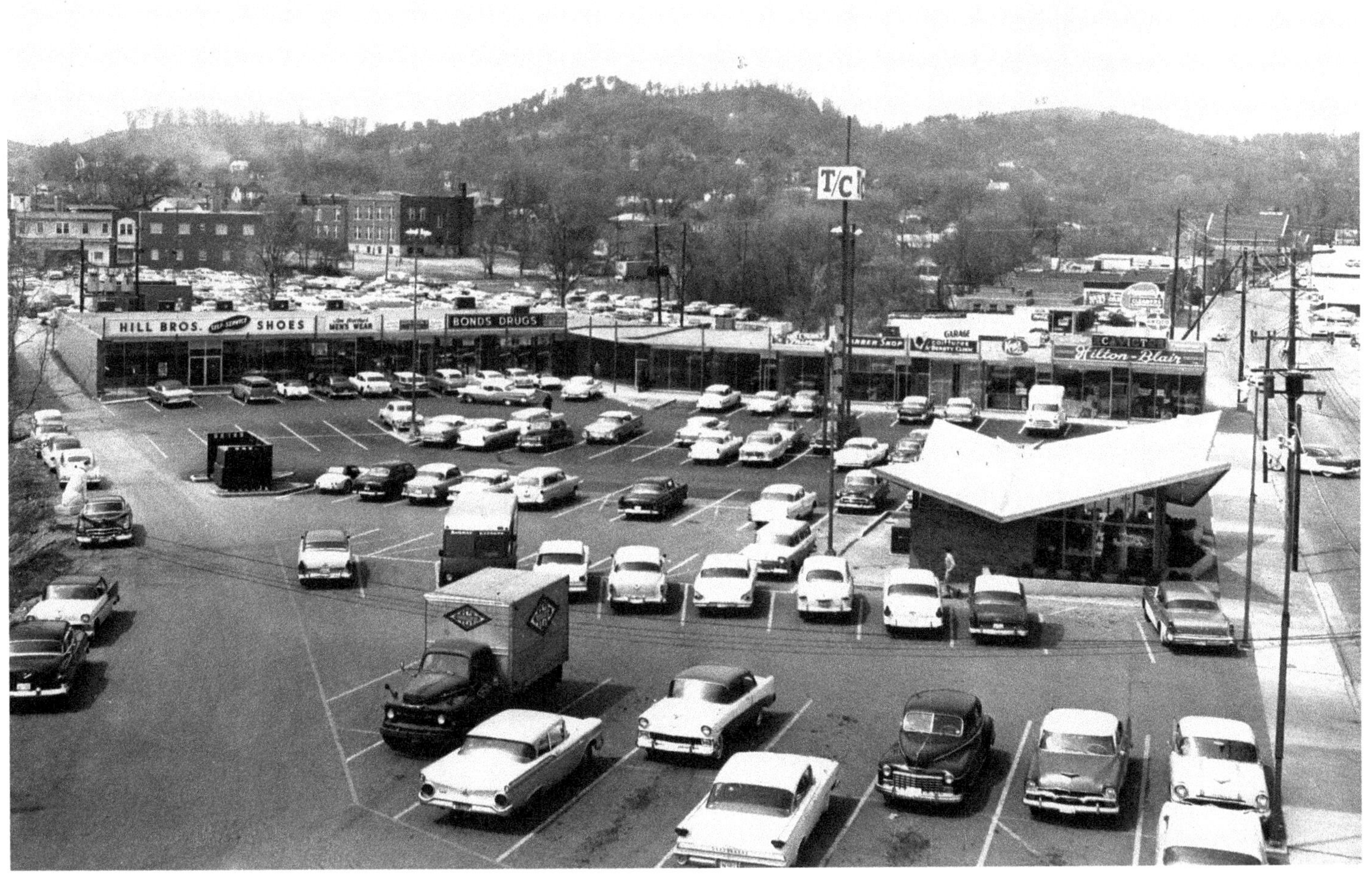

Seen here around 1960, the Town and Country shopping center is a good example of strip malls, essentially a row of retail shops housed within a single connected building with plate-glass fronts and an adjacent large parking area. Hills Brothers Shoes is now a Mexican eatery, Taco Mamacita. The free-standing building with the angled roof, the Longhorn Restaurant, continues today to serve good southern breakfasts and delicious grilled sandwiches.

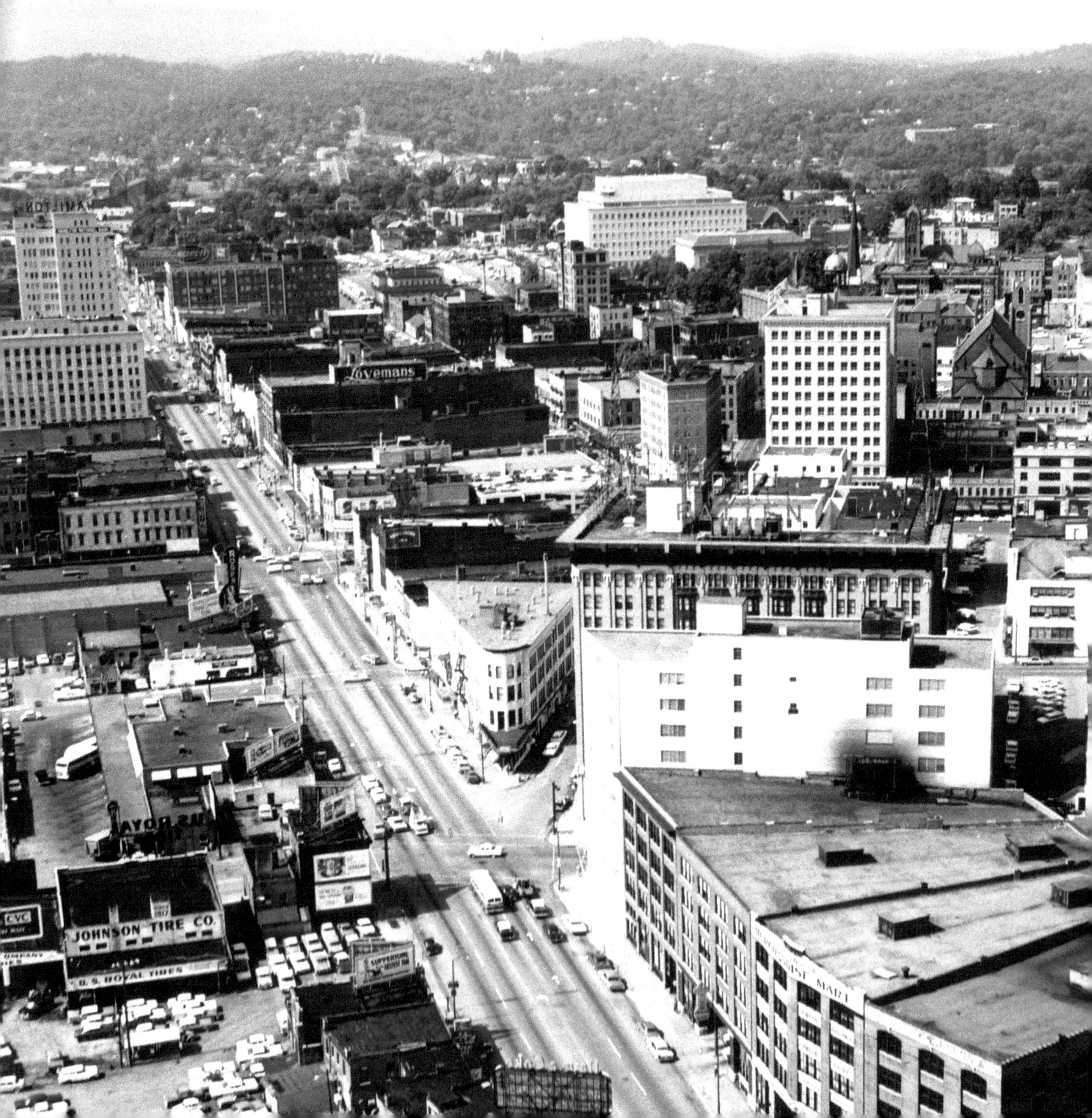
Lovemans
JOHNSON TIRE CO.
U.S. ROYAL TIRES

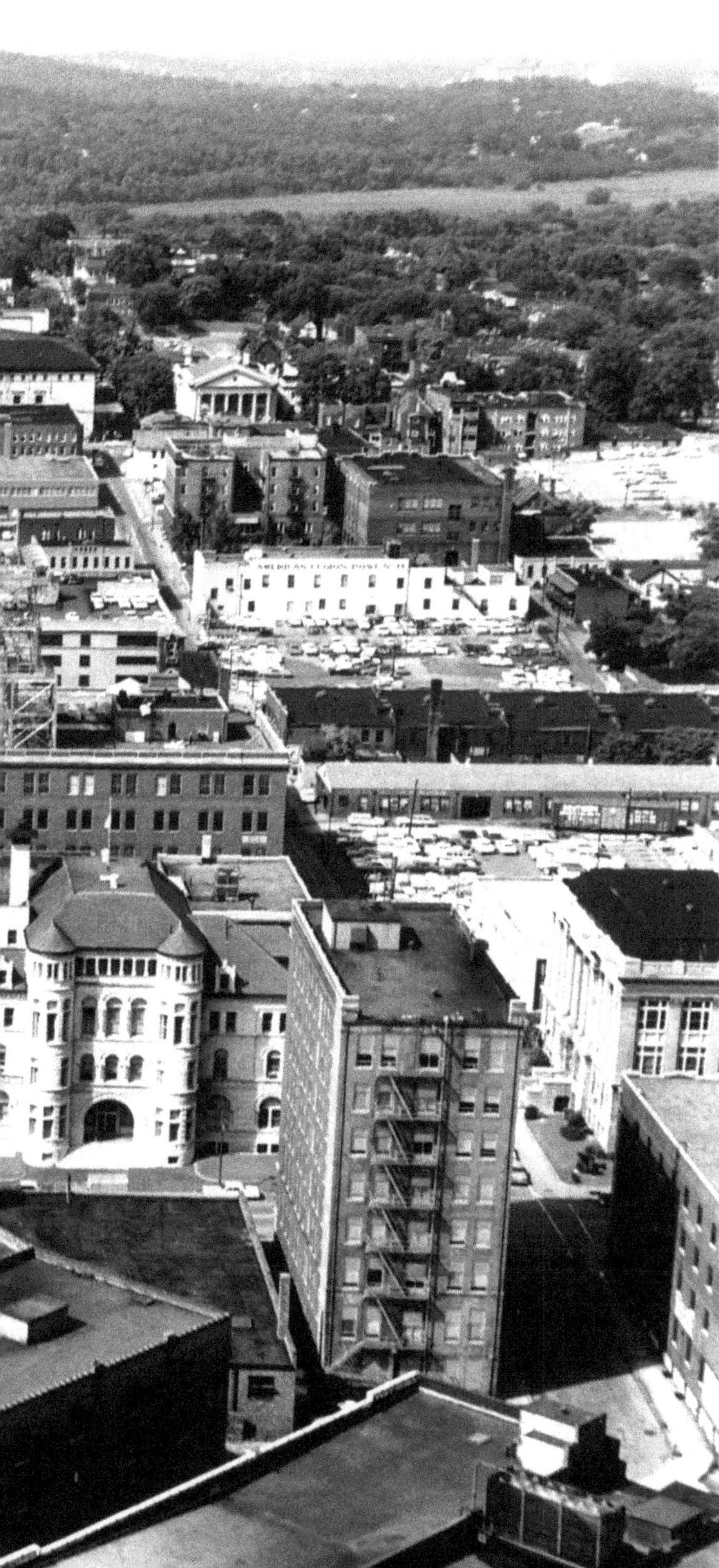

This aerial view of Market Street facing north from Twelfth Street around 1960 depicts the road as it runs through the heart of downtown to the Tennessee River. The conjoined buildings at bottom are today known as Warehouse Row, the building behind them with the two tower-like columns on the facade is the Custom House, and to the left is the Hotel Patten.

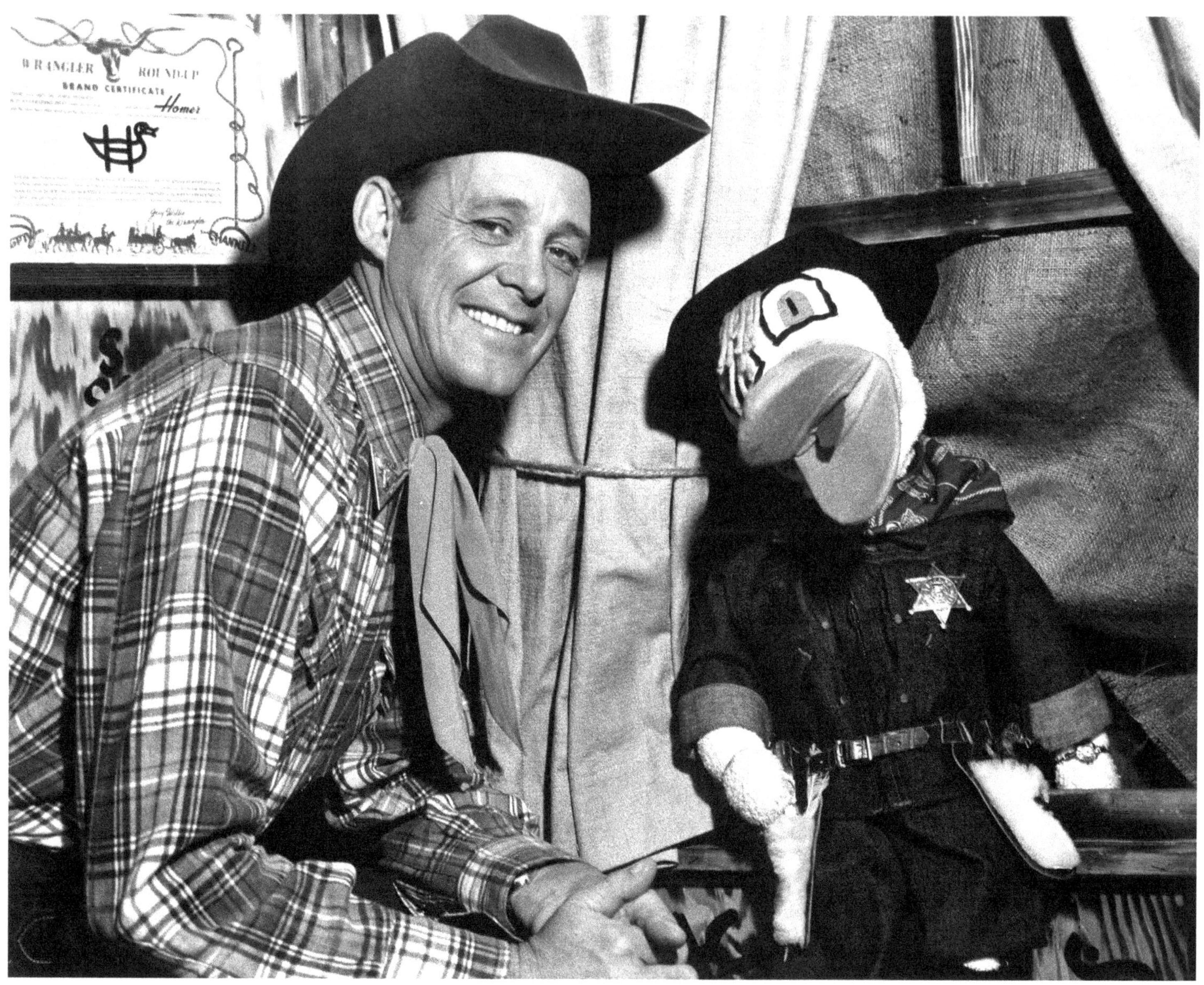

A staple of children's shows was long a talking puppet, and this one happens to be a gunslinging duck with a badge, furry holsters, and a mop of hair on his brow. Here around 1960, a good-looking cowboy, possibly Guy Willis, is a guest star on *The Tom and Homer Show,* which ran on WRGP, now WRCB-TV. In the background, a Wrangler Round-Up Certificate hangs on the wall.

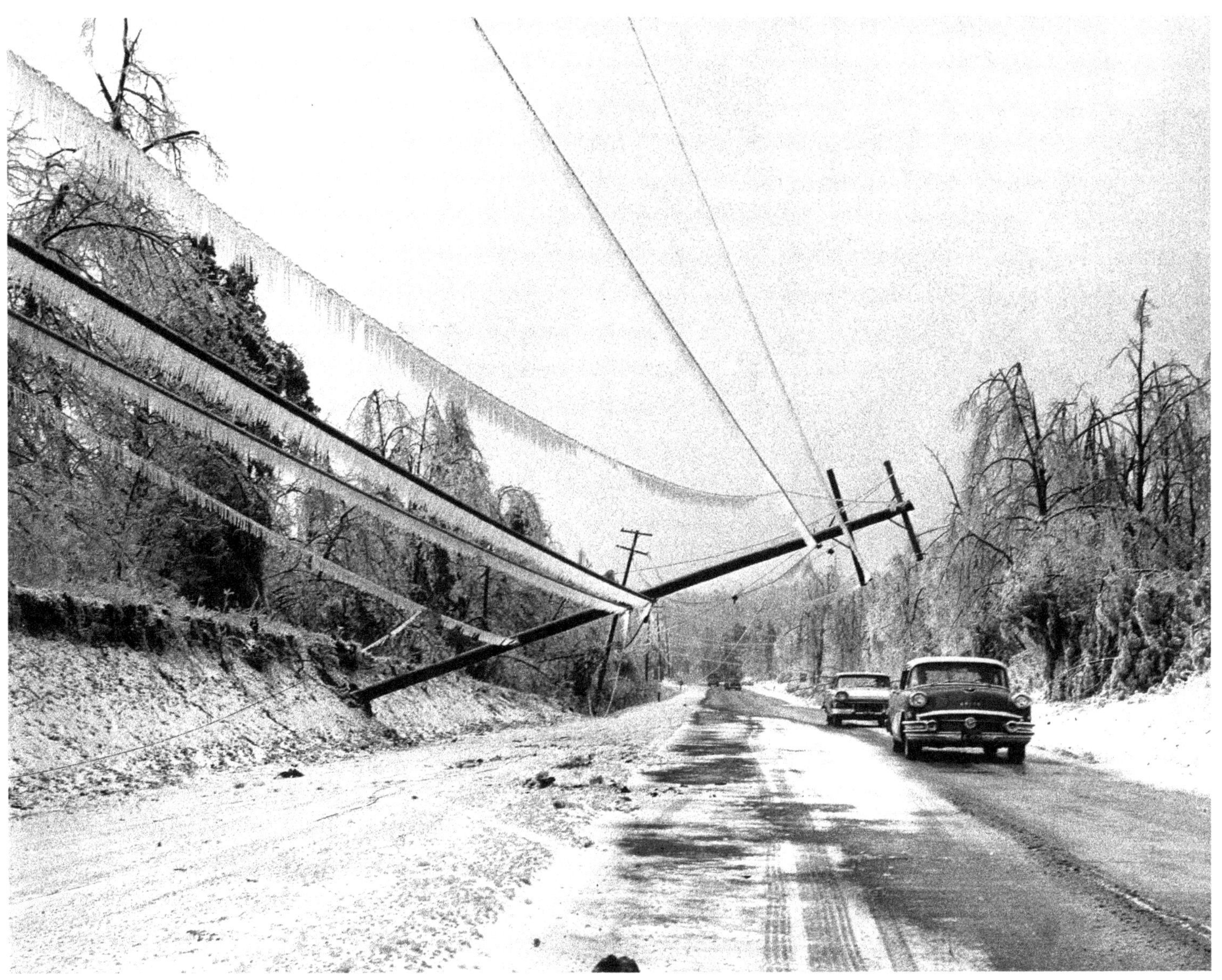

The mountains skirting the city get snow in the winter, often just a dusting of the powdery stuff. Residents are comfortable with that kind of weather. What is scary is the heavy, slippery ice that forms quickly when rain freezes and covers the roads. In March 1960, Walden's Ridge was paralyzed with heavy ice formations that wreaked havoc for days on the denizens of the upper elevations.

The civil rights movement in Chattanooga was marked by smaller protests and negotiations than those in towns like Birmingham and Memphis. A distinct turning point in city politics came in February 1960 during several days of sit-ins by high school students. Using classic civil disobedience techniques, they marched into lunch counters and sat down, hoping to be served and make an important point.

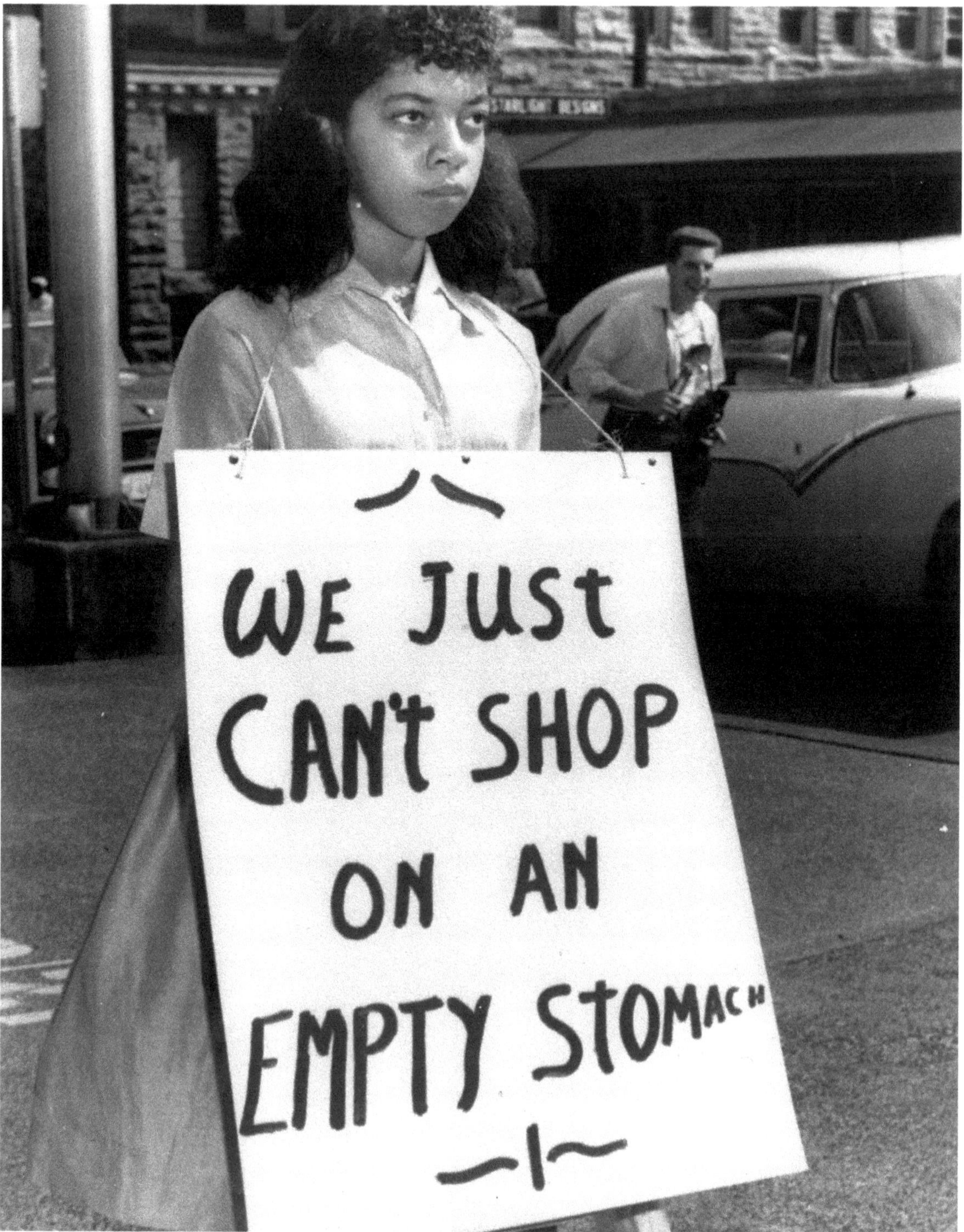

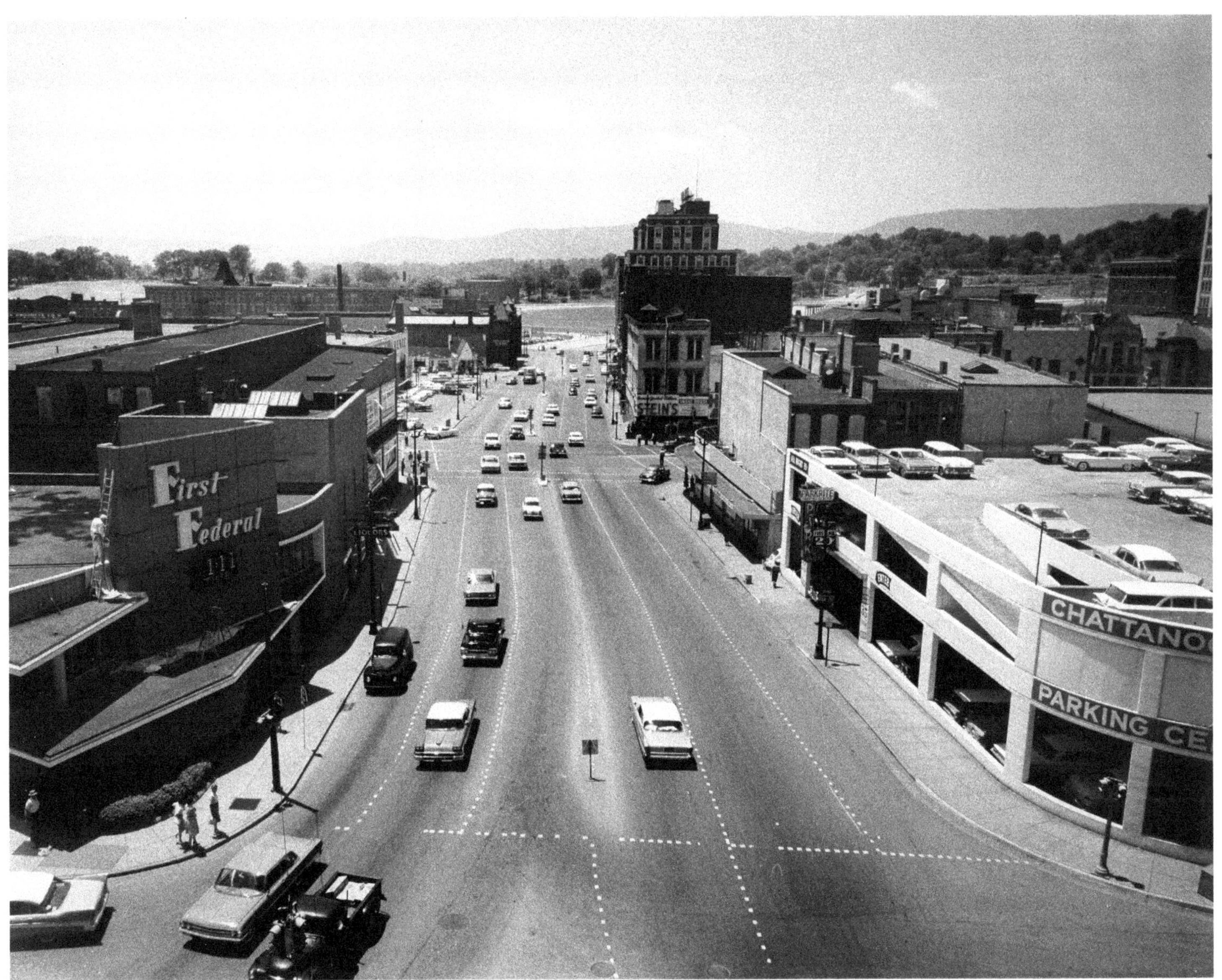

This long, westward facing view of Ninth Street shows the First Federal Bank on the left with its "electronic" clock and the Parkrite Parking Center on the right. The tall building in the distance to the right is the Read House. By the 1980s, as fewer shoppers came downtown, the parking garage was razed and replaced with a plaza with a performing stage and the Waterhouse pavilion. This view was recorded in 1961.

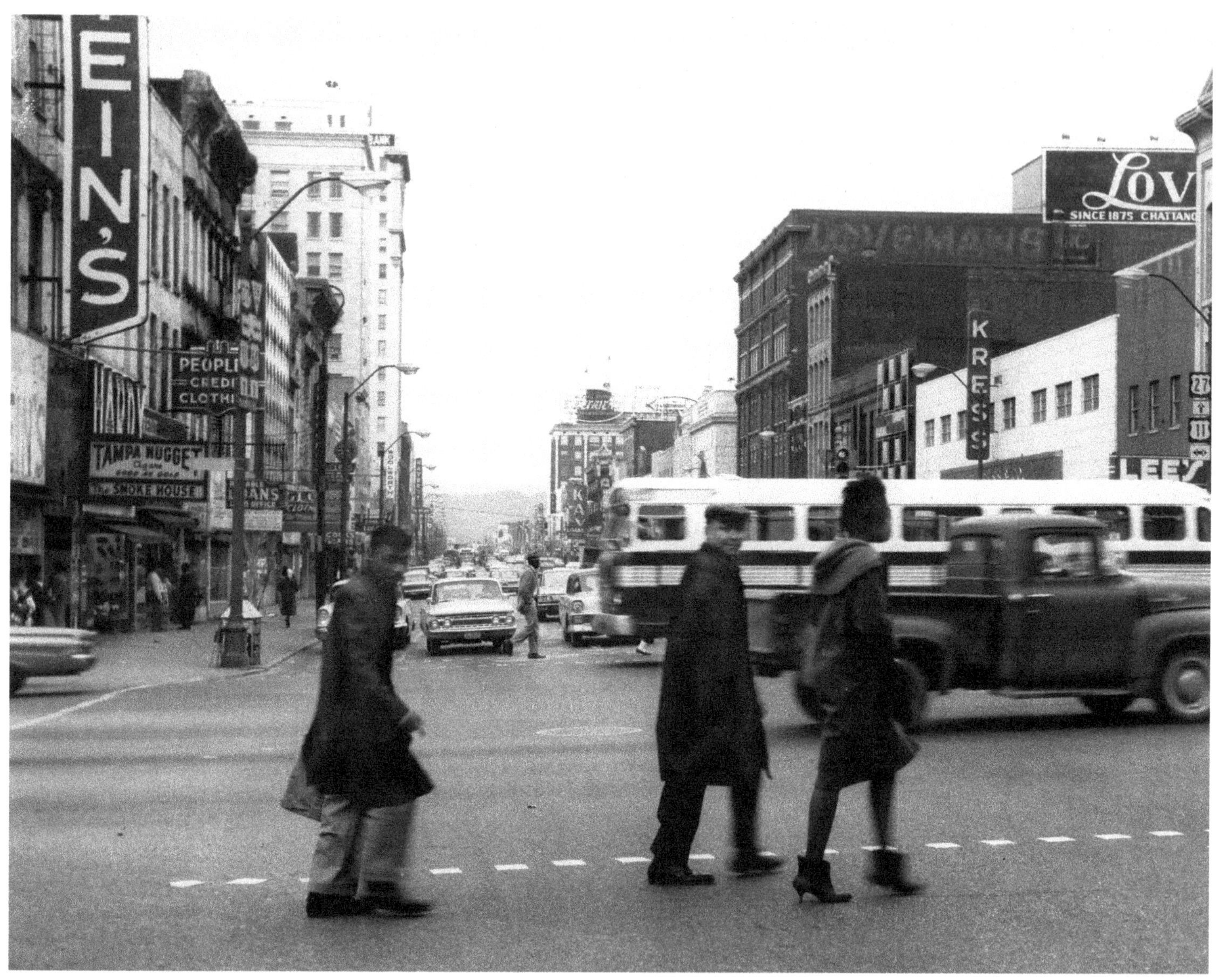

A busy day downtown on Market Street was the norm in the early 1960s as this photograph indicates. "Fighting downtown traffic" was part of life in the city. Part of the old Loveman's sign is visible in the upper-right corner next to the Kress's store. A sign on the left for Tampa Nugget cigars advertises the local tobacconist, the Smoke House.

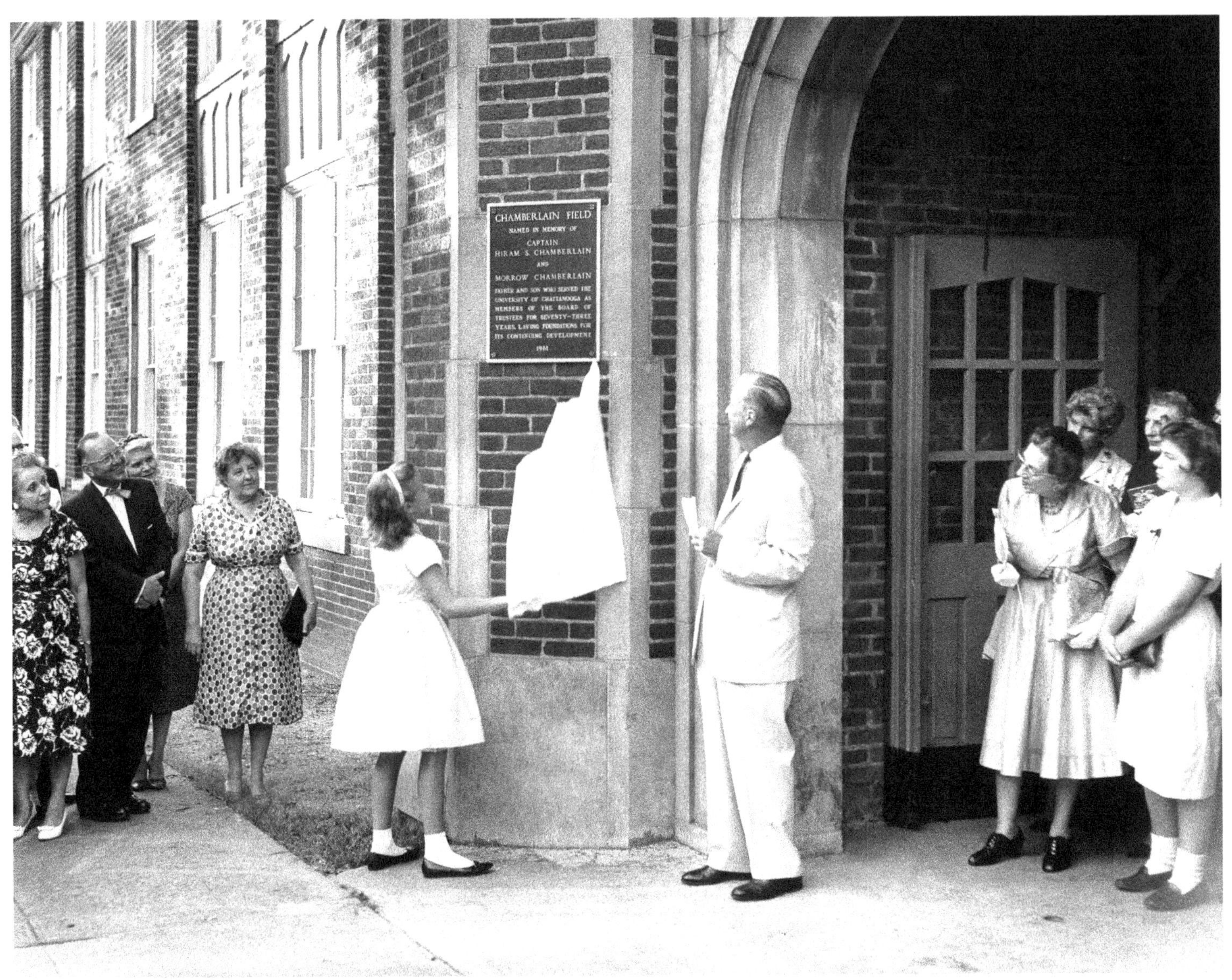

The University of Chattanooga was founded in the city in 1886 and located on a knoll on McCallie Avenue. Its small campus grew and eventually included a football gridiron, which fielded some competitive teams over the years guided by coaching legend Scrappy Moore. Here a plaque is dedicated in 1961 on the Oak Street side of the field to Hiram S. and Morrow Chamberlain, prominent citizens and enthusiastic supporters of the school.

It goes without saying that the memory of the Civil War is ever present in Chattanooga. One of the memorable tales of the conflict centered on the heist of the locomotive the *General.* Stolen by Yankee raiders while Confederate soldiers ate breakfast in Big Shanty, Georgia, the engine wound up in Chattanooga in 1901, a prize gem and local attraction at the Union Depot across from the Read House for more than half a century.

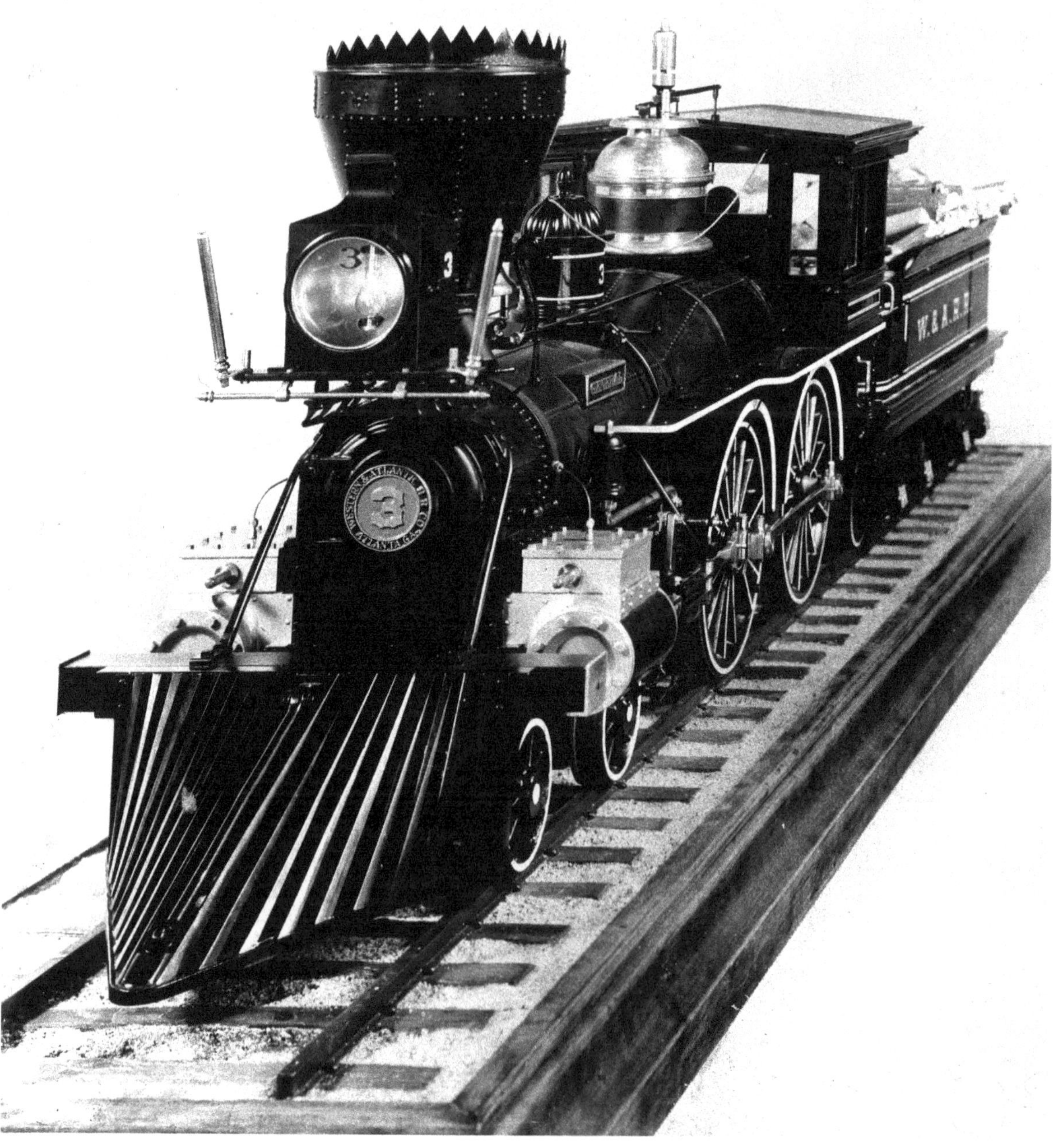

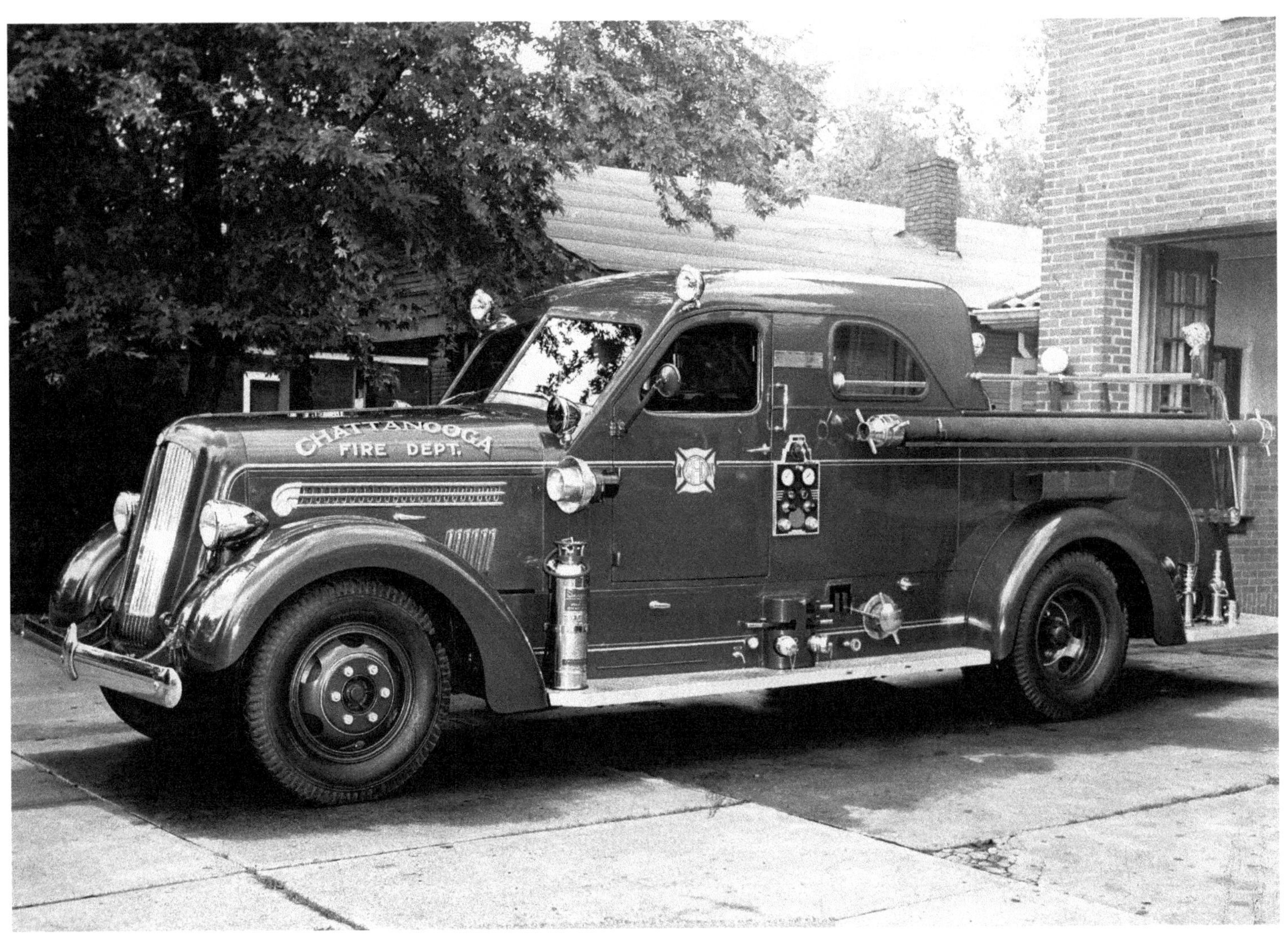

This vintage fire engine looks well taken care of and ready to roll around 1961. More likely though, it is something of a museum piece and a point of pride for the local fire fighters who are assigned to the precinct station. The name of the side, "McInturff," probably refers to George L. McInturff, Commissioner of Public Works from 1947 to 1967.

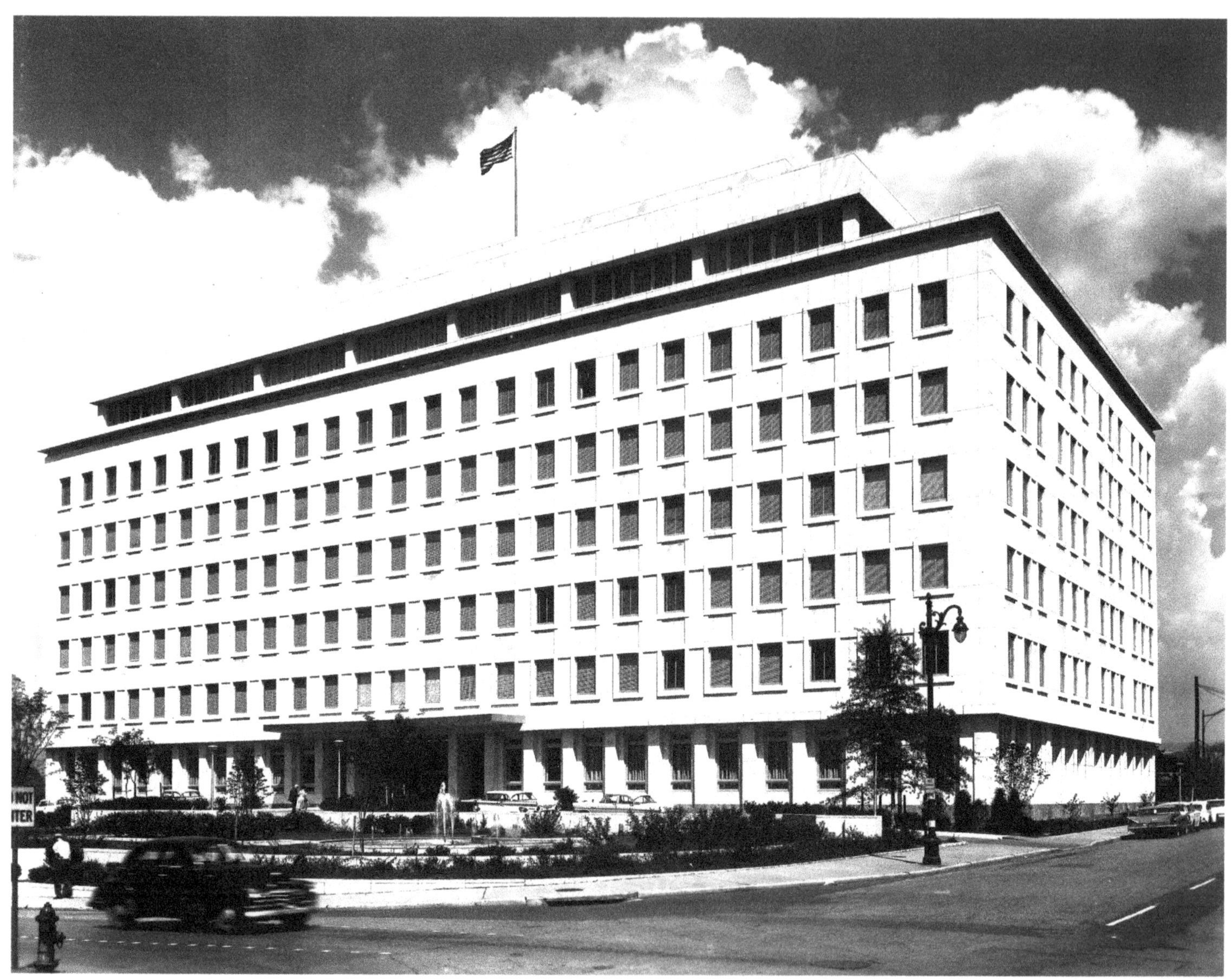

One of the city's oldest family-owned businesses and largest employers is the Provident Life and Accident Insurance Company, founded in 1887 by Thomas Maclellan. Originally headquartered on Broad Street in the aptly named Maclellan Building, the company specialized in "uninsurables" and later in the disability benefits market. The company had relocated to this modern, marble-faced box by 1960, across from the county courthouse on Fountain Square.

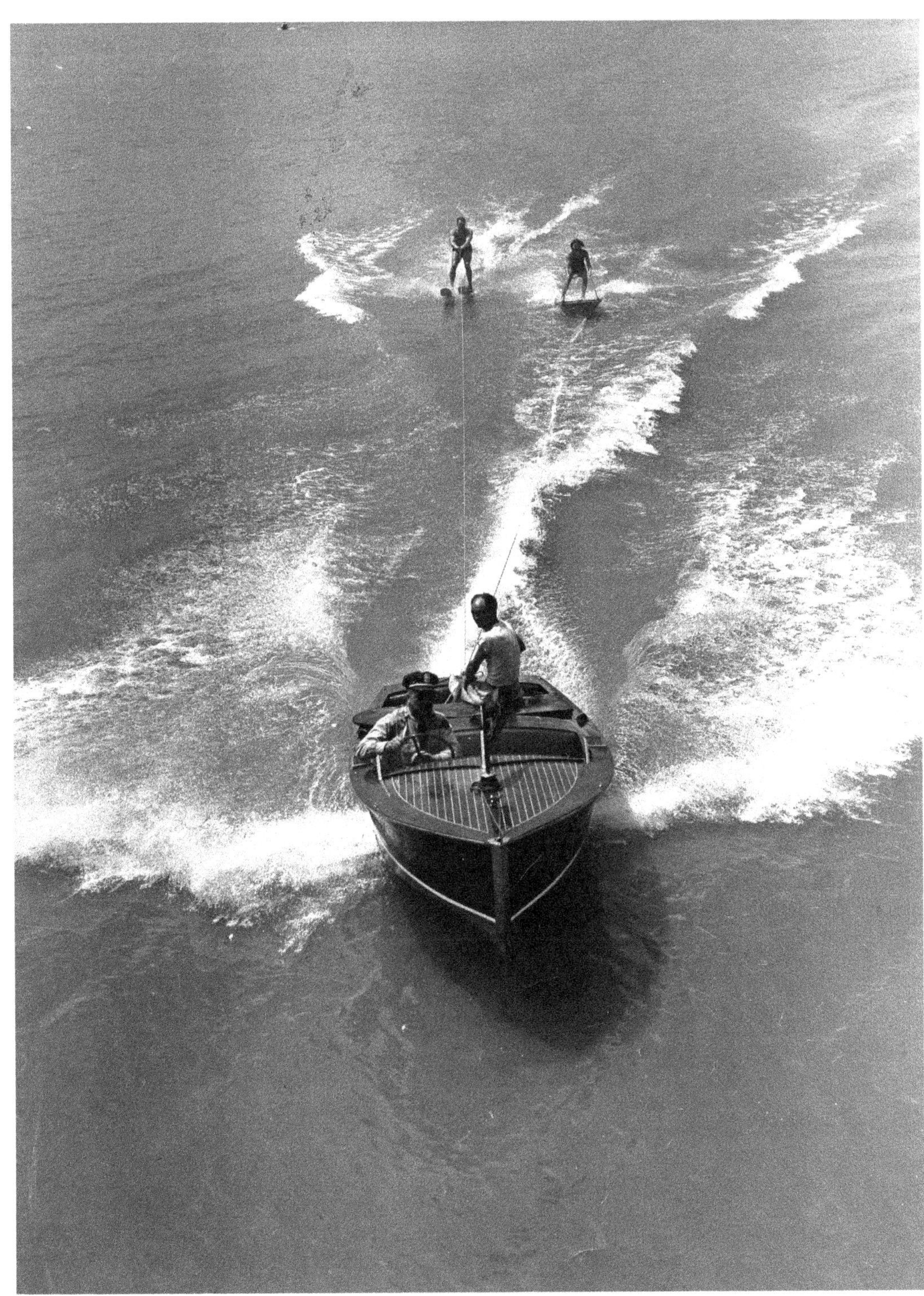

Life is good when you're flying across the water on a summer's day on Chickamauga Lake. The lake was formed by the newly completed Chickamauga Dam in 1940 and was actually one of the goals of the Tennessee Valley Authority in building the system. Providing electricity was the primary reason for the dam, but providing recreation and fishing for local residents was deemed important as well. This view was recorded in 1962.

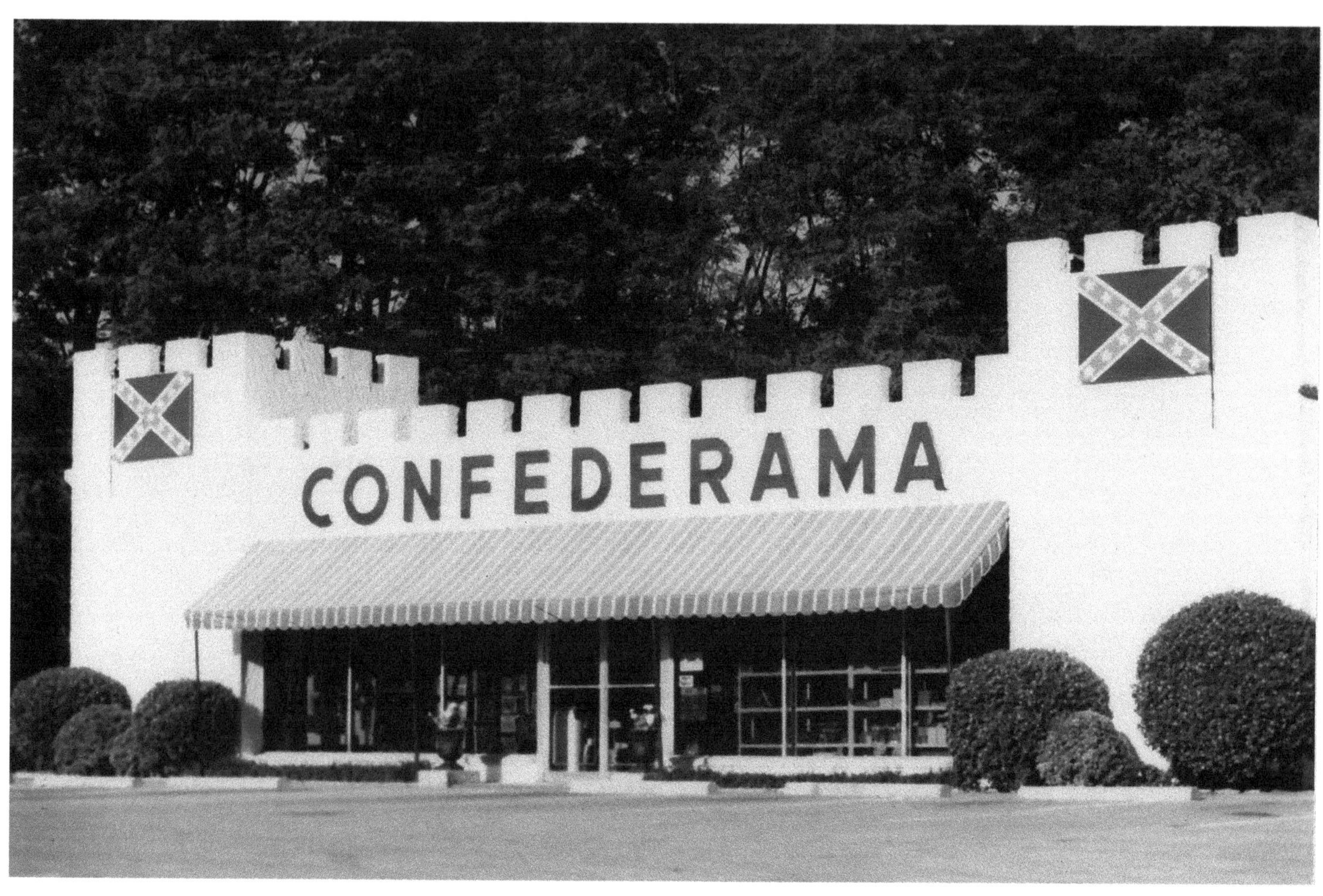

Confederama was located for years in St. Elmo and housed a large table that replicated to scale the geography of Chattanooga with thousands of small soldiers, horses, and wagons in formations indicating the positioning of Union and Confederate troops during the siege of the city. The building's facade was complete with towers and crenelations and proudly displayed the rebel flag in a time before political correctness deemed the symbol offensive.

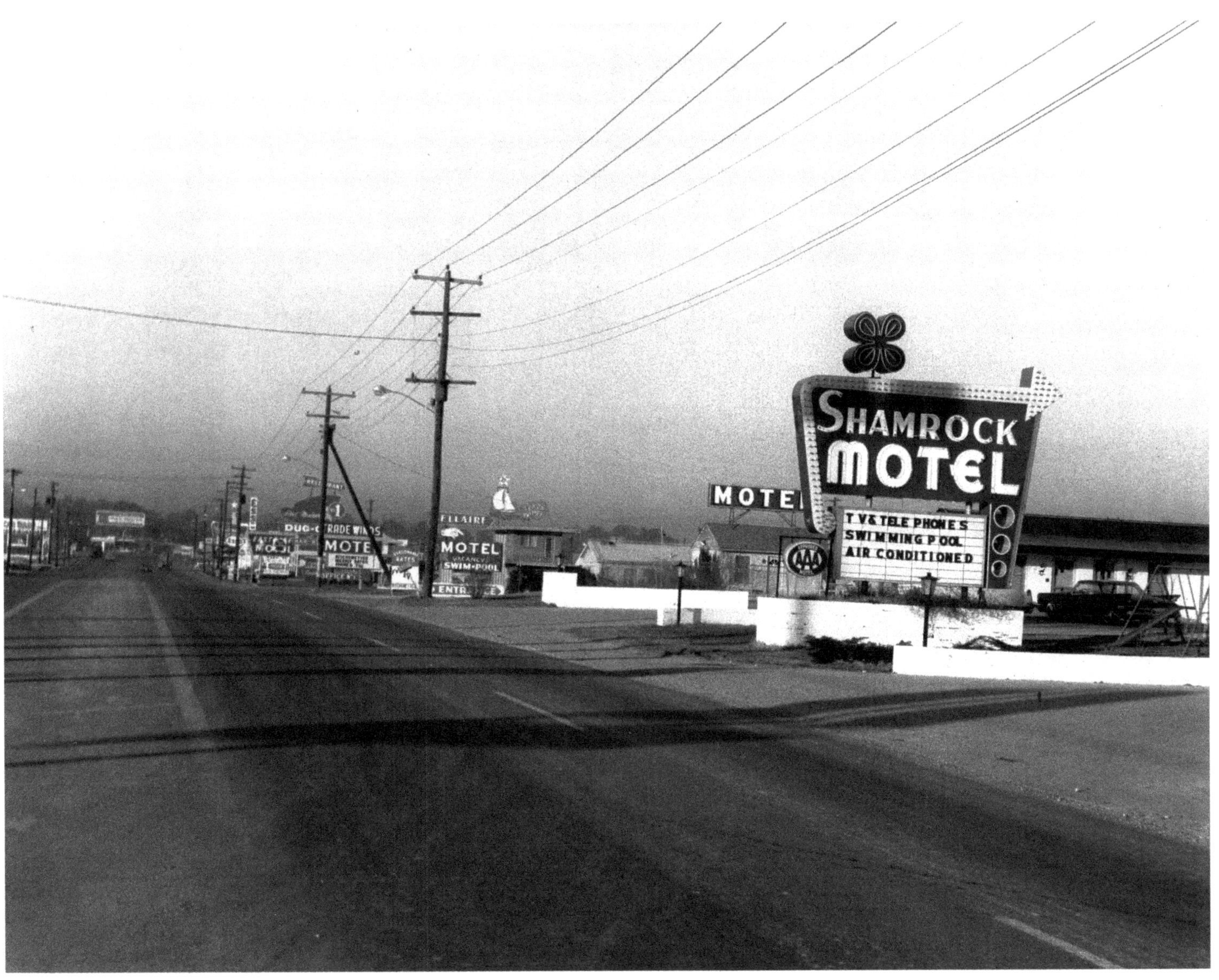

Brainerd Road is one of Chattanooga's most traveled roads as it heads southeast out of town. But 50 years ago, the highway past the Krispy Kreme was on the outskirts of the city and a good place to stop, stretch, and spend the night. With television, a swimming pool, and air conditioning, and prices that beat those of the established hotels downtown, places like the Shamrock Motel were enticing.

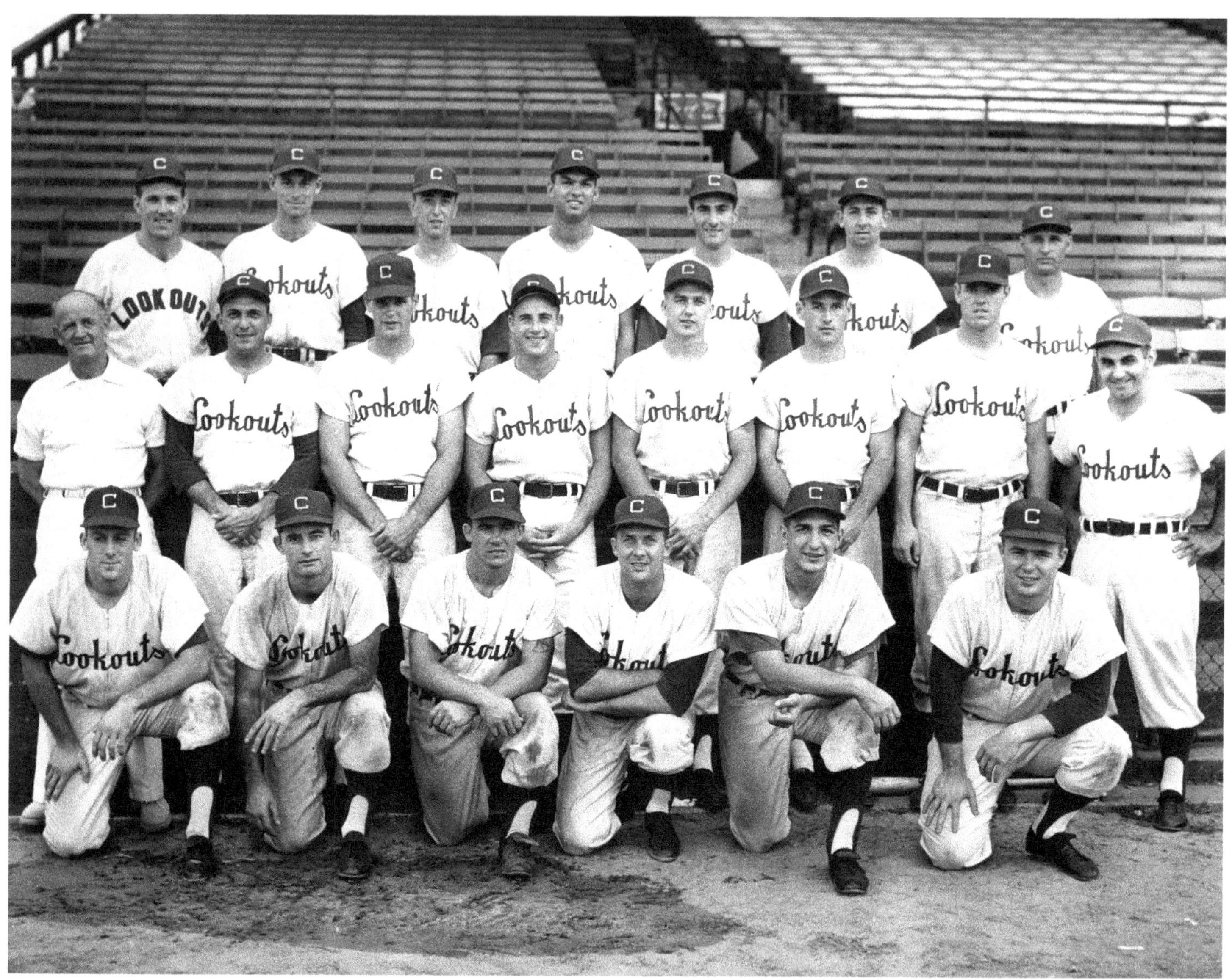

Baseball has thrived for generations in southeast Tennessee, and the home team since 1885 has been the Chattanooga Lookouts. Named for the famous mountain that overlooks the city, the ball club played in Engel Stadium from 1930 to 1999, fielding such greats as Harmon Killebrew and Ferguson Jenkins. In 1961, the year this photograph was made, they were the toast of the town when they took the Southern Association title in a hard fought pennant race.

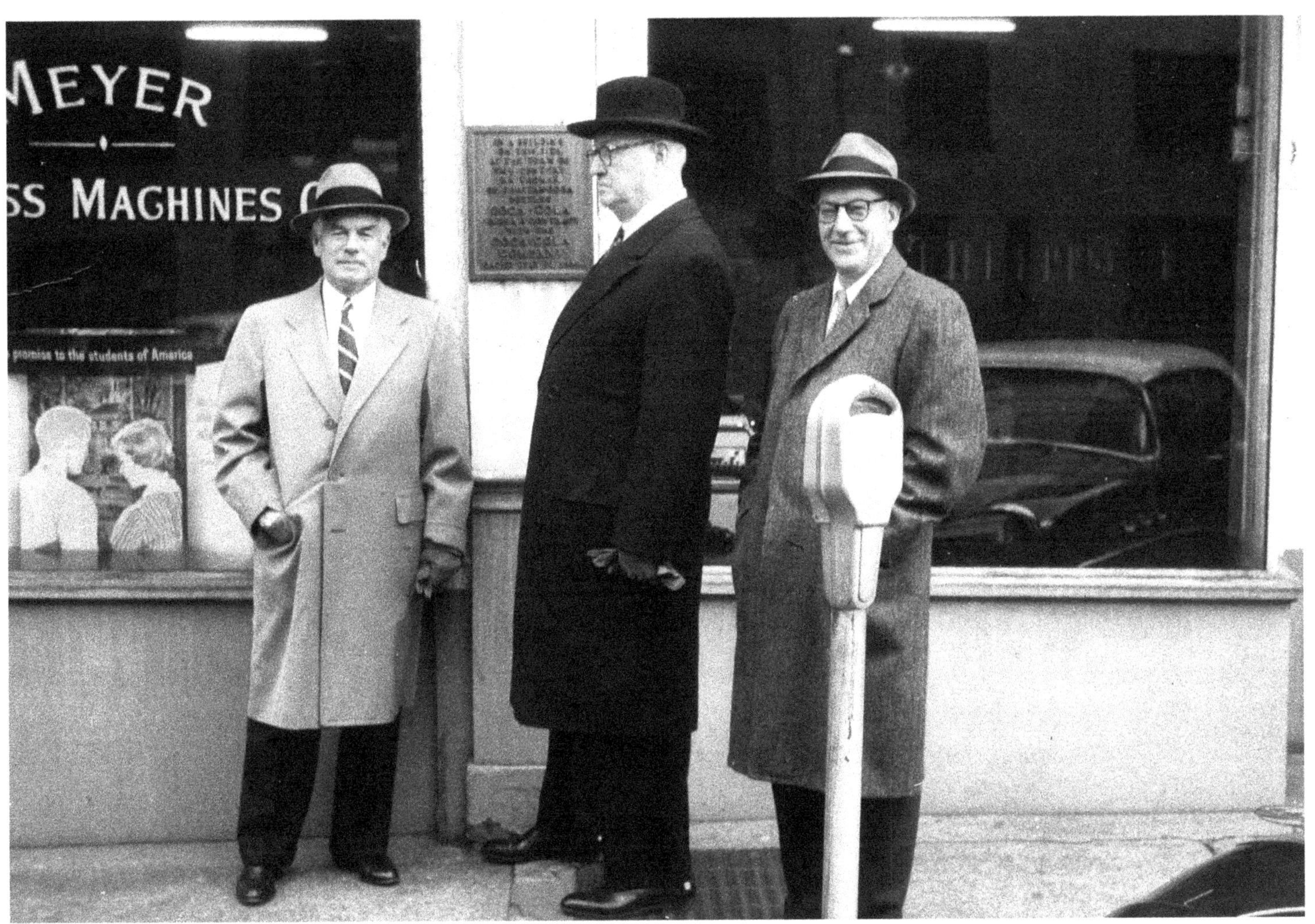

Around 1962, three gentlemen stand on Patten Parkway at the original site of the bottling operation for that famous, fizzy beverage, Coca-Cola. To the left is DeSales Harrison, chairman of the board of the Chattanooga Coca-Cola Bottling Company, and to the right is Sebert Brewer, president of the same. The statuesque figure in the center is James Aloysius Farley, Postmaster General for Franklin D. Roosevelt and influential leader of Coca-Cola International for decades.

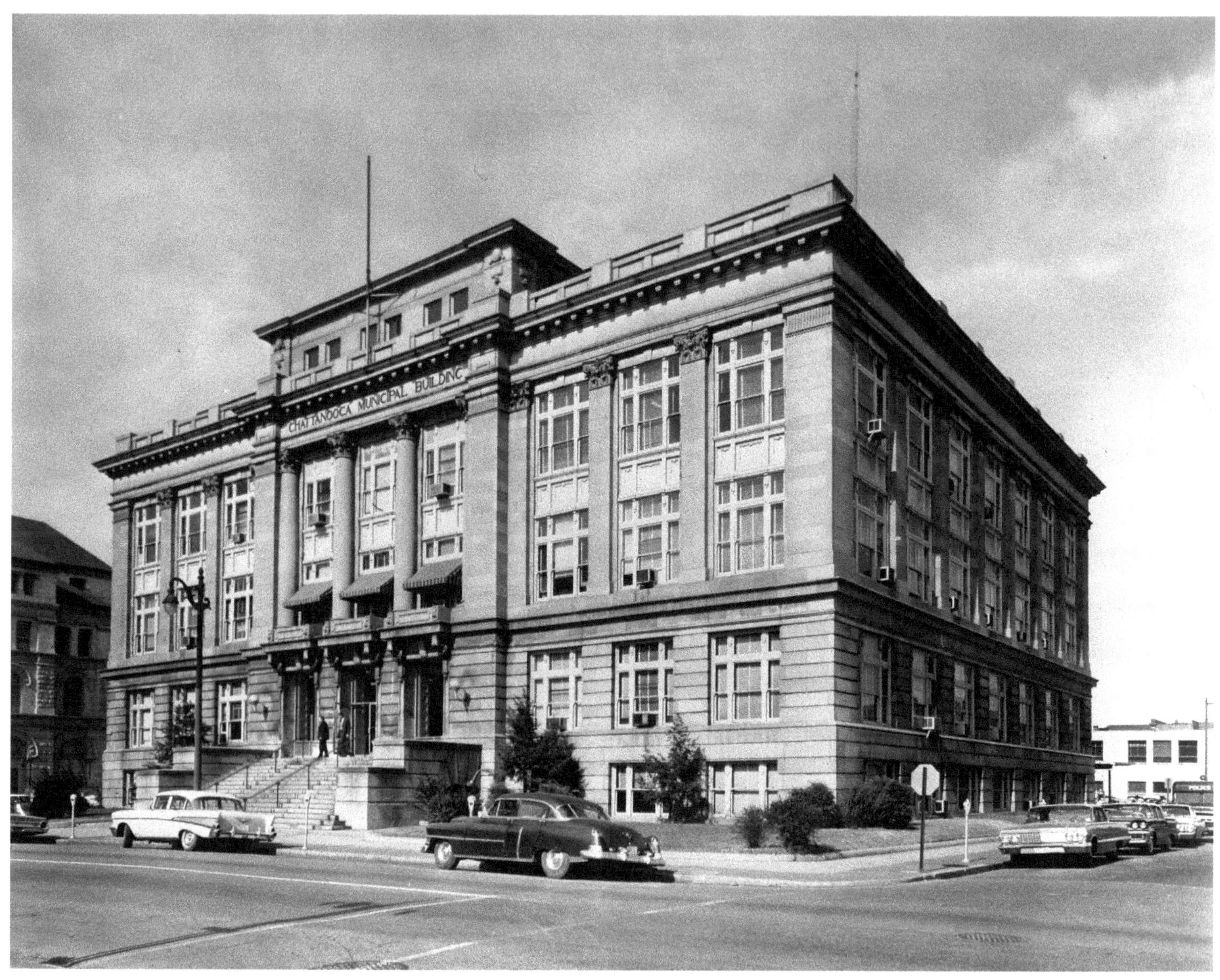

In 1908 the city was booming. New neighborhoods were being built and people were leaving the countryside for steady industrial work in town, where jobs were plentiful. That year a stately, new city hall with beautiful glass work inside opened on East Eleventh Street to provide the mayor and his men respectable quarters to process tax collections and expedite requests for permits. This is a view of the building as it looked around 1962.

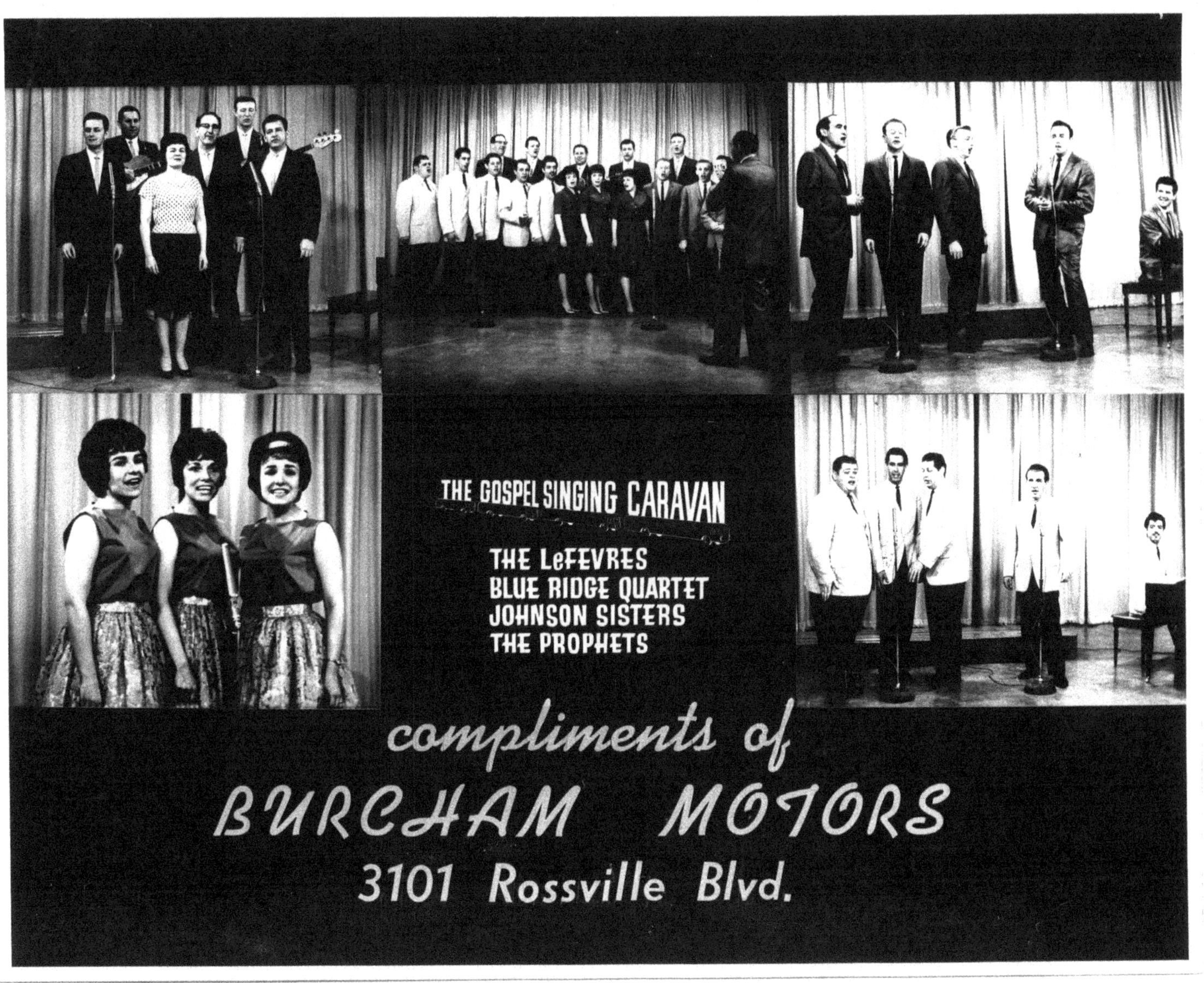

Old-time gospel music has been popular in east Tennessee for generations and is no stranger to regional television. This promotional photograph from 1963 highlights a "gospel singing caravan." Quartets and family groups have always been a staple of this style of harmonizing. The LeFevres, who produced syndicated television shows out of Atlanta, are ranked among the great practitioners of this southern gospel tradition.

One of Lookout Mountain's iconic shapes is Sunset Rock, seen here around 1963. Viewed from below, it was compared by past generations to the profile of a Native American "chief." For many folks it is simply a good place to watch a sunset, since the jutting stone faces west toward Raccoon Mountain. These days, mountain climbers who enjoy "bouldering" find scaling the precipice an exhilarating challenge.

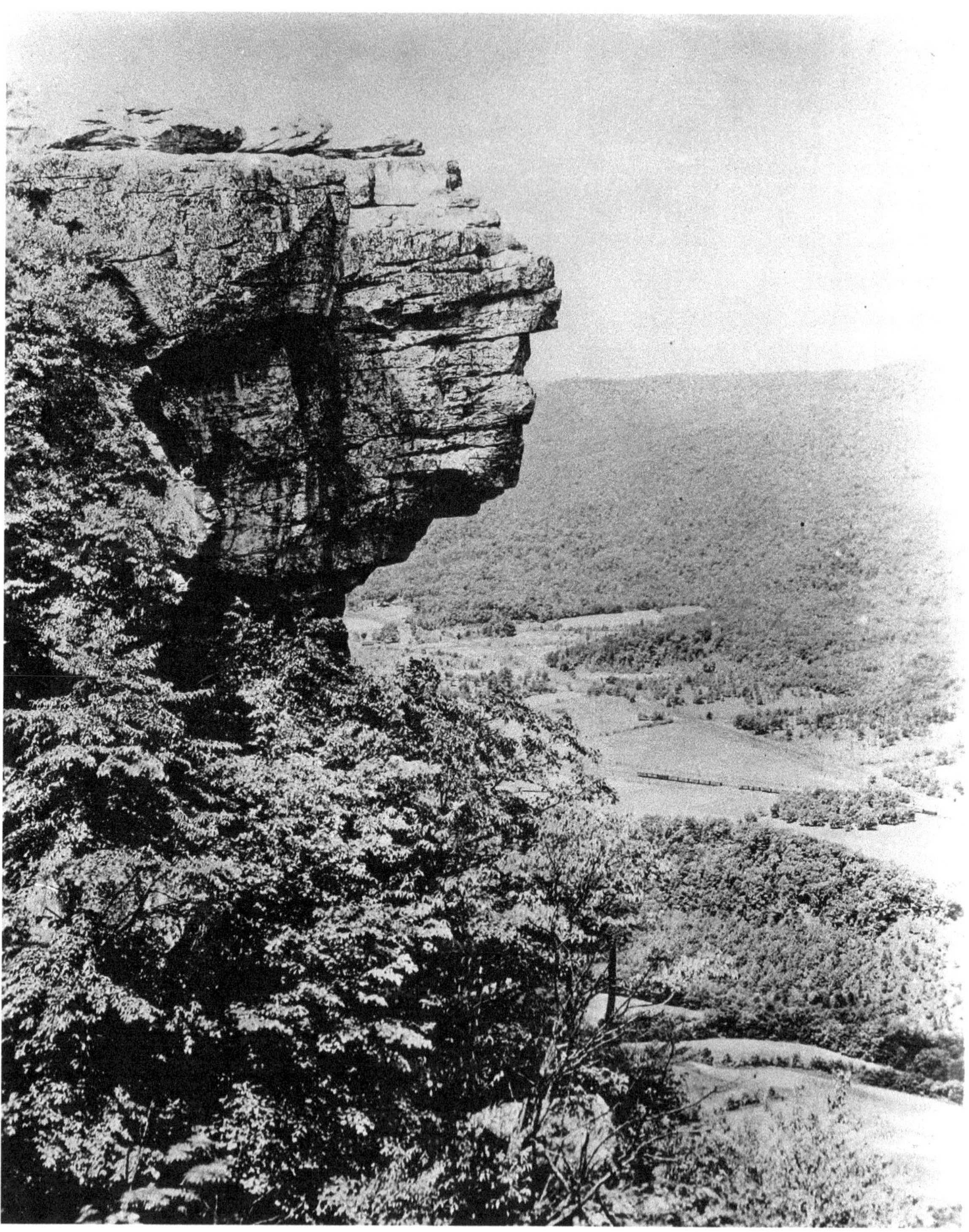

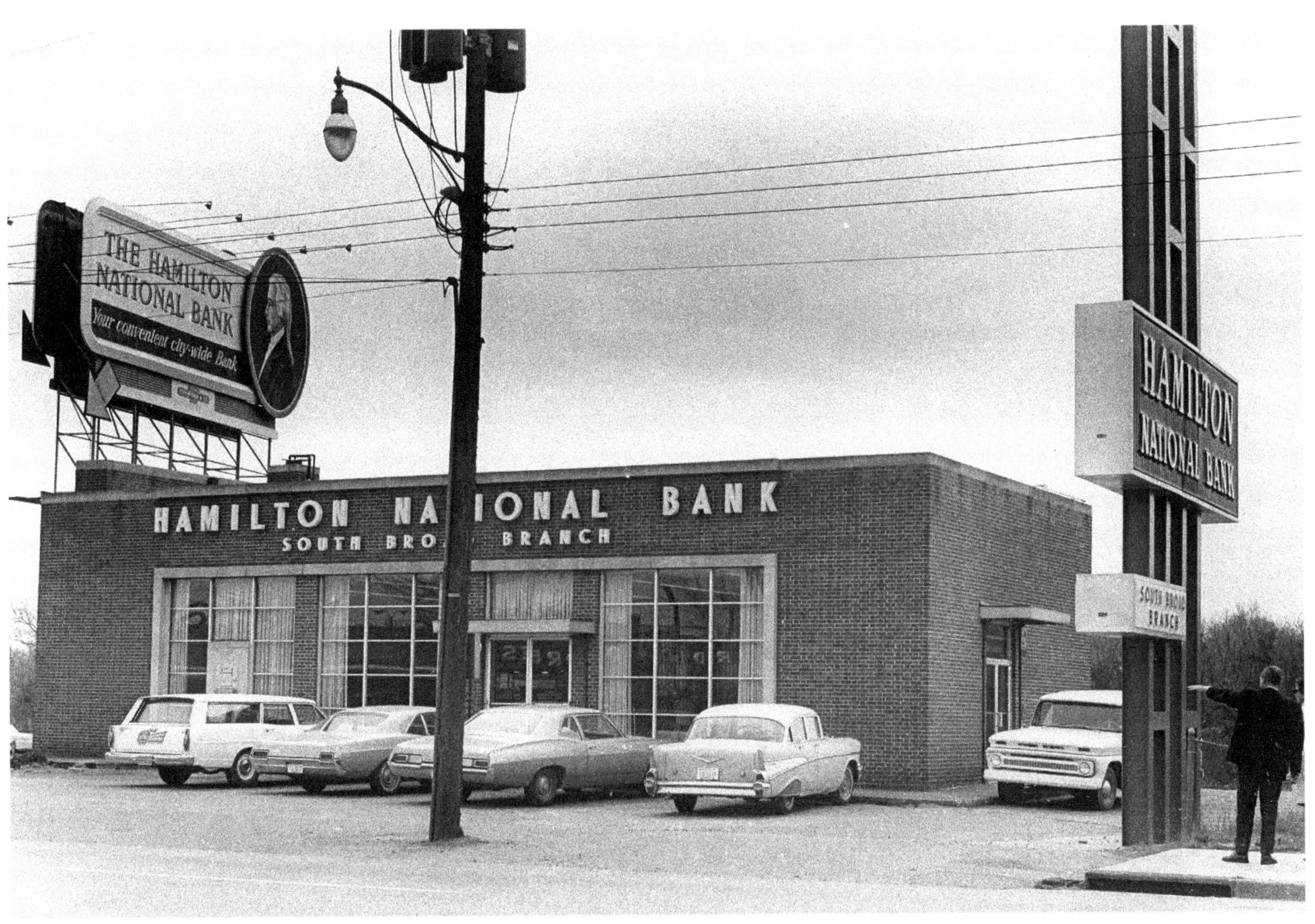

Hamilton County was, of course, named for Alexander Hamilton, first Secretary of the Treasury, whose picture is displayed in a large oval on a billboard above this small bank building. Banks were traditionally headquartered in large buildings downtown, but as suburbia grew in the fifties, small "branch" locations opened in the greater area to serve the public and draw in more deposits. This branch is open for business around 1963.

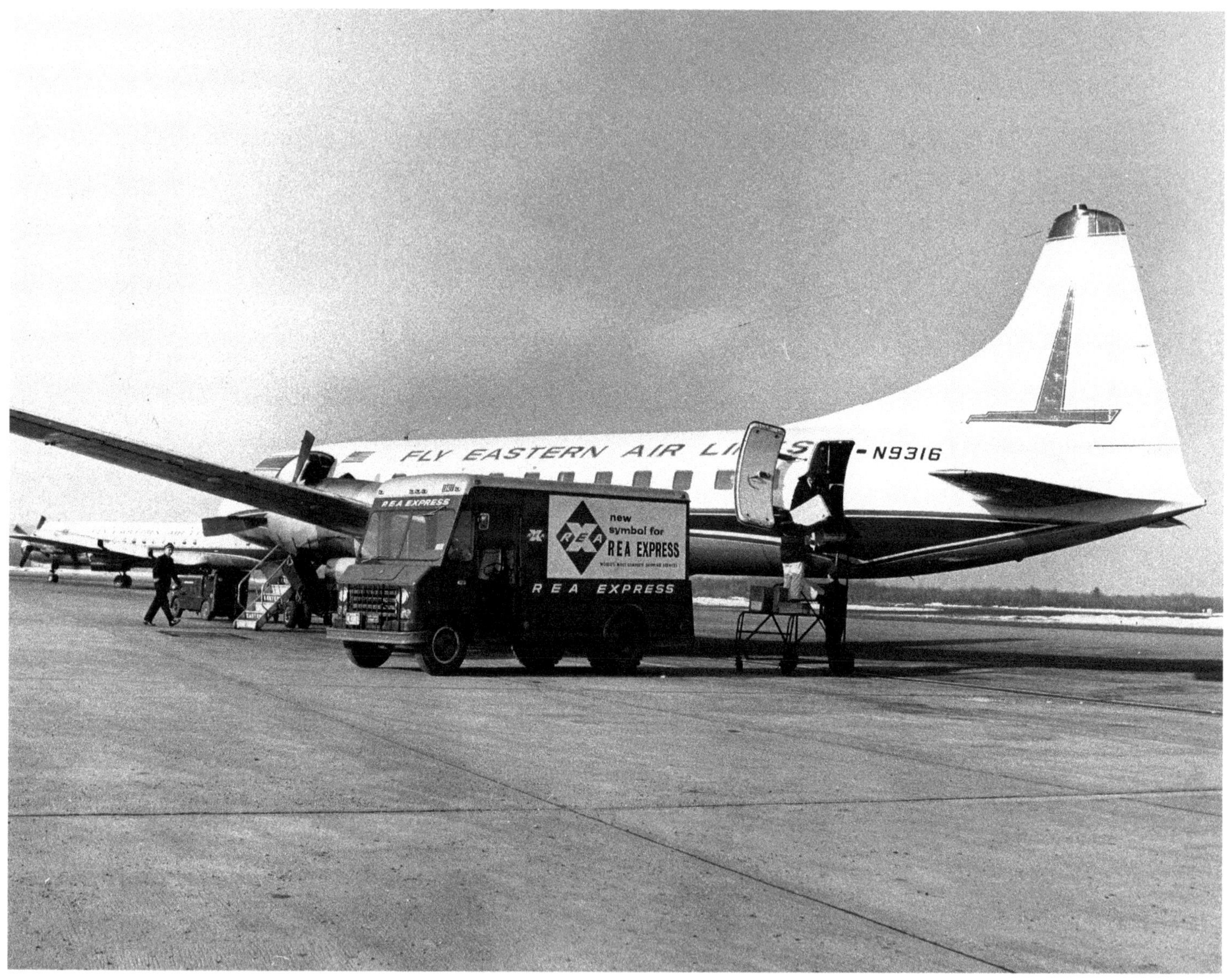

For decades Eastern Air Lines was one of the dominant air carriers in the United States. Both Eastern and Delta had hubs in nearby Atlanta and competed to serve Chattanooga at Lovell Field. The town's original airfield was Marr Field, something of a converted cow pasture. Mayor Ed Bass pushed for a modern facility and Lovell Field opened east of town in 1930 on farmland near South Chickamauga Creek. These Eastern Air Lines planes were photographed in 1964.

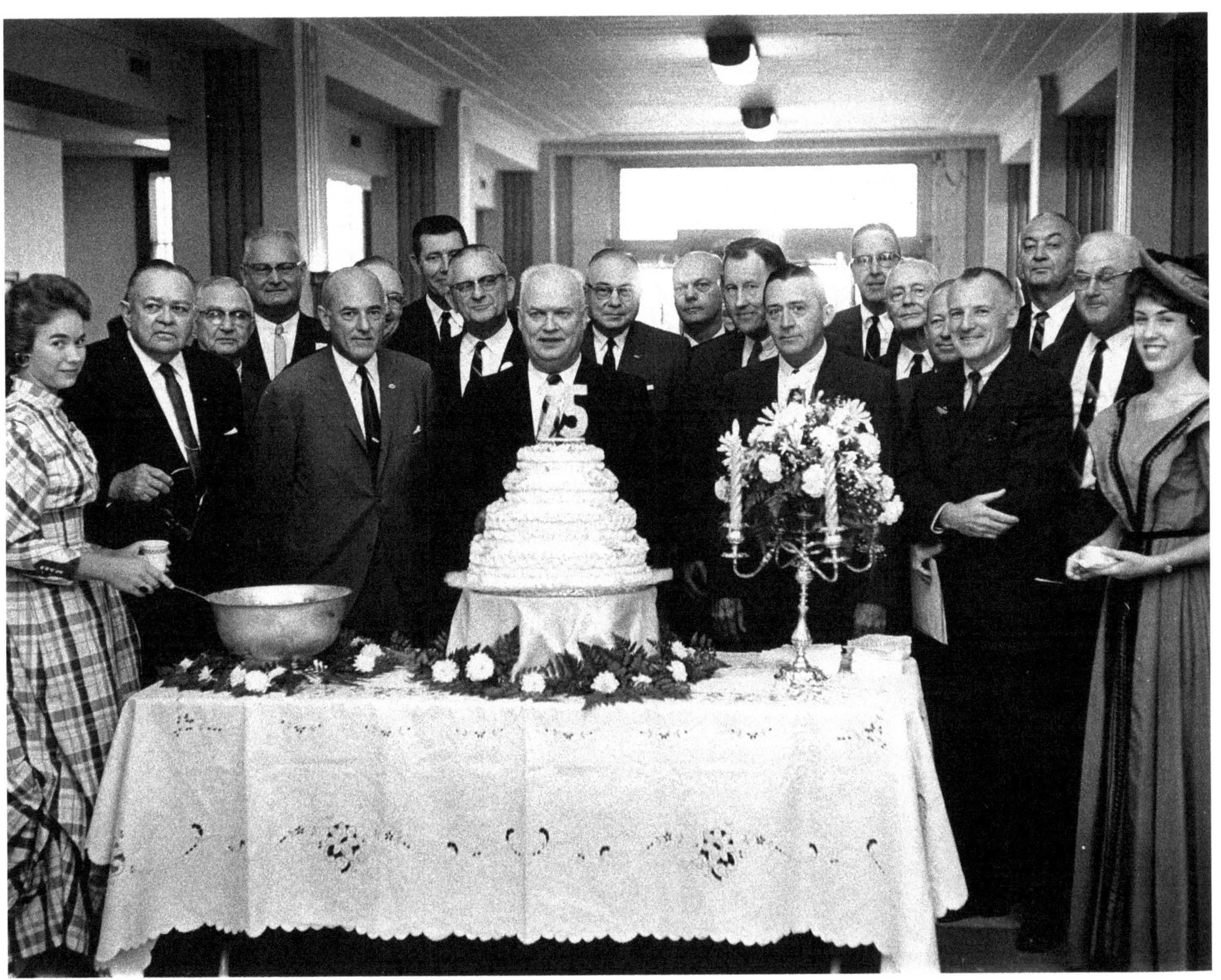

The Hamilton National Bank was a prominent financial institution in the 1960s as the large 75th anniversary cake denotes. Prominent guests of the 1964 celebration in this image include W. E. Brock, H. Clay Johnson, and John Kruesi. Banking then was a man's profession and women who worked in banks generally served as tellers and secretaries.

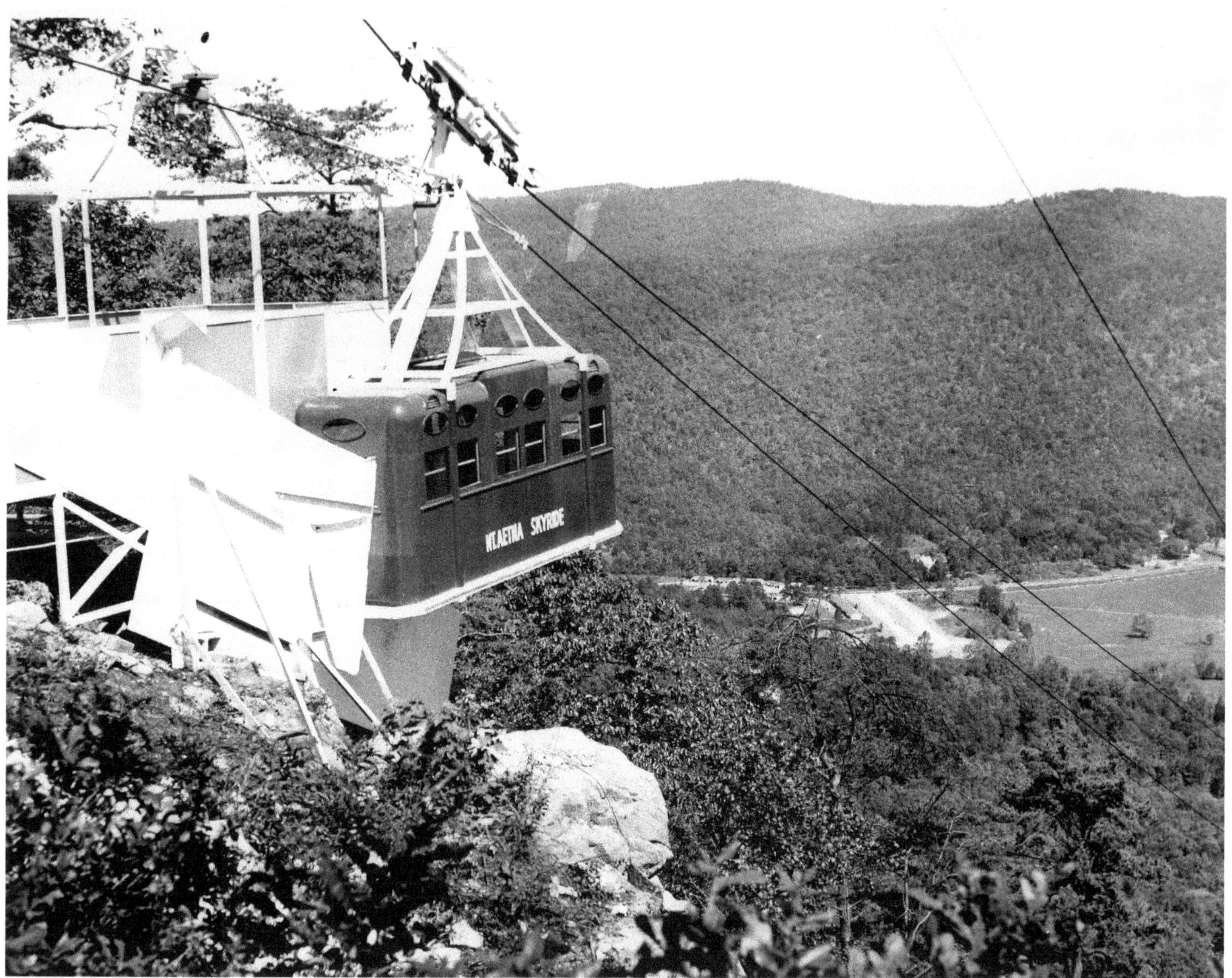

Lookout Mountain has its railway incline and for some time Raccoon Mountain had its airborne version, the Mt. Aetna Skyride. Seen here around 1965, the year it opened, the suspended cable car ride complemented the tourist attraction called Crystal Cave in the Lookout Valley, but a year later the terminal at the bottom of the ride went up in flames. Though it was replaced, the sky cabs could not generate enough popularity to remain in business and closed in 1984.

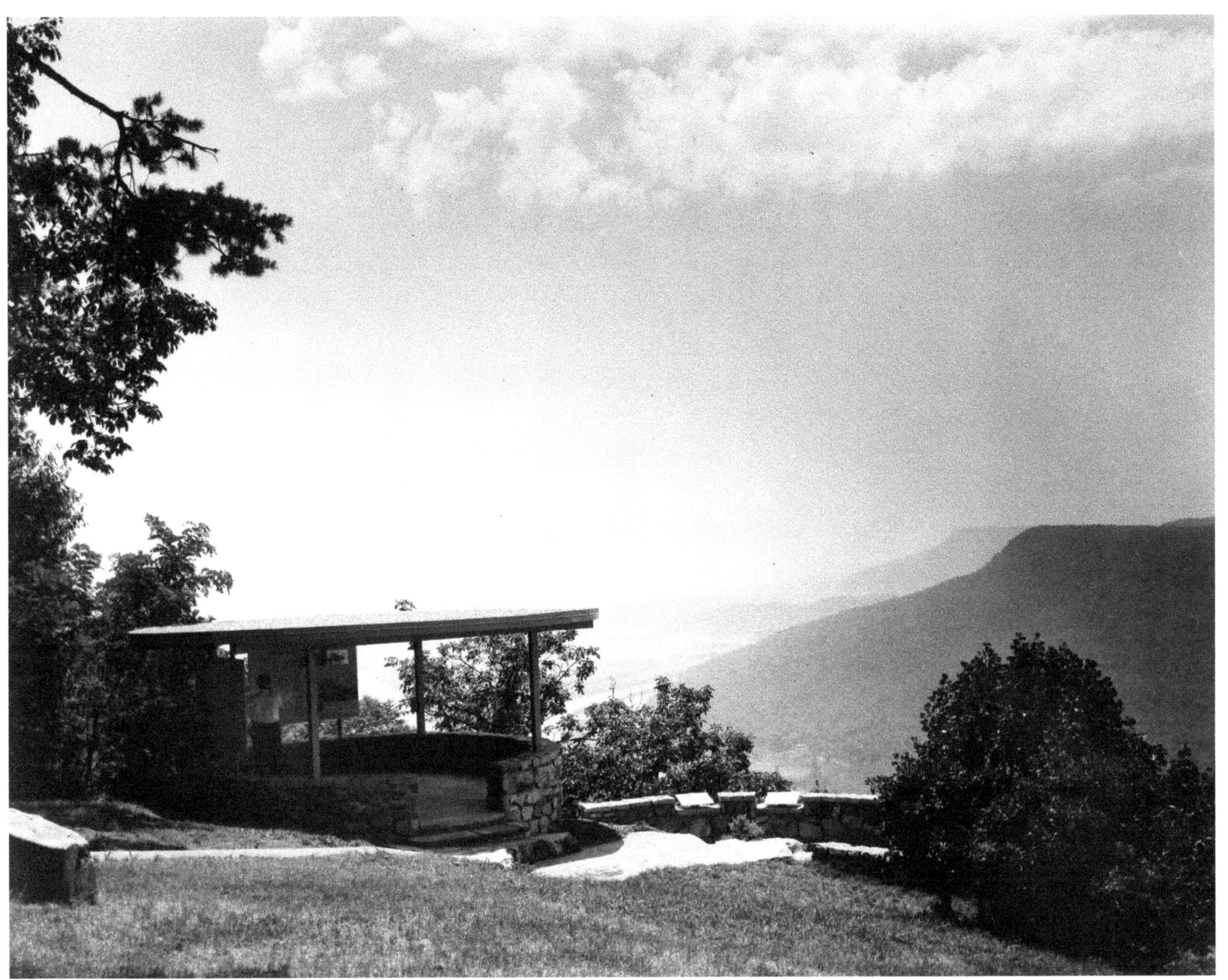

In the Civil War, Signal Mountain served as a route into Chattanooga for Yankee supply trains. Its southern tip became a place where signal corps could communicate with other troops about placement and strategy because of the clear view of the river valley below. Known as Signal Point, it became a park in 1948 thanks to the Signal Mountain Garden Club and later was folded into the Chickamauga and Chattanooga National Military Park. This is Signal Point around 1966.

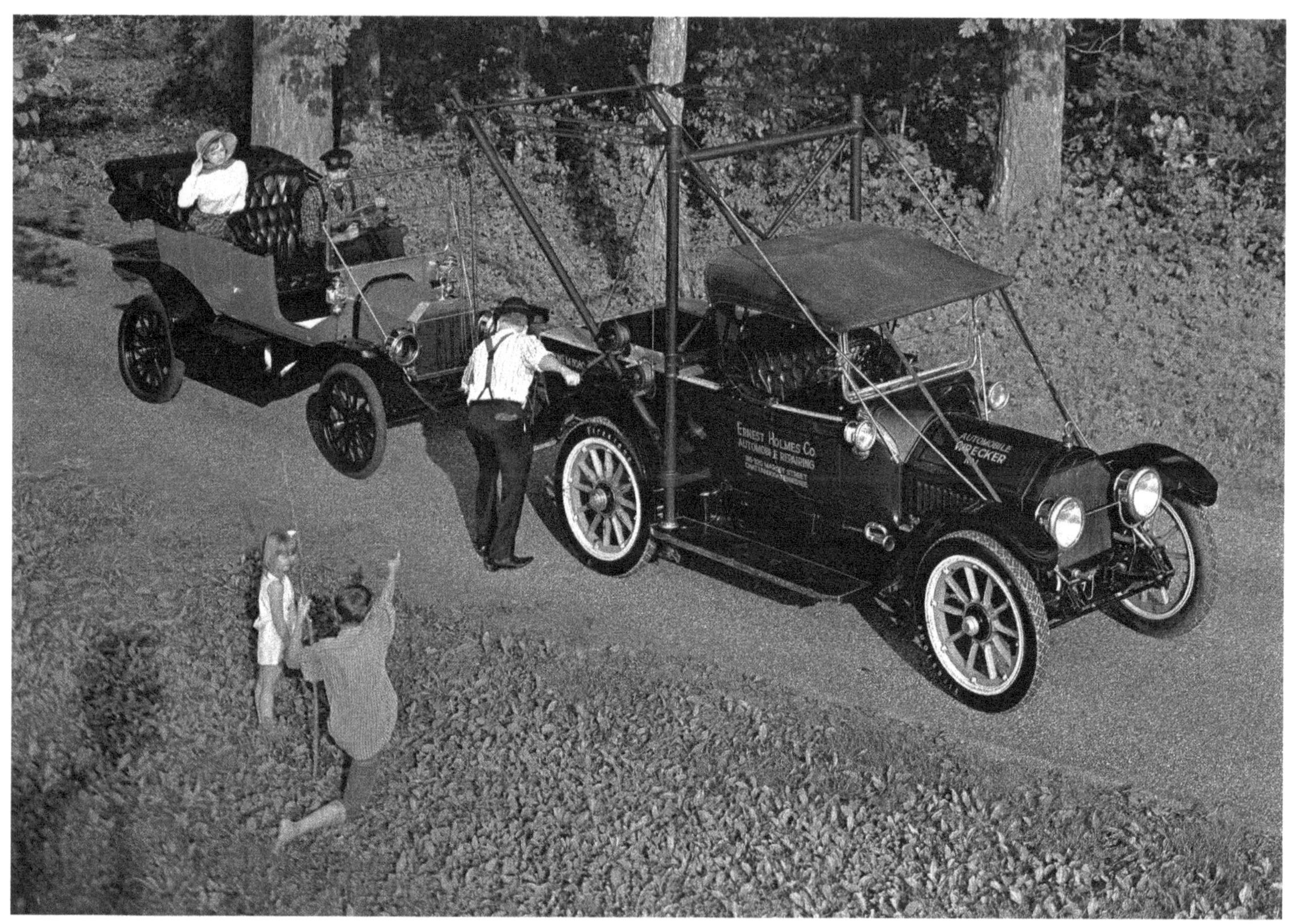

This 1966 reenactment of an automobile wrecker towing a car pays homage to one of Chattanooga's entrepreneurs, Ernest Holmes, inventor of the tow truck. In the early days of the automobile, this rescue vehicle could be a life saver. In a mountainous region like Tennessee, where wet roads, tall hills, and primitive brakes were standard, Holmes's tow truck seemed to fulfill the proverb that "necessity is the mother of invention."

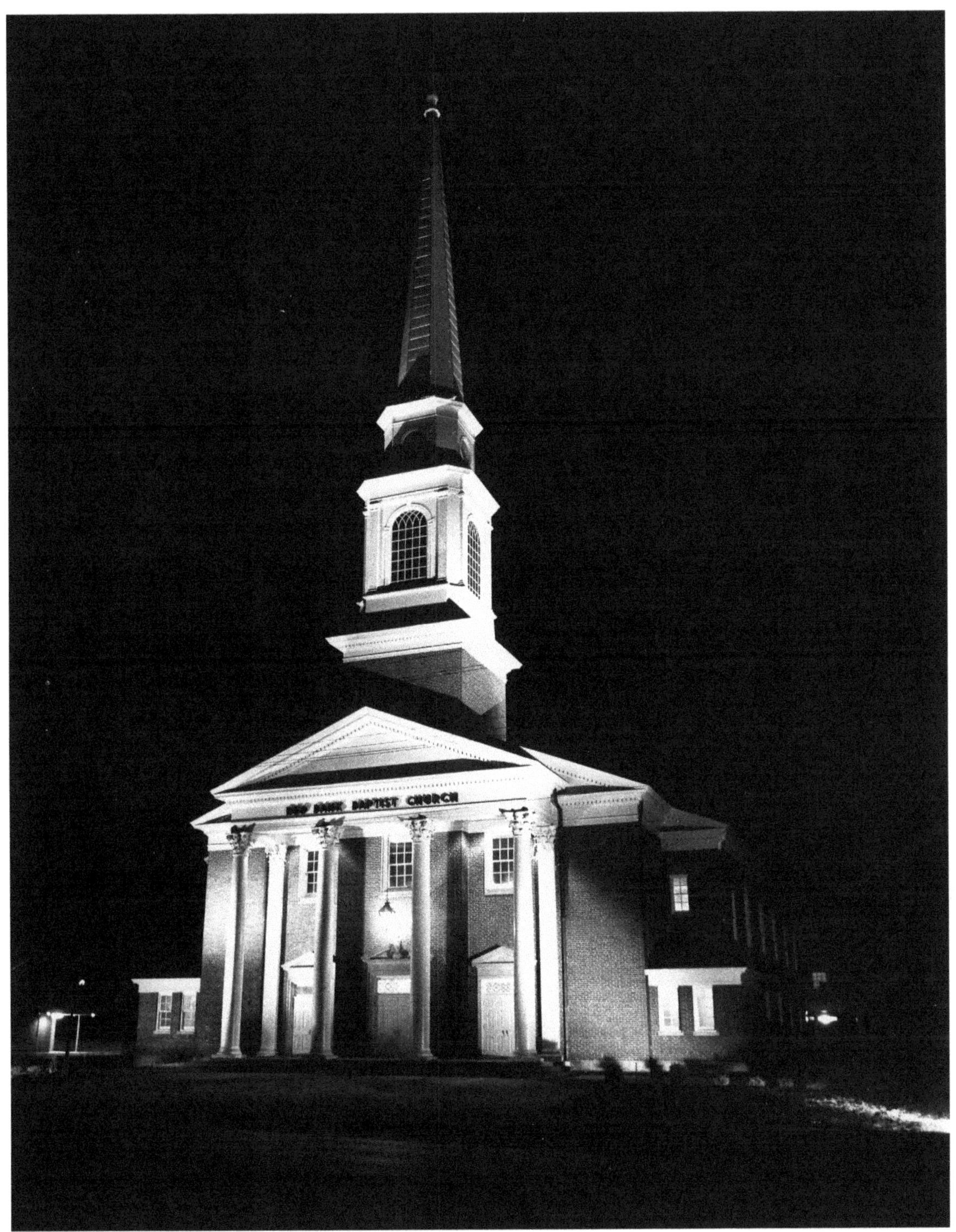

A dramatic night view of the Red Bank Baptist Church on Dayton Boulevard around 1967 reveals a modern interpretation of Classical style religious architecture, complete with columns, pediment, and a soaring spire. Churches of many traditions are a common sight around the city, where established congregations of the Church of Christ, Baptists, Methodists, and Presbyterians predominate, along with a fair number of other spiritual traditions.

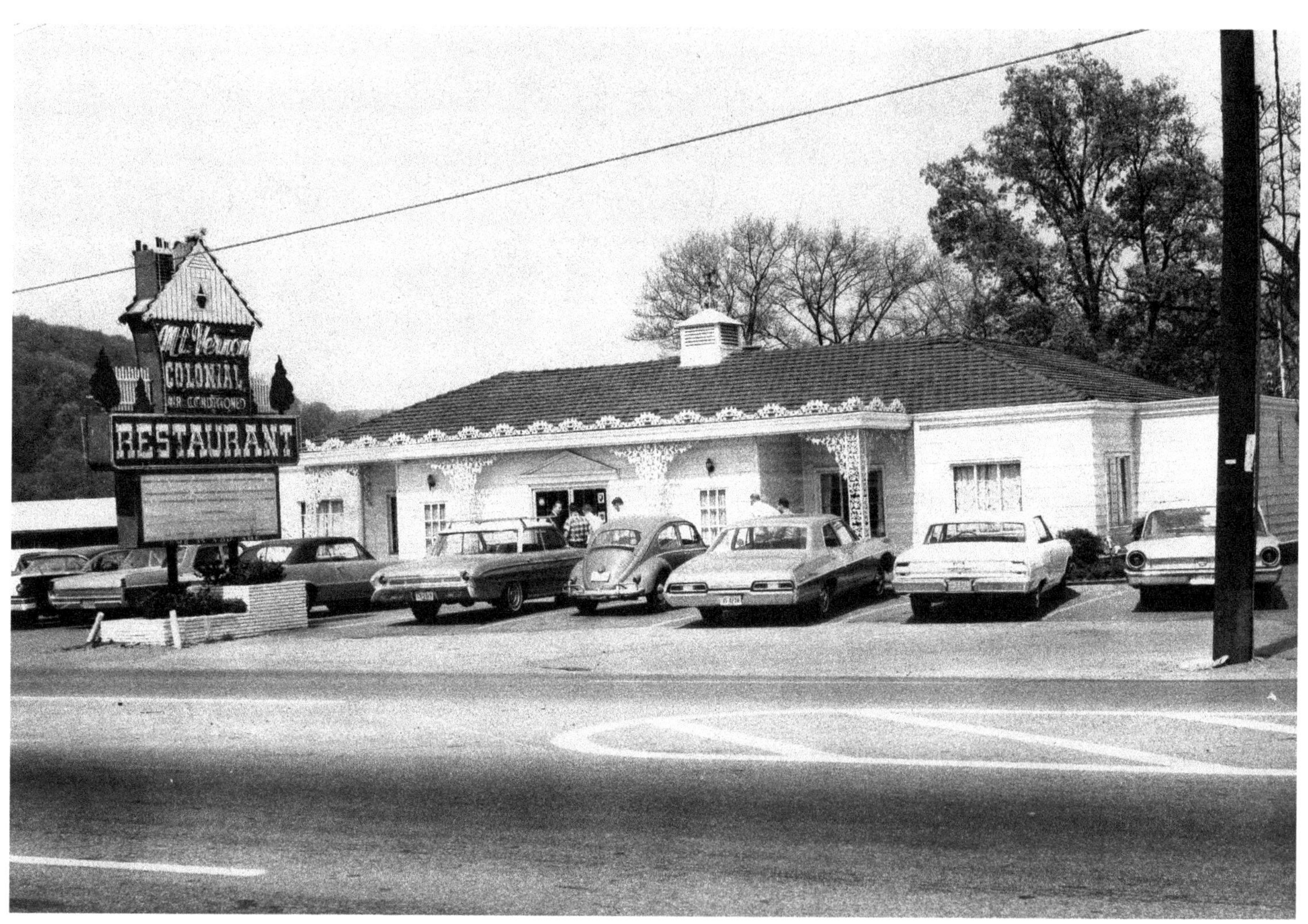

One of Chattanooga's best southern-style dining establishments is the Mount Vernon Restaurant at the foot of Lookout Mountain. With a small cupola on the rooftop, the restaurant makes reference to George Washington's home in Virginia. Inside, a quiet atmosphere with tasteful decor complements well-prepared dinners of vegetables and traditional fare, such as field peas, casseroles, and fried chicken, which have made this a local favorite since 1955. Hungry Chattanoogans have filled the parking lot in this image recorded around 1967.

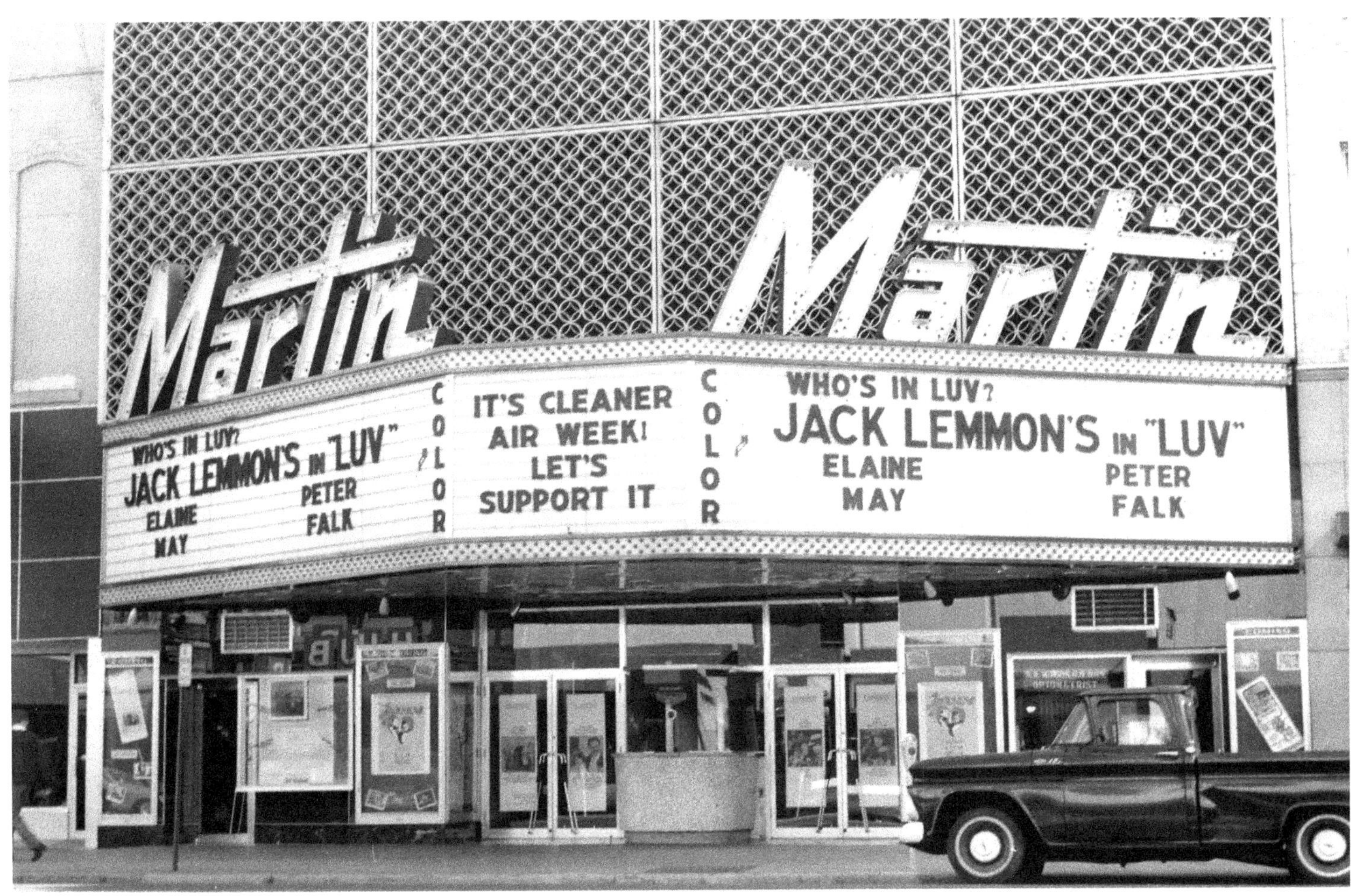

The Martin Theater's marquee announces "It's cleaner air week ! Let's support it" to passers-by on Market Street. In the sixties, film houses had only one, very large screen (fondly recalled by moviegoers unimpressed with the small screens of today) and usually served Coca-Cola, popcorn, and a candy bar. Cartoons preceded the movie; there were few trailers and, thank goodness, no advertisements. Playing here in 1967 is the new release *Luv,* starring Jack Lemmon.

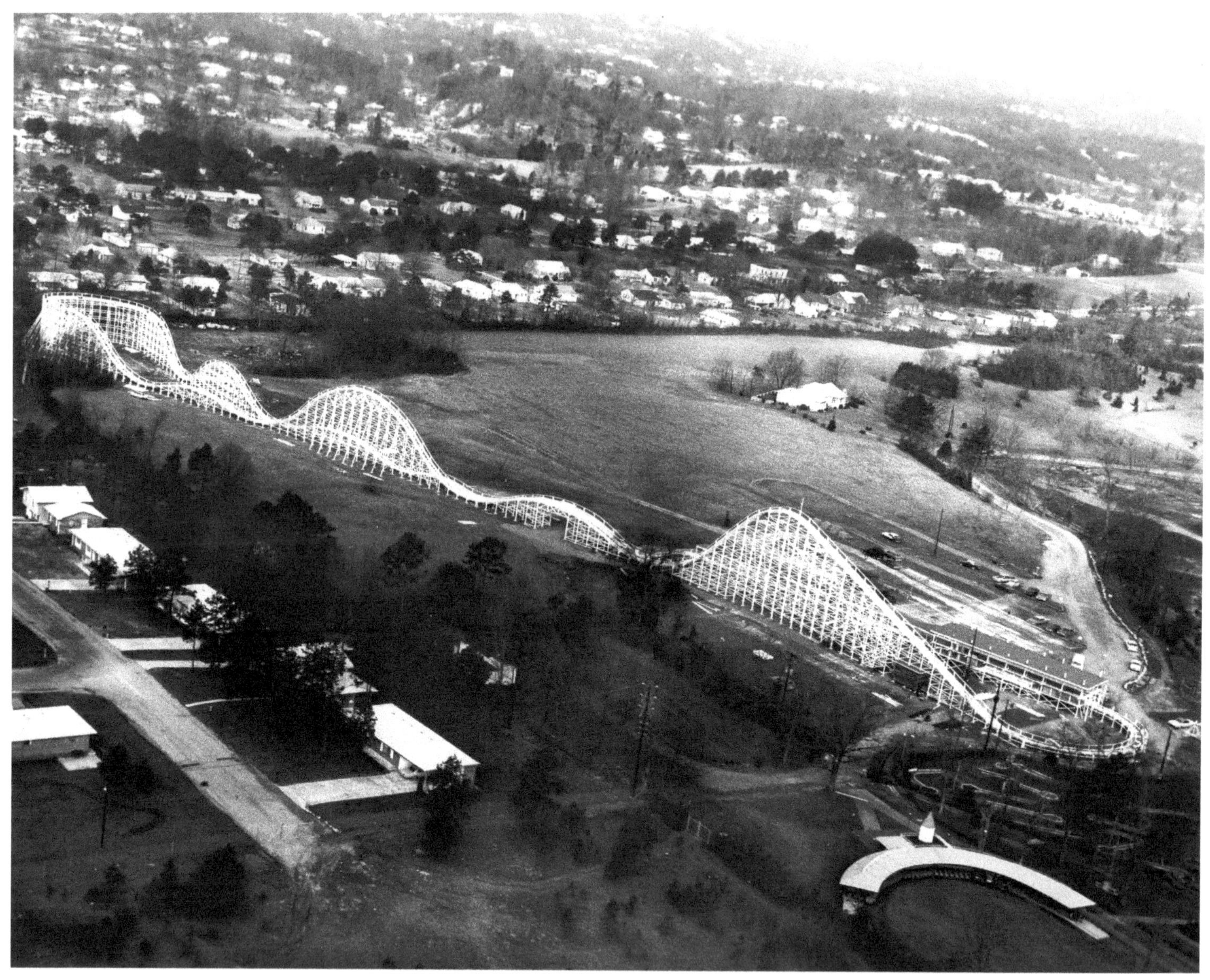

State fairs are always fun, but fleeting. Something of a permanently situated fair, Lake Winnepesaukah became Chattanooga's version of outdoor fun. Begun in 1925 and still operated today by the Dixon family, the park was built around a lake and featured the Boat Chute. Added in 1967 was a roller coaster, the Cannon Ball, that whipped riders up, down, and all around over its shiny rails.

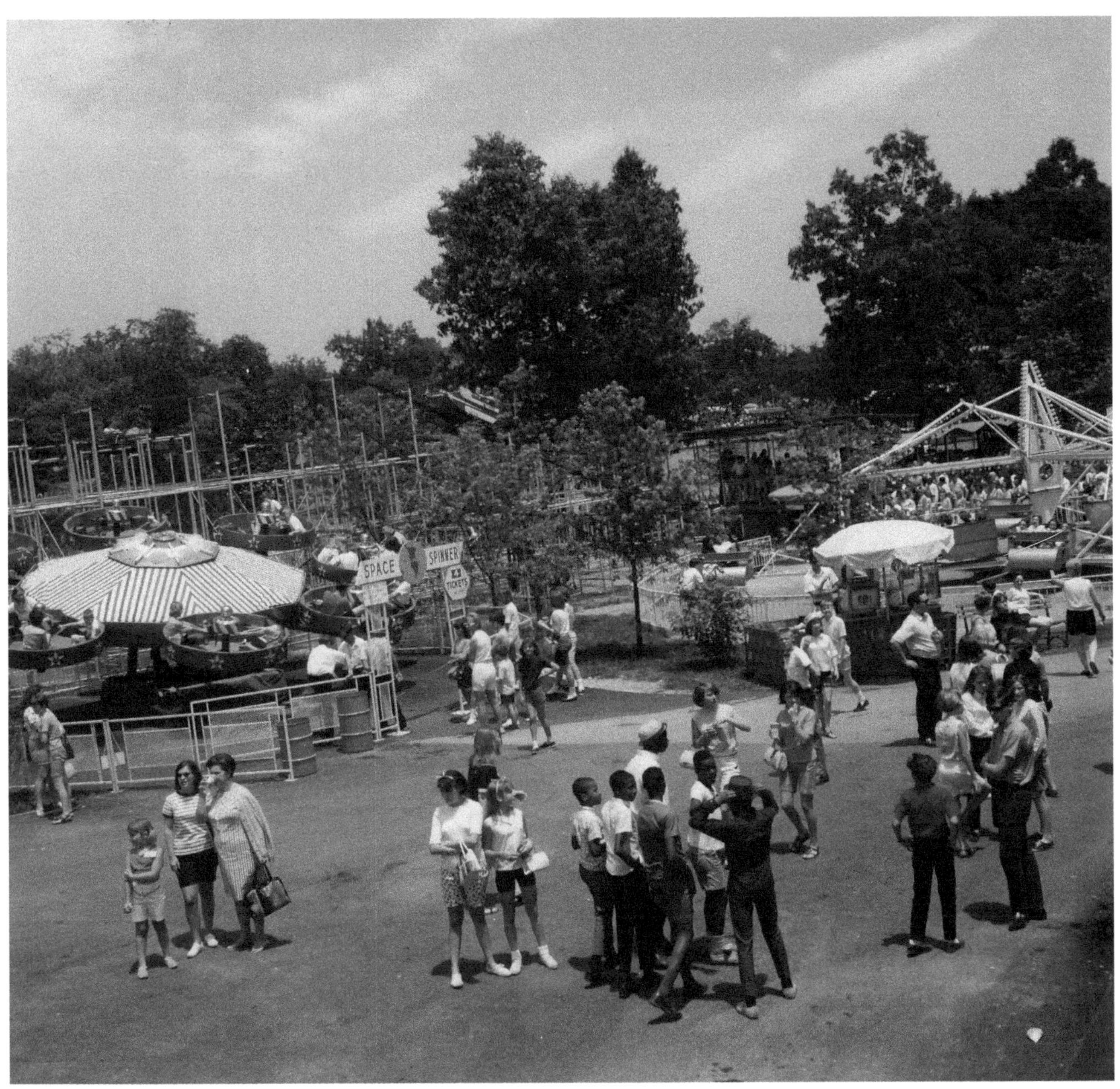

With rides and attractions primarily aimed at attracting families, Lake Winnie as it is known locally is a leading hangout for teenagers. Plenty of room, fun, food, and reasonably priced tickets make it a natural place for kids to meet and have aimless fun. Although considered a Chattanooga attraction, Lake Winnepesaukah is actually just over the Tennessee border in Rossville, Georgia.

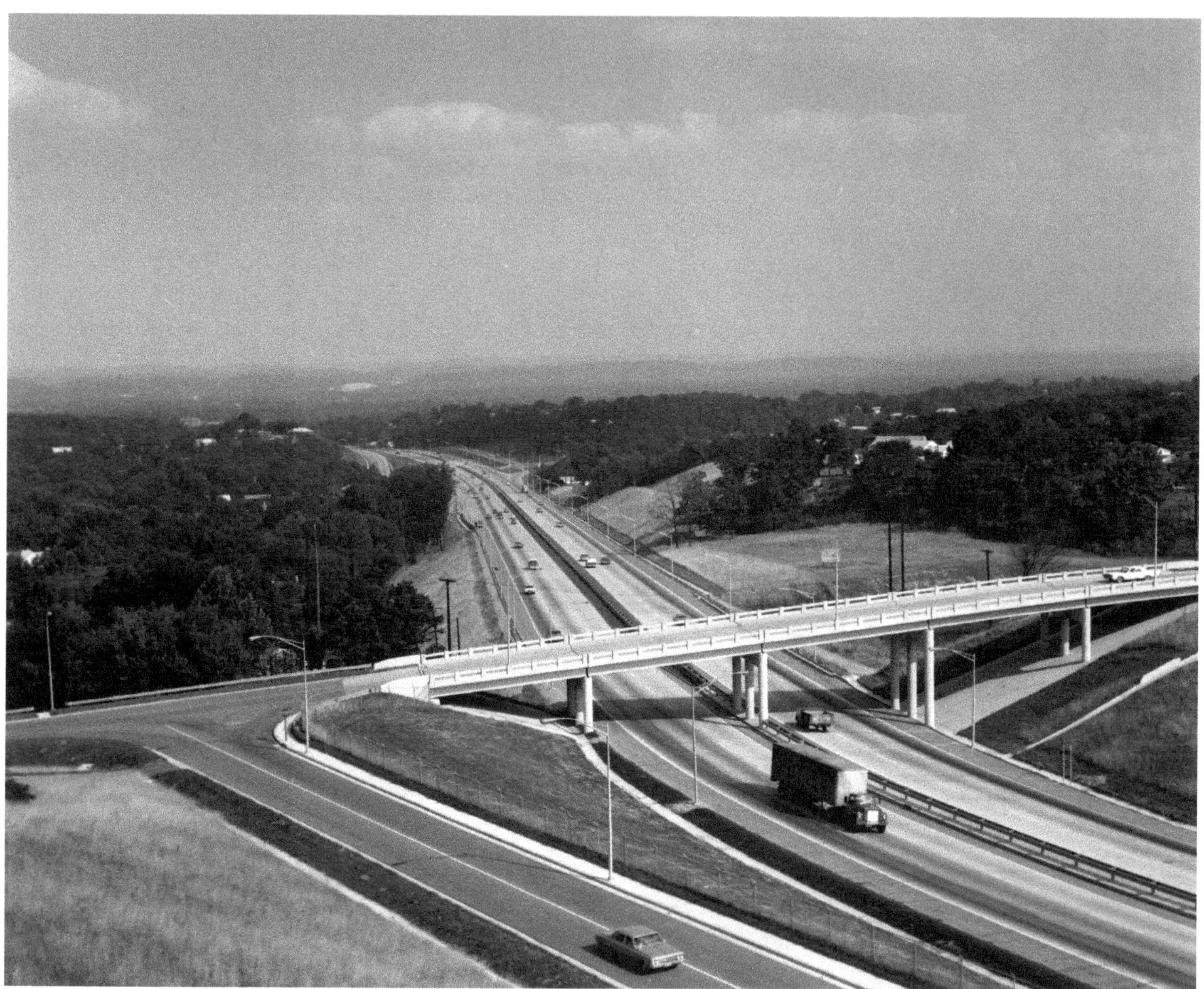

Looking at photographs of the modern interstate system that was built in the fifties and sixties, one is struck with the clean, almost pristine newness of the concrete roadways. In this view from 1967, greenery abounds and towering billboards are completely absent from the roadsides. Chattanooga lost a good deal of housing to this project, but being part of the highway system was vital to the city's commercial viability in the twentieth century.

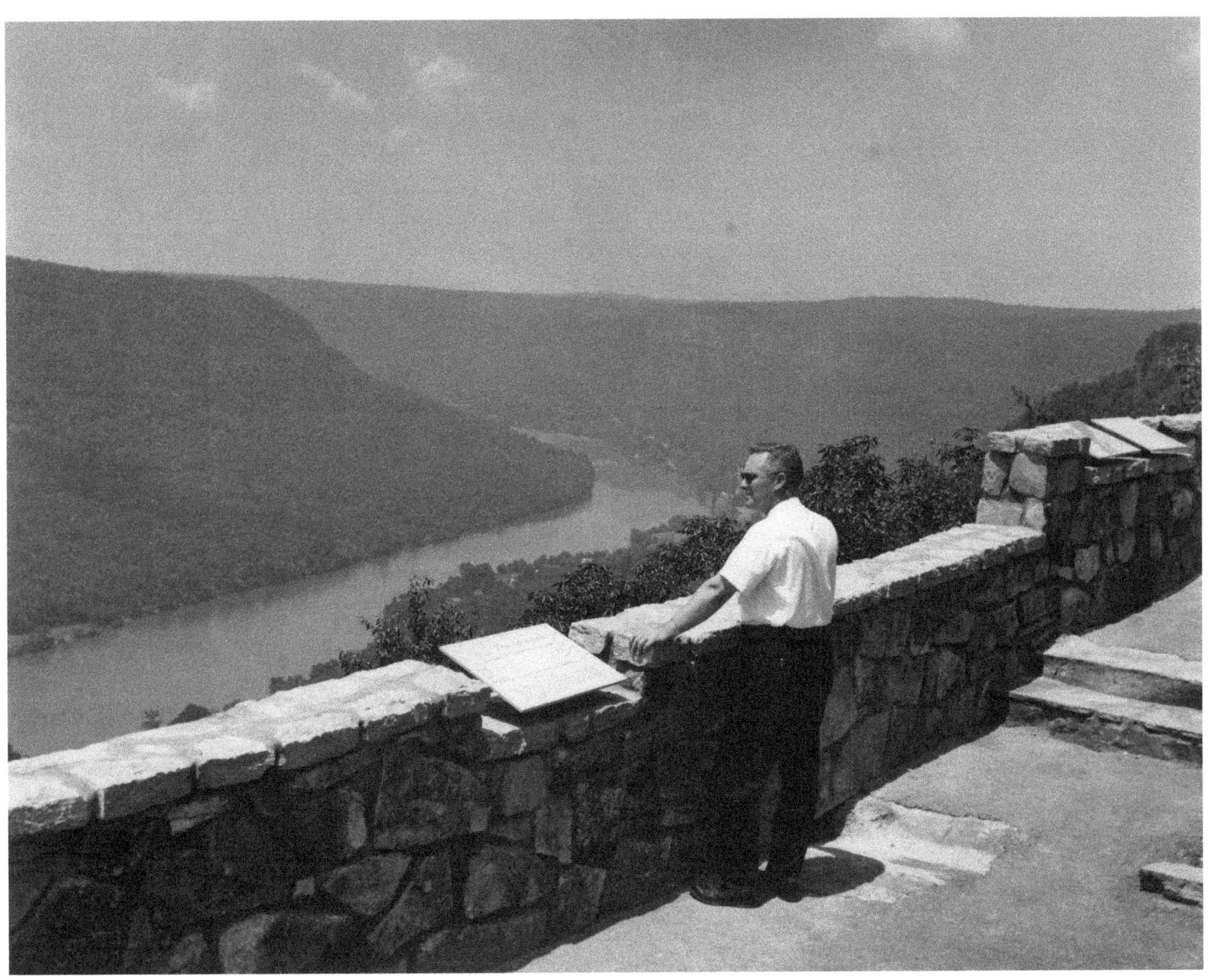

On the city's western edge is the beginning of the Grand Canyon of the Tennessee River. From here the river winds toward Alabama through a meandering series of long turns more than 20 miles long that take the water through the Tennessee River Gorge. Names like the Skillet, Deadman's Eddy, the Kettle, and the Suck recall the lethal rapids and uncertain currents that thwarted early settlers' journeys along the river.

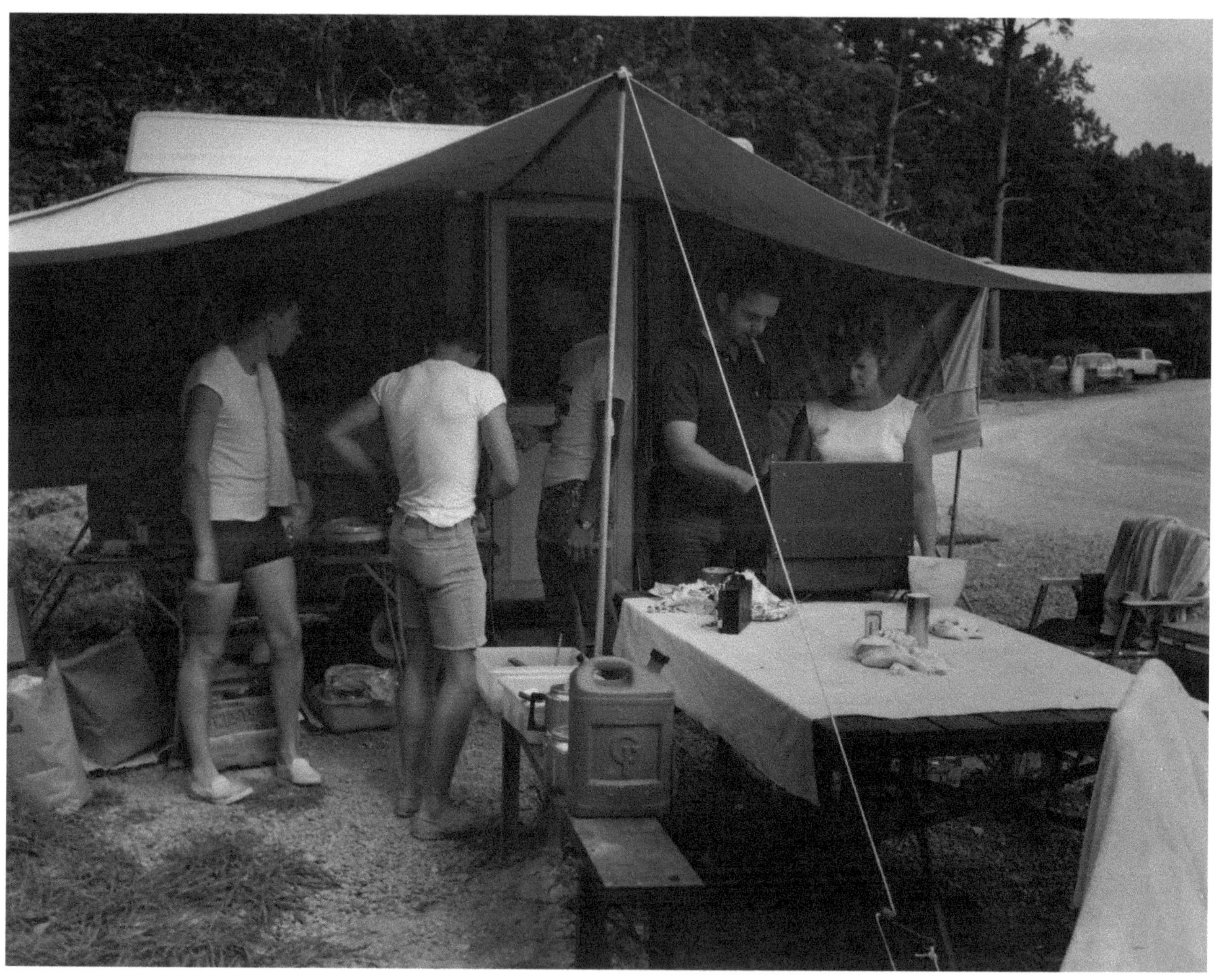

In the days before reinforced nylon, collapsible chairs, and freeze-dried food, campers had to pack some heavy equipment just to enjoy a weekend near home. These folks at Chickamauga Lake, where the swimming and fishing are good and the weather is warm, appear to be set up and ready to cook on their portable propane stove.

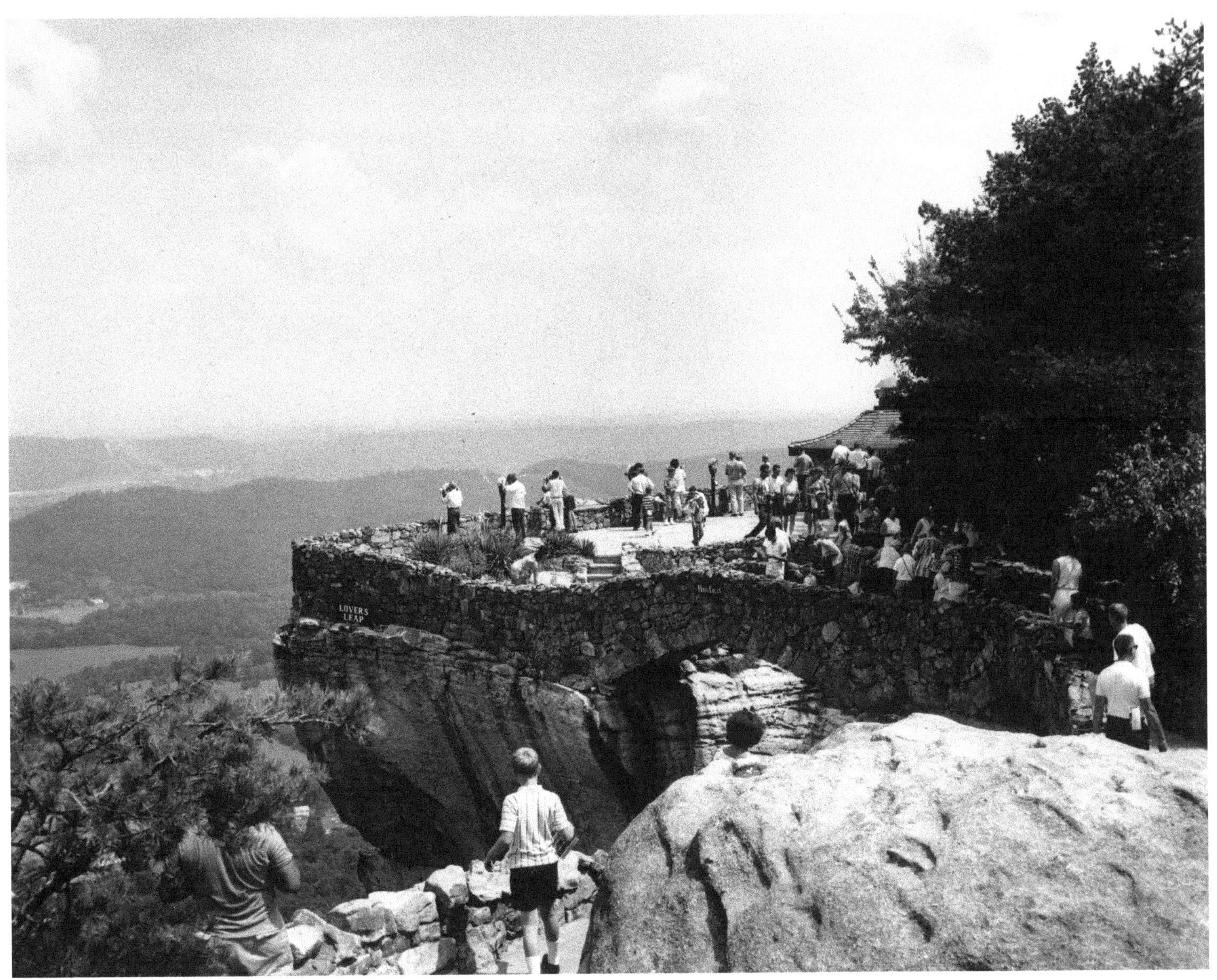

Lover's Leap at Rock City is located at the end of a path that winds through some stunning rock formations. A questionable legend about a Native American youth and his desperate love for a young woman from a rival tribe has been oft repeated for generations as the source for this name. Its veracity is as foggy as the claim that one can see seven states from the stone prominence.

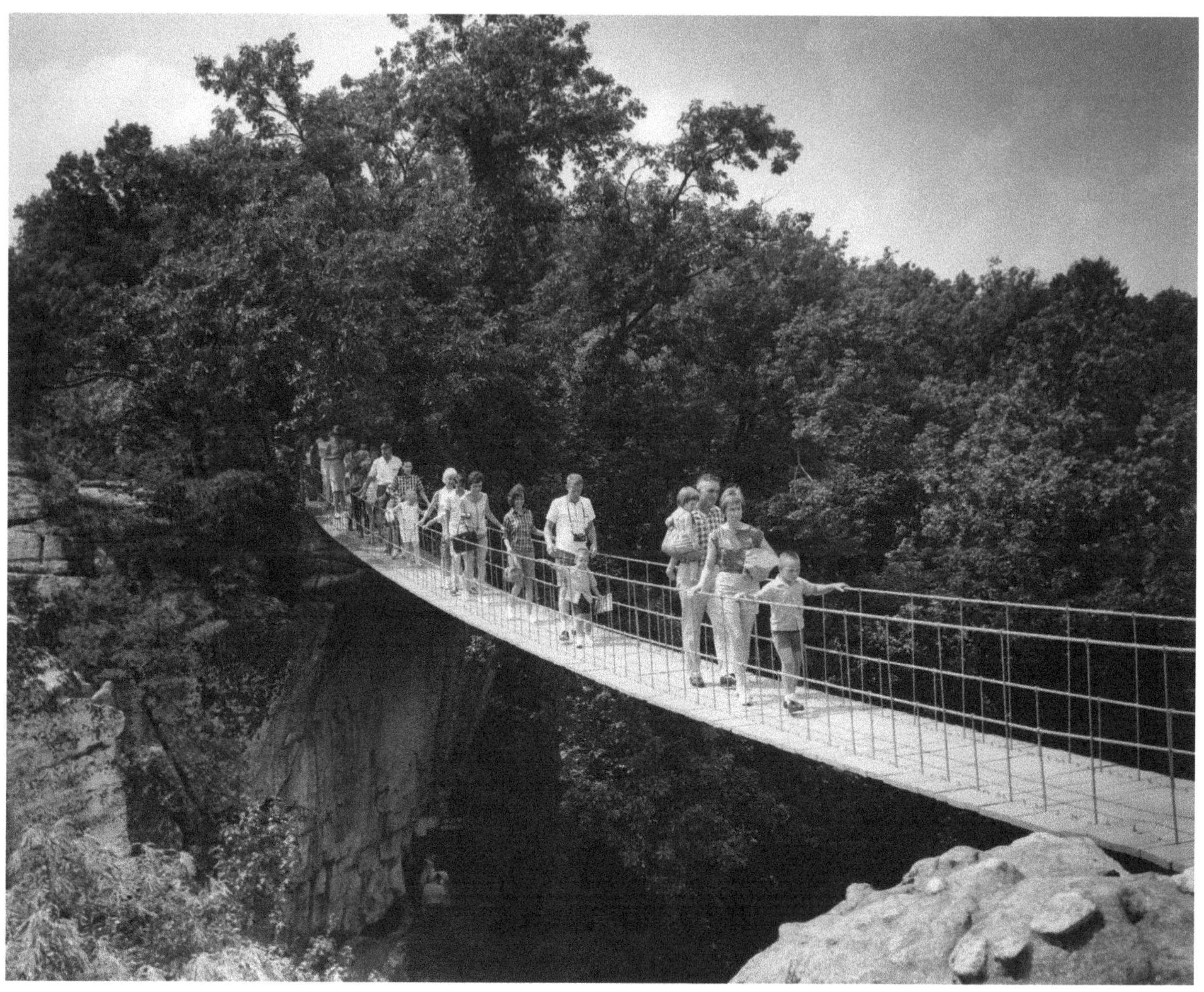

The first written description of the Rock City area was penned by missionary Daniel S. Butrick in 1823, who called it "a citadel of rocks." Not only do guests at Rock City have to slide through "Fat Man's Squeeze," they must also gingerly cross the "Swinging Bridge" between the enormous stones. Known for its bouncing motion, the bridge has handrails that the boy in front is gripping tightly.

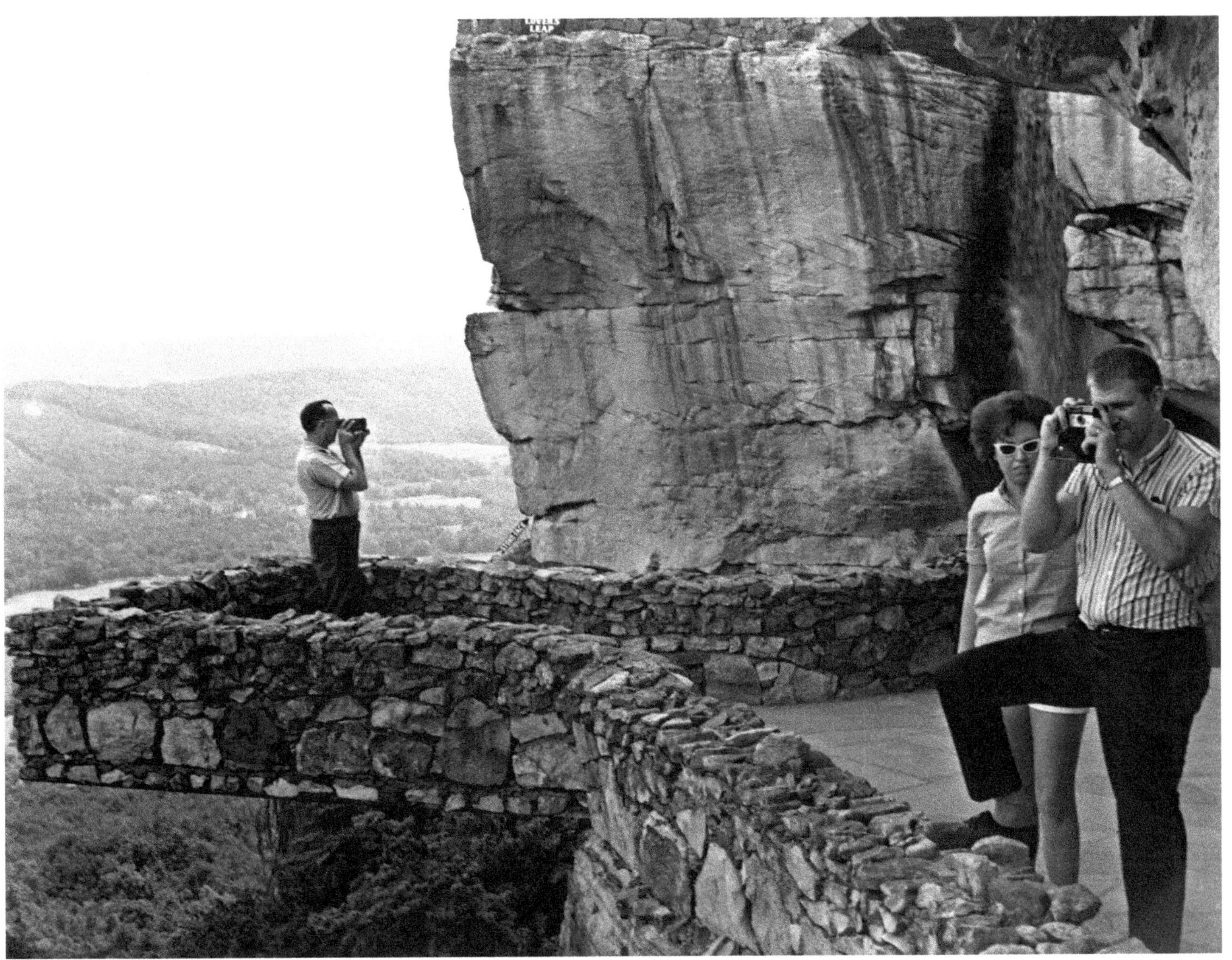

Rock City lends itself to walking, climbing, even speculation about the nature of geology and creation. But it is also a fabulous opportunity to take photographs of the vistas, the rock formations, and your own family. While one couple take a picture from the bluff, the man behind them aims his 8mm film at the waterfall, clearly entranced with his subject.

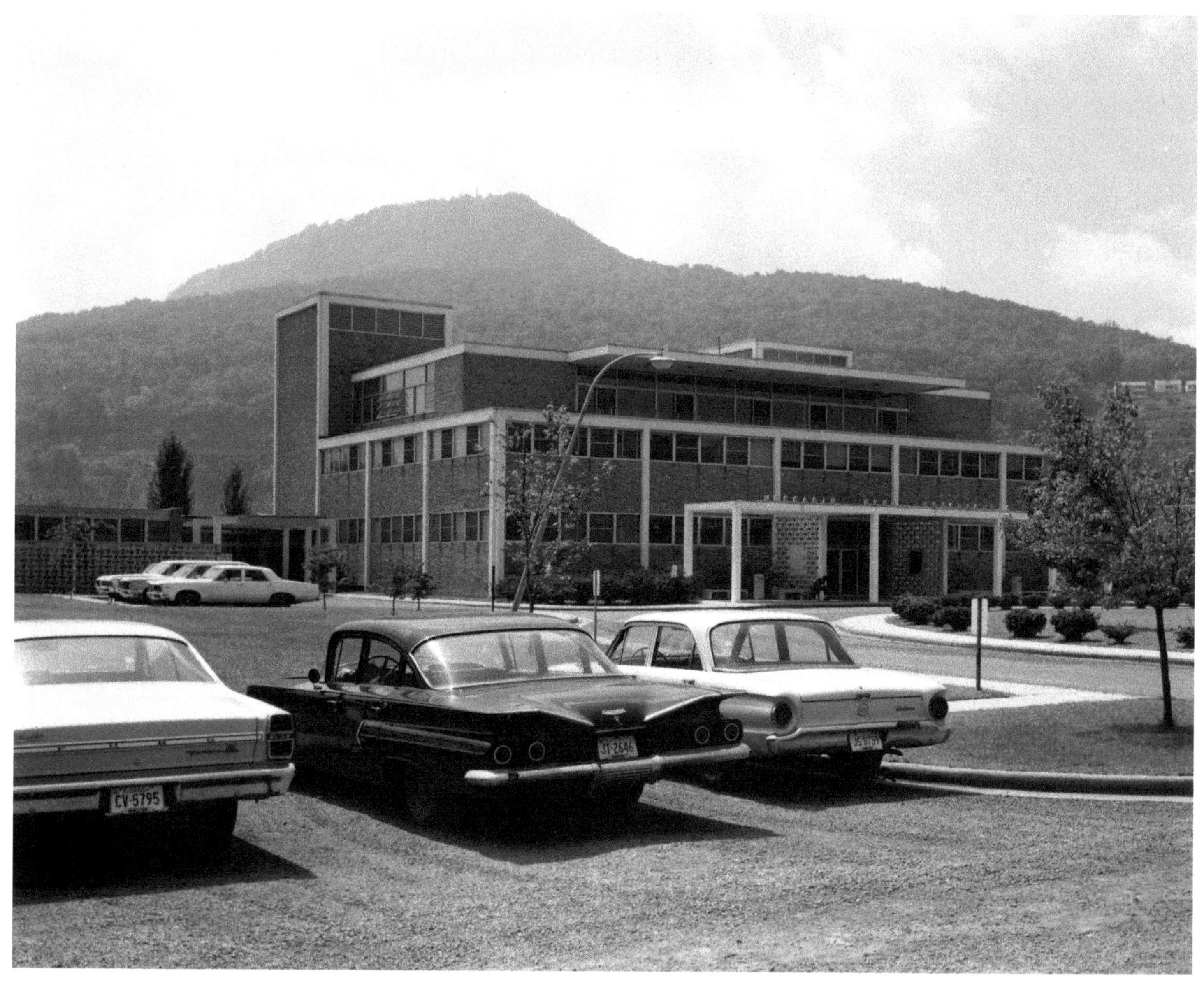

Mental illness has been shunted aside from public view for centuries. So when it came time to build a facility in east Tennessee to treat people with emotional difficulties, it is no surprise that the project was located in an out-of-the-way area. Moccasin Bend Psychiatric Hospital opened in Chattanooga in 1961 at the end of a solitary road on the bend as an intensive treatment facility with 150 beds.

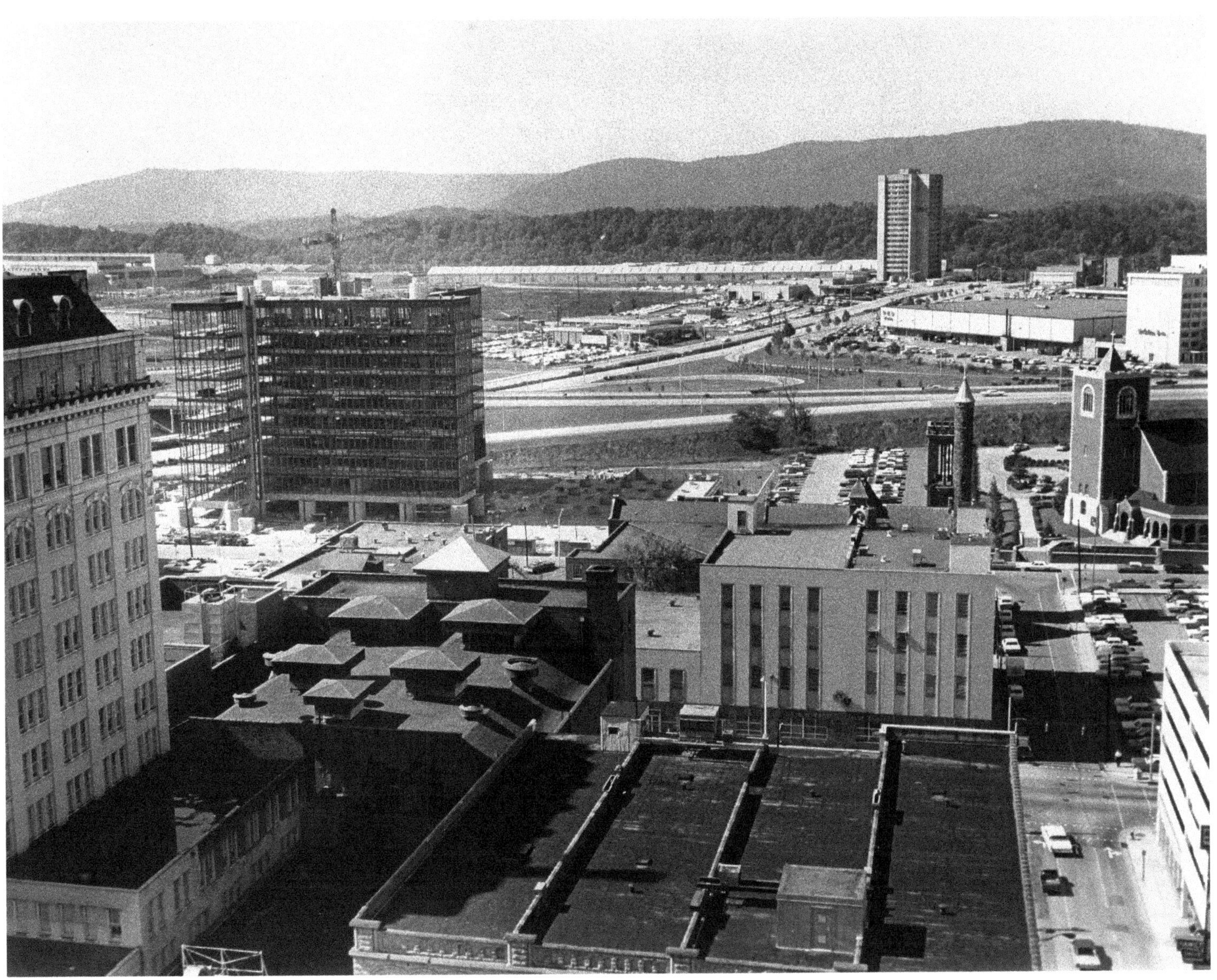

Urban renewal was in full swing by the mid-sixties as this view from 1968 facing west from atop Broad Street makes clear. Under construction on Chestnut Street (to the left) is one of the first important buildings by famed Atlanta architect John Portman, a structure finished in highly reflective, copper-colored glass. Beyond is the "Golden Gateway," an area for shops and car dealerships built after the south end of Cameron Hill was flattened.

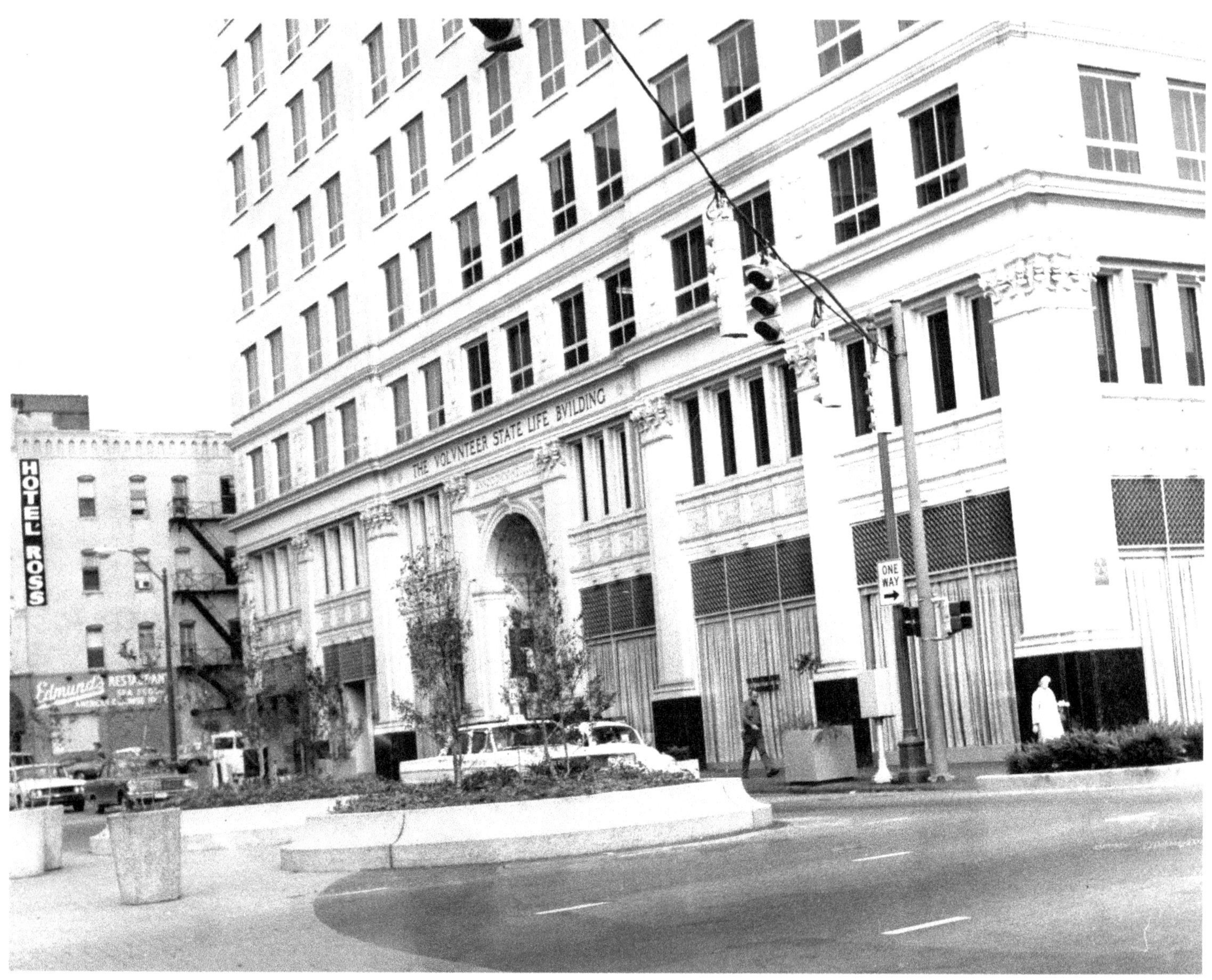

With the decline of downtown areas all over the nation came efforts to lure businesses and shoppers back to the cities. One of Chattanooga's efforts was to beautify intersections, such as this one at Georgia Avenue and Ninth Street with its concrete, circular planter and a brick walkway, to make the city greener and more hospitable. Standing at the intersection is the Volunteer State Life Insurance Building, underwritten by Z. C. Patten, which opened in 1917 as the tallest structure in the city. The building and planter are seen here around 1968

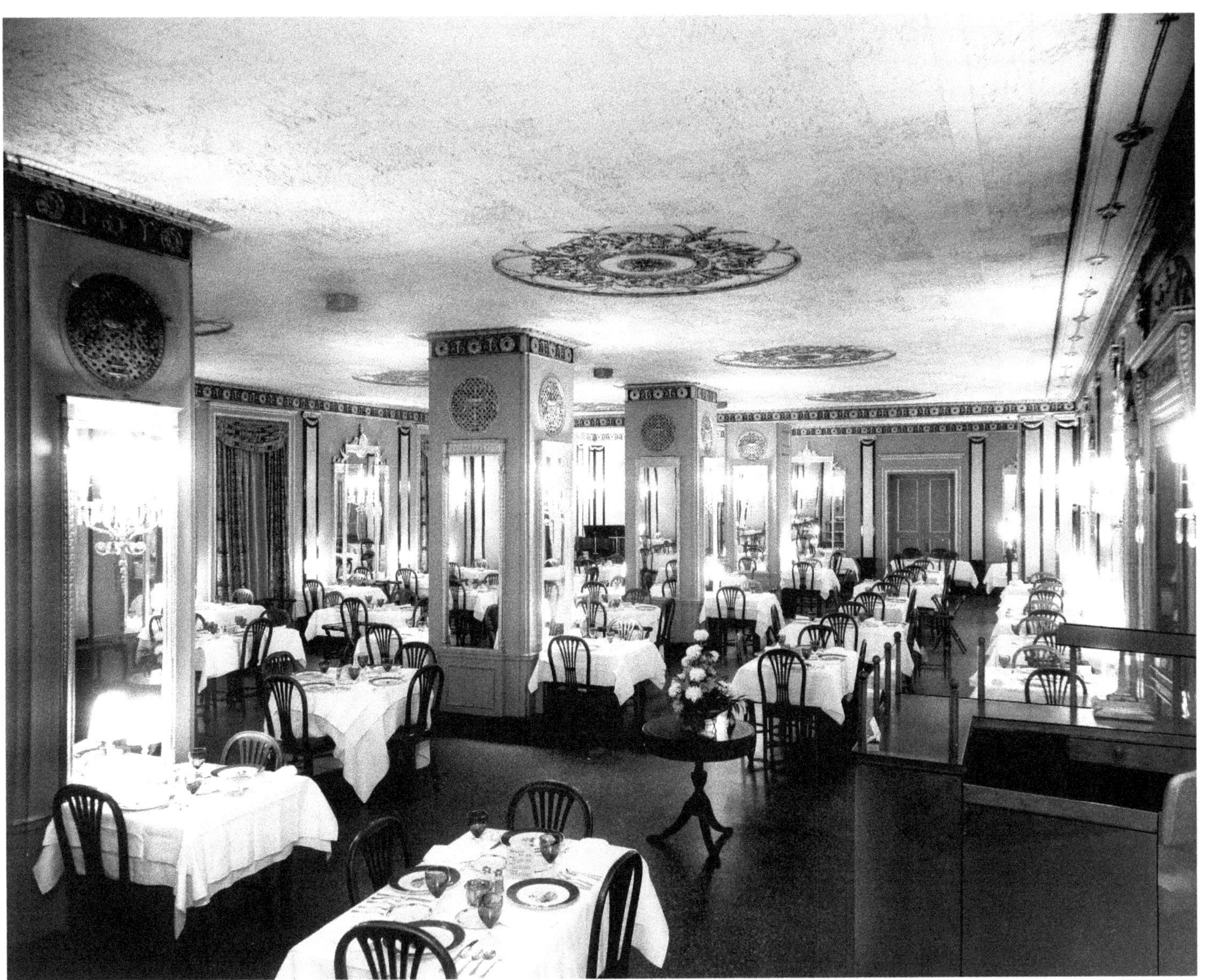

Elegant dining has always thrived in certain places, and in the sixties a seated dinner with linen table cloths, tasteful lighting, and well spoken waiters was assured in the Green Room at the Read House. Built in 1871, then razed and rebuilt in 1926, Samuel Read's hotel prided itself as being the best in town, and the service and food in the Green Room always set the standard for fine dining. This is the Green Room around 1968. Only blocks away from the Tennessee Aquarium, today the Read House is owned and operated by Sheraton.

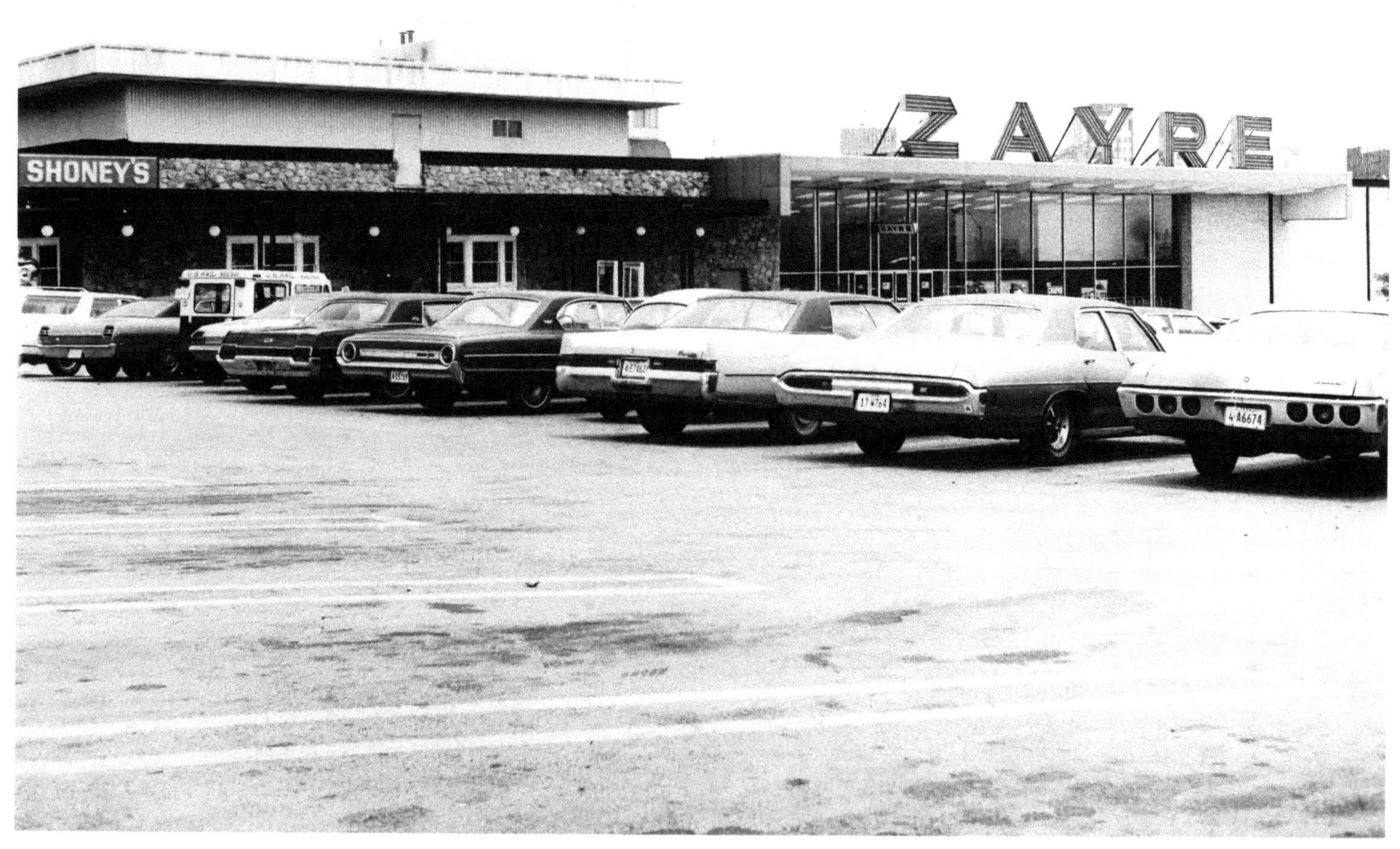

With government urban renewal came the replacement of old housing with fresh parking lots and new retail stores on Chattanooga's west side. On West Ninth Street, a shopping center was constructed with a Shoney's Restaurant. Beside it was one of the modern, mass retailers of the sixties, Zayre's, full of a wide variety of moderately priced wares and few sales associates, all under rows and rows of fluorescent lighting. This was the scene around 1969.

New Visions of Old

(1970–1979)

By 1970 the city was changing. People were moving to the suburbs or to other parts of the country. Overall population was declining. Chattanooga's economic engine of heavy industry was faltering as foreign imports and cheap labor overseas eliminated area jobs. Even the Chattanooga Coca-Cola Bottling Company, long a staple of the downtown landscape on Broad Street, moved to Amnicola Highway in 1970. An era ended on May 1, 1971, when the L&N train, the Georgian, made its last run, ending local passenger service. TVA, however, was still ascendant as a government agency and began construction on a power facility, the Sequoyah Nuclear Power Plant, north of town, as well as the less conspicuous Raccoon Mountain Pumped-Storage Hydro Plant.

A new mayor, Robert Walker, struggled as businesses fled downtown for shopping centers in Brainerd and in Hixson. Racial conflict boiled over when a Wilson Pickett concert in May 1971 became the flash point for a race riot that brought the national guard into the city. Nevertheless, attempts to make over Market Street and the downtown area yielded some success. Miller Park was created at Market and Ninth streets as an urban park; Miller Plaza followed, becoming an enduring Friday night gathering spot for music and entertainment. In 1976, a new state-of-the-art public library opened on Broad Street. Chattanooga elected Marilyn Lloyd as its first woman to serve in Congress. In sports a young student named Reggie White was astonishing the public with his football prowess at Howard High, setting a course for a legendary career in the NFL. And Baylor graduate Roscoe Tanner gained international fame on the tennis court with his big left-handed serve.

In 1978, the Walnut Street Bridge was declared unsafe and readied for the wrecking crew. But the proposed demolition outraged Chattanoogans and they rose to defend this gray lady. The span was saved and became "the walking bridge," a pedestrian thoroughfare. The preservation of this link to the past inspired citizens to study the city's natural heritage in the Tennessee River Gorge, Moccasin Bend, and the riverway and consider the positive source of city origins. Meetings began and a common vision arose that would begin to build on the past to create a better day for the city by the river.

Outside of a horse and buggy ride, few things are as old-fashioned as riding a paddleboat on a lake on a summer's eve, but that is exactly what Lake Winnepesaukah offers to summer visitors. Of course it may not be a serene and peaceful ride, since the amusement park centers on the lake and offers water rides that elicit screams and whoops from the excited crowds. These paddlers are enjoying a sunset around 1970.

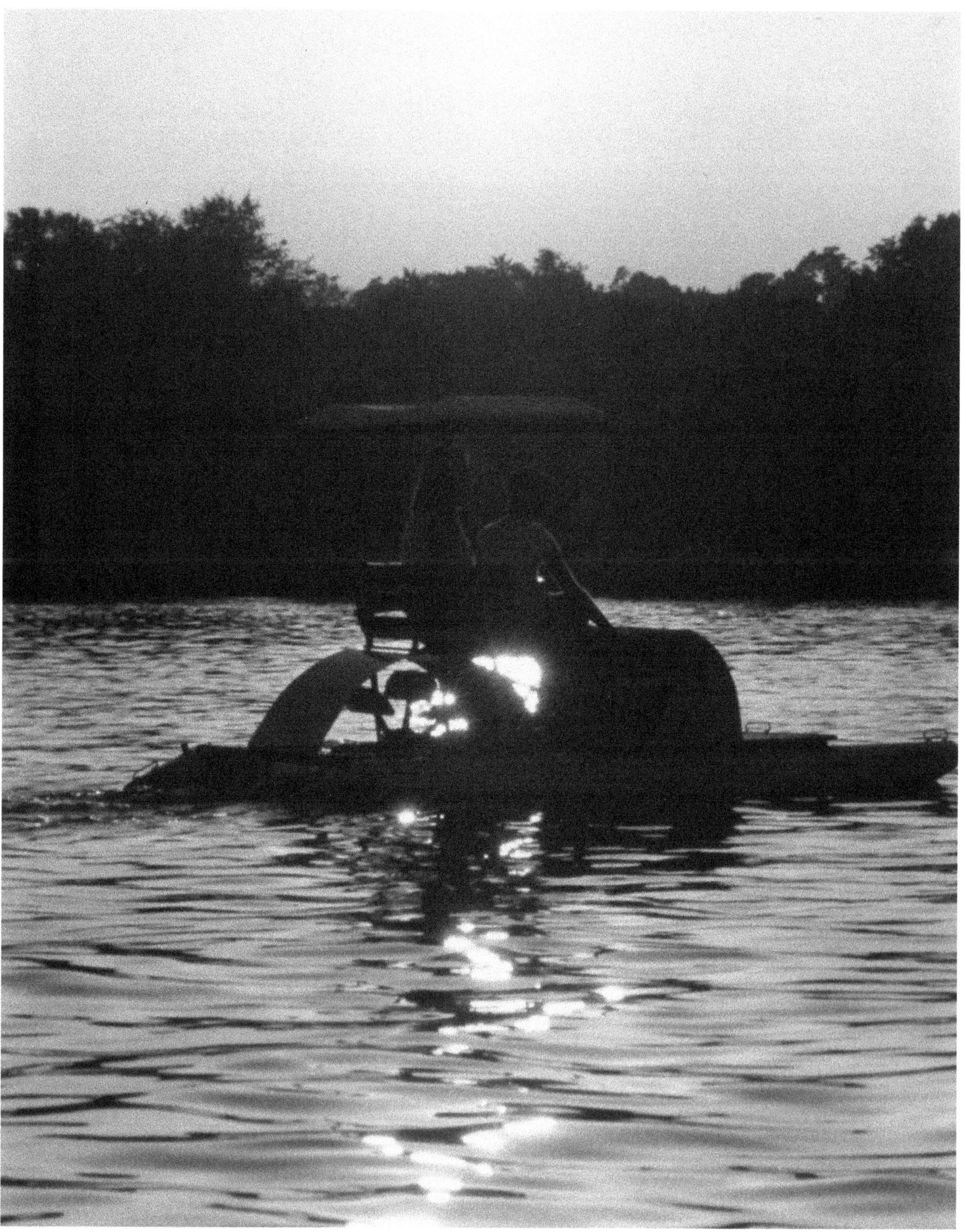

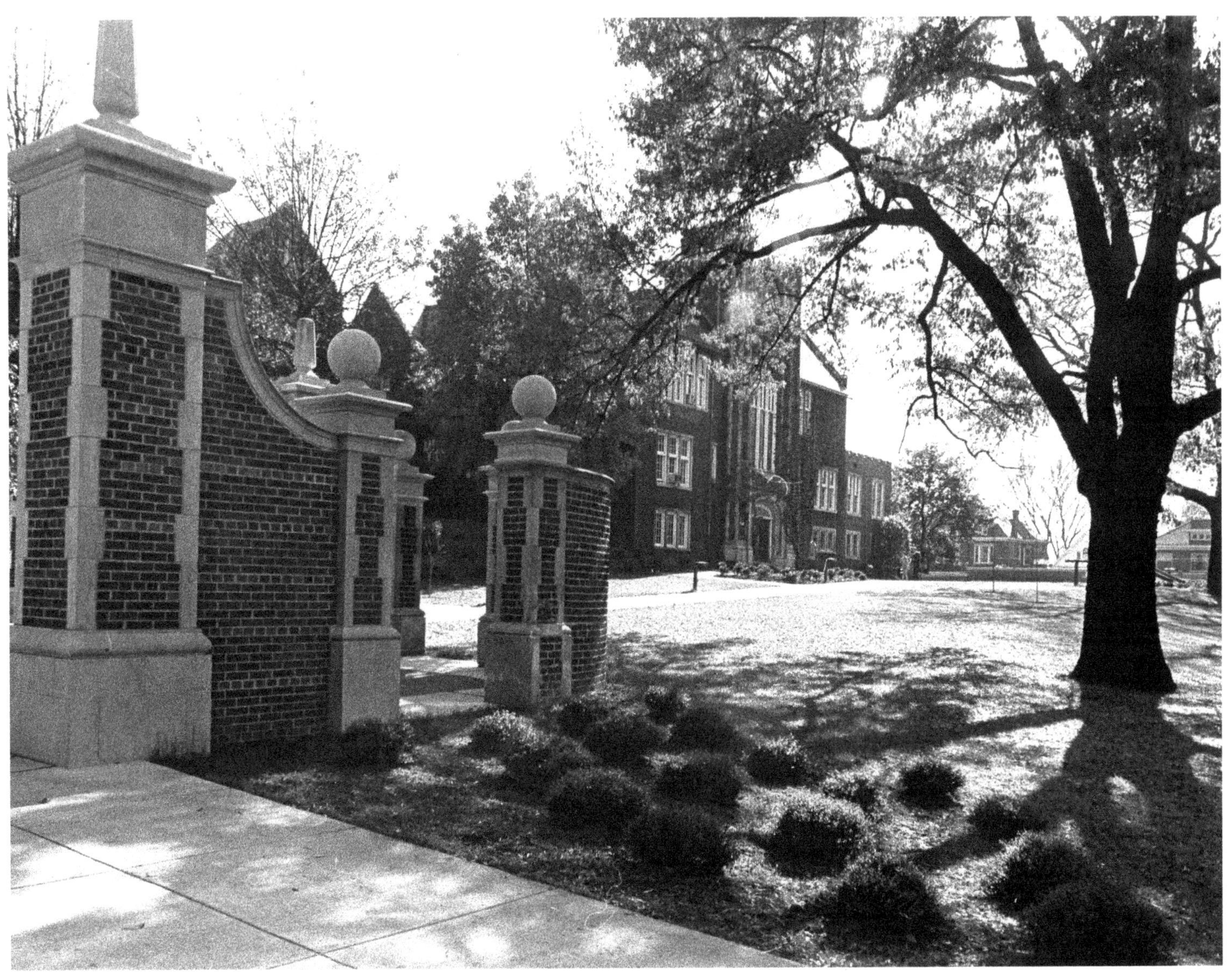

The University of Chattanooga began on this hillock on McCallie Avenue. The original structure, an enormous Victorian edifice called Old Main, was demolished, making way for the pictured Founders Hall in 1916 and giving this part of the campus the classic appearance of a liberal arts institution with an open lawn and gracious trees arching over the bricked walks. This view of the campus was recorded around 1970.

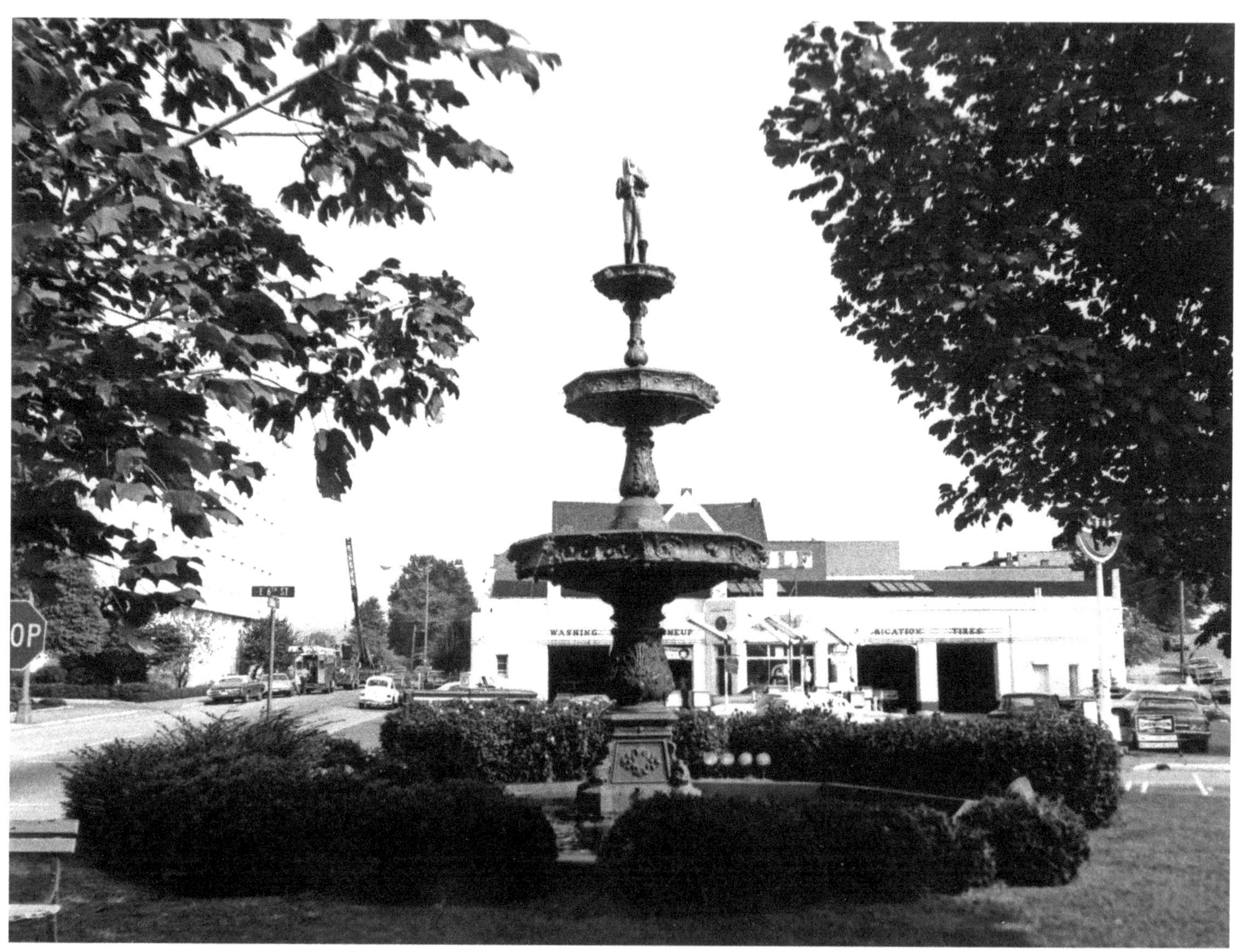

A solemn, understated, three-tiered fountain rises on a triangle of grass near the old Gulf Station on Georgia Avenue. Dedicated in June of 1888 and known as the Fireman's Fountain, the monument stands as a testimony to the bravery of two men, William Peak and Henry Iler, who answered a call of distress on Market Street and lost their lives fighting the ferocity of the blaze.

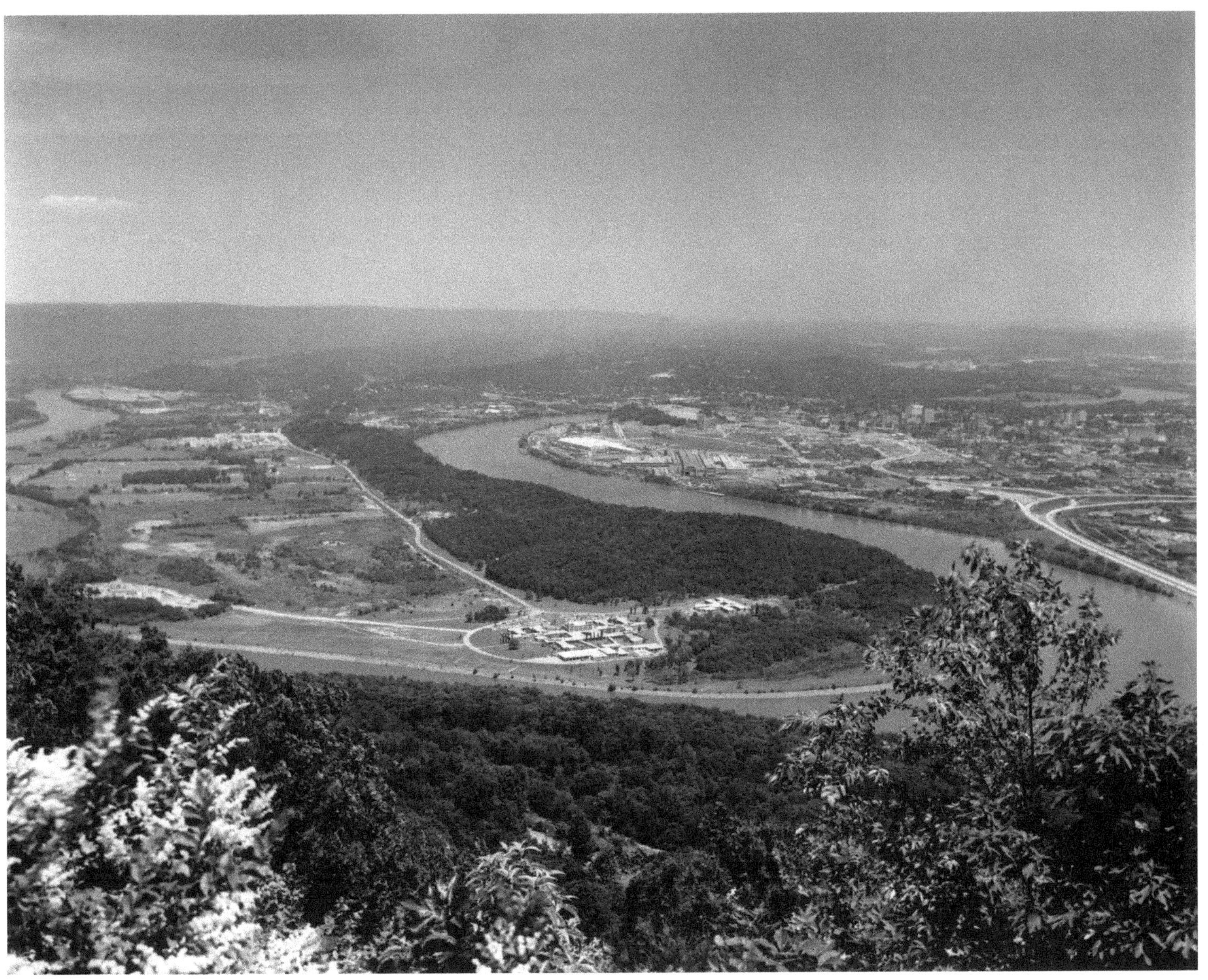

This long view from Lookout Mountain in June 1970 depicts the river with a part of Moccasin Bend visible below and the recently built mental health complex in the lower portion of the image near the riverbank. In the farther bend is the city itself, revealing industry all along the edge of the waterway with Walden's Ridge in the distance.

The entrance at Ruby Falls is called Cavern Castle, seen here around 1971. With a tourist attraction that was underground, a singular, eye-catching entrance on the topside was important to bringing in visitors. Built of stone that was dredged out of the ground from the drilling that was necessary to find the cave waterfall deep in the earth, the castle-like edifice became an identifiable and memorable landmark.

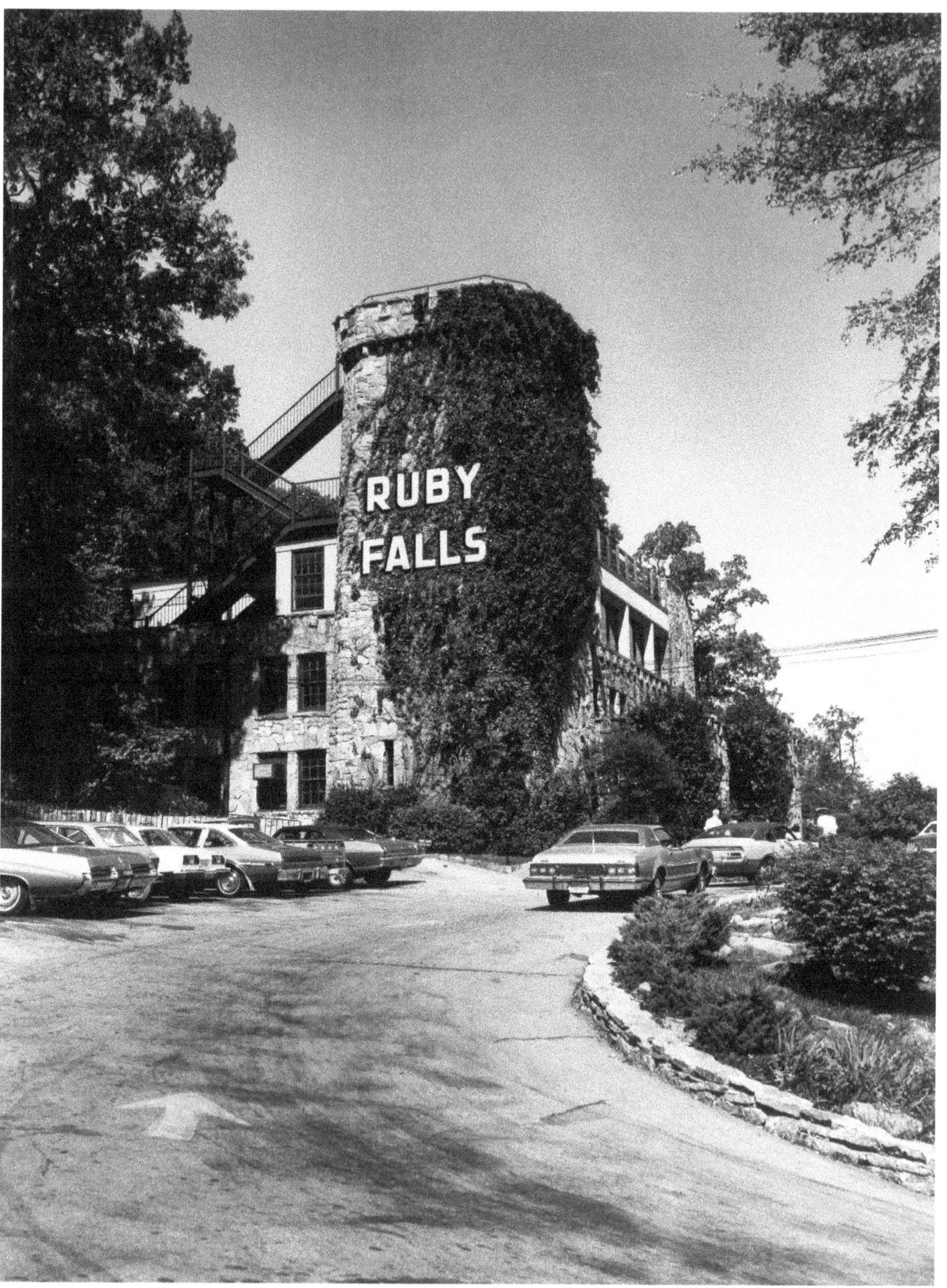

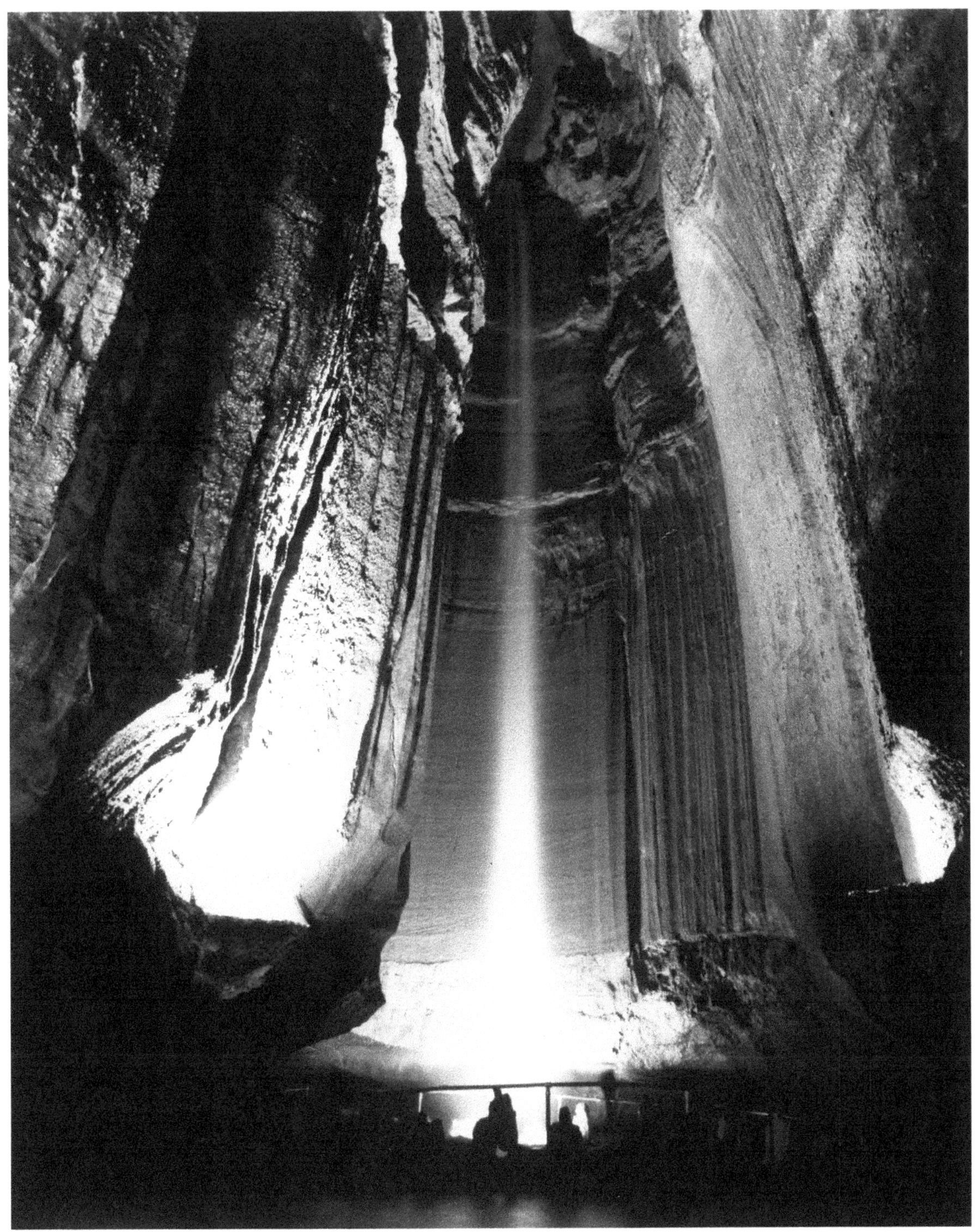

The trek into Ruby Falls is a remarkable walk through some evocative formations like "arctic mirage." The end of the path is a spectacular room that soars 145 feet to the ceiling, revealing a long cascade of water that is dramatically lit. The source of the water remains a mystery and never fails to impress visitors, even those folks who have come back for a second look.

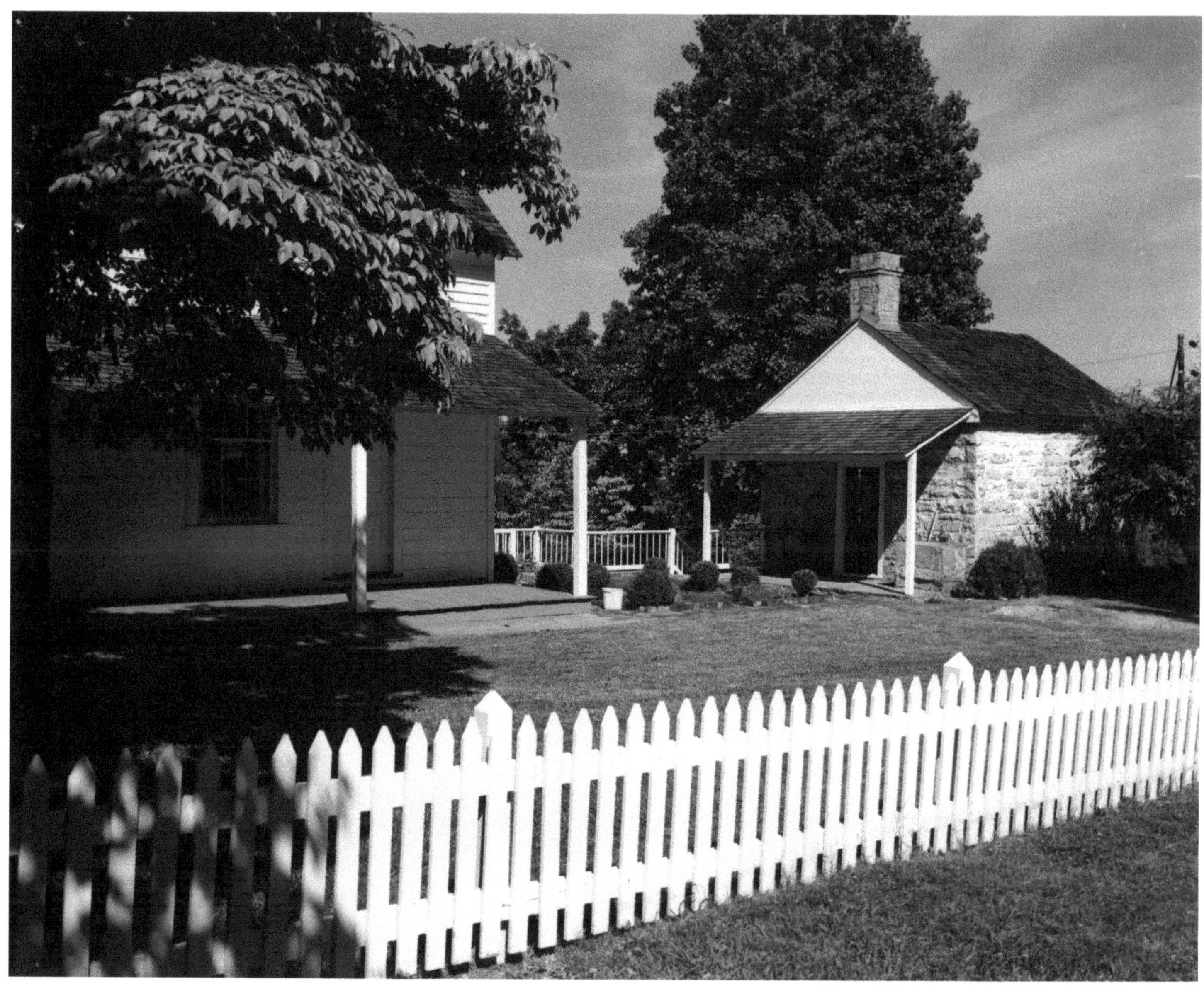

The Robert Cravens House was the home of the iron master who built a furnace on the bluffs near the present-day Hunter Museum of American Art. Chances are that the house looks better in this view from June 1970 than it did when Cravens lived here. A much needed restoration effort in the 1950s stabilized these structures and cleaned them up to make them presentable to the public.

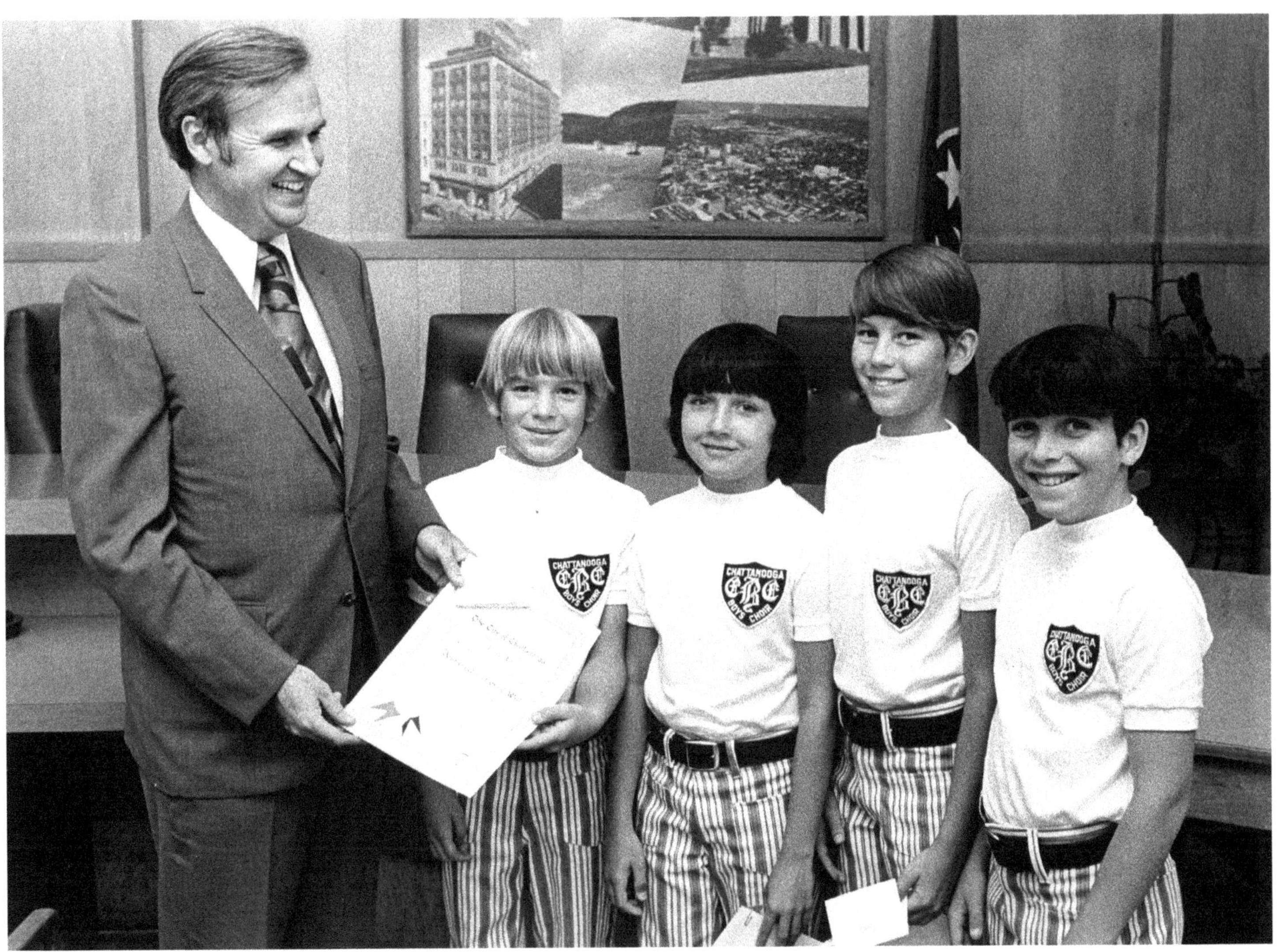

The Chattanooga Boys Choir is one of the city's great independent arts organizations, tracing its origins to 1954. A perennial favorite at Christmastime with their holiday concerts, the CBC has appeared in numerous countries and cities. Mayor Robert Kirk Walker presents these young lads with an "Ambassador of Goodwill" certificate on June 26, 1972, for representing the town so well on their travels.

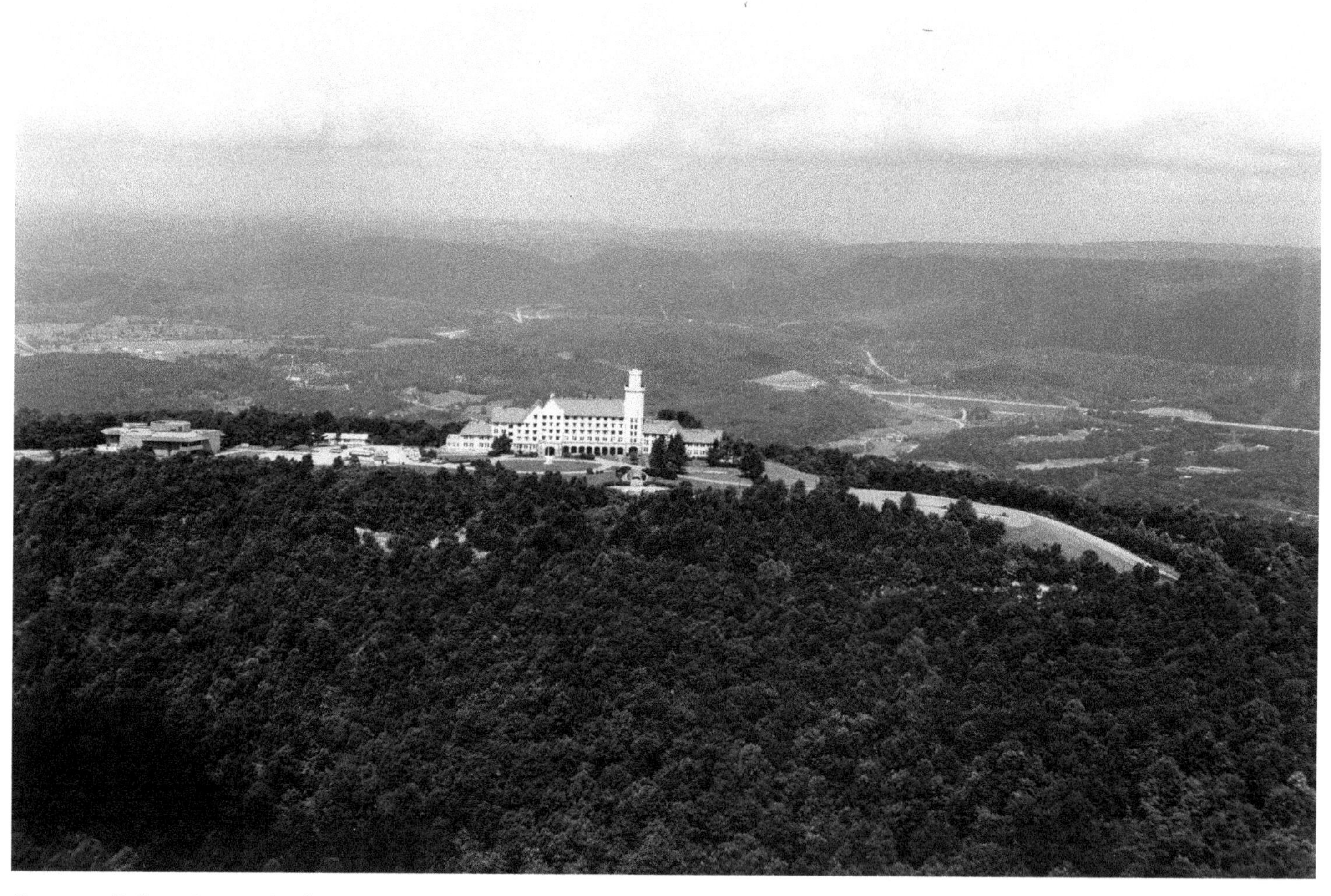

Covenant College sits atop Lookout Mountain on its western side and is the most prominent landmark visible to travelers approaching Chattanooga on I-24. Founded in 1955 in California as a Christian institution of higher learning, the school moved to its present location in 1965. The college was originally the Lookout Mountain Hotel, built in 1928 by Paul Carter. It wound up bankrupt during the hard times of the Great Depression and struggled to operate successfully for years before becoming the college it is today. This 1971 aerial view of the college faces Sand Mountain.

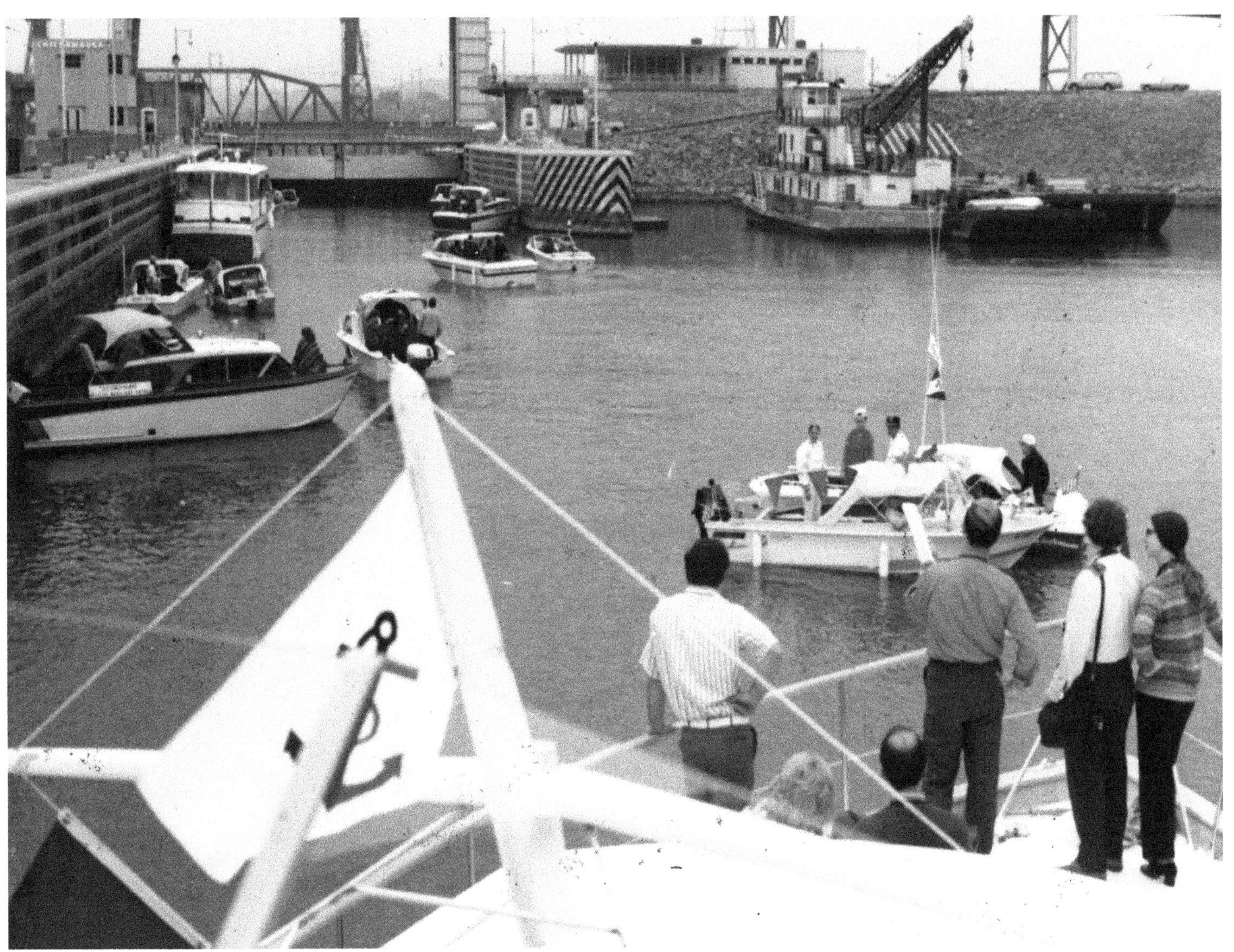

Traveling the great Tennessee waterways is a pleasure available to anyone with a worthy boat. These folks are lining up in the Chickamauga Lock in 1971, which is part of the Chickamauga Dam, and are preparing to be lowered to the next phase of the river below the lake. From there they can cruise into Chattanooga or downriver into Alabama.

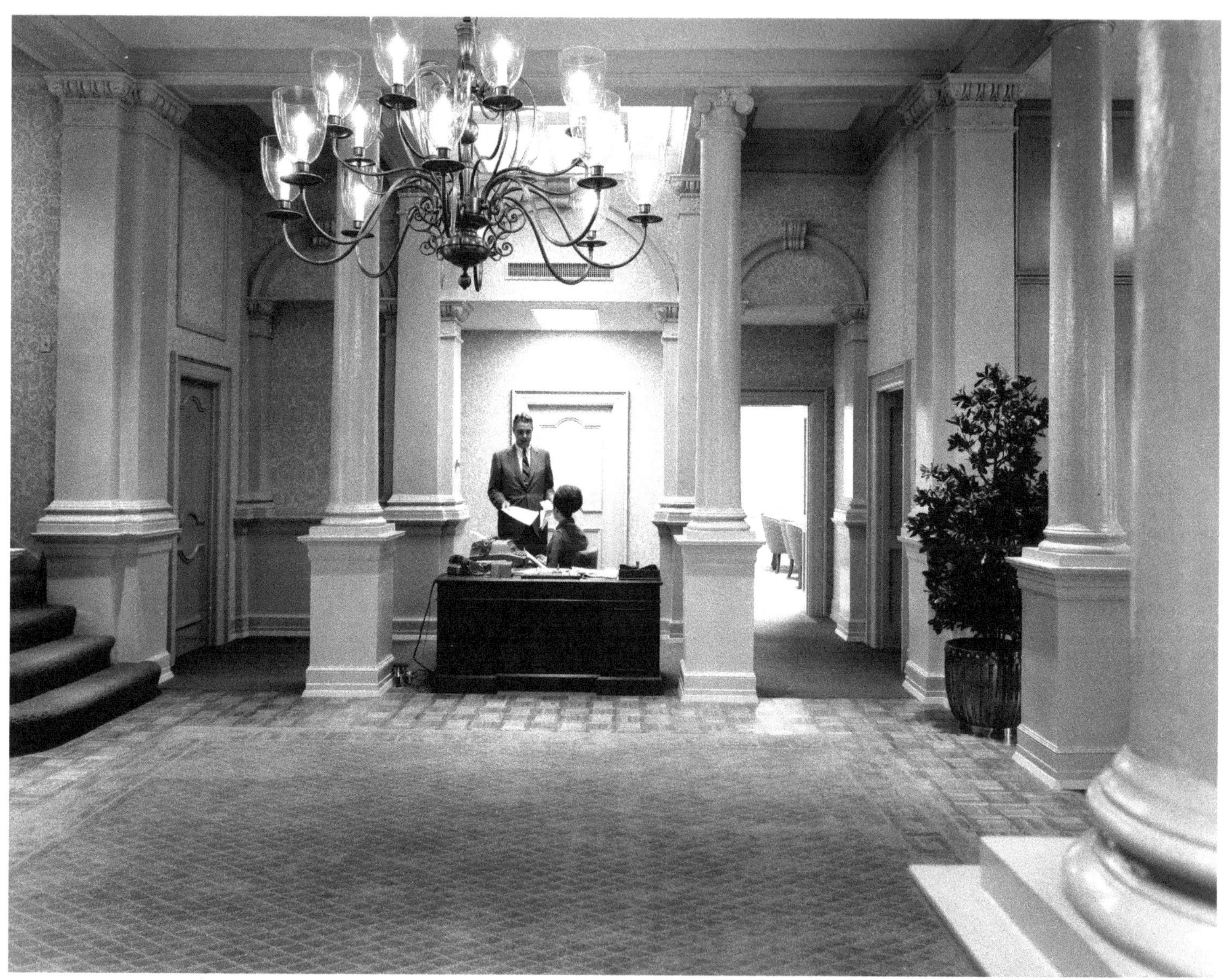

Chattanooga's first freestanding public library was built at the corner of Georgia Avenue and Eighth Street. Underwritten by the steel magnate and philanthropist Andrew Carnegie, the library was located across from the *Chattanooga Times* newspaper building. By 1941 the collection had moved, but the neo-Classical building remained. In 1971, the North American Royalties company occupied the library building, where a receptionist is seen here speaking to Gordon L. Smith, Jr., a principal in the company.

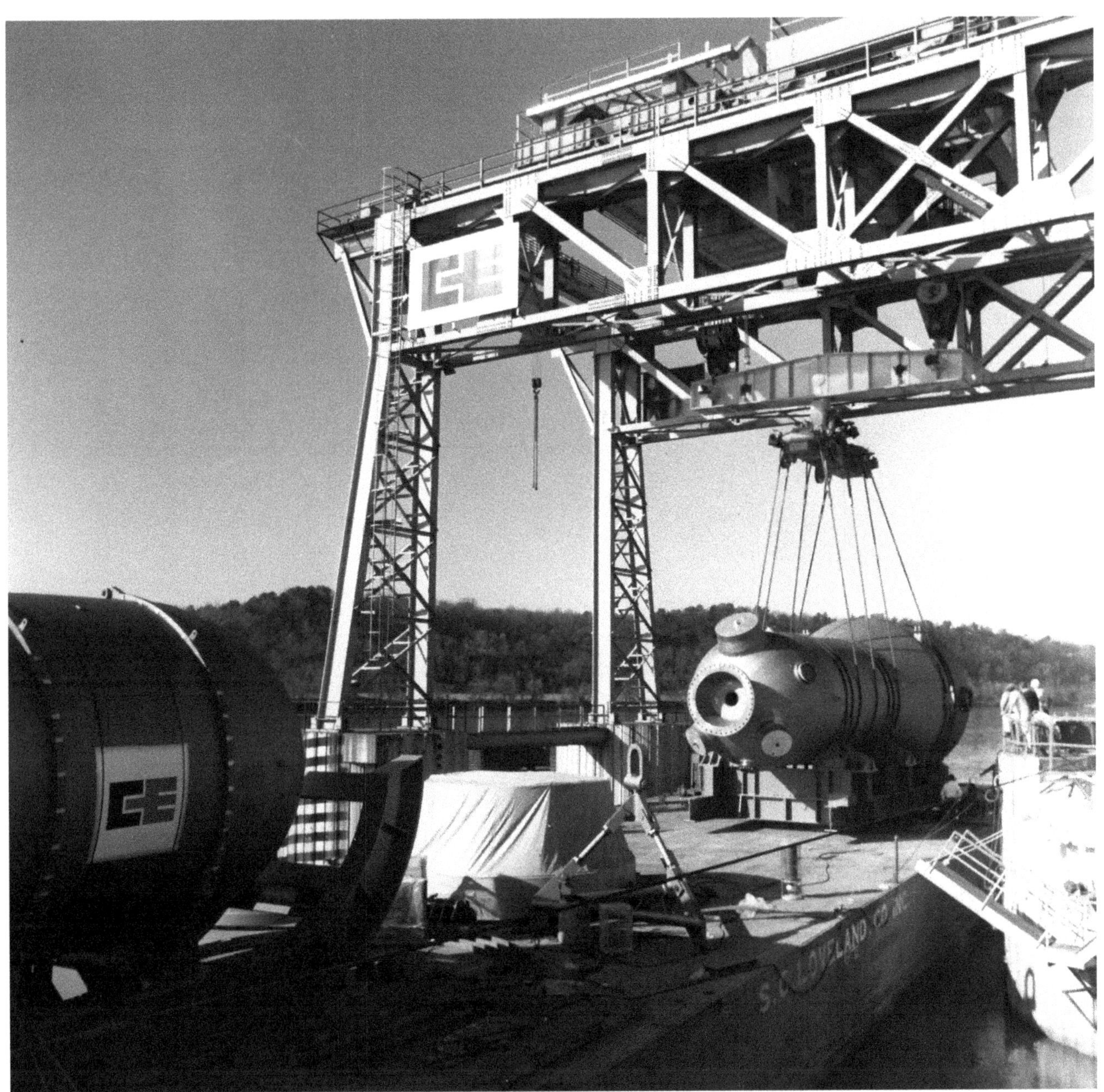

Rivers rarely come to mind nowadays as the "highways" they are. In Chattanooga, a number of facilities have been located on the river for just that reason. Here in 1971 a reactor vessel for a nuclear plant is placed on a barge for transport at the river terminal of Combustion Engineering. The company was known as Hedges, Walsh, and Weidner with origins in the nineteenth century in the cast-iron business.

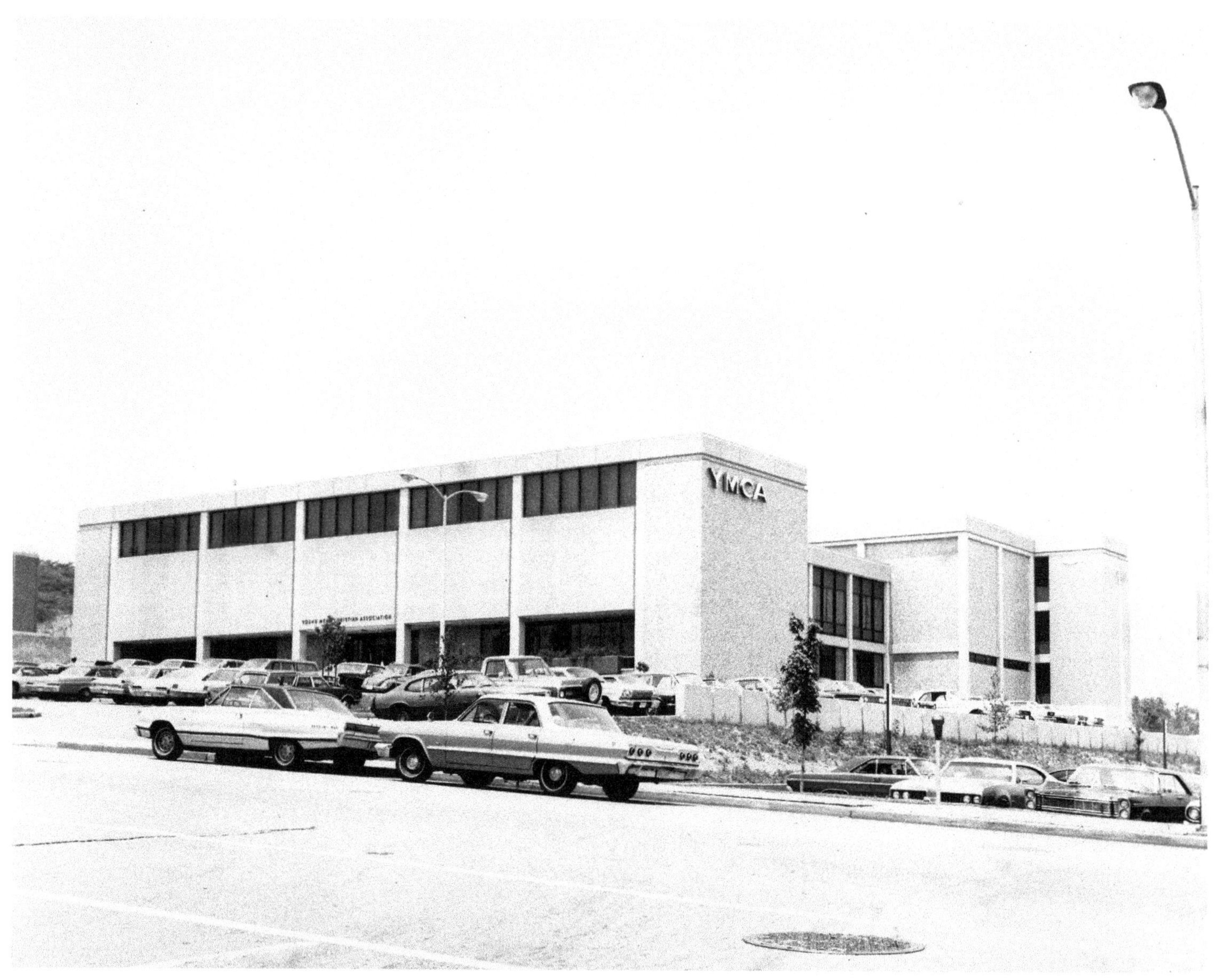

Every town of any size has a Y.M.C.A., and Chattanooga is no exception. Located for years next to the original public library on Georgia Avenue, "the Y" featured an indoor pool, an uncommon accommodation for its day. By the 1960s, wear and tear were evident, and a new facility was constructed on West Sixth Street with a much larger pool, weight rooms, and space for group activities. This is the new Y.M.C.A. as it looked around 1972.

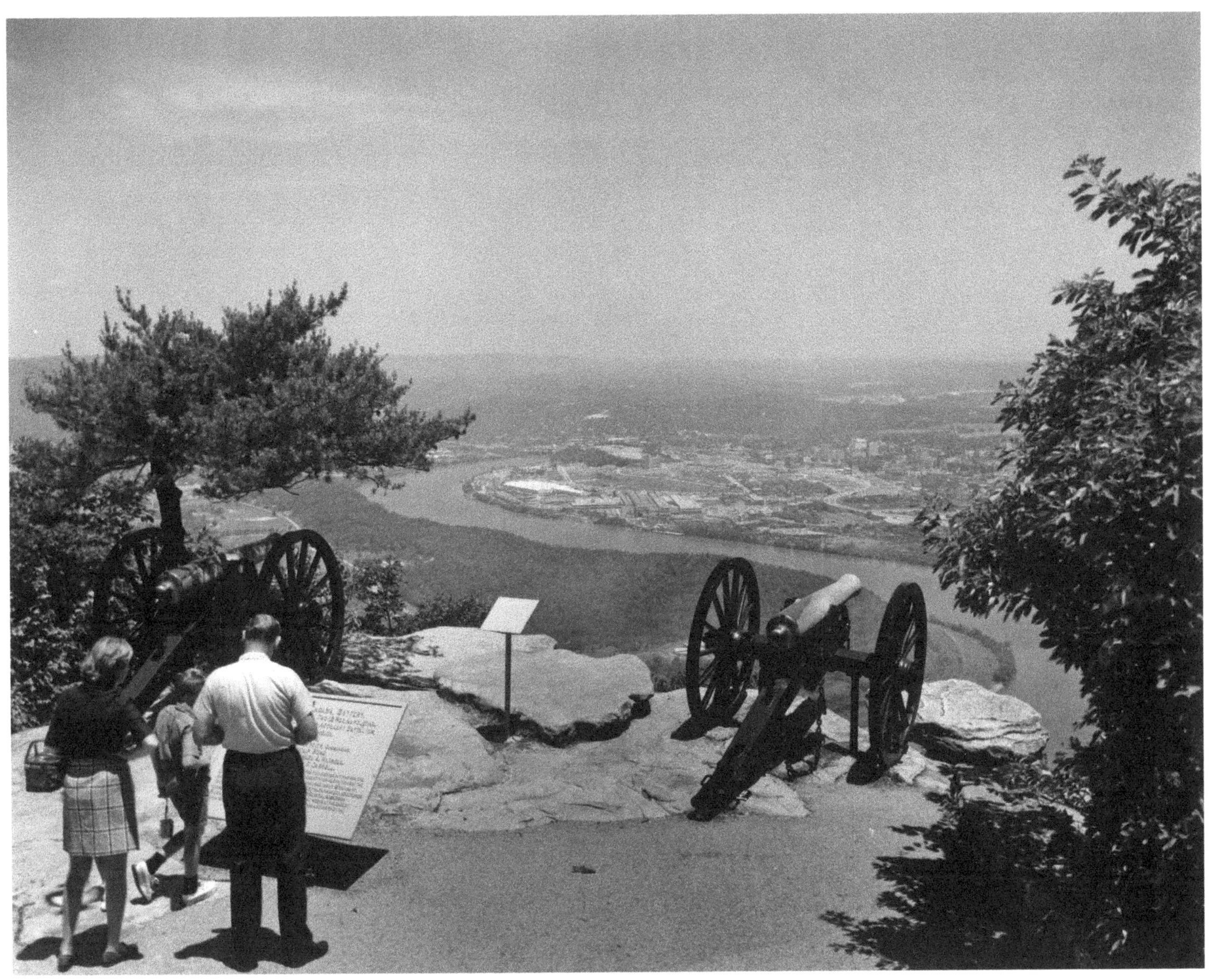

Point Park on the "point" of Lookout Mountain is a part of Chickamauga and Chattanooga National Military Park and as such is replete with cannon emplacements and large metal plaques with detailed inscriptions of the historic struggle that took place on this land. During the Civil War, the commanding height of this position gave the occupying Confederates a strategically advantageous bird's-eye view of all Federal movements below. These visitors are touring the park in May 1972.

Rising majestically on the side of Lookout Mountain is the New York monument, seen here in May 1972. Situated on a flat length of ground called Cravens Terrace, the memorial commemorates the courage and determination of the New York soldiers who secured this land during the Civil War. In the "Battle Above the Clouds," it was here that the soldiers helped send Confederate troops up the grade to the mountaintop to make one last stand before they went into full retreat from the Union infantry.

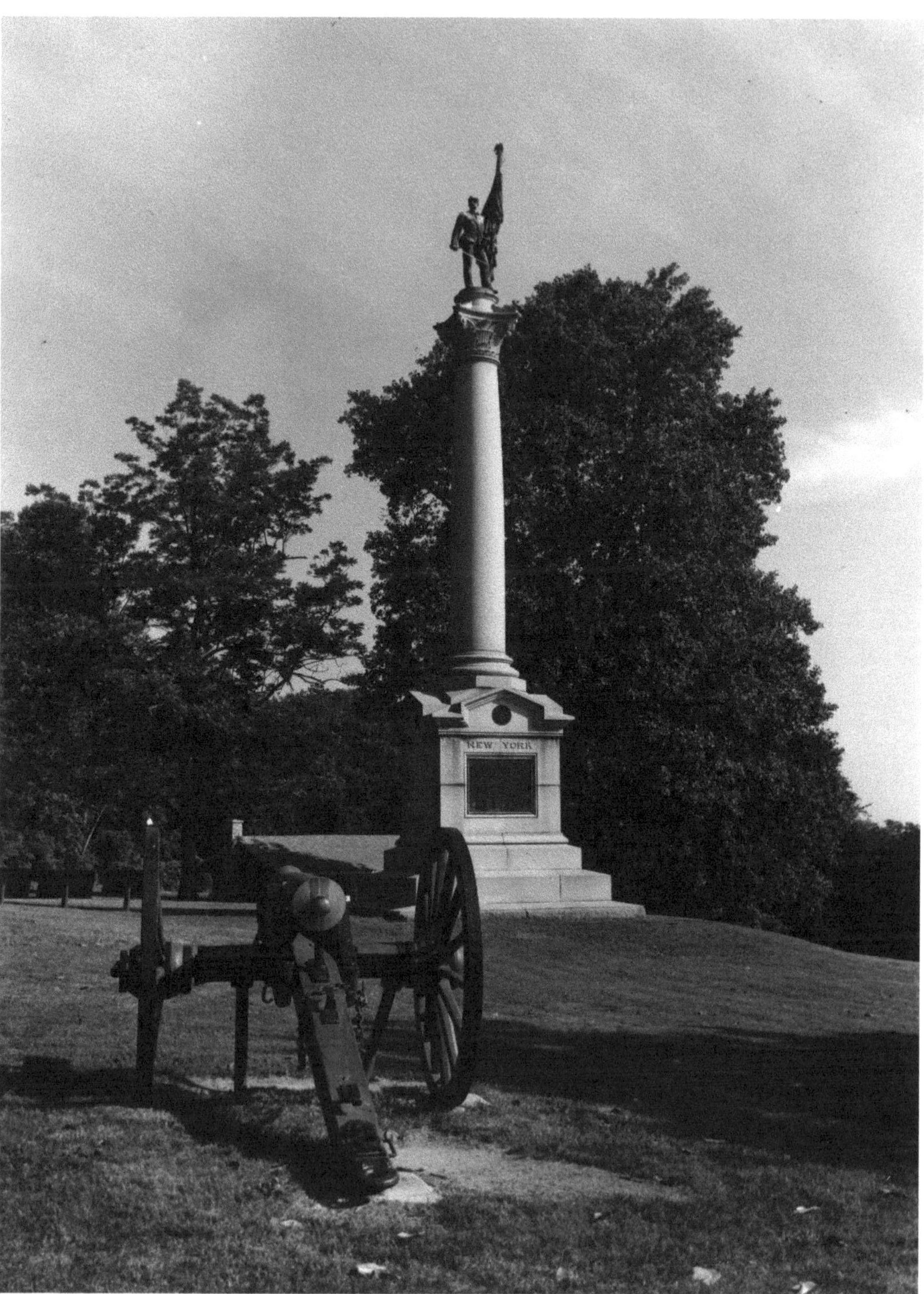

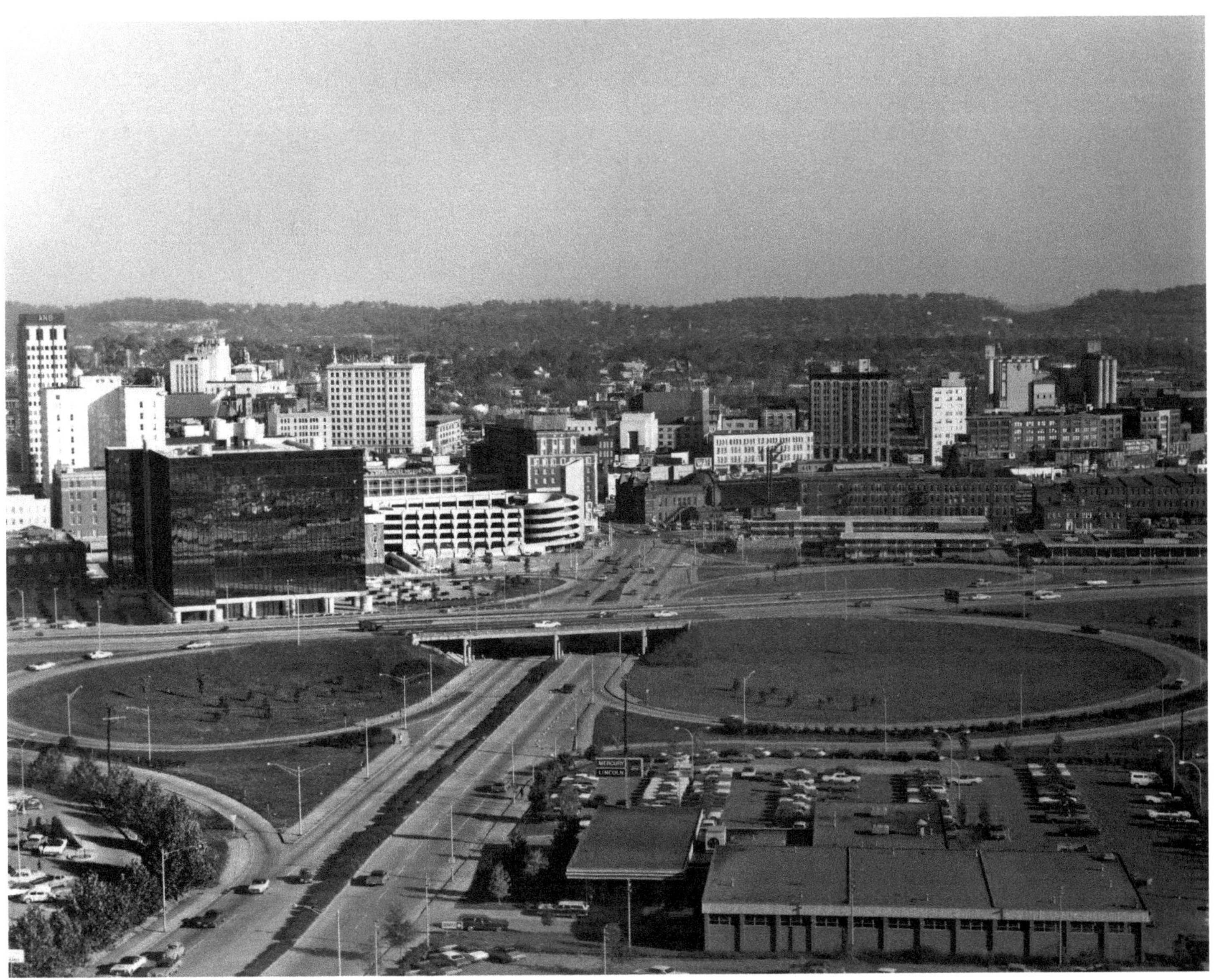

Chattanooga's west side was one of the largest residential neighborhoods downtown for generations, but construction of the interstate system changed all that. City leaders considered the weathered homes to be slums and had them removed through eminent domain. By the early 1970s, the old neighborhoods had been converted to avenues of concrete, car dealerships, and retail establishments. This is a view of the area in 1973.

The Hamilton National Bank has been a fixture on Market Street since its opening in 1911 as a striking Beaux Arts–style building designed by local architect R. H. Hunt. But by the 1950s, sleek and simple was becoming the preferred architectural look for downtown buildings, and in 1965 it was decided that a new facade, seen here in January 1973, would do wonders for business. The change did not prevent bankruptcy, and the bank closed in 1976.

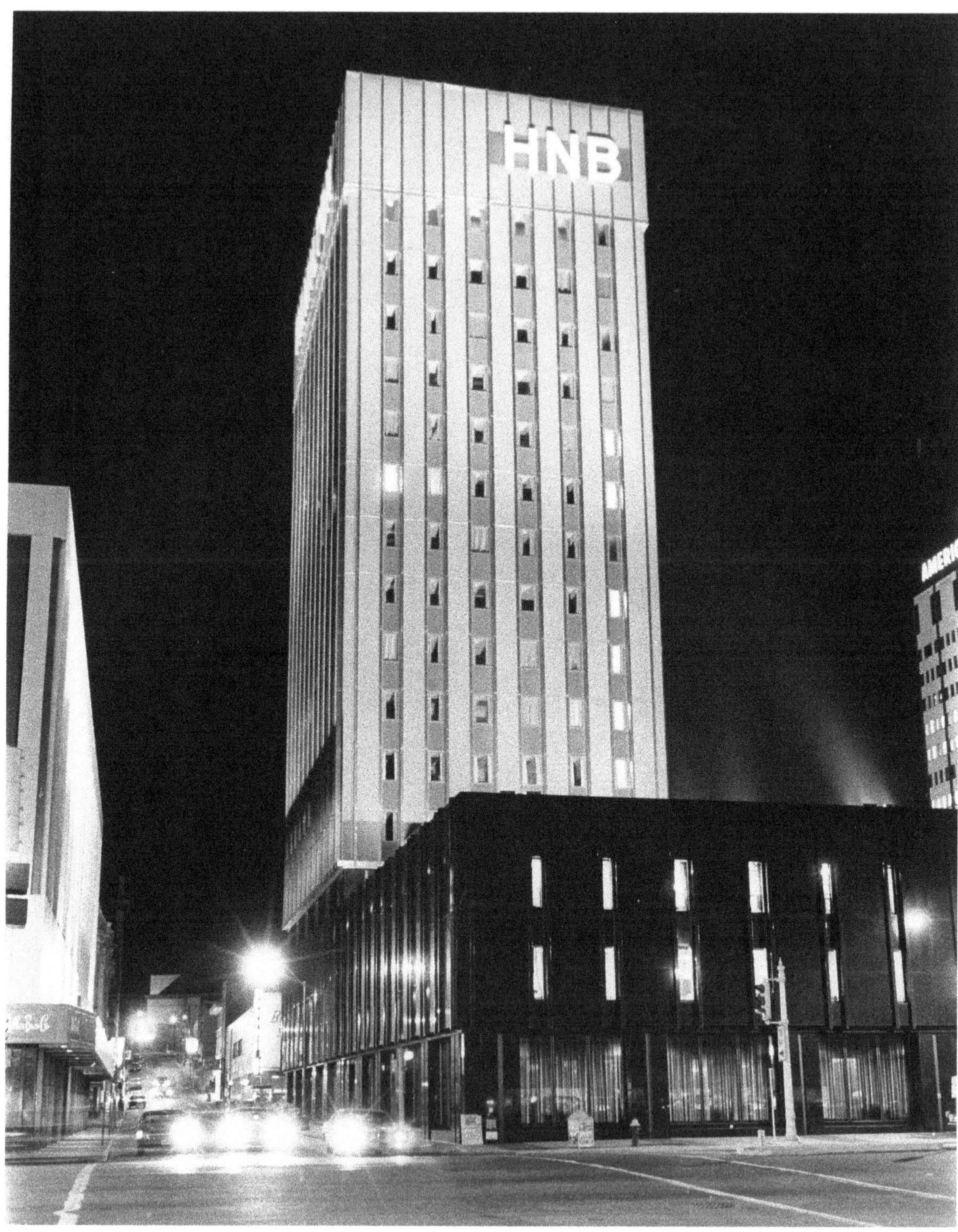

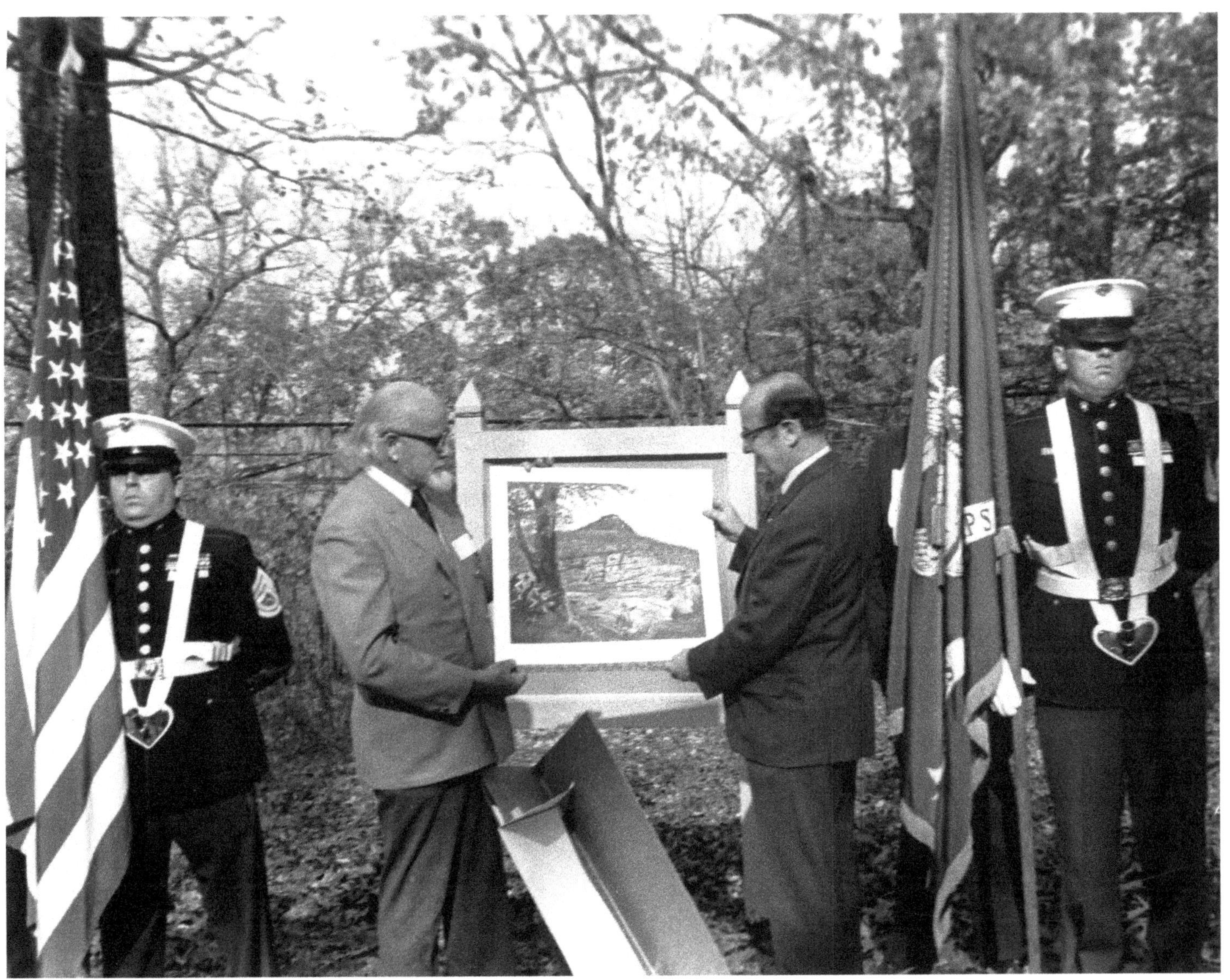

Chattanooga has long claimed that the "Last Battle of the Revolution" was fought on Lookout Mountain between John Sevier's Tennessee troops and pro-British Native Americans in 1782. Today there is some contention about the meaning of that skirmish. Nonetheless, on November 19, 1973, Congressman Lamar Baker (right) accepted this painting by Chattanooga artist George Little—owner of the Little Art Shop—at a ceremony commemorating this historic event.

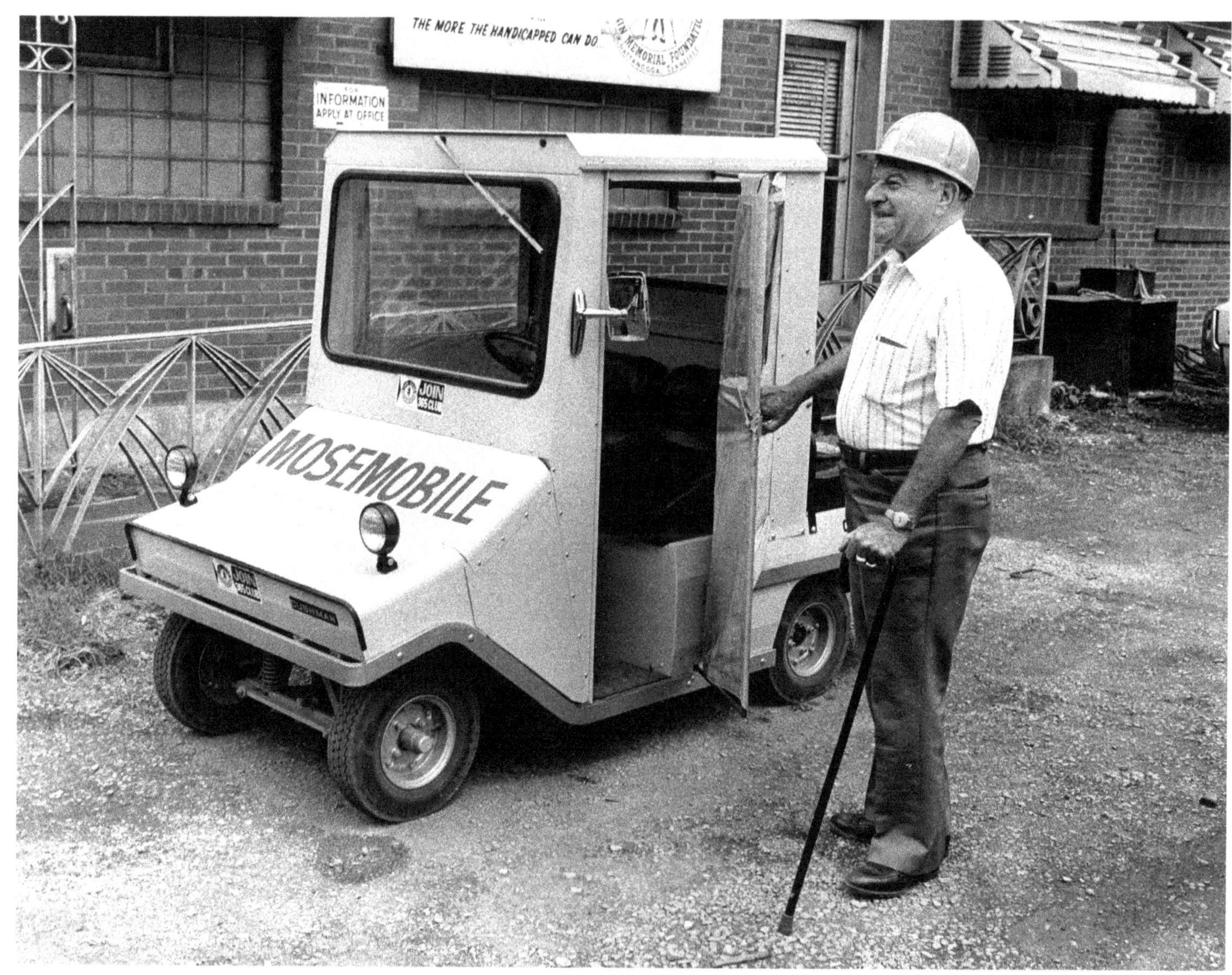

In 1942, Garrison Siskin made a religious promise to God that he would help other people. When his brother, Mose, heard this, he told Garrison, "If it's your promise, it's my promise." Together they built the Siskin Memorial Clinic containing facilities for therapy and training for the handicapped in Chattanooga. Pictured here around 1970 is Mose Siskin and his Mosemobile, used in their supply company, Siskin Steel.

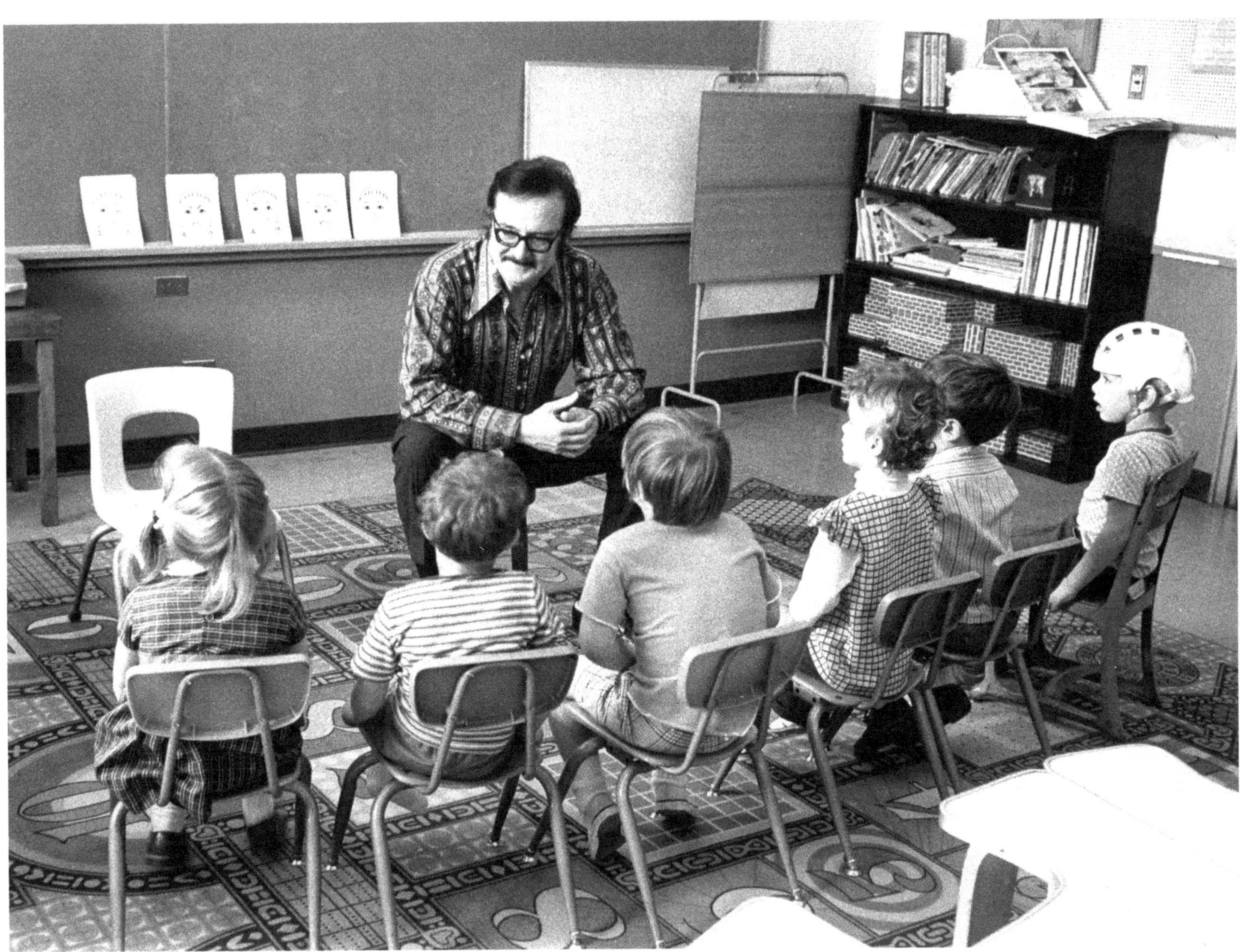

Entertainer Steve Allen sits and talks to children at the Siskin Children's Institute in 1973. The organization is the result of the work of two brothers, Mose and Garrison Siskin, who opened the rehabilitation center in 1959 for people with physical disabilities and developmental difficulties. One part of the facility included young children long before "special needs" programs became part of mainstream education.

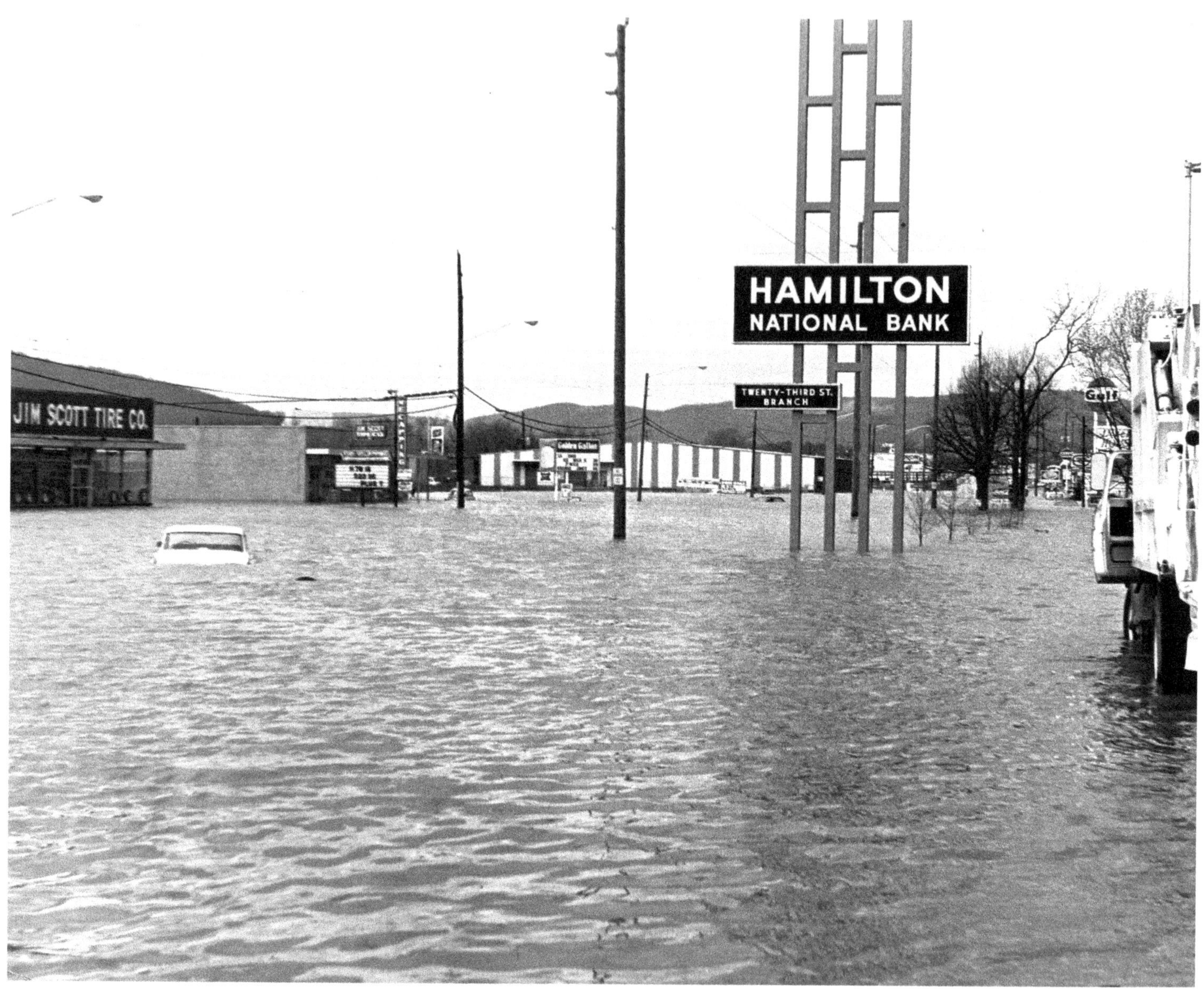

The flood of 1973 wrought some of the worst damage from water that Chattanooga has sustained in the last 40 years. These businesses on Twenty-third Street were under water for several days. During heavy, sustained downpours, the land around Twenty-third Street can also be inundated by water running off the six-lane interstate highway nearby. Chattanooga has experienced flooding from the time it was founded. Before TVA began building dams in the 1930s, the raging water could be devastating to life and property. Even today, lowlands can easily be swamped when Mother Nature rains and rains. Twenty-third Street is one part of town, along with Brainerd and Alton Park, that is usually hard hit when the creeks overflow.

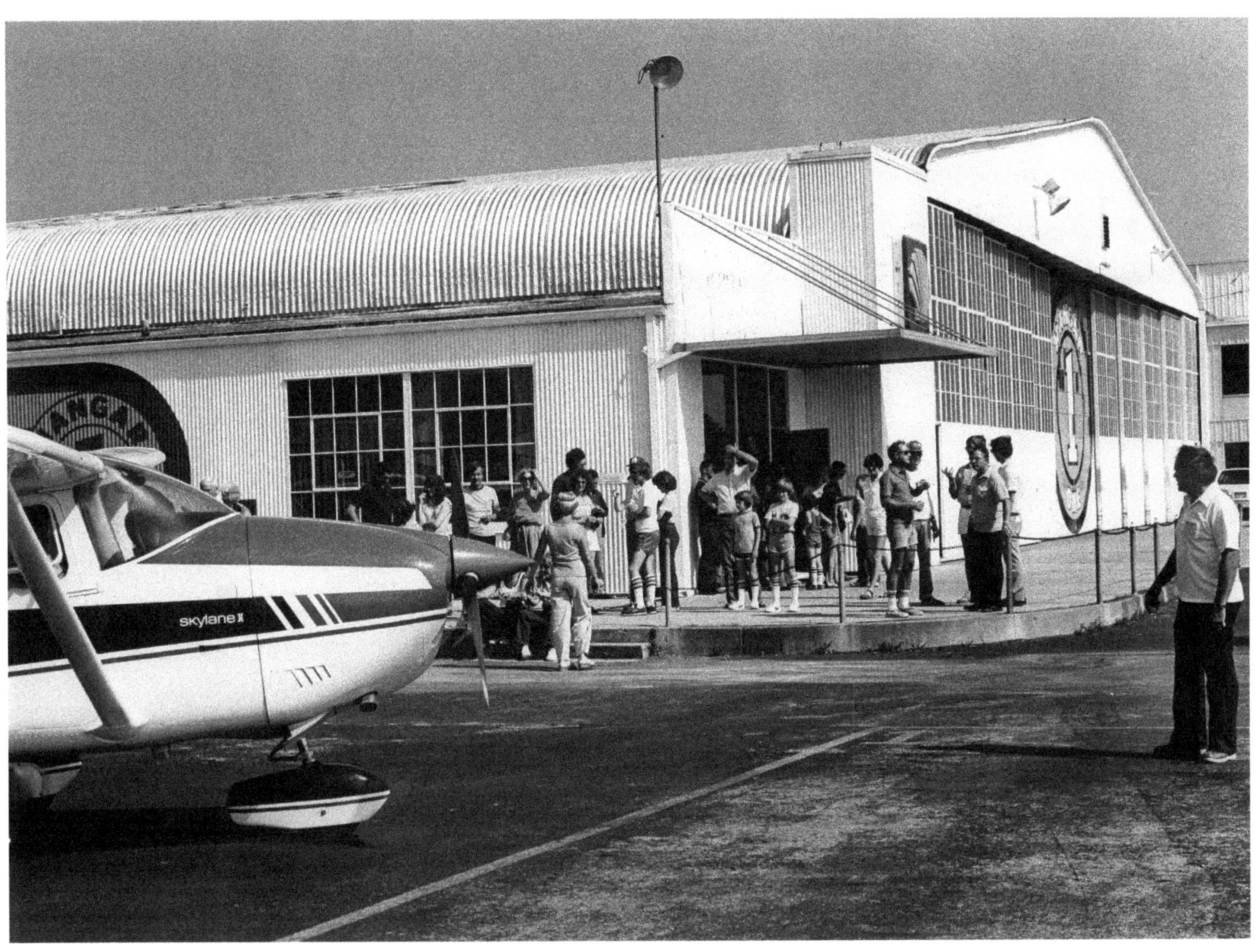

Around 1974, students and adults wait at Hangar One at Lovell Field as different groups are given airplane rides to raise money for the Orange Grove School. A truly inspirational agency, the Orange Grove Center was begun in 1953 by Chattanoogans seeking ways to better the lives of disabled children and now serves both children and adults with intellectual disabilities.

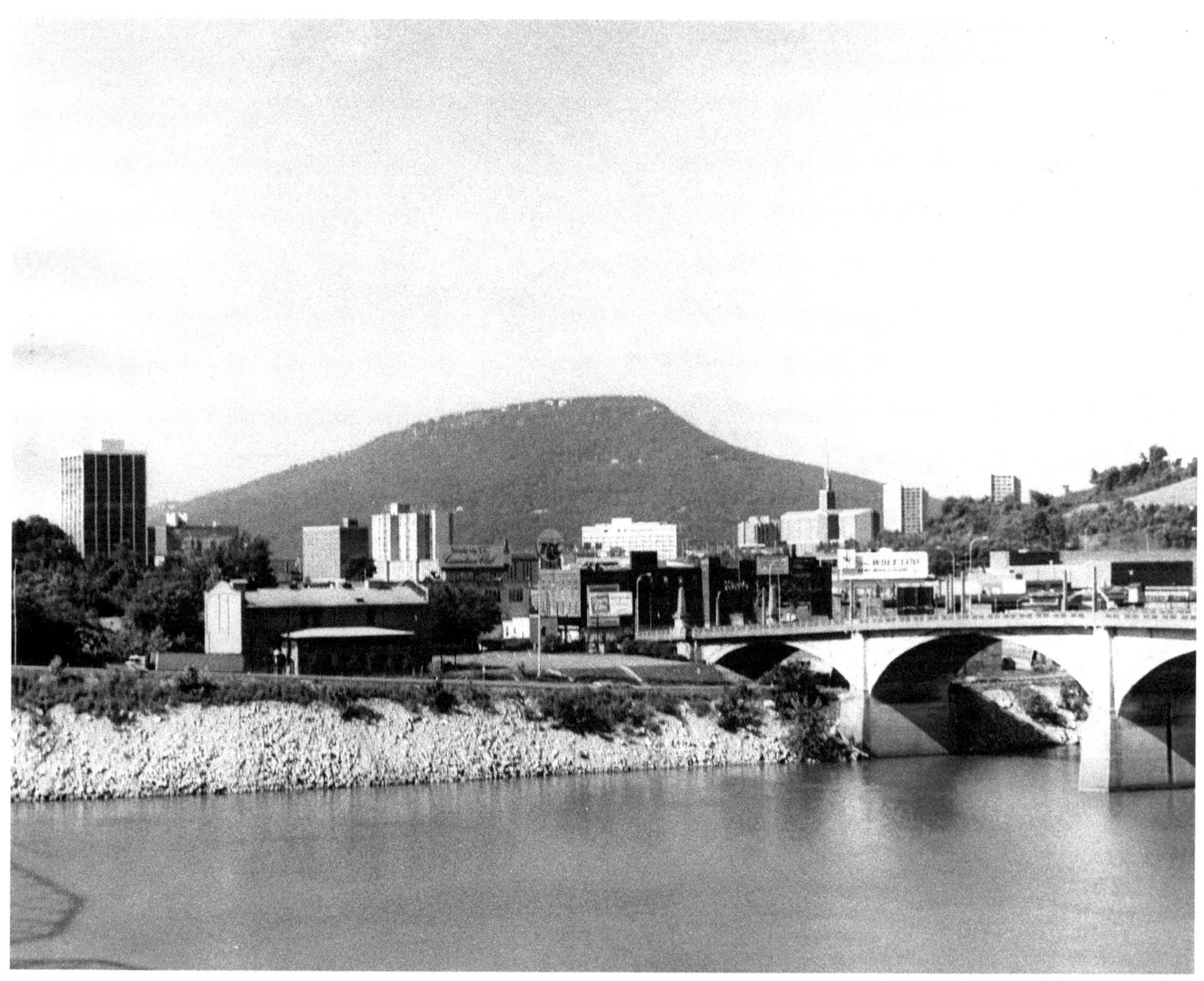

Chattanooga's waterfront in the mid-seventies looked unused and uninviting. The long, low building to the left, an Alhambra Shrine Temple, was later replaced with riverfront apartments, and the John Ross Bridge to the right has been joined by the popular Tennessee Aquarium. Today, walkways and piers line the water. Lookout Mountain rises in the background.

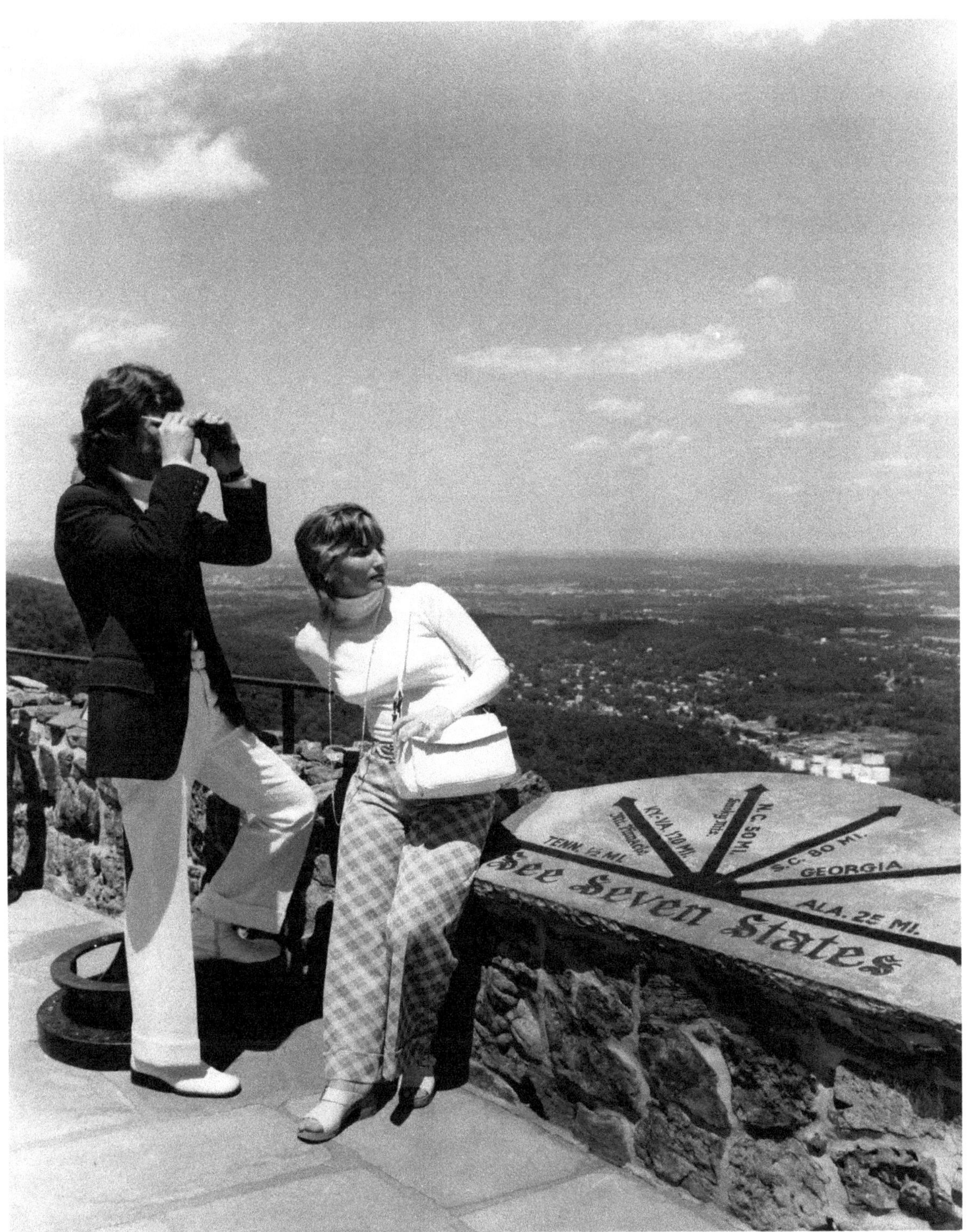

With binoculars in hand and sporting the fashions of the seventies, this gentleman peers into the distance searching for a glimpse of another state. The well-known sign, which encourages visitors to "see seven states," sits on a wall at Lovers Leap at Rock City Gardens and has served as a motto for the Lookout Mountain attraction for decades. The ability to view these seven states has always depended on very clear weather and uncanny eyesight.

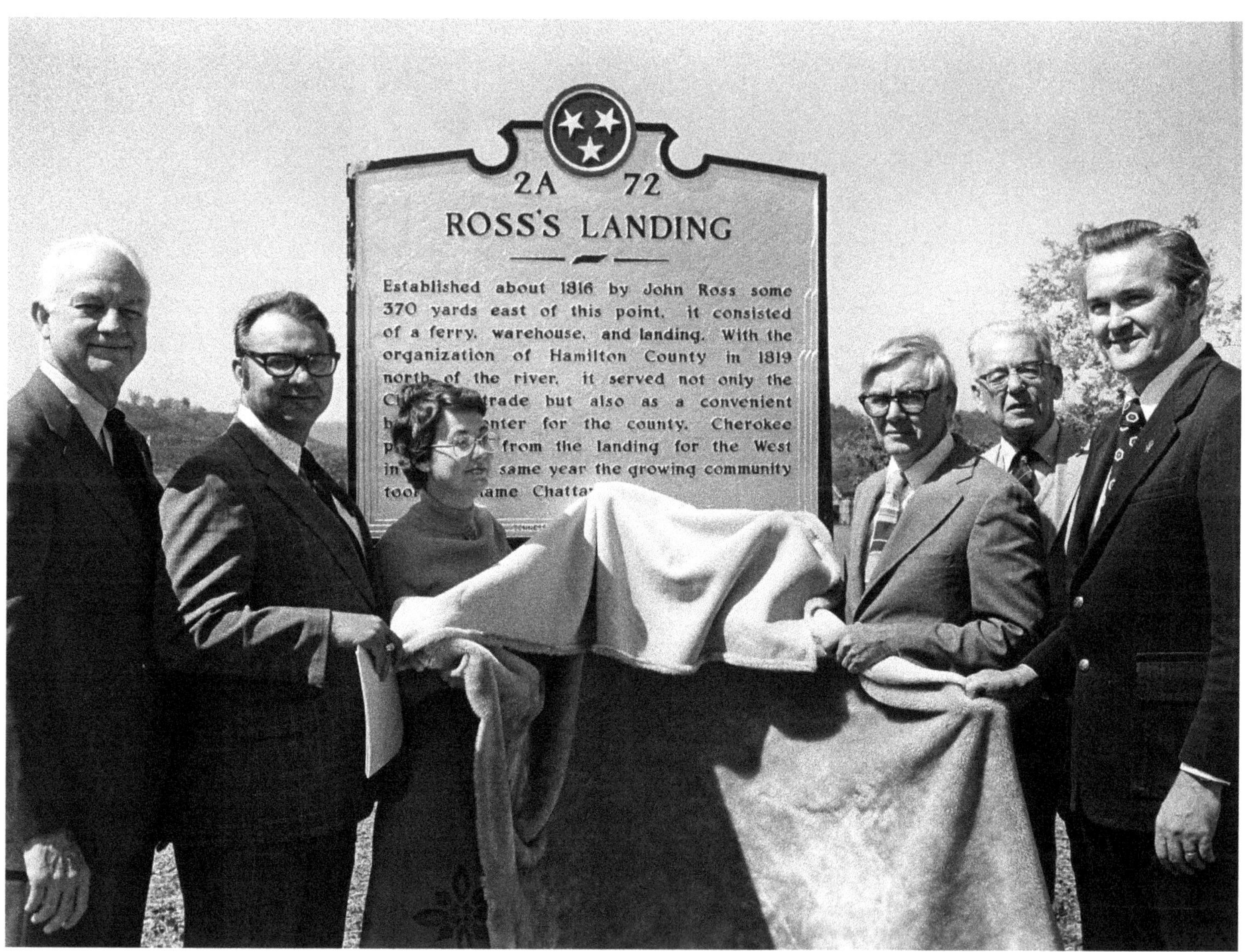

Ross's Landing has long been accepted as the starting point for the permanent settlement of Chattanooga. Essentially a warehouse operated by John Ross, who would become chief of the Cherokee nation, it was established in 1816. Standing beside the marker on April 9, 1976, left to right, are Dudley Porter, County Judge Don Moore, Joan Franks, Stanley Lewis of Baylor School, the historian Dr. James Livingood, and Mayor Charles "Pat" Rose.

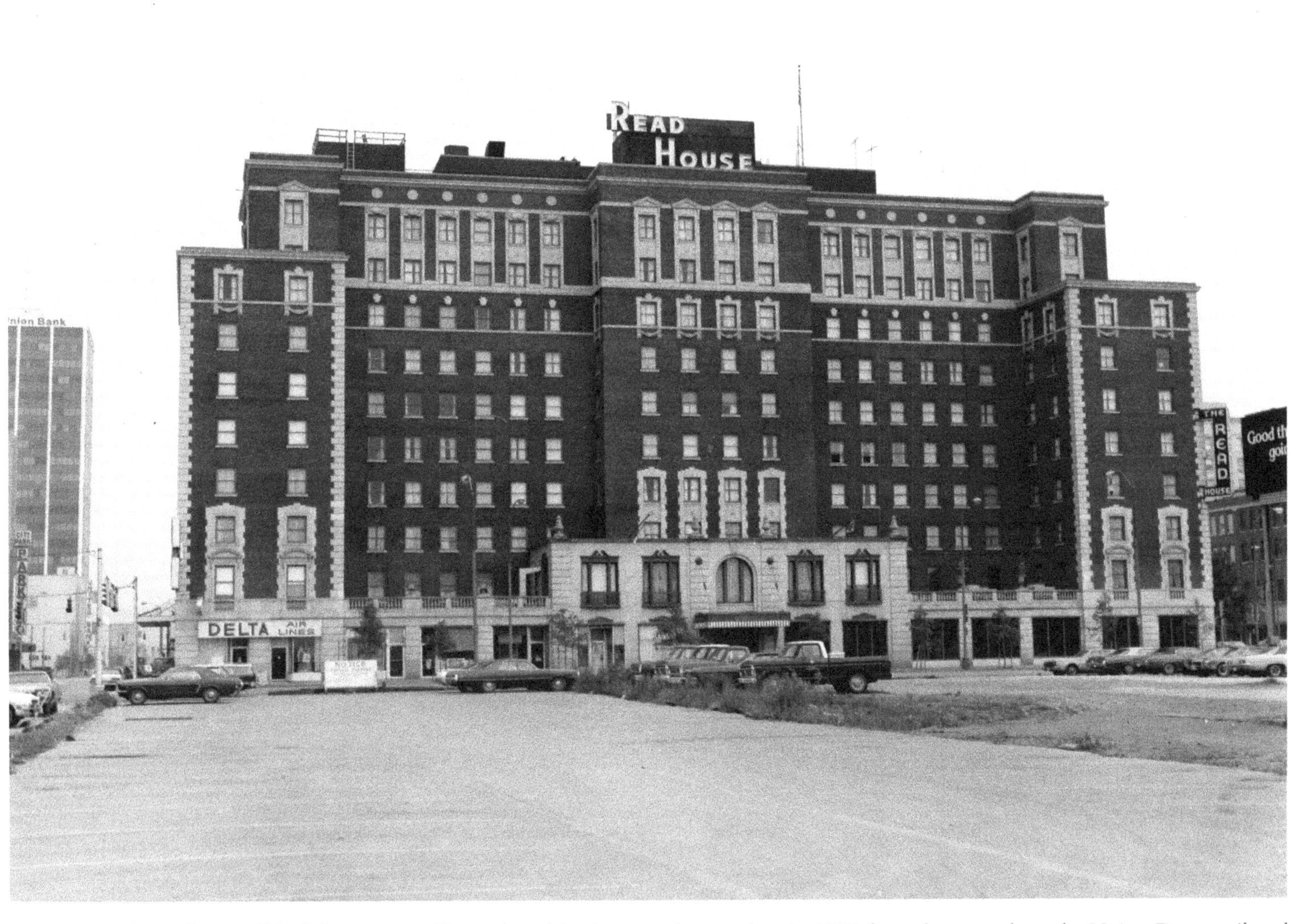

Delta Airlines still had downtown offices when this photograph was taken in 1976 from the spot where the Union Depot railroad station once stood. Demolished in 1973, the depot faced the Read House, seen here and built in 1926. This building succeeded the first hotel of that name, erected in 1871 by Samuel Read and John Thomas, which in turn had replaced the Civil War–era Crutchfield House.

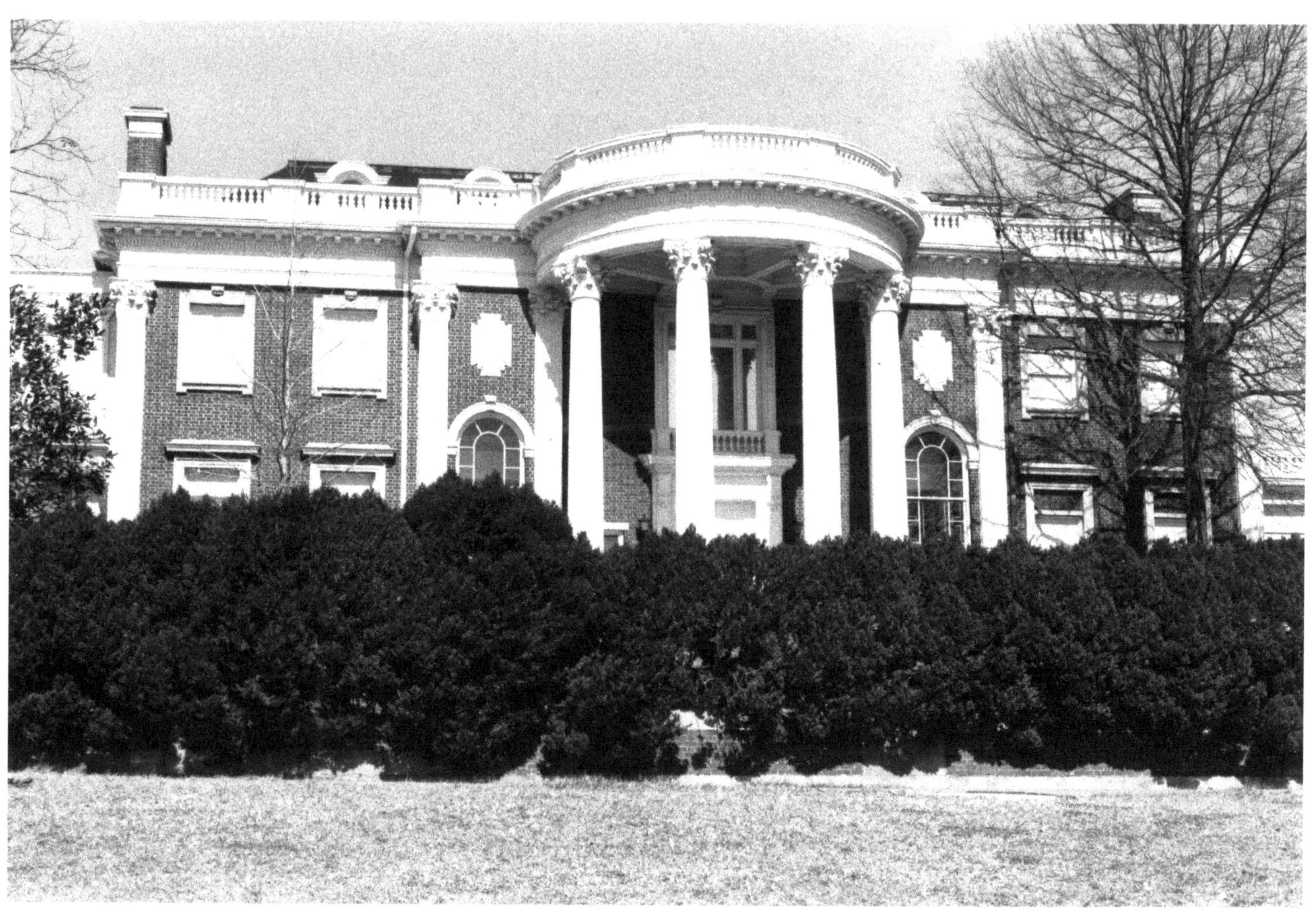

George Thomas Hunter, an heir to the Chattanooga Coca-Cola Bottling Company fortune, was the last resident of the Ross-Faxon house. In his will he directed that his home be converted to an art museum. Situated downtown on the bluff overlooking the river, the 1906 residence became the Hunter Museum of American Art in 1952 and gained a fine reputation for the quality and depth of its collection. This is the museum in 1976.

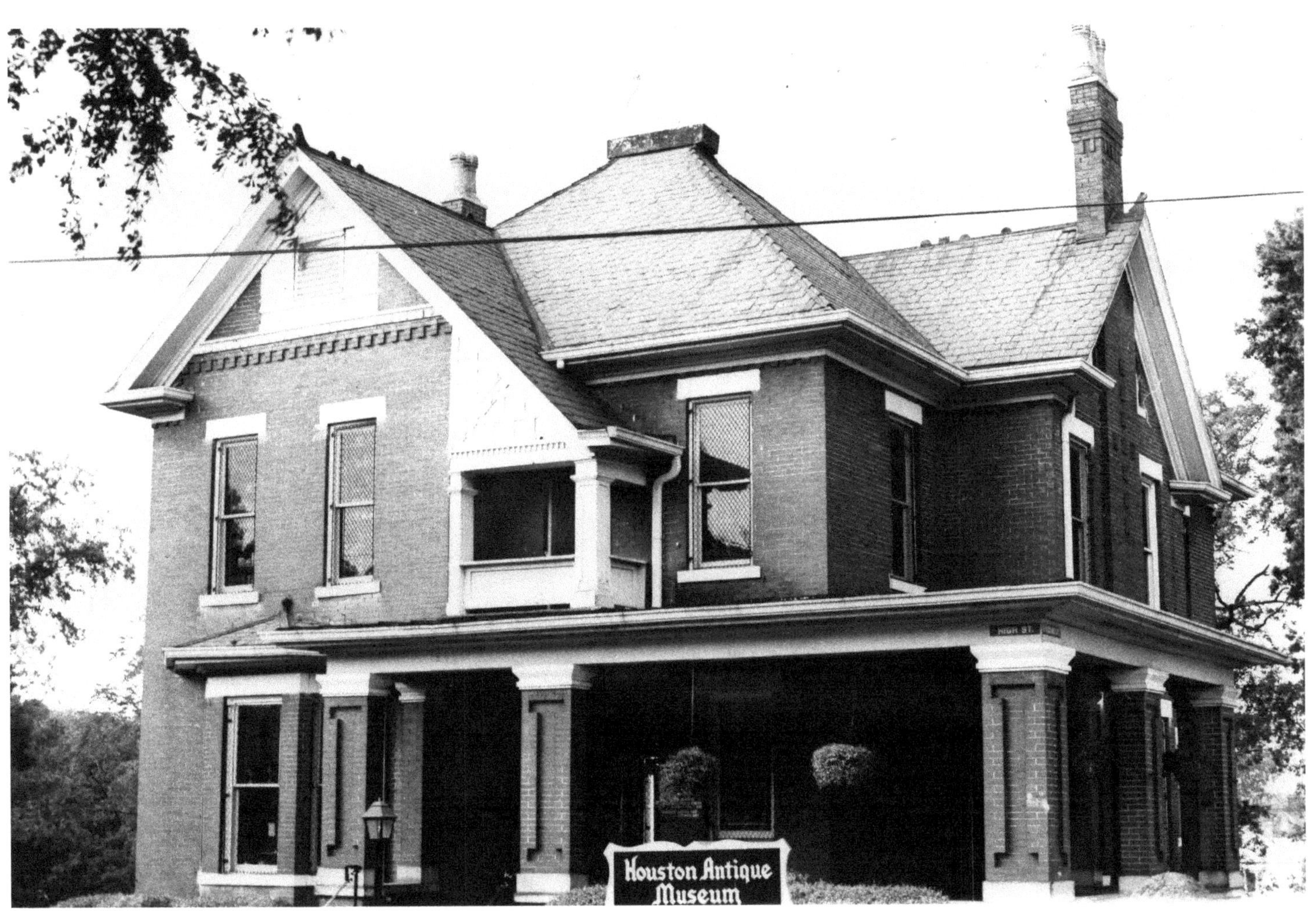

Anna Safley Houston was a colorful, gregarious antiques dealer known as "Antique Annie" whose mission in life was to collect things. Over her lifetime, she accumulated 15,000 glass pitchers, and at least 9 husbands. A savvy businesswoman, Houston built a collection consisting primarily of glassware of all kinds, which she bequeathed to the city of Chattanooga. Later evaluated as a unique and valuable American treasure, much of the colorful glass is displayed in this house on High Street, which has served as a museum since 1968.

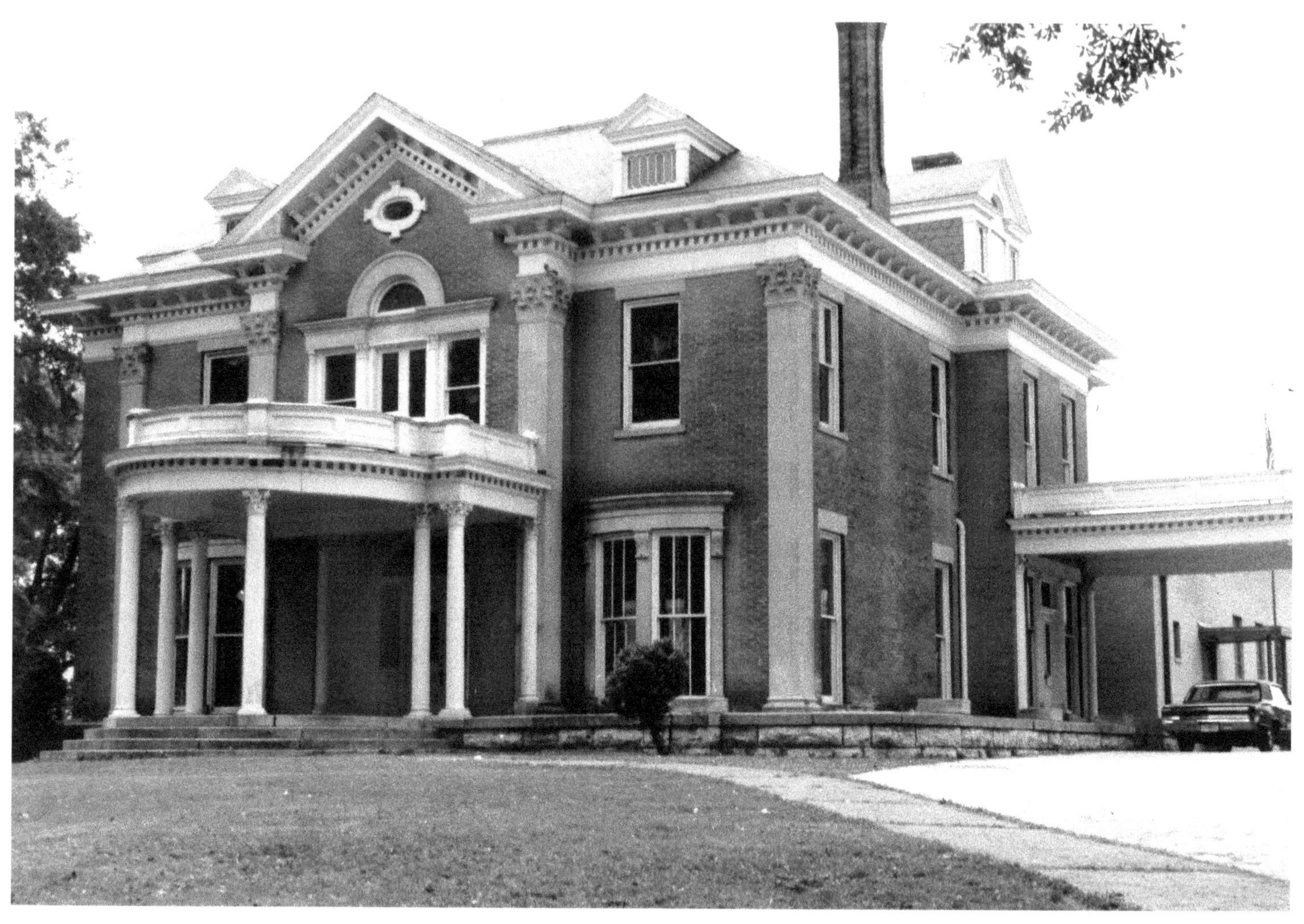

This stately brick house on Vine Street, which today is a Masonic temple, was once the home of Jo Conn Guild. He was an outspoken proponent of private electric power in the early twentieth century and served as president of the Tennessee Electric Power Company. His most ambitious and difficult project was the construction of the Hales Bar Lock and Dam in 1913, the first multipurpose dam on the Tennessee River.

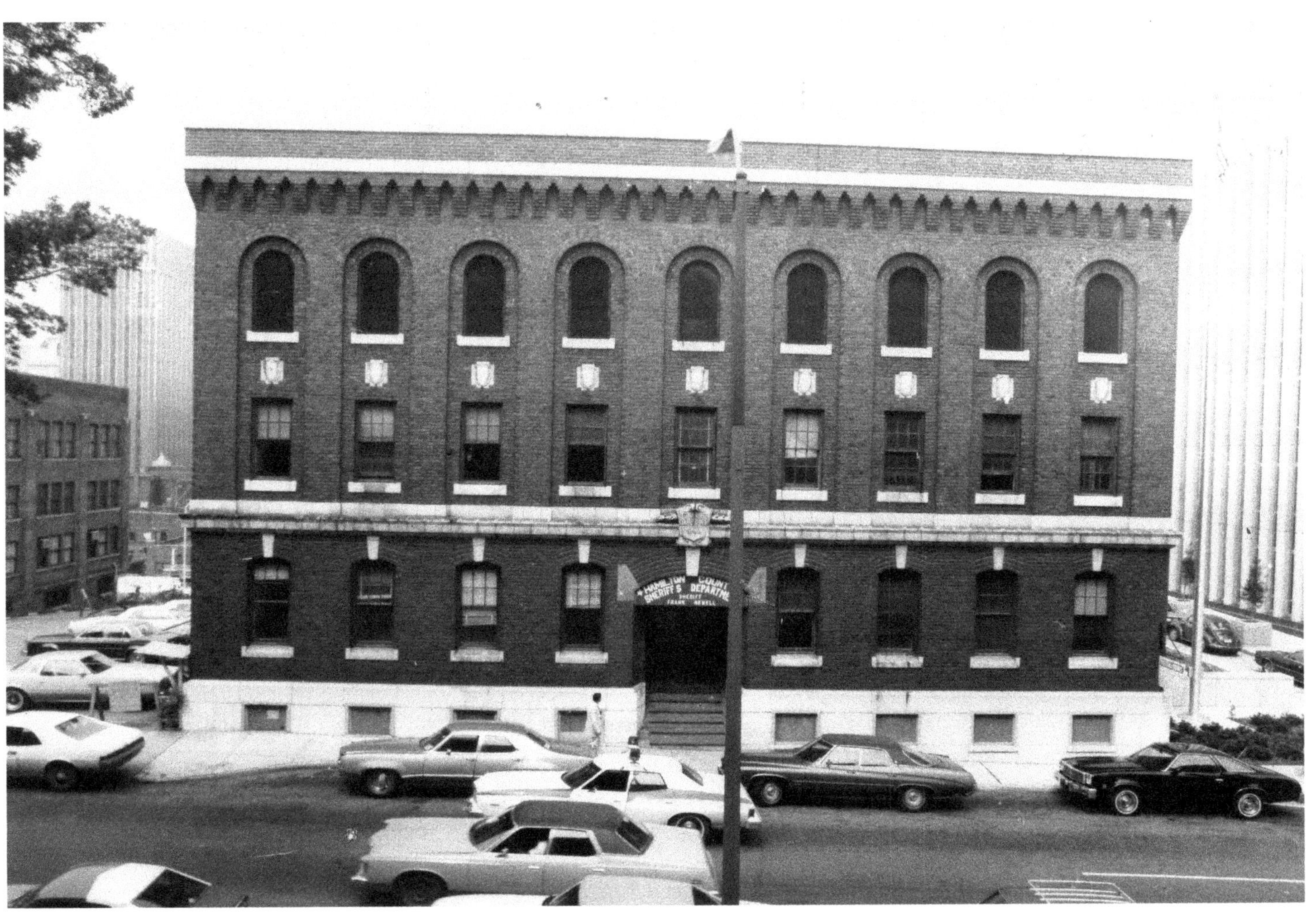

The old Hamilton County Jail on Walnut Street stood across from the Hamilton County Courthouse, whence this photograph was taken. A well-built structure when it opened in 1913, by the 1970s the facility had seen more escapes than the public wanted to hear about. It went the way of the wrecking ball and was replaced with a newer jail next door.

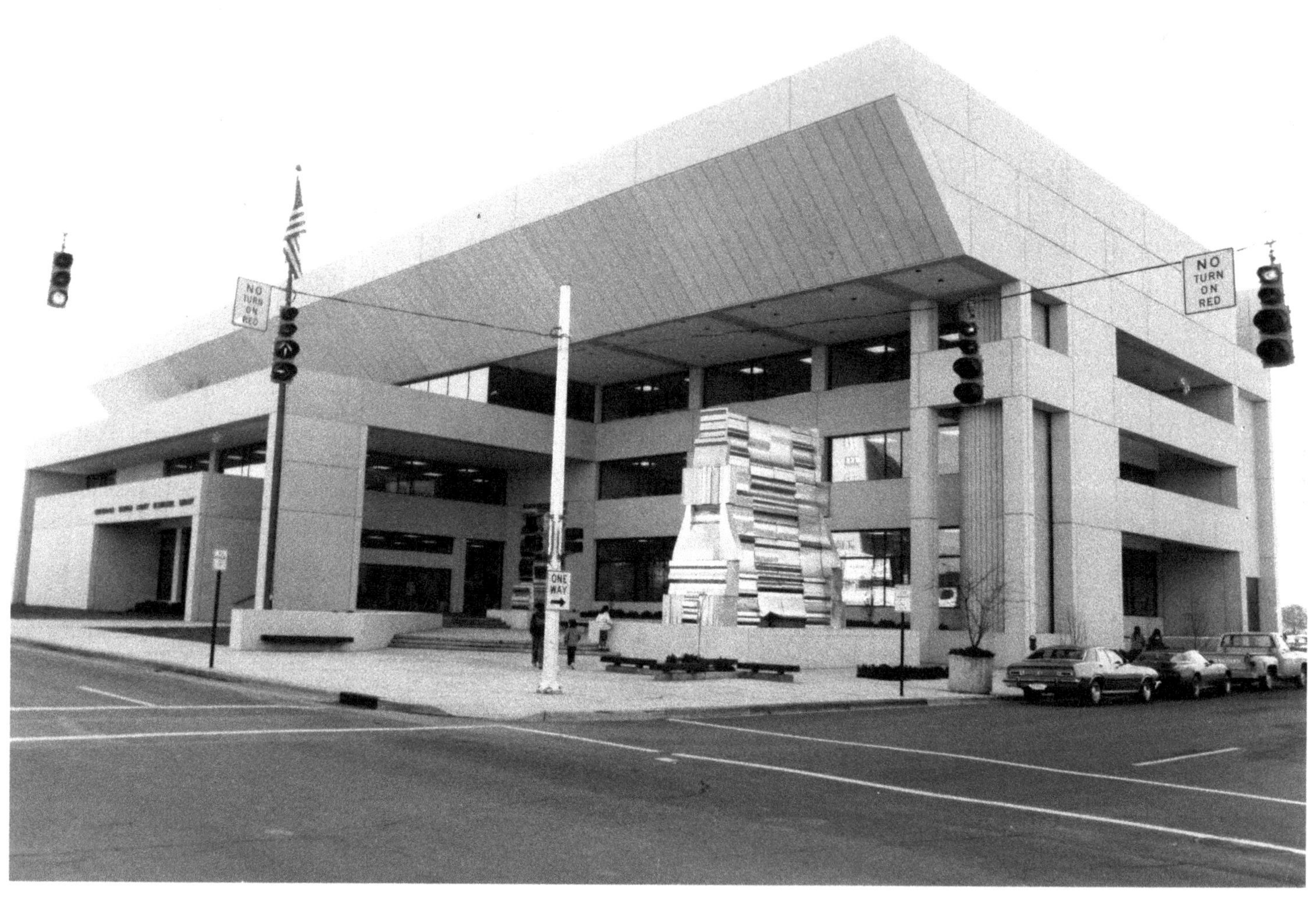

Where steam engines once sounded their shrill whistles, now search engines ply quietly through networks of data. For generations this site was covered with rail lines into the city, but as Chattanooga's fortunes changed in the 1970s so did its landscape. This land on Broad Street was chosen as the home for the new Chattanooga–Hamilton County Bicentennial Library, fittingly dedicated in 1976.

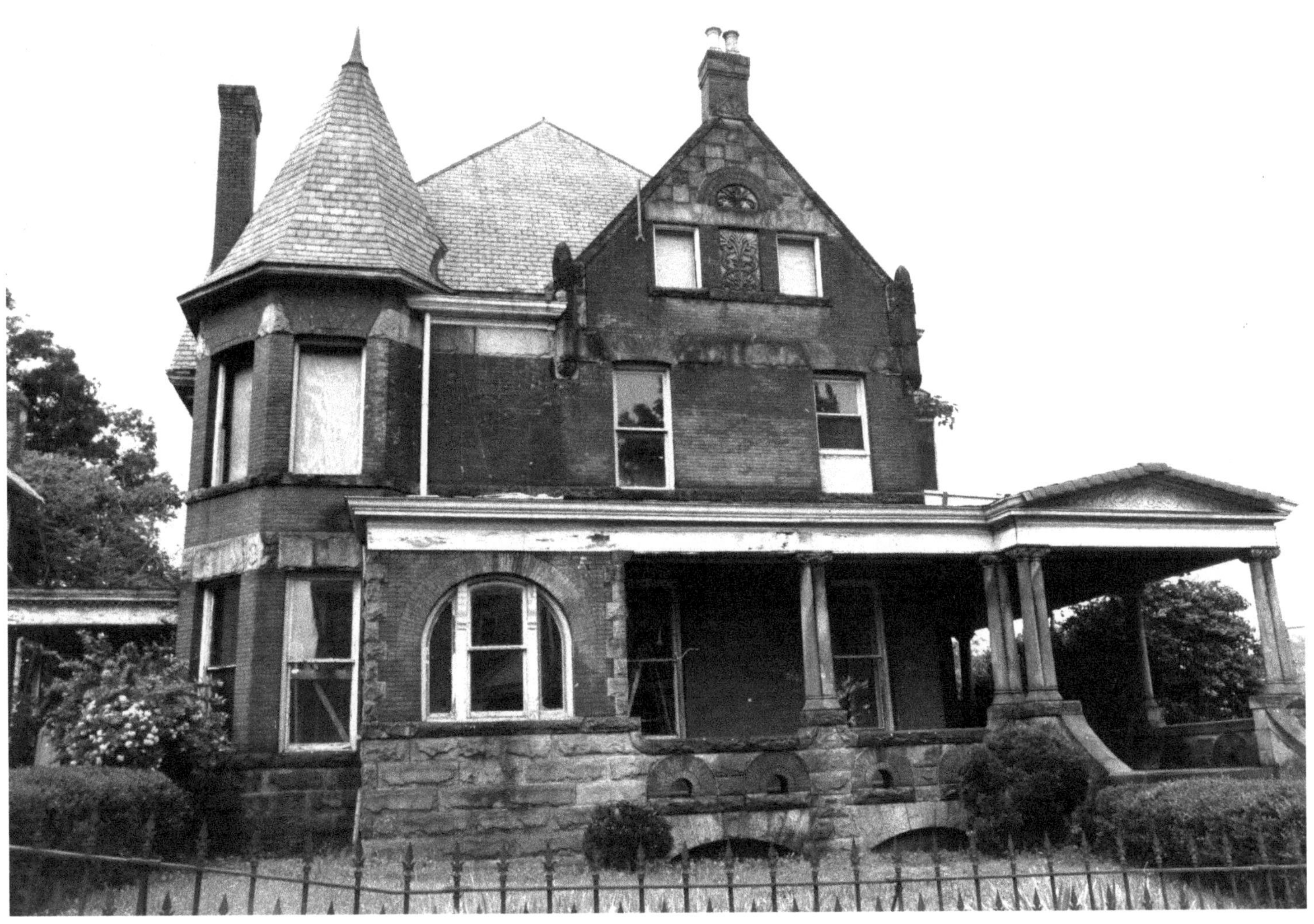

Vine Street is home to some of the city's finest turn-of-the-century residences. Built in 1891, this brick and stone mansion had grown quite shabby by 1976, before the renovation movement began in the Fort Wood neighborhood. It served as the home of Major Joseph Warner, a banker and utilities commissioner, and his wife, Alice. Warner Park, several blocks east of this site, is named in his honor.

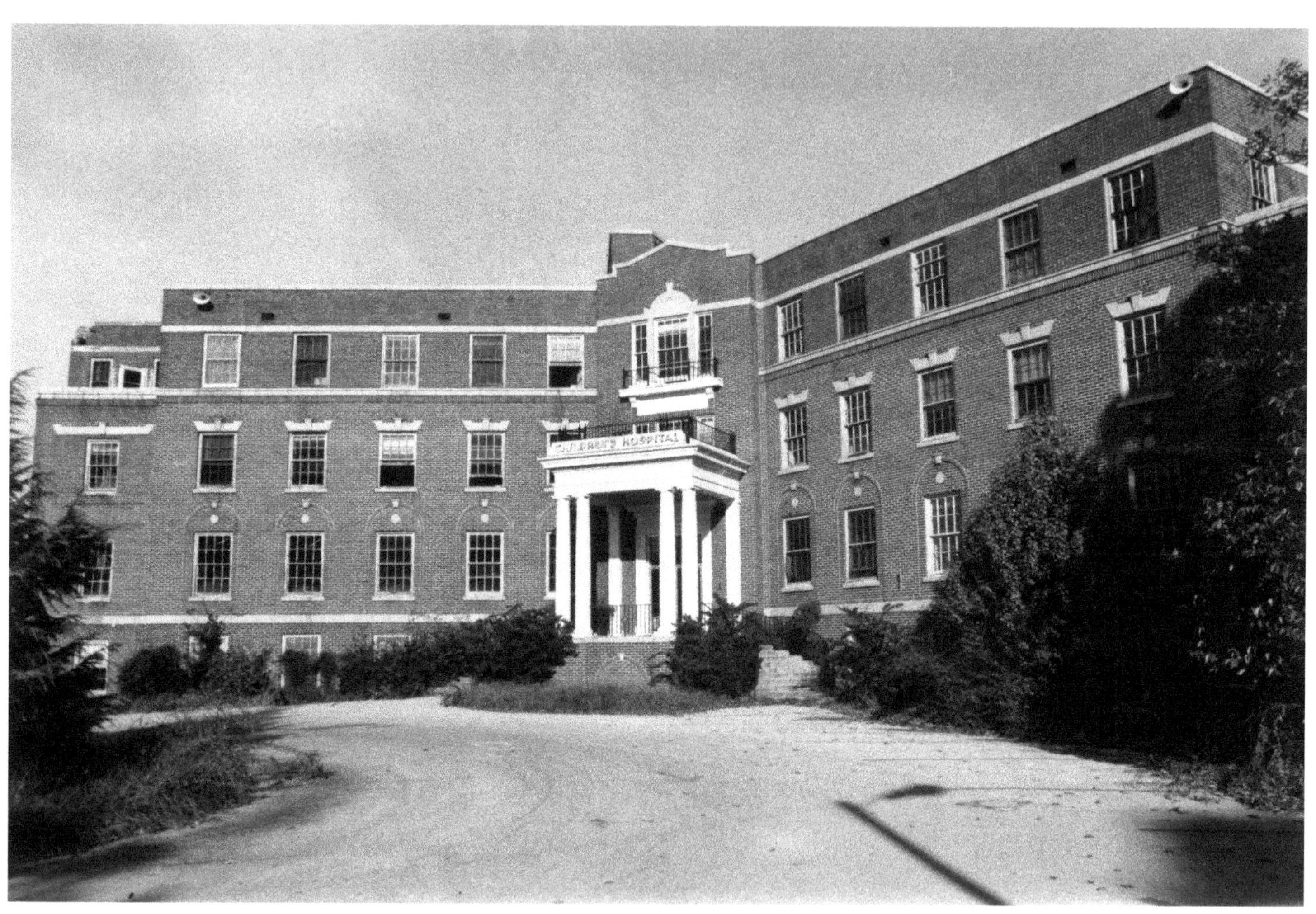

Mayor T. C. Thompson had an abiding interest in children's welfare, working constantly to raise private and public money for a children's hospital where children with needs regardless of income would be served. Opened in 1929, the specialty hospital was located in the Glenwood neighborhood near Missionary Ridge and had 89 beds. But by the seventies it had become untenable and in a wise move became part of Erlanger Hospital.

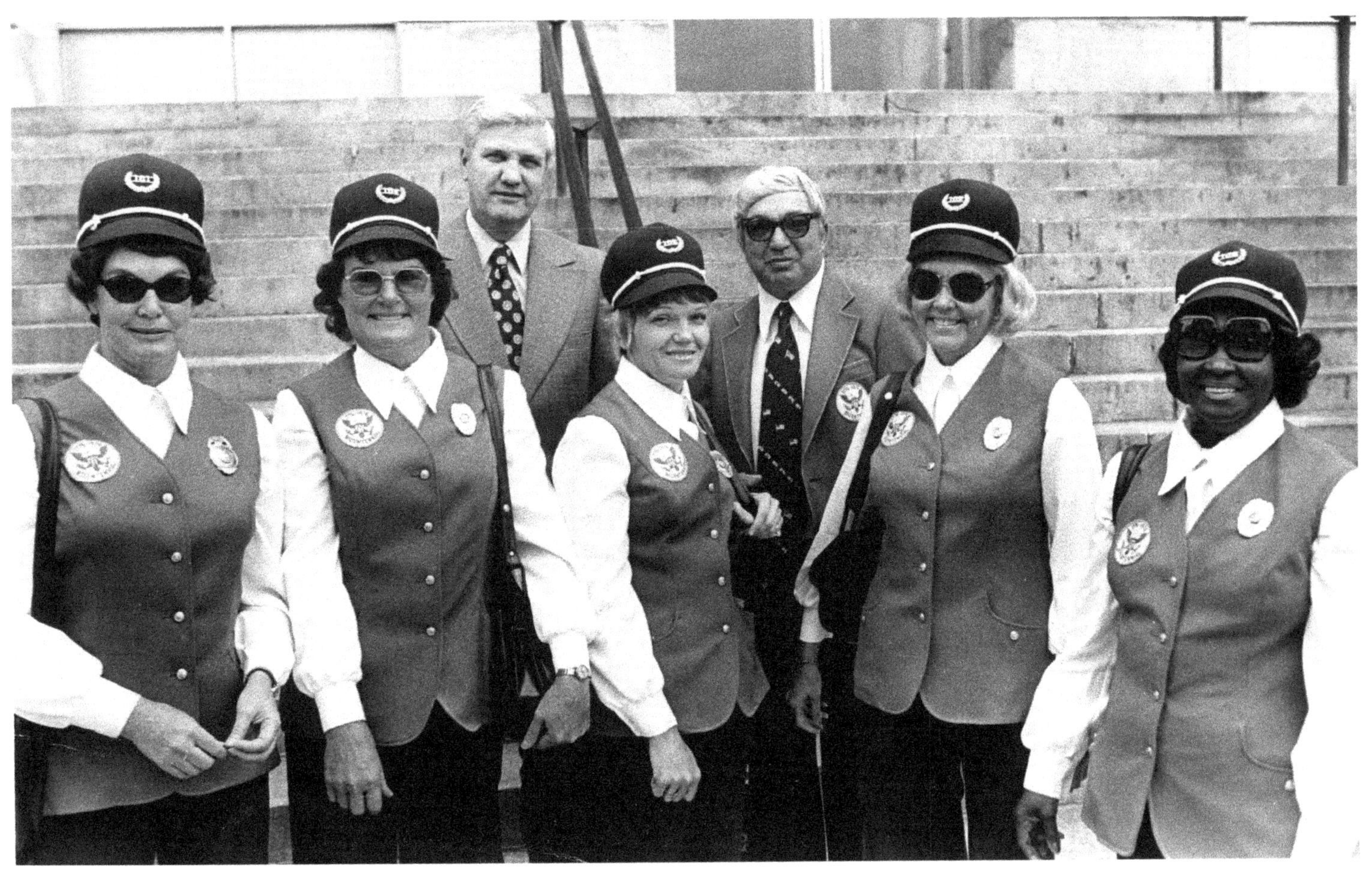

In the 1970s, women were working in increasing numbers at jobs that had been primarily the domain of men. One new wrinkle in police work was the presence of women as "meter maids"on city streets, checking automobiles to see if their parking meters were paid up. Mayor Gene Roberts and an assistant pose here with a uniformed squad of enforcers on the steps of the local municipal building around 1977.

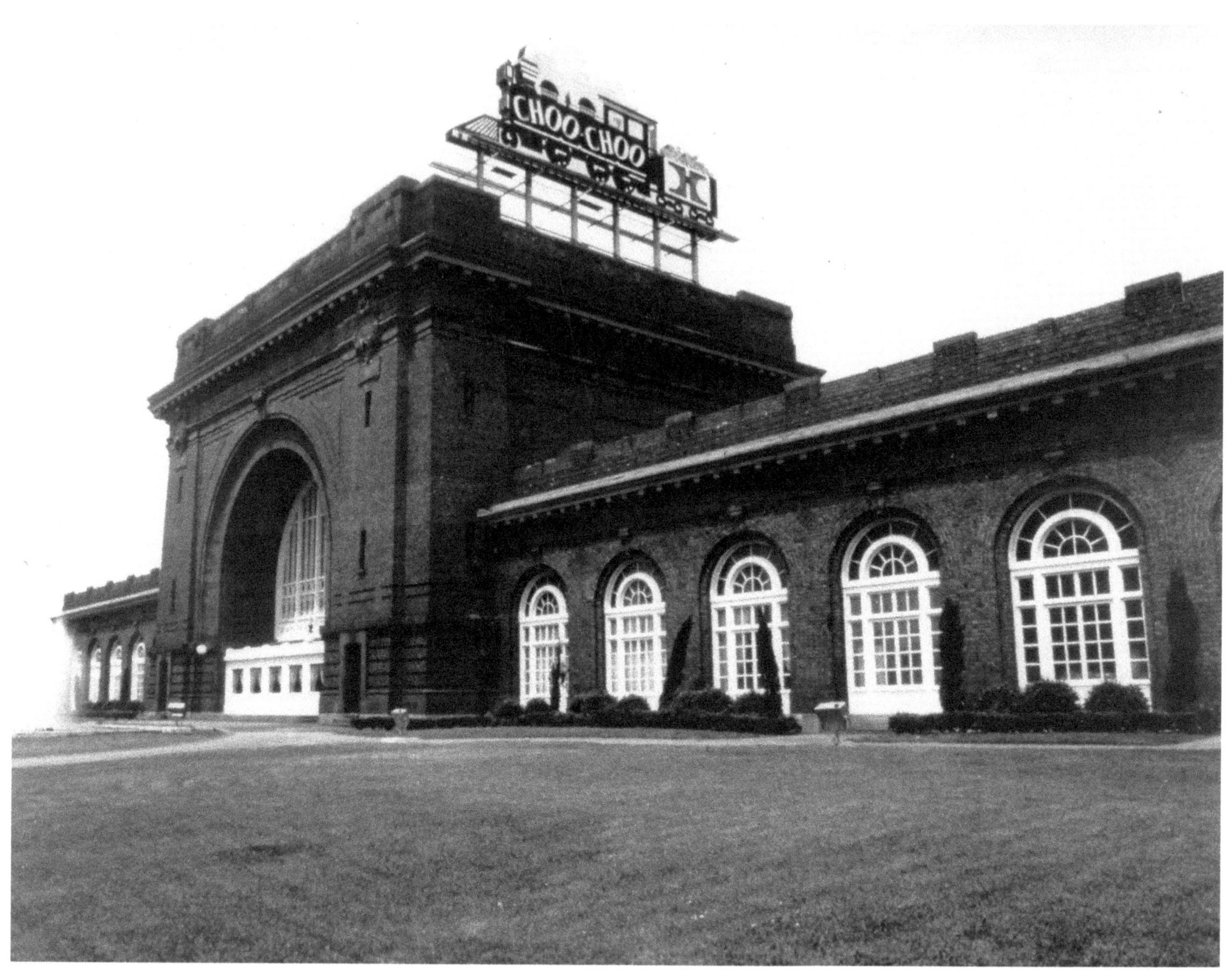

In the twentieth century, Chattanooga had two main train depots: the first, Union Depot across from the Read House, was demolished in the early seventies; the second, the Terminal Station, survived the demise of passenger rail service and reopened in 1973 as the Chattanooga Choo-Choo, with dining facilities and sleeper cars for overnight stays and a large neon sign above its roof. Originally opened in 1909, it features a spectacular domed interior over the main lobby.

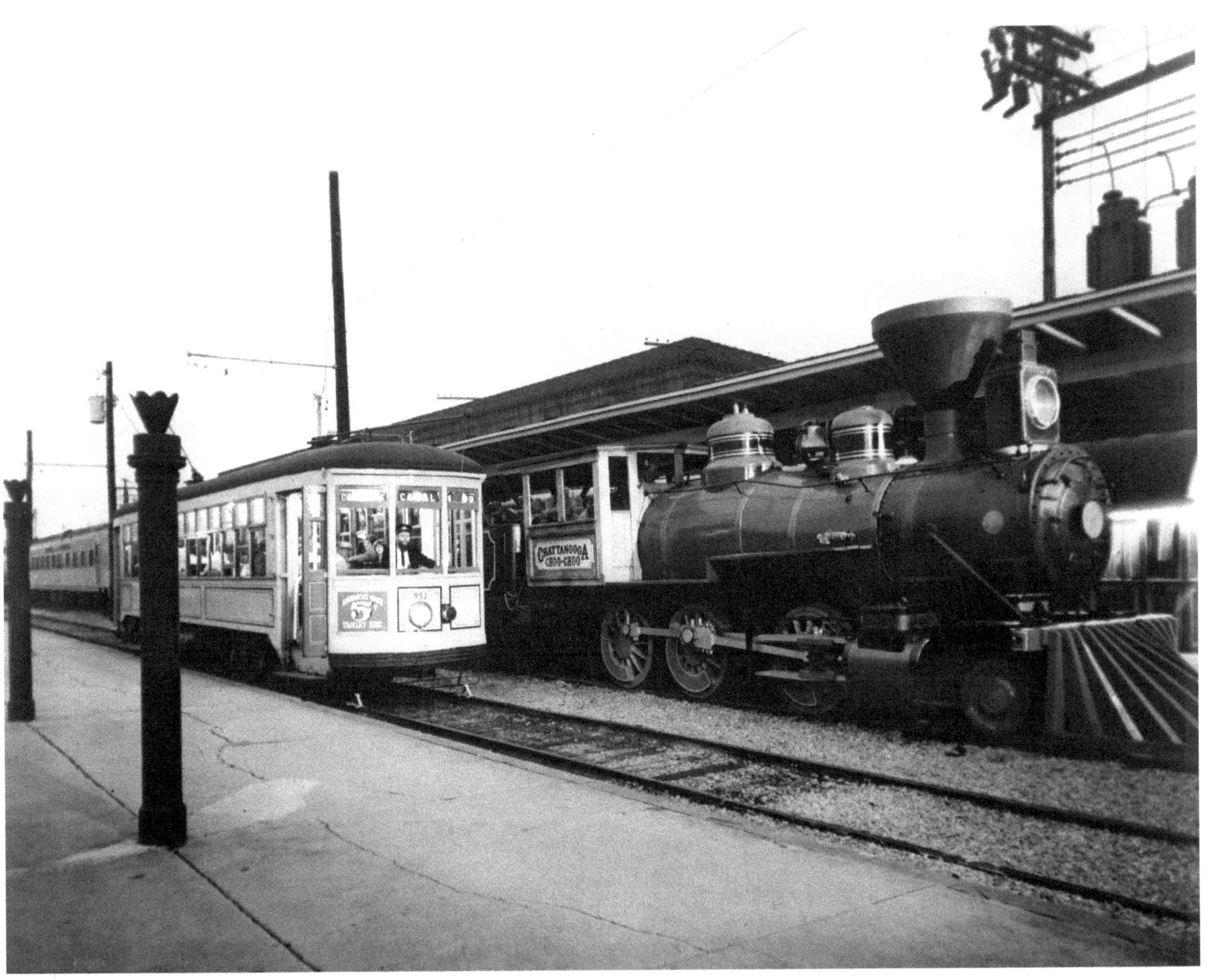

Rabbi David Steinberg, a historian and collector of Chattanooga railroad history, operates a trolley for passengers as they glide into the Chattanooga Choo-Choo. The tracks behind the station at the complex feature walkways, gardens, a shop, and benches for sitting and taking it all in. Aside from the Tennessee Valley Railroad Museum, the Choo-Choo is Chattanooga's most tangible remnant of the rail era, which literally put the city "on the map."

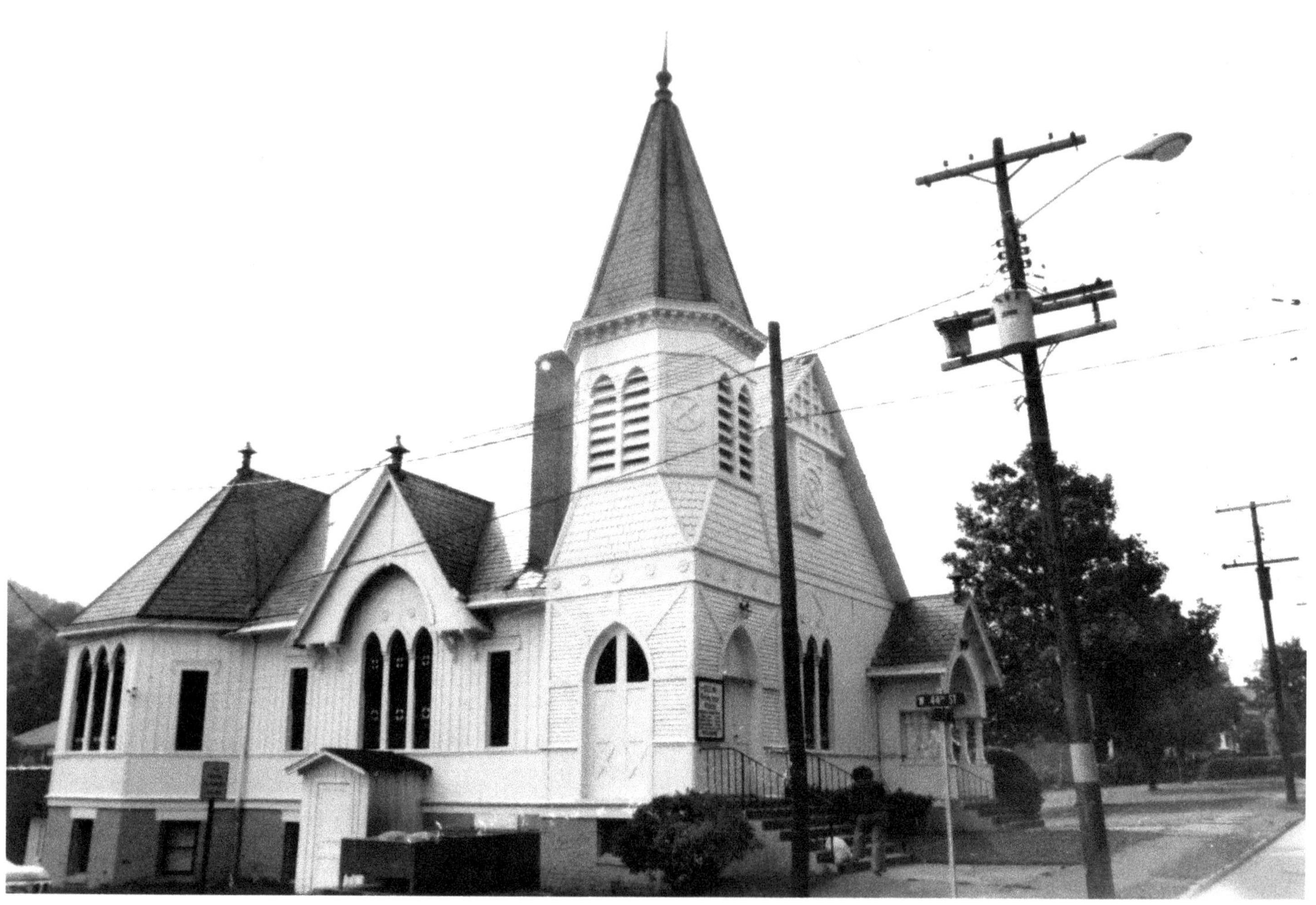

St. Elmo is considered Chattanooga's first suburb, beginning during the boom years of the late 1880s and early 1890s. Still a picturesque neighborhood today, its main thoroughfare, Tennessee Avenue, boasts a number of beautiful churches with a true diversity of architecture among them. The St. Elmo Presbyterian church, which opened in 1889, displays unique Craftsman-style features in the exterior woodwork, beautiful elongated windows, and a captivating corner tower. This is the church as it looked in 1976.

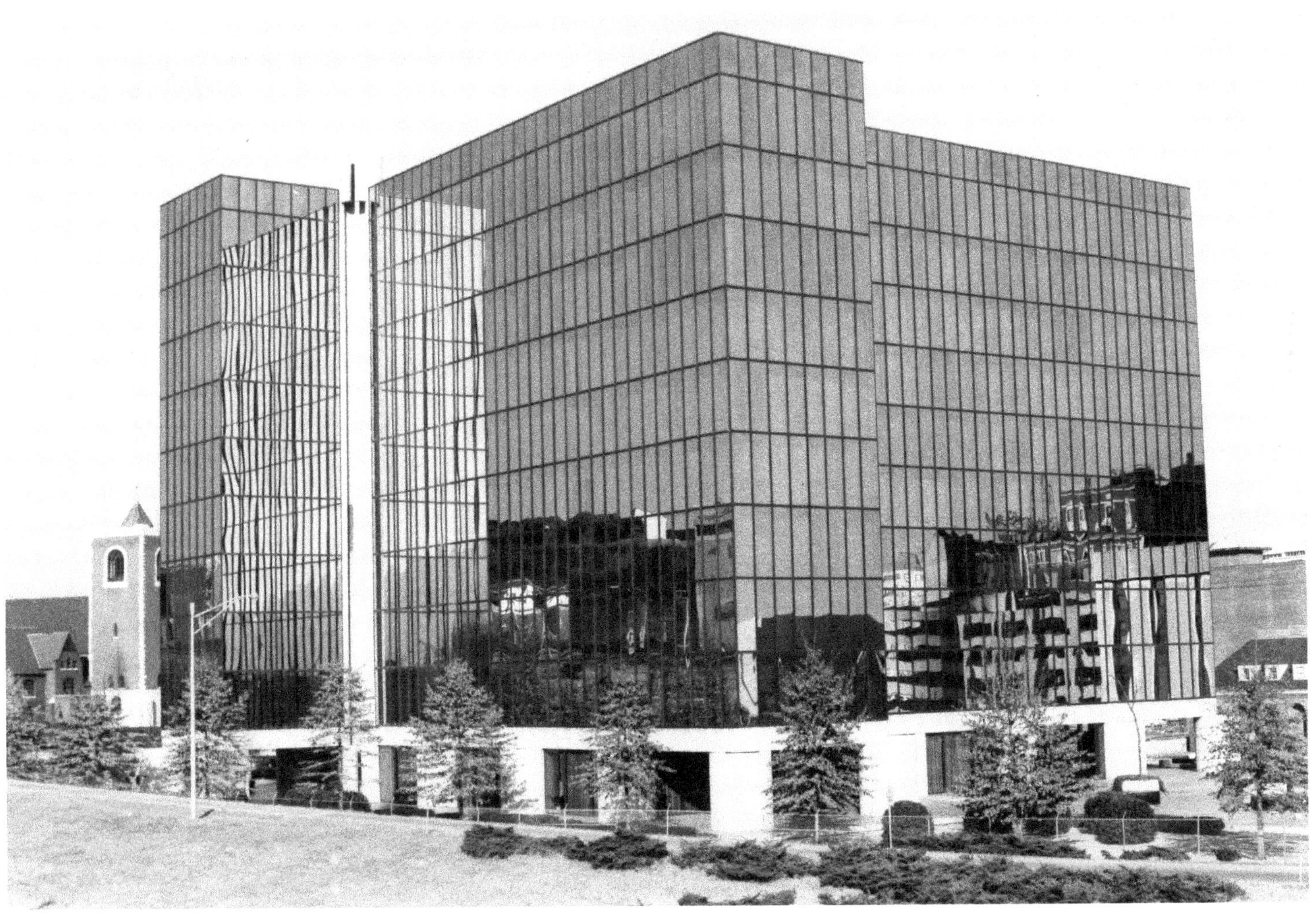

When the James Building, designed by R. H. Hunt, was built on Broad Street in 1907, it was considered Chattanooga's first skyscraper. Similarly, the Blue Cross Blue Shield building on Chestnut Street might be thought of as the city's first landmark modern building. The work of Atlanta architect John Portman, it opened in 1968 with gleaming, copper-colored skin that reflected automobiles speeding past it on the adjacent interstate.

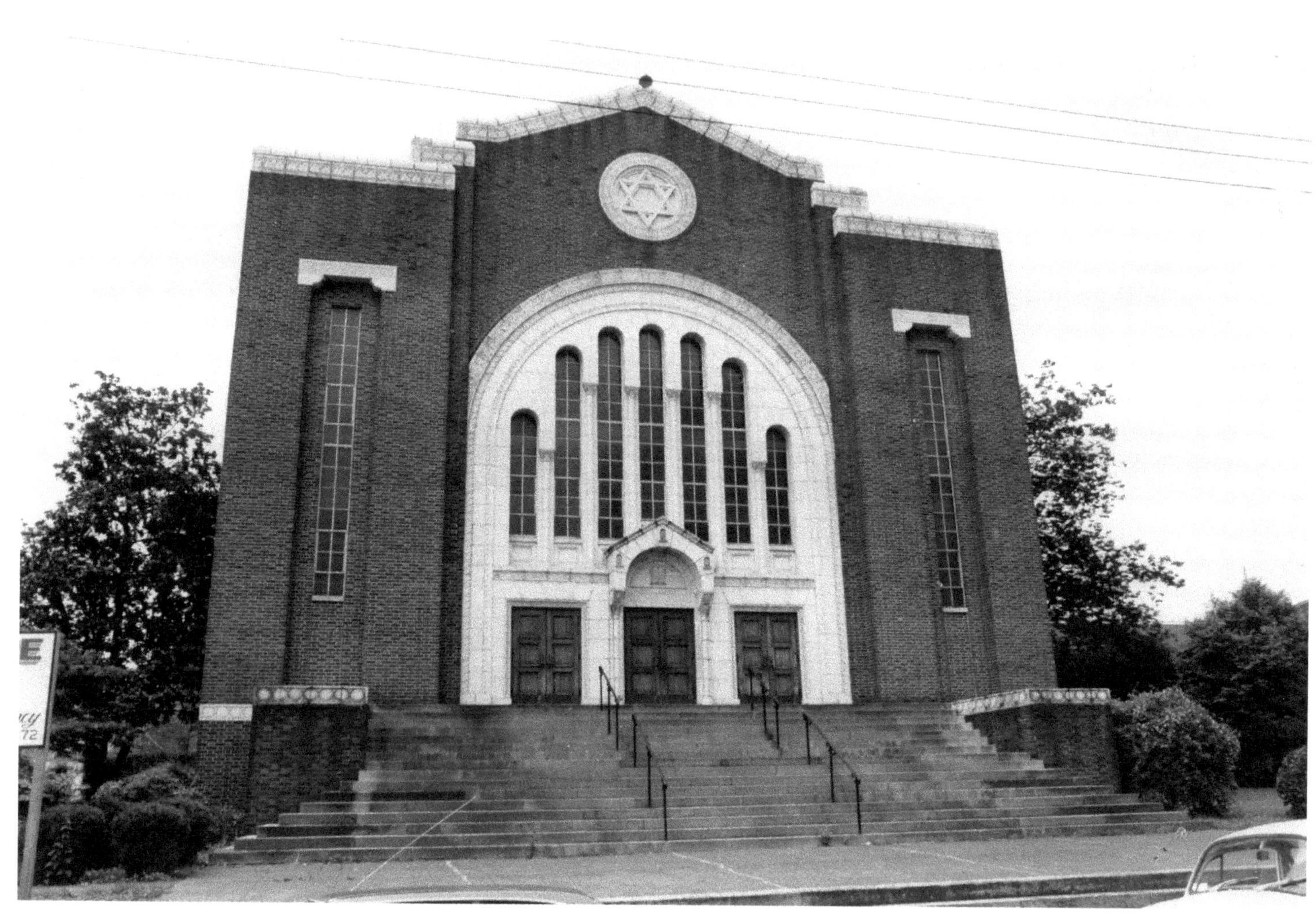

The Vine Street neighborhood downtown was vibrant prior to the suburbanization that took place in the sixties and seventies. This Jewish synagogue was located at 534 Vine Street and became the B'Nai Zion congregation in 1924; it was founded as B'Nai Chien in 1888. When the congregation decided to move to McBrien Road in Brainerd, the old synagogue was sold to the university in 1975, the year of this photograph, and eventually torn down.

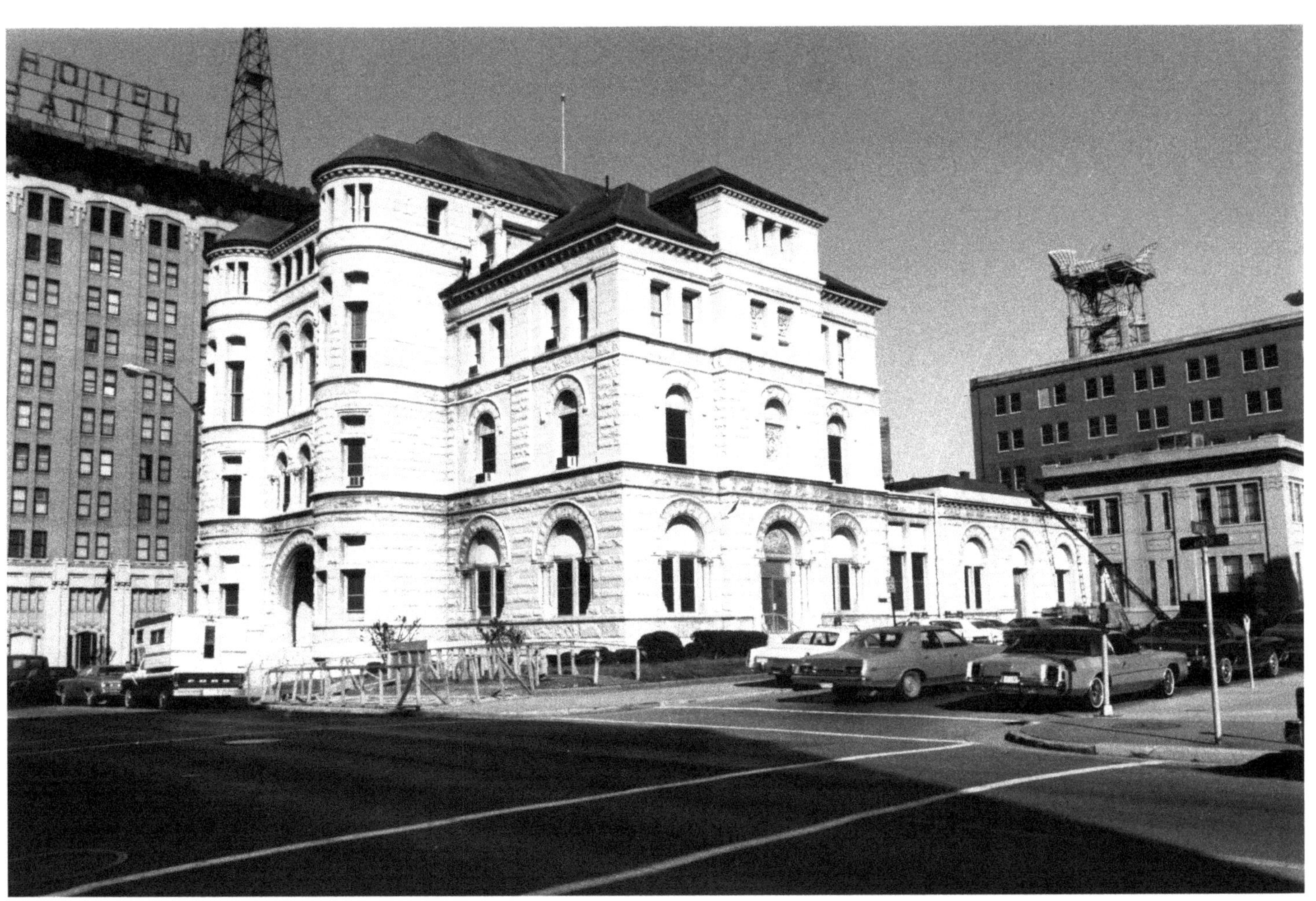

The Custom House stands on East Eleventh Street, a monument in stone to the city's first, notable resurgence after the Civil War. An impressive example of Richardsonian architecture, it was completed in 1893 at the end of a boom period in Chattanooga. The Post Office was located here until 1933; the site then became the home of a newer federal agency, the Tennessee Valley Authority, in 1934.

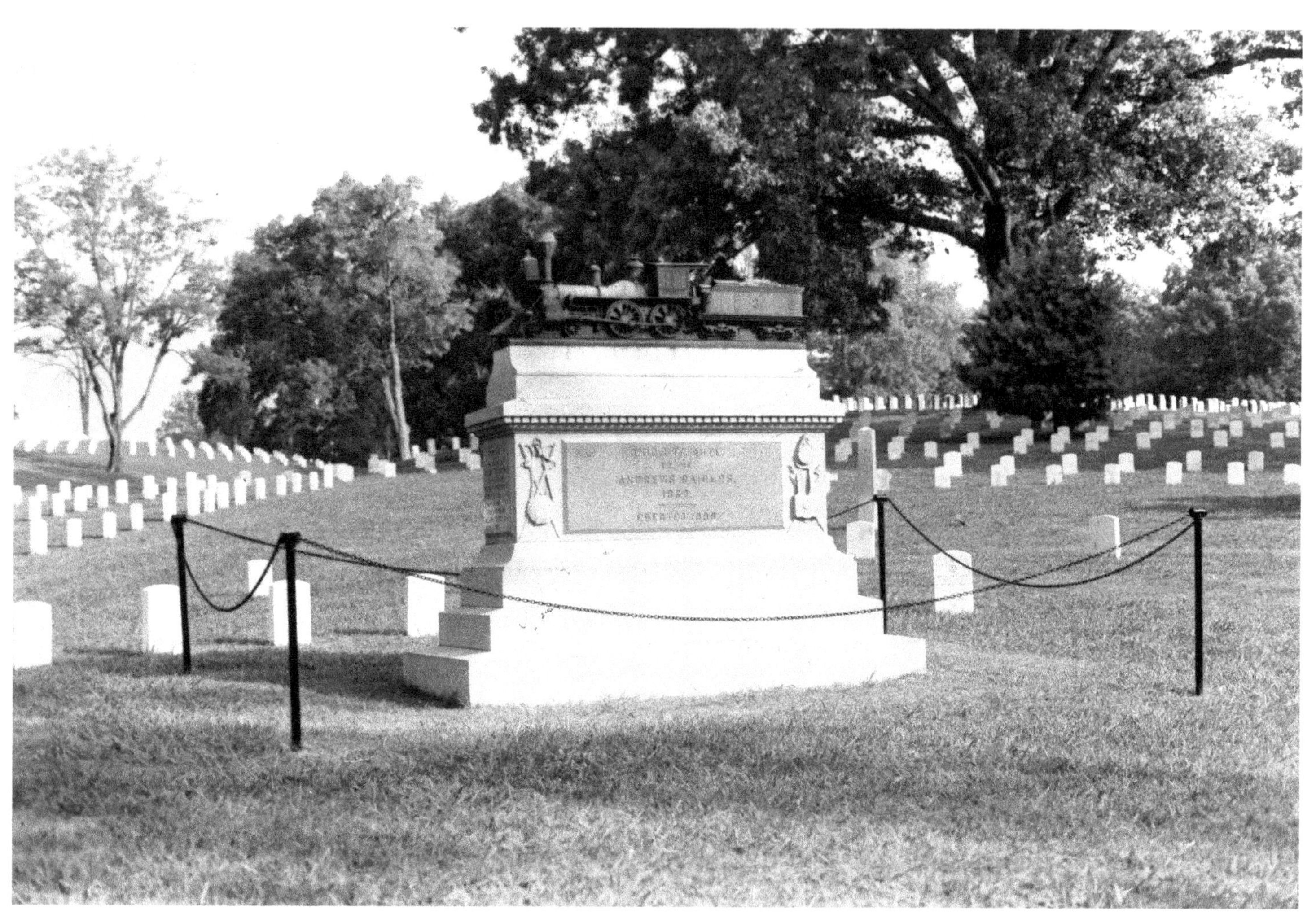

The National Cemetery on Bailey Avenue has one particular monument built in 1890 featuring a small reproduction of the Civil War engine the *General* and its coal car, which commemorates the story of Andrews' Raiders. During the war, James Andrews and his Union men stole the engine from the depot in Kennesaw, Georgia, and went full bore toward Chattanooga, doing all the damage they could to the rail line before they were captured. This image was recorded in 1976.

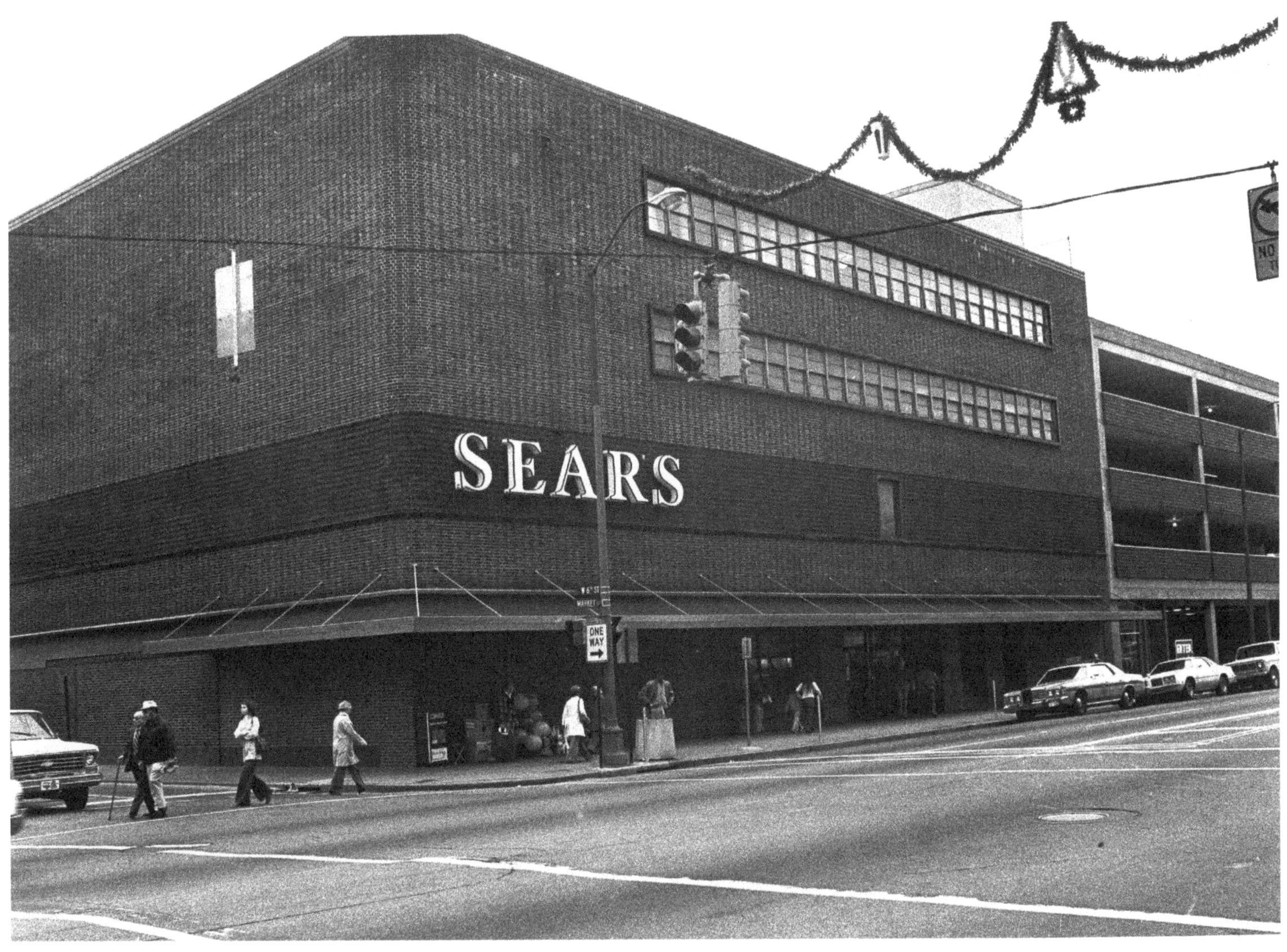

The original caption to this photograph reads "Sears Celebrates 50 Years Downtown," and this store on the corner of Broad and Sixth is evidence that the retail giant had a thriving presence in the urban core. But even by the mid-1970s, many shoppers had already taken their business elsewhere, and the Sears Company would eventually vacate the premises and head to the malls.

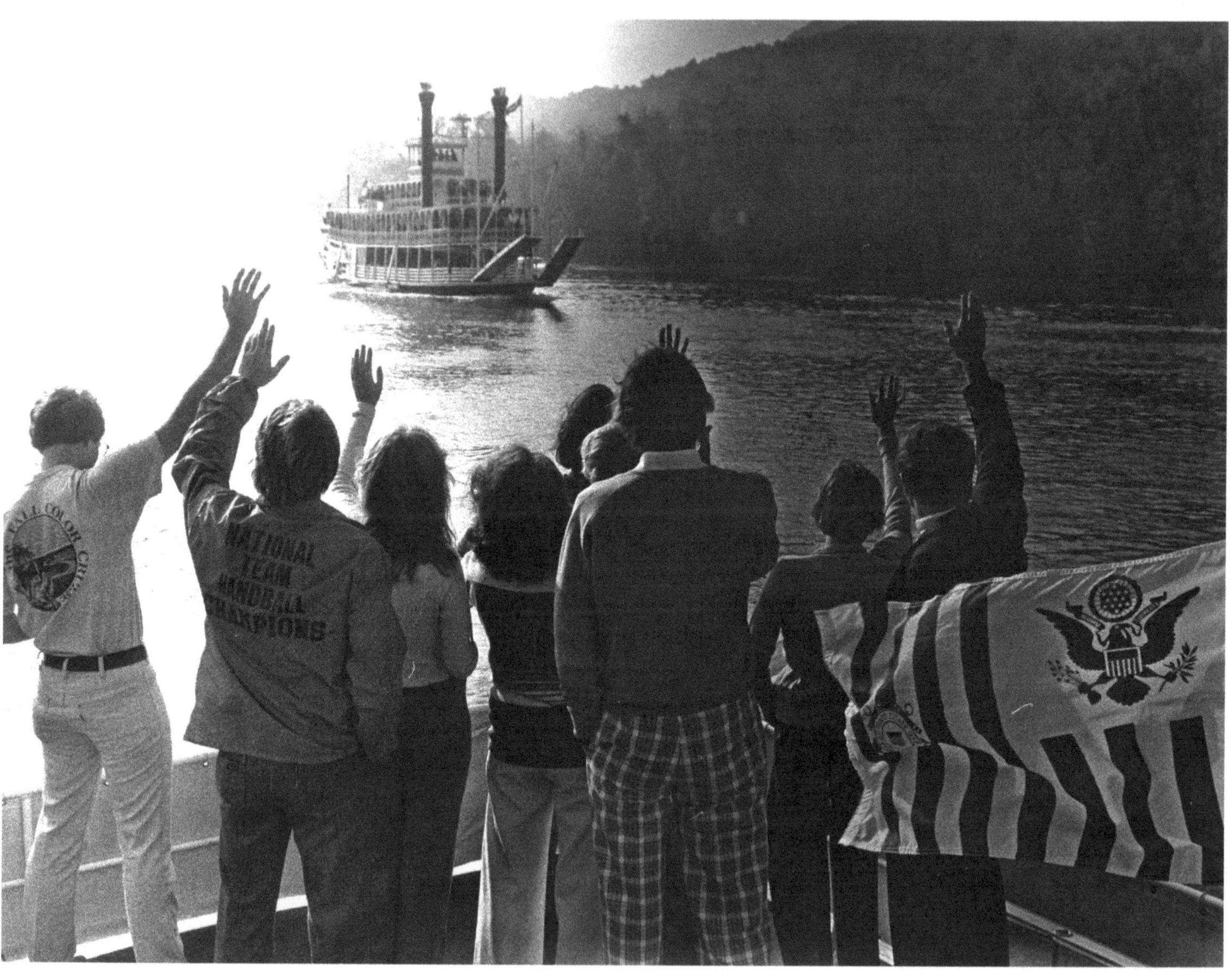

In the seventies, the environmental movement was having an impact on the city. Not only was the city making real strides in cleaning up the environment, people were beginning to value the natural heritage of the valley. One outcome was the annual Fall Color Cruise on the Tennessee River. Here folks wave at the *Julia Belle Swain* as it meanders down the river gorge to Nickajack on a sunny afternoon around 1974.

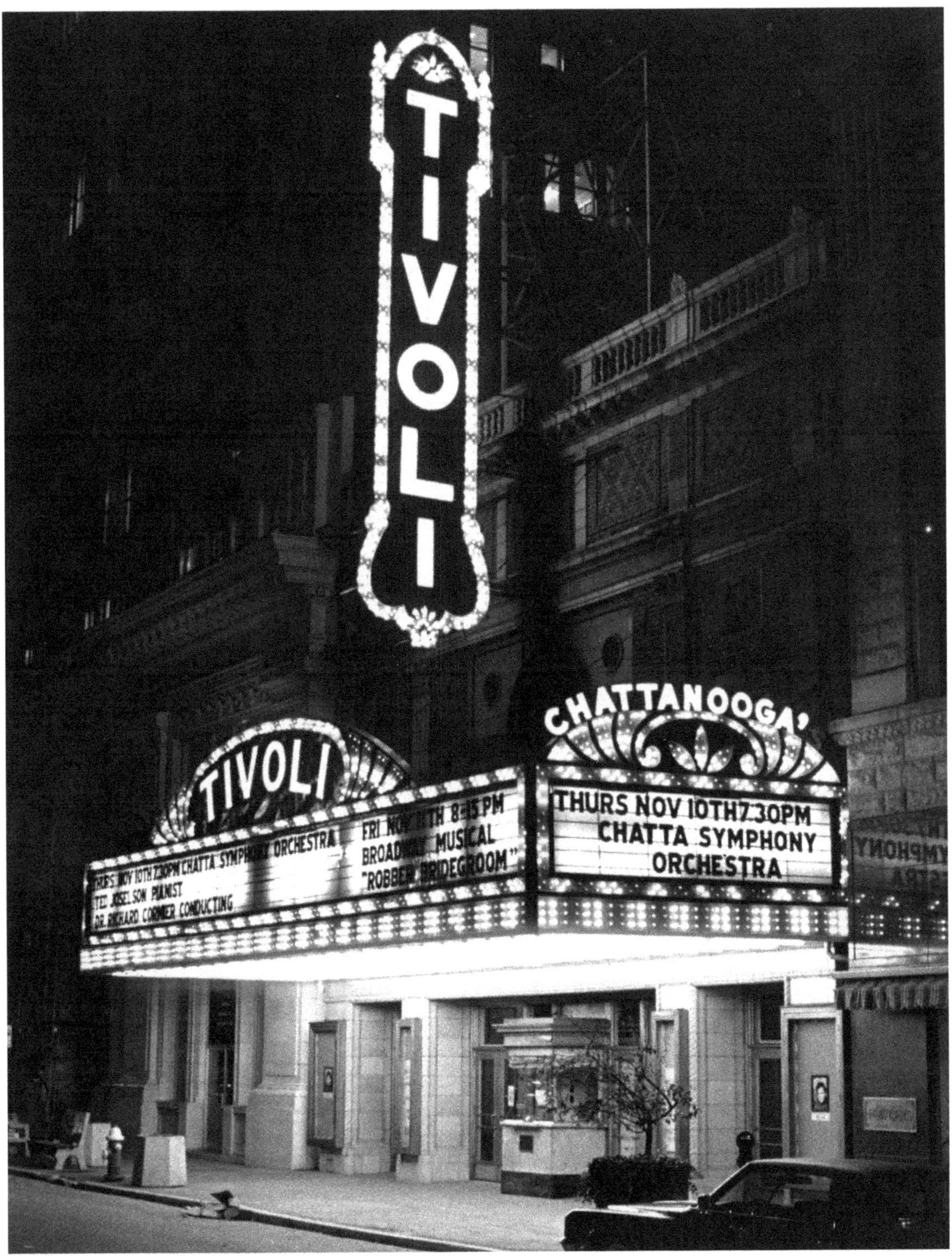

One of Broad Street's enduring landmarks is the Tivoli Theatre, a 1920s Beaux Arts edifice that one of the architects, George Rapp, called "a cavern of many-colored jewels." The home of the Chattanooga Symphony Orchestra, its interior is richly embellished with ornate, golden plaster work and crystal chandeliers. Originally a movie palace, it was one of the first public venues in the nation to offer air conditioning, a novelty at the time. The theater is seen here one evening in 1977.

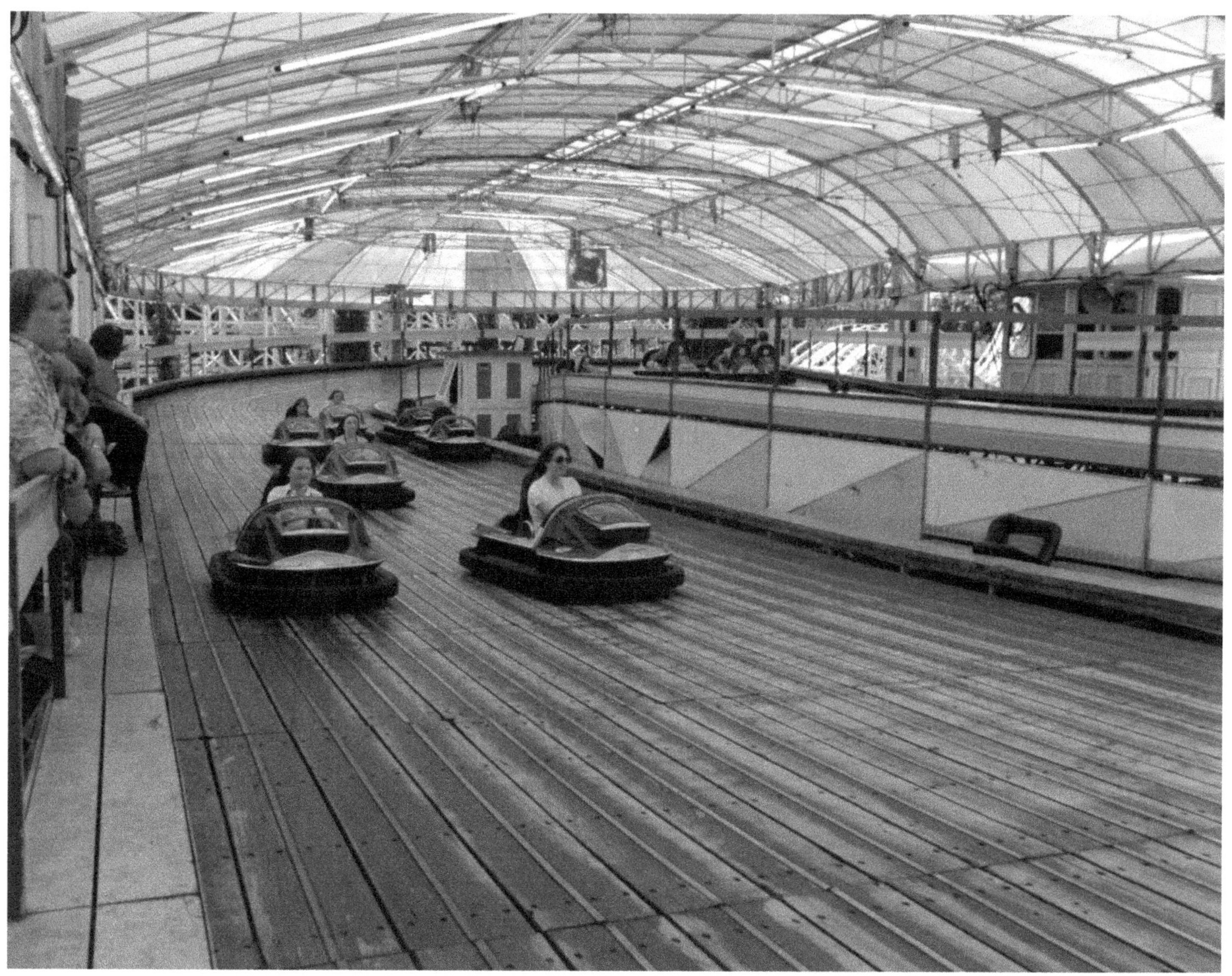

Lake Winnepesaukah offers some old-fashioned fun at an old-fashioned price. In addition to bumper cars, the park gave these racing fans something to enjoy in 1978. This long oval and the families hanging on the rail may not be the Talladega raceway, but for plenty of kids—and some adults—"Lake Winnie's" Indy 500 car ride on a hot summer afternoon was close enough.

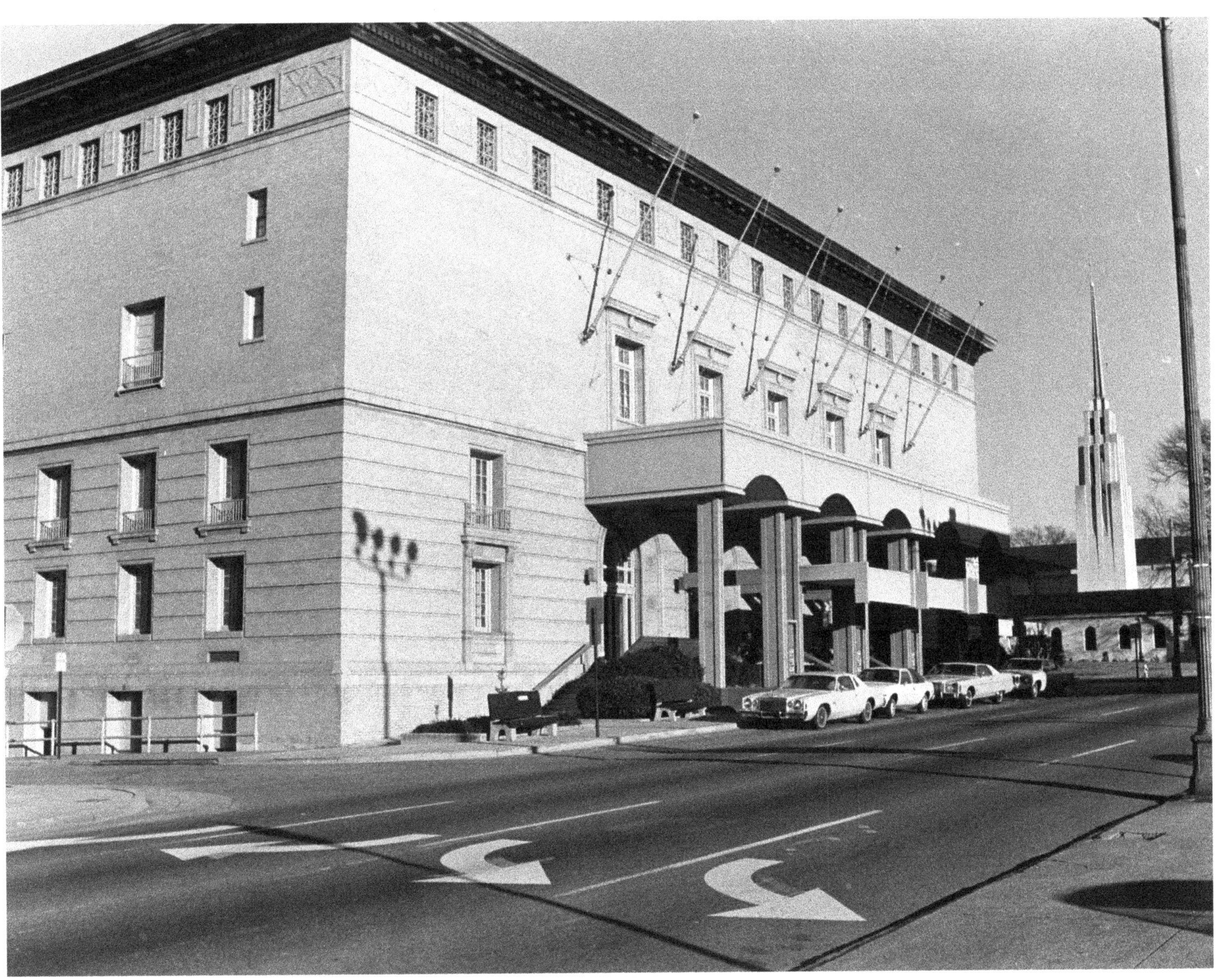

The city's largest space for performances is the Soldiers and Sailors Memorial Auditorium on McCallie Avenue, one of the town's oldest thoroughfares. In 1971, the board of directors denied the staging of the rock music hit *Hair* on grounds of obscenity. The promoters sued and the case went to the Supreme Court. In the background around 1978 stands the concrete spire of the First Centenary United Methodist Church, opened in 1973.

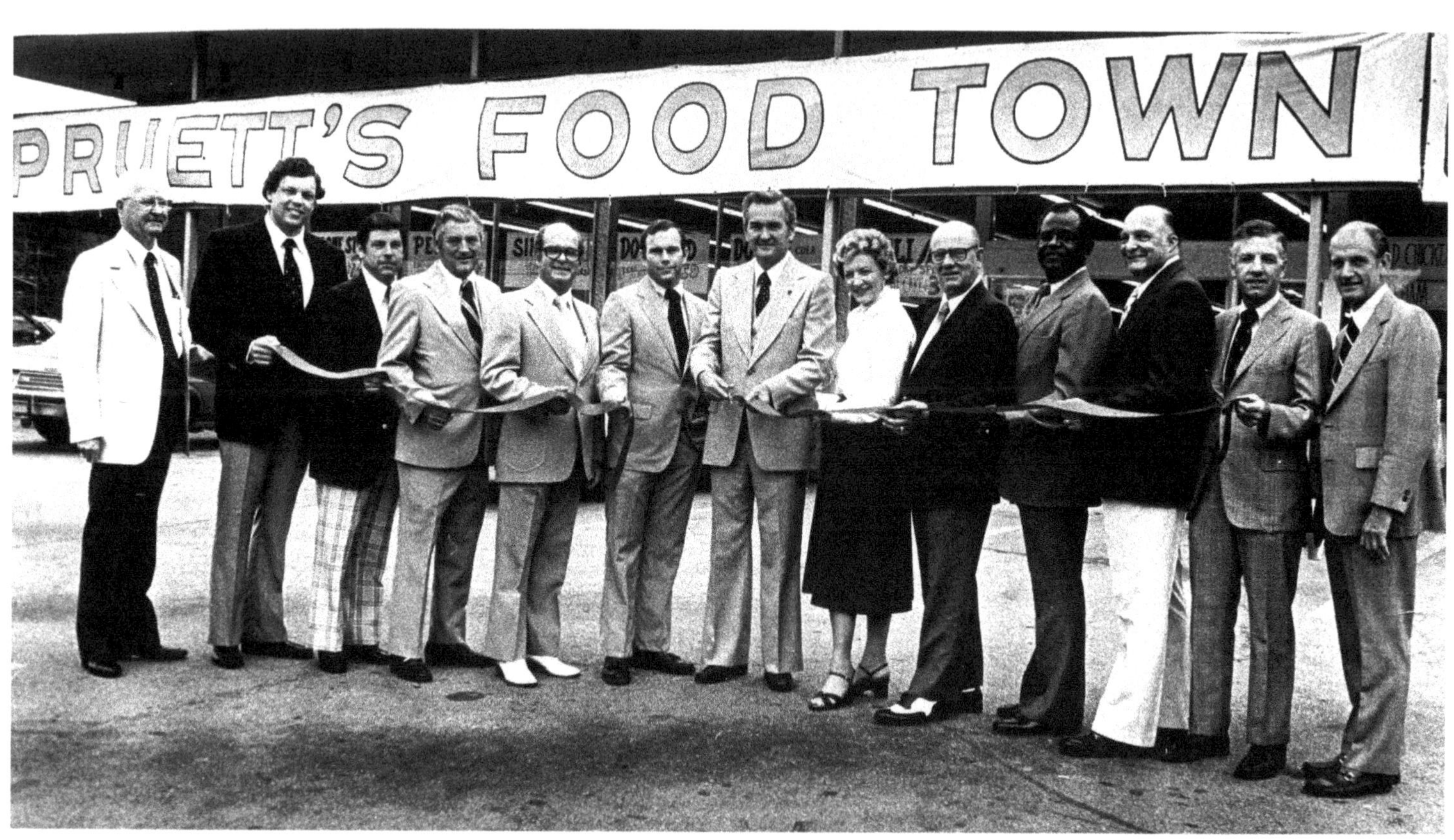

When the mayor shows up for a grand opening, the occasion must be important. The Pruett family has operated one of the longest running and most successful grocery businesses in Chattanooga, and it is still prospering today. Standing in front of the Highway 58 store in 1979 are Mayor Pat Rose, in the very center; Charles Pruett to his left; Rachel Pruett to his right; and founder A. C. Pruett to her right.

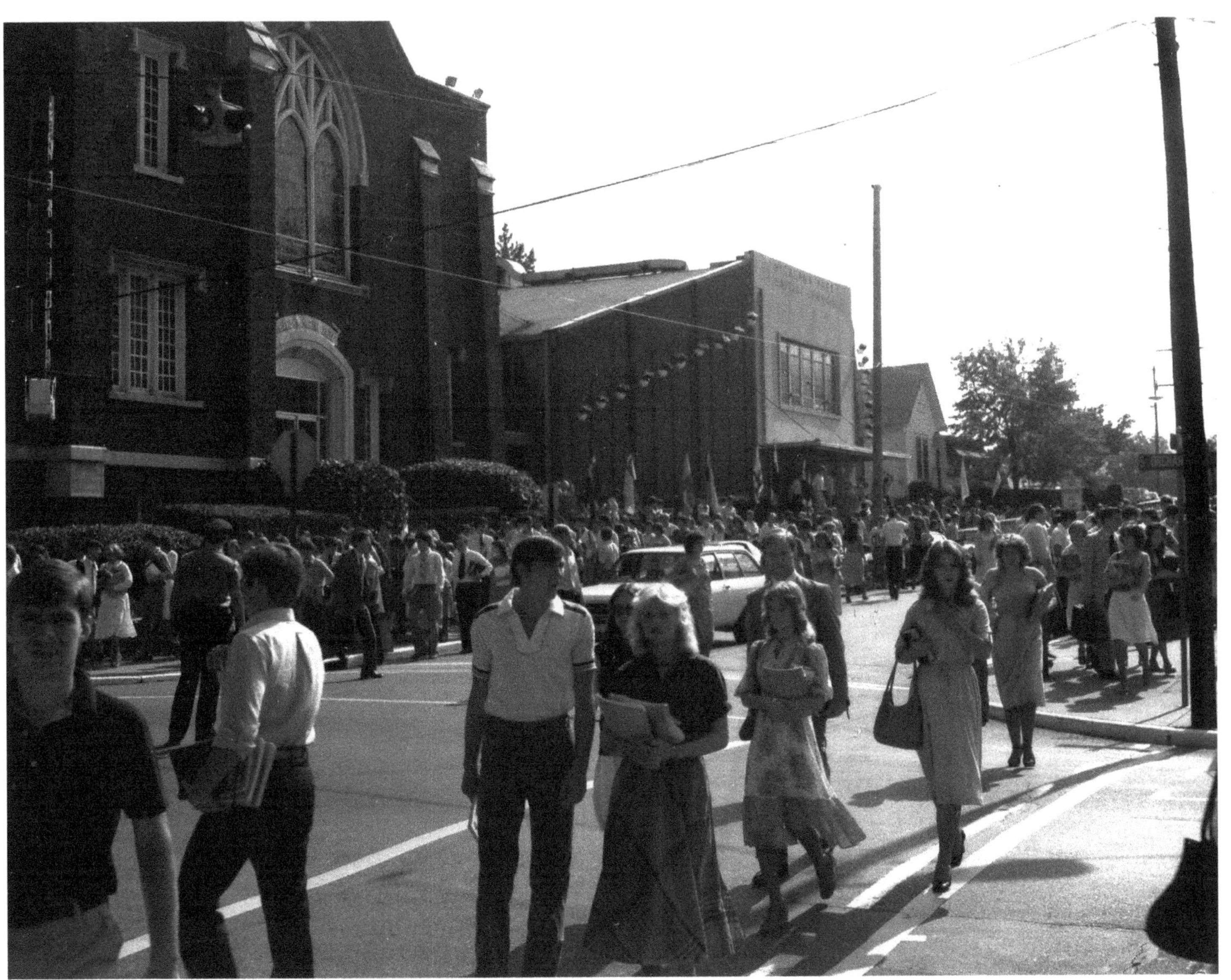

Students at Tennessee Temple University stroll between classes on Orchard Knob Avenue on a sunny day in 1979. The school, whose motto is "Distinctively Christian," traces its roots to the Phillips Memorial Chapel, visible on the left, where church services began in 1922. Located in the Highland Park neighborhood, the school grew slowly at first but expanded rapidly in the 1970s, becoming an accredited four-year university with a strong emphasis on biblical studies.

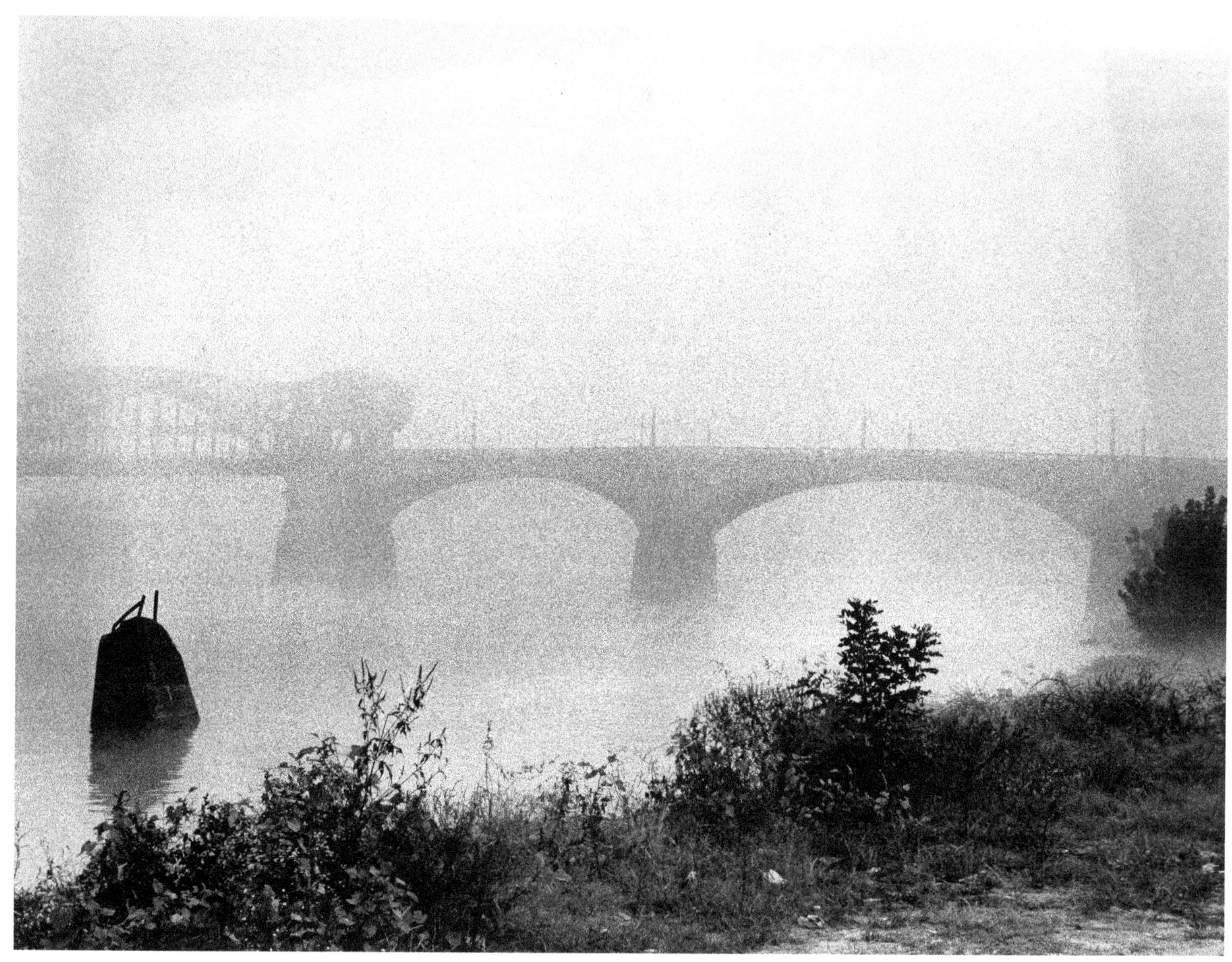

A dense, early morning fog enfolds the Market Street Bridge around 1979, making it difficult to tell where the mist ends and the bridge begins. Occasionally, the vapory air is sufficiently opaque that it obscures the mountaintops. Caution is the watchword when the fog sits "on silent haunches" and roads around the river must be driven.

Notes on the Photographs

These notes, listed by page number, attempt to include all aspects known of the photographs. Each of the photographs is identified by the page number, photograph's title or description, photographer and collection, archive, and call or box number when applicable. Although every attempt was made to collect all data, in some cases complete data may have been unavailable due to the age and condition of some of the photographs and records.

ii **Point Park Panorama, 1953**
Courtesy of Tennessee State Library and Archives
DB 15937

vi **The Plaza Hotel on Market Street**
Chattanooga-Hamilton County Bicentennial Library
00001353

x **Visitors to Ruby Falls**
Chattanooga-Hamilton County Bicentennial Library
00002495

2 **The Incline's Ton of Steel Cable**
Chattanooga-Hamilton County Bicentennial Library
00003917

3 **Chattanooga Amateur Thespians**
Cox Family Collection

4 **Stone House with Cannons**
Chattanooga-Hamilton County Bicentennial Library
00005055

6 **Interstate Insurance Office Building**
Chattanooga-Hamilton County Bicentennial Library
00004021

7 **Highland Park Station Post Office Staff**
Cox Family Collection

8 **The Patten Parkway**
Chattanooga-Hamilton County Bicentennial Library
00003981

9 **Spring Frog Cabin**
Chattanooga-Hamilton County Bicentennial Library
00003912

10 **Chattanooga Shoe Shine Day Contest, 1950**
Chattanooga-Hamilton County Bicentennial Library
00003957

11 **Ernest Peckinpaugh and His Fly Tiers**
Courtesy of Tennessee State Library and Archives
DB 16841

12 **Members of the Art Study Club**
Chattanooga-Hamilton County Bicentennial Library
00002385

13 **Picnickers at Booker T. Washington Park**
Courtesy of Tennessee State Library and Archives
DB 22564

14 **Another Source of Power**
Chattanooga-Hamilton County Bicentennial Library
00003990

15 **Natural Gas Stove Promotion, 1950**
Chattanooga-Hamilton County Bicentennial Library
00003991

16 **Well-wishers at Trackside**
Chattanooga-Hamilton County Bicentennial Library
00004012

17 **Servicemen Bound for Camp Pendleton**
Chattanooga-Hamilton County Bicentennial Library
00004029

18 **A Portrait of the Baroness d'Erlanger**
Chattanooga-Hamilton County Bicentennial Library
00004988

19 **The Founders Hall Clock**
Chattanooga-Hamilton County Bicentennial Library
00004031

20 **Veterans Day Ceremony**
Chattanooga-Hamilton County Bicentennial Library
00004015

21 **Market Street at Christmastime**
Chattanooga-Hamilton County Bicentennial Library
00004172

22 **A Good Day to Fish at Chickamauga Lake**
Chattanooga-Hamilton County Bicentennial Library
00004056

23 **Blaze at Kirk's Supermarket, 1951**
Chattanooga-Hamilton County Bicentennial Library
00001166

24 **Lookout Mountain's Police Force**
Chattanooga-Hamilton County Bicentennial Library
00004039

25 **Margaret Truman with Members of the Orchestra**
Chattanooga-Hamilton County Bicentennial Library
00003182

26 **Rogers Theater**
Chattanooga-Hamilton County Bicentennial Library
00004036

27 **Rogers Theater no. 2**
Chattanooga-Hamilton County Bicentennial Library
00004052

28 **Trackside at the Cox & Lawson Railroad**
Cox Family Collection

29 **Cox & Lawson Engineers**
Cox Family Collection

30 **Field-trial Bird Dog Competition, 1951**
Chattanooga-Hamilton County Bicentennial Library
00004057

31 **Greyhound Bus Station on Market Street**
Chattanooga-Hamilton County Bicentennial Library
00004044

32 **Market Street North from Ninth Street, 1951**
Chattanooga-Hamilton County Bicentennial Library
00004169

33 **Krystal and the Rogers Theater Block**
Chattanooga-Hamilton County Bicentennial Library
00001354

34 **Olan Mills Studios**
Chattanooga-Hamilton County Bicentennial Library
00004059

35 **Future Farmers of America Convention**
Chattanooga-Hamilton County Bicentennial Library
00004068

36 **Southern Coach Lines Bus**
Chattanooga-Hamilton County Bicentennial Library
00001454

37 **South on Market Street**
Chattanooga-Hamilton County Bicentennial Library
00004171

38 **No Hunting Signage at Chapin Sanctuary**
Chattanooga-Hamilton County Bicentennial Library
00004158

39 **Floodwaters at St. Elmo, 1951**
Chattanooga-Hamilton County Bicentennial Library
00004072

40 **View from Missionary Ridge**
Courtesy of Tennessee State Library and Archives
DB 15922

41 **Cavalier Corporation Employees**
Courtesy of Tennessee State Library and Archives
DB 20661

42 **Bottling Coca-Cola**
Courtesy of Tennessee State Library and Archives
DB 20652

43 **Vending Machines for Coca-Cola**
Courtesy of Tennessee State Library and Archives
DB 20664

44 **Brock Candy Assembly Line**
Courtesy of Tennessee State Library and Archives
DB 20648

45 **Brock Candy Cooking Vats**
Courtesy of Tennessee State Library and Archives
DB 20642

46 **Jelly Bean Polisher**
Courtesy of Tennessee State Library and Archives
DB 20640

47 **The E. I. Du Pont de Nemours Plant**
Courtesy of Tennessee State Library and Archives
DB 20638

48 **The Privateer Yacht Club**
Courtesy of Tennessee State Library and Archives
DB 24036

49 **View from the Upper Incline Station**
Courtesy of Tennessee State Library and Archives
DB 15939

50 **Two Chattanooga Banks**
Chattanooga-Hamilton County Bicentennial Library
00004514

51 **Cruising the River to Watts Bar Village**
Courtesy of Tennessee State Library and Archives
DB 24413

52 **Westward on Eleventh Street, 1954**
Chattanooga-Hamilton County Bicentennial Library
00001307

53 **Dedication of the Chickamauga Bridge**
Chattanooga-Hamilton County Bicentennial Library
00001379

54 **The Scenic City**
Chattanooga-Hamilton County Bicentennial Library
00004412

55 **Concrete Parking Garage on Cherry Street**
Chattanooga-Hamilton County Bicentennial Library
00001368

56 **Field House at Warner Park**
Chattanooga-Hamilton County Bicentennial Library
00005752

57 **The Central Block Building**
Chattanooga-Hamilton County Bicentennial Library
00001336

58 **Effron's New Facade**
Chattanooga-Hamilton County Bicentennial Library
00004719

59 **At Ninth and Market, 1955**
Chattanooga-Hamilton County Bicentennial Library
00002076

60 **Hamilton County Courthouse**
Chattanooga-Hamilton County Bicentennial Library
00004685

61 **Rocky Courts Cabins Roadside Inn**
Chattanooga-Hamilton County Bicentennial Library
00005715

62 **Lovell Field Tower**
Chattanooga-Hamilton County Bicentennial Library
00004479

63 **Busy Day on Market Street, 1955**
Chattanooga-Hamilton County Bicentennial Library
00001351

64 **The Town and Country Restaurant**
Chattanooga-Hamilton County Bicentennial Library
00001296

65 **Frazier Avenue**
Chattanooga-Hamilton County Bicentennial Library
Heiner
00001298

66 **High School Art Club Trip**
Cox Family Collection

67 **Automobiles on the Wilkes T. Thrasher Bridge**
Chattanooga-Hamilton County Bicentennial Library
00001496

68 **Morning Traffic at Georgia and Ninth**
Chattanooga-Hamilton County Bicentennial Library
00004416

69 **Home of the Electric Power Board**
Chattanooga-Hamilton County Bicentennial Library
00004642

70 **United States Post Office at Georgia Avenue**
Chattanooga-Hamilton County Bicentennial Library
00001357

71 **Farrar's Hosiery**
Chattanooga-Hamilton County Bicentennial Library
00001369

72 **Horse Auction at Sam O'Neil's**
Chattanooga-Hamilton County Bicentennial Library
00000603

73 **Incline Station at the Summit, 1956**
Chattanooga-Hamilton County Bicentennial Library
00001576

74 **Scene at the Home Plate Cafeteria**
Chattanooga-Hamilton County Bicentennial Library
00002095

75 **Patten Parkway and Volunteer Life**
Chattanooga-Hamilton County Bicentennial Library
00001372

76 **Moccasin Bend from Lookout Mountain**
Chattanooga-Hamilton County Bicentennial Library
00002648

78 **Campers at Harrison Bay State Park**
Chattanooga-Hamilton County Bicentennial Library
00005741

79 **Lookout Mountain Museum**
Chattanooga-Hamilton County Bicentennial Library
00005728

80 **Cravens Terrace Monument**
Chattanooga-Hamilton County Bicentennial Library
00005809

81 **Chickaroonie**
Chattanooga-Hamilton County Bicentennial Library
00002209

82 **Mort Lloyd**
Chattanooga-Hamilton County Bicentennial Library
00002221

83 **Top 10 Dance Party**
Chattanooga-Hamilton County Bicentennial Library
00002254

84 **The Bob Brandy Show**
Chattanooga-Hamilton County Bicentennial Library
00002183

85 **Members of the Symphony Orchestra**
Courtesy of Tennessee State Library and Archives
DB 16027

86 **Drake Motor Court**
Chattanooga-Hamilton County Bicentennial Library
00005699

87 **Near the Summit on the Incline**
Chattanooga-Hamilton County Bicentennial Library
00005487

88 **Rock City Promotions**
Chattanooga-Hamilton County Bicentennial Library
00005572

89 **Dedication Day at the Restored Cravens House**
Chattanooga-Hamilton County Bicentennial Library
00005115

90 **The Battle Recounted**
Courtesy of Tennessee State Library and Archives
DB 15978

91 **Creeping Around the Subterranean Falls**
Courtesy of Tennessee State Library and Archives
DB 30358

92 **Country Music Performers**
Courtesy of Tennessee State Library and Archives
DB 30359

93 **Inside at the Confederama**
Courtesy of Tennessee State Library and Archives
DB 30361

94 **Scene at harry Porter Flight School**
Chattanooga-Hamilton County Bicentennial Library
00004464

95 **Service at Hunter Hall**
Chattanooga-Hamilton County Bicentennial Library
00004134

96 **The Hotel Northern**
Chattanooga-Hamilton County Bicentennial Library
00004114

97 **Evening View from Missionary Ridge**
Chattanooga-Hamilton County Bicentennial Library
00004118

98 **Construction of an Interstate Highway**
Chattanooga-Hamilton County Bicentennial Library
00002657

99 **Aerial View of Erlanger Hospital**
Chattanooga-Hamilton County Bicentennial Library
00004991

100 **Home of the Mountain City Club**
Chattanooga-Hamilton County Bicentennial Library
00004113

101 **Remembrances of Antebellum Hoopskirts**
Chattanooga-Hamilton County Bicentennial Library
00002382

102 **Brown's Tavern**
Chattanooga-Hamilton County Bicentennial Library
00005072

103 **Melting Ice from the Walnut Street Bridge**
Chattanooga-Hamilton County Bicentennial Library
00004629

104 **Luther Masingill**
Chattanooga-Hamilton County Bicentennial Library
00002227

106 **In Front of the Read House, 1960**
Chattanooga-Hamilton County Bicentennial Library
00004144

107 **Cannon at the Brotherton House**
Courtesy of Tennessee State Library and Archives
DB 19322

108 **Concave Bank Building on the North Shore**
Chattanooga-Hamilton County Bicentennial Library
00000272

109 **Town and Country Shopping Center**
Chattanooga-Hamilton County Bicentennial Library
00002123

111 **Aerial View Facing North**
Chattanooga-Hamilton County Bicentennial Library
00000009

112 **The Tom and Homer Show**
Chattanooga-Hamilton County Bicentennial Library
00002501

113 **Ice Storm Aftermath on Walden's Ridge**
Chattanooga-Hamilton County Bicentennial Library
00002078

114 **Civil Rights Demonstrator**
Courtesy of Tennessee State Library and Archives
DB 26085

115 **View of Ninth Street, 1961**
Chattanooga-Hamilton County Bicentennial Library
00004424

116 **Busy Day on Market Street**
Chattanooga-Hamilton County Bicentennial Library
00001337

117 **Dedication of Plaque at the University**
Chattanooga-Hamilton County Bicentennial Library
00001754

118 **The General**
Chattanooga-Hamilton County Bicentennial Library
00001410

119 **Vintage Fire Engine**
Chattanooga-Hamilton County Bicentennial Library
00004950

120 **Provident Insurance Company**
Chattanooga-Hamilton County Bicentennial Library
00000826

121 **A Day on Chickamauga Lake**
Chattanooga-Hamilton County Bicentennial Library
00001530

122 **Outside at Confederama**
Chattanooga-Hamilton County Bicentennial Library
00004640

123 **Brainerd Road**
Chattanooga-Hamilton County Bicentennial Library
00001284

124 **The Chattanooga Lookouts, 1961**
Chattanooga-Hamilton County Bicentennial Library
00001982

125 **Chattanooga Bottling Dignitaries**
Chattanooga-Hamilton County Bicentennial Library
00002327

126 **The Municipal Building**
Chattanooga-Hamilton County Bicentennial Library
00004677

127 **Old-time Gospel Vocalists**
Chattanooga-Hamilton County Bicentennial Library
00002206

128 **Sunset Rock, 1963**
Chattanooga-Hamilton County Bicentennial Library
00005441

129 **Branch of Hamilton National Bank**
Chattanooga-Hamilton County Bicentennial Library
00004593

130 **Eastern Air Lines Plane at Lovell Field**
Chattanooga-Hamilton County Bicentennial Library
00001440

131 Hamilton Bank 75th Anniversary Cake
Chattanooga-Hamilton County Bicentennial Library 00004532

132 The Mt. Aetna Skyride
Chattanooga-Hamilton County Bicentennial Library 00005747

133 Signal Point, 1966
Chattanooga-Hamilton County Bicentennial Library 00005751

134 Wrecker Reenactment
Chattanooga-Hamilton County Bicentennial Library 00005263

135 Red Bank Baptist Church
Chattanooga-Hamilton County Bicentennial Library 00000844

136 The Mount Vernon Restaurant
Chattanooga-Hamilton County Bicentennial Library 00001687

137 The Martin Theater on Market Street
Chattanooga-Hamilton County Bicentennial Library 00000803

138 Lake Winnepesaukah
Chattanooga-Hamilton County Bicentennial Library 00005763

139 Lake Winnepesaukah no. 2
Chattanooga-Hamilton County Bicentennial Library 00005767

140 New Interstate Roadway
Courtesy of Tennessee State Library and Archives DB 15188

141 Grand Canyon of the Tennessee River
Courtesy of Tennessee State Library and Archives DB 24983

142 Campers at Chickamauga Lake
Courtesy of Tennessee State Library and Archives DB 23200

143 Lover's Leap at Rock City
Courtesy of Tennessee State Library and Archives DB 15835

144 Rock City Swinging Bridge
Courtesy of Tennessee State Library and Archives DB 15837

145 Amateur Photographers at Rock City
Courtesy of Tennessee State Library and Archives DB 15987

146 Moccasin Bend Psychiatric Hospital
Courtesy of Tennessee State Library and Archives DB 15402

147 Urban Renewal in Full Swing
Chattanooga-Hamilton County Bicentennial Library 00004438

148 Beautified Intersection at Georgia and Ninth
Chattanooga-Hamilton County Bicentennial Library 00001449

149 The Green Room at the Read House
Chattanooga-Hamilton County Bicentennial Library 00005040

150 Zayre
Chattanooga-Hamilton County Bicentennial Library 00000735

152 Sunset by Paddleboat
Chattanooga-Hamilton County Bicentennial Library 00005765

153 University of Chattanooga, 1970
Chattanooga-Hamilton County Bicentennial Library 00001753

154 Fireman's Fountain
Chattanooga-Hamilton County Bicentennial Library 00004974

155 View of the City from Lookout Mountain, 1970
Courtesy of Tennessee State Library and Archives DB 15840

156 Cavern Castle at Ruby Falls
Chattanooga-Hamilton County Bicentennial Library 00005602

157 Waterfall at Ruby Falls
Chattanooga-Hamilton County Bicentennial Library 00005611

158 The Cravens House, 1970
Courtesy of Tennessee State Library and Archives DB 19554

159 Mayor Walker and the Chattanooga Boys Choir
Chattanooga-Hamilton County Bicentennial Library Walker Collection #240

160 Aerial View of Covenant College
Chattanooga-Hamilton County Bicentennial Library 00005022

161 Boaters at Chickamauga Lock
Chattanooga-Hamilton County Bicentennial Library 00001151

162 The Carnegie Library Refitted, 1971
Chattanooga-Hamilton County Bicentennial Library 00005328

163 Nuclear Reactor Vessel on Barge
Chattanooga-Hamilton County Bicentennial Library 00005250

164 The New Y.M.C.A.
Chattanooga-Hamilton County Bicentennial Library 00000956

165 Revisiting Civil War History at Point Park
Courtesy of Tennessee State Library and Archives DB 15847

166 New York Monument
Courtesy of Tennessee State Library and Archives DB 19567

167 West Side Interstate
Courtesy of Tennessee State Library and Archives DB 16005

168 Hamilton National Bank, 1973
Chattanooga-Hamilton County Bicentennial Library
00004501

169 "Last Battle of the Revolution" Commemoration
Chattanooga-Hamilton County Bicentennial Library
00005398

170 Mose Siskin and His Mosemobile
Chattanooga-Hamilton County Bicentennial Library
Stone Collection
#232

171 Steve Allen at Siskin Institute
Chattanooga-Hamilton County Bicentennial Library
00001708

172 Flood of 1973 at Twenty-third Street
Chattanooga-Hamilton County Bicentennial Library
00001251

173 Lovell Fund-raiser for Orange Grove School
Chattanooga-Hamilton County Bicentennial Library
00004474

174 Waterfront in the Mid-1970s
Chattanooga-Hamilton County Bicentennial Library
00004449

175 See Seven States
Chattanooga-Hamilton County Bicentennial Library
00005596

176 Ross's Landing Historical Marker
Chattanooga-Hamilton County Bicentennial Library
00005750

177 Delta Airlines Downtown Office
Chattanooga-Hamilton County Bicentennial Library
00005038

178 Hunter Museum of American Art
Chattanooga-Hamilton County Bicentennial Library
00005723

179 Houston Antique Museum
Chattanooga-Hamilton County Bicentennial Library
00005719

180 Masonic Temple on Vine Street
Chattanooga-Hamilton County Bicentennial Library
00005133

181 Hamilton County Jail on Walnut Street
Chattanooga-Hamilton County Bicentennial Library
00005289

182 Bicentennial Library, 1976
Chattanooga-Hamilton County Bicentennial Library
00005313

183 Joseph Warner Home in Fort Wood
Chattanooga-Hamilton County Bicentennial Library
00005223

184 Glenwood Children's Hospital
Chattanooga-Hamilton County Bicentennial Library
00005001

185 Meter Maids
Chattanooga-Hamilton County Bicentennial Library
Stone Collection
#170

186 The Chattanooga Choo Choo
Chattanooga-Hamilton County Bicentennial Library
00004839

187 The Choo Choo Trolley
Chattanooga-Hamilton County Bicentennial Library
00004843

188 St. Elmo Presbyterian Church, 1976
Chattanooga-Hamilton County Bicentennial Library
00004907

189 Blue Cross Blue Shield Building on Chestnut Street
Chattanooga-Hamilton County Bicentennial Library
00004634

190 Vine Street Synagogue
Chattanooga-Hamilton County Bicentennial Library
00004862

191 The Custom House on East Eleventh
Chattanooga-Hamilton County Bicentennial Library
00004694

192 National Cemetery Marker with the General
Chattanooga-Hamilton County Bicentennial Library
00004816

193 Sears Downtown 50th Year
Chattanooga-Hamilton County Bicentennial Library
00000660

194 Julia Belle Swain Fall Color Cruise
Chattanooga-Hamilton County Bicentennial Library
00001398

195 The Historic Tivoli Theatre, 1977
Chattanooga-Hamilton County Bicentennial Library
00000940

196 Lake Winnie Indy 500
Chattanooga-Hamilton County Bicentennial Library
00000200

197 Soldiers and Sailors Memorial Auditorium
Chattanooga-Hamilton County Bicentennial Library
00004707

198 Pruett Food Town Grand Opening
Chattanooga-Hamilton County Bicentennial Library
00000625

199 Between Classes at Tennessee Temple University
Chattanooga-Hamilton County Bicentennial Library
00001744

200 Morning Fog at the Market Street Bridge
Chattanooga-Hamilton County Bicentennial Library
00004609

HISTORIC PHOTOS OF CHATTANOOGA IN THE 50s, 60s, AND 70s

Nestled in a valley beside the Tennessee River and surrounded by the southern Appalachian mountains, Chattanooga is truly Tennessee's most scenic city. With the experience of the Great Depression and World War II still strong in memory, and the legacy of the long ago Civil War still percolating, Chattanoogans would grapple with the new realities of postwar America while preserving much of what had given the city its unique aura.

In this companion volume to *Historic Photos of Chattanooga,* William F. Hull leads a tour past many Chattanooga landmarks from recent times, reminiscing with Chattanoogans who can remember and informing those new to the city who may not. Nearly 200 images reproduced in vivid black-and-white, with captions and introductions, show the Tivoli Theatre, Rock City, Dupont, Chickamauga Lake, Lovell Field, the Hunter Museum, Coca-Cola Bottling, Krystal, Erlanger Hospital, the Chattanooga Lookouts, radio legend Luther Masingill—still broadcasting today after 70 years—and, of course, the Chattanooga Choo Choo, among countless other subjects from yesteryear that remain key to the city's past and present.

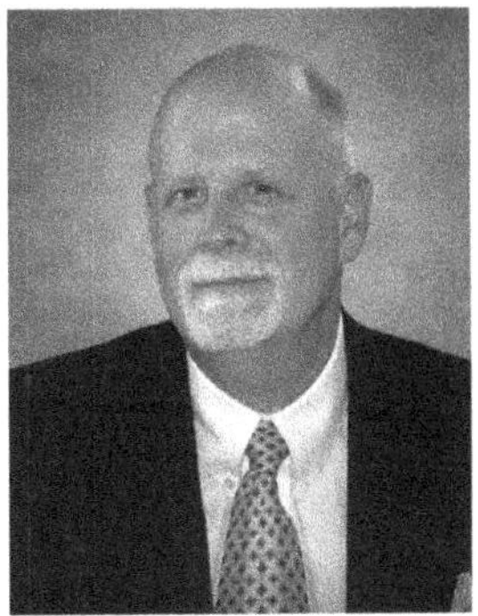

William F. Hull has been working in the history museum field for the past 25 years. As staff photographer for the Atlanta History Center he was involved with the preservation of historic images and served as curator for several exhibits dealing with the cultural importance of photography. A native of Chattanooga, he attended Baylor School and graduated from Vanderbilt University. As the collections manager at the Chattanooga Regional History Museum for five years, he was the curator of two exhibits and oversaw the care and development of the museum's permanent collection.

Hull has written *Historic Photos of Chattanooga,* also available from Turner Publishing, a look at one hundred years of Chattanooga history through black-and-white images, many of them published for the first time. His other books include *Chattanooga: Then and Now* (2008) and *Images of America: Lookout Mountain* (2009).

Hull lives in North Chattanooga with his wife, Eleanor, their two sons, and a parrot.

WWW.TURNERPUBLISHING.COM

www.ingramcontent.com/pod-product-compliance
Lightning Source LLC
LaVergne TN
LVHW060609110826
845154LV00003B/58

* 9 7 8 1 6 8 4 4 2 1 2 7 5 *